Viktor Shklovsky's Heritage in Literature, Arts, and Philosophy

Viktor Shklovsky's Heritage in Literature, Arts, and Philosophy

Edited by Slav N. Gratchev
and Howard Mancing

Introduction by Irina Evdokimova

LEXINGTON BOOKS
Lanham • Boulder • New York • London

Published by Lexington Books
An imprint of The Rowman & Littlefield Publishing Group, Inc.
4501 Forbes Boulevard, Suite 200, Lanham, Maryland 20706
www.rowman.com

6 Tinworth Street, London SE11 5AL

Copyright © 2019 by The Rowman & Littlefield Publishing Group, Inc.

All rights reserved. No part of this book may be reproduced in any form or by any electronic or mechanical means, including information storage and retrieval systems, without written permission from the publisher, except by a reviewer who may quote passages in a review.

British Library Cataloguing in Publication Information Available

Library of Congress Cataloging-in-Publication Data Available

ISBN 9781498597920 (cloth : alk. paper)
ISBN 9781498597944 (pbk : alk. paper)
ISBN 9781498597937 (electronic)

∞™ The paper used in this publication meets the minimum requirements of American National Standard for Information Sciences Permanence of Paper for Printed Library Materials, ANSI/NISO Z39.48-1992.

Contents

List of Figures vii

Introduction 1
   Irina Evdokimova

Part I: Shklovsky's Heritage in Literature

1 Thinking in Images, Differently: Shklovsky, Yakubinsky, and the Power of Evidence 11
   Michael Eskin

2 The Odyssey of Viktor Shklovsky: Life after Formalism 27
   Basil Lvoff

3 The Eternal Wonderer or Who Was Viktor Shklovsky? 41
   Slav N. Gratchev

4 Defamiliarization in Translating Lewis Carroll's *Wonderland* 51
   Victor Fet and Michael Everson

5 Shklovsky and Narrative Theory 65
   David Gorman

6 *Ostranenie* and Genre: Semiotic Subversions in *The Crying of Lot 49* and "Death and the Compass" 79
   Melissa Garr

7 Shklovsky and Things, or Why Tolstoy's Sofa Should Matter 93
   Serguei Alex. Oushakine

8 The Motherland Will Notice Her Terrible Mistake*: Paradox of Futurism in Jasienski, Mayakovsky and Shklovsky 109
   Norbert Francis

9	Framing and Threading Non-Literary Discourse into the Structure of Cervantes's *Don Quixote II* *Rachel Schmidt*	125
10	Shklovsky and World Literature *Grant Hamilton*	139
11	Racism and Robots: Defamiliarizing Social Justice in Rosa Montero's *Tears in the Rain* and the Twenty-First Century *Steven Mills*	151

Part II: Shklovsky's Heritage in Arts

12	Shklovsky's Dog and Mulvey's Pleasure: The Secret Life of Defamiliarization *Eric Naiman*	169
13	Reading Viktor Shklovsky's "Art as Technique" in the Context of Early Cinema *Annie van den Oever*	189

Part III: Shklovsky's Heritage in Philosophy

14	Shklovsky as Philosopher for Tynyanov *Alexander Markov*	207
15	Shklovsky as a Technique: Literary Theory and the Biographical Strategies of a Soviet Intellectual *Ilya Kalinin*	219
16	From a New Seeing to a New Acting: Viktor Shklovsky's Ostranenie and Analyses of Games and Play *Holger Pötzsch*	235

Appendix: List of Russian Transliterated Titles	253
Index	259
About the Contributors	273

List of Figures

Fig. 16.1   Playing Civilians in *This War of Mine*: Day-mode. 243

Fig. 16.2   Playing Civilians in *This War of Mine*: Night-mode.   244

Introduction

Irina Evdokimova

This volume celebrates 100 years of Viktor Shklovsky's heritage: in 1918 when Shklovsky decided not to participate in politics anymore, he started his life-long career as a literary critic, writer, and screenwriter. At that time no one knew that he would become one of the most original, penetrating, and controversial literary critics of the twentieth century.

This book aims to examine the heritage of Viktor Shklovsky in a variety of disciplines. To achieve this end, we drew upon colleagues from eight different countries across the world—the United States, Canada, Russia, England, Scotland, Germany, Norway, and China—in order to bring the widest variety of points of view on the subject. But we also wanted this book to be more than just another collection of essays of literary criticism: we invited scholars from different disciplines—literature, cinematography, and philosophy—who have dealt with Shklovsky's heritage and saw its practical application in their fields. Therefore, all these essays are written in a variety of humanist academic and scholarly styles, all engaging and dynamic. And that is as it should be.

Perhaps for the first time, Viktor Shklovsky will be discussed from the point of view of such a wide range of approaches and methodologies. A primary objective was to articulate the enduring relevance and heritage of the great and varied works of Shklovsky during more than half a century, from the early 1920s to the mid-1970s. His work in aesthetics, philosophy, linguistics, history, and theory of literature are present here, as understood by a wide variety of distinguished scholars. In our case, we have chosen to minimize the editors' voices; we have imposed no strict definition of what we think Shklovsky's heritage should be on the contributors but have given them complete freedom to discuss the concept in their own terms, in their own style, in their own voice.

Much has been written on Shklovsky, and this book will take another look, from the angle of sixteen different perspectives, at the heritage of one of the most prominent thinkers of the twentieth-century, and perhaps open a new critical discourse that may well contribute to reshaping our current understanding of one of the most original literary figures—the Russian Formalist Viktor Borisovich Shklovsky.

In chapter 1 Michael Eskin aims to accomplish four things: (1) remedy the dearth of research on Shklovsky's dialogue with Yakubinsky, and more specifically, outline the latter's role as the methodological 'brains' that enabled Shklovsky's "Art as Device" to be perceived as the founding document of Russian Formalism; (2) revisit Shklovsky's earliest essays—"The Resurrection of the Word," "Potebnya," and "Art as Device" in light of their debt to and creative appropriation of Yakubinsky's work; (3) reread Shklovsky's polemic against Alexander Potebnya in light of his appropriation of Yakubinsky's work *and* in light of the ubiquitous presence of Husserlian phenomenology in Russia at the time; (4) argue that Shklovsky's entire "formalist" approach can be understood as an extroverted phenomenological reduction premised on the life-enhancing, *emotive* power of *evidence* offered up by the poetic text, which *impacts* the reader, hearer, etc. by way of the dynamic of the classical notion of *enargeia* (rendered into Latin as "evidence" by Cicero).

In chapter 2 Basil Lvoff argues that, having weathered a parade of scholarly movements from Structuralism to Deconstruction and modern trends, Viktor Shklovsky's legacy has remained relevant thanks to its perennial principle of defamiliarization. The author maintains that literary critics tend to underestimate Shklovsky's fifty-year-long odyssey after his public, albeit forced and ostensible, recantation of Formalism. Therefore, the period from 1930 to 1984 is in the limelight of this chapter, which aims to outline the arc of Shklovsky's post-Formalist evolution. At the same time, the chapter compares Shklovsky's major works after 1930 with his earlier ones that share similar theoretical or generic features. For example, the densely theoretical *Theory of Prose* (1925/1929) is juxtaposed with *Bowstring: On the Dissimilarity of the Similar* (1970); the epistolary novel *Zoo, or Letters Not about Love* (1923) is compared to its later, sanitized edition and *Letters to a Grandson* (published in 2002); some parallels are also drawn between Shklovsky's 1929 and 1963 books on Leo Tolstoy.

In chapter 3 Slav Gratchev analyzes a series of interviews with Viktor Shklovsky that were conducted in 1967–1968 by professor Victor Duvakin in Moscow. Many years had to pass before the recording could become a book that truly reflects the spirit of times—when the most dramatic events of the twentieth century were happening in Russia and the USSR. This is a slice of Russian micro-history but even more trustworthy because it relies on the living voice of that history, the voice of a real participant in events that for the longest time in the USSR could not be openly discussed. Shklovsky, besides being a well-known and brilliant literary theorist, was a friend and interlocutor of many famous people whose lives and deaths, up to these days, remain a mystery to us. Through these informal dialogues that are not constrained by censorship or fear, we will be able to shed some more light on the real characters, instincts, habits, and views of those people. By "listening" to these dialogues, one will see the reflection of history in the eyes of a real witness who, in most cases, was just a good fellow citizen and suffered during those times, like thousands of others. This essay will talk in detail about these dialogues.

Chapter 4 by Victor Fet and Michael Everson problematizes the Russian Formalist concept of defamiliarization, or estrangement, in literature and art—a concept that has been adopted recently as a strategy in literary translation. The authors argue their point by examining the concept of defamiliarization in translations of Lewis Carroll's *Alice's Adventures in Wonderland* (1865), one of the most translated English literary texts. Fet and Everson suggest that any attempt to translate this famous book that is often referred to as "untranslatable wordplay" has always faced the issue of handling defamiliarization, and they show how two differing approaches were used in two Russian versions translated by Nina Demurova. Therefore, the chapter discusses various approaches in which the translators handle defamiliarization following the tradition established by Lewis Carroll himself.

David Gorman in chapter 5 examines and interrogates Shklovsky's ideas about narrative with the aim of treating them not only as part of a finished record, but also as having continued potential for narratology. First, his essay delineates a basic corpus of Shklovsky's work on narrative during the era of Russian Formalism (primarily *Theory of Prose* [1925, 1929]); it also addresses the difficulties of discerning Shklovsky's ideas about narrative because his style was that of a creative writer rather than an academic critic. Gorman argues that Shklovsky developed a number of general aesthetic concepts, which he applied to literary narrative in his Formalist writings. The second part of this essay deals with topics of this kind, including the history of art as a discontinuous movement "from uncle to nephew" (including such notions as canonization and parody), the distinction between material and form (popularized as *fabula/sujet*), and defamiliarization. The last part of the essay turns our attention to Shklovsky's engagement with narrative, to his methods of folkloristic as well as literary criticism, including motifs, plot types, and device versus motivation.

In chapter 6 Melissa Garr engages us with Thomas Pynchon's *The Crying of Lot 49* and Jorge Luis Borges's "Death and the Compass," and explores how the authors deliberately defamiliarize the genre itself by using symbols to lure the main characters into fake mysteries that end ambiguously in the middle of the labyrinth of clues, with no way out. The author argues that the investigators actively create mysteries that are in themselves red herrings, or semiotic subversion of the genre's tropes and expectations.

By applying Shklovsky's critical frameworks to these works, this essay will highlight semiotic subversions in postmodern detective fiction and symbolic representations of law and order.

Chapter 7 by Serguei Oushakine discusses a series of texts in which Shklovsky in the 1930s laid out the basics of the art of writing: *Tekhnika pisatel'skogo remesla* (The Technique of the Writer's Craft, 1930) and *Kak pisat' stsenarii: posobie dlia nachinayushchikh stsenaristov s obraztsami stsenariev raznogo tipa* (How to write a screenplay: a textbook for beginning screenwriters with templates of various screenplays, 1931). While the first one provided a collection of elemental rules with instructive vignettes, explaining how to produce a reasonable and professional text, the second one offered a crash course on how to produce plays for a quickly expanding cinematic industry. The third essay *Kak my pishem* (How We Write, 1930) proposed a self-reflective observation on fifteen years of his own writing career, emphasizing his montage-like approach to building the narrative. The essay aims to revisit these three didactic texts by reading them through Shklovsky's own "theory of prose." In a sense, his manuals were aimed to operationalize his famous maxim that the ultimate goal of art is "to renew the process of making a thing" by breaking down "the process of making" into manageable stages and operations. Consequently, the essay explores what these basic elements of the writer's craft were; to what extent was Shklovsky capable of instrumentalizing the insights and devices that he discovered during his reading of Tolstoy and alike for a larger audience? Or, to put it simply, did his "theory of prose" have any practical—*prosaic*—application?

Chapter 8 by Norbert Francis turns our attention to Russian Futurism, an avant-garde current that surprised readers and writers alike during the years of social ferment leading up the 1917 revolution. In particular, the participants in the movement themselves had no idea what events would have in store for them. Three among them, Bruno Jasienski, Vladimir Mayakovsky and Viktor Shklovsky, are representative of the literary upheaval and explosion of creativity that we look back to as a turning point in literature. Taken together for comparison, a study of their work also gives us an idea of the confusion of the time, how outcomes often seemed strangely arbitrary, and how events took unexpected turns. On another level, the route taken by each writer, nevertheless, is consistent with the overall direction of art and culture during the Soviet era. Shklovsky, authors argue, perhaps was the writer who most directly challenged the assumptions of early Socialist Realism (more precisely its precursors) who survived to reflect on the history, and precisely on an interesting aspect of this history—the relationship between the Futurists and Russian Formalism. The essay explores in detail. The discussion of their work will turn on three important historical studies that trace the course of the revolution and the course of parallel literary currents.

In chapter 9 Rachel Schmidt proposes that in his *Theory of Prose* (1990), Viktor Shklovsky demonstrated how Miguel de Cervantes structured his novel *Don Quixote de la Mancha* part 1 through a combination of framing and threading. Framing allowed the author to inset stories that at first glance do not share an obvious connection with the journey of the main characters, Don Quixote and Sancho Panza, whereas threading assimilated the motif of the interpolated stories to the frame. Shklovsky noted, that without these techniques, Don Quixote's speech on the Golden Age (book 1, chap 11) is "essentially out of place." This essay argues that in *Don Quixote* book 2 threading and framing allowed Cervantes to incorporate important non-literary genres of his period that govern masculinity and politics into the literary plot; that Cervantes structured his book 2 (chapters 1–24) around the nonliterary discourses of the *ars moriendi* (the art of the good death), *verdadera honra* (true honor), the political *arbitrio* (a form of reform-minded treatise) with its emphasis on *razón de estado* (reason of state), and even the art of swordsmanship.

In chapter 10 Grant Hamilton turns our attention to the influence that Shklovsky's work has had on the field of world literature. Working from the proposition that the sense of defamiliarization that attends the experience of reading world literature is not so much a matter of writerly technique as it is a constitutive feature of the literature itself, Hamilton begins by stressing the significance of Shklovsky's notion of *ostranenie* to discussions of world literature. Following this, he moves into a discussion of the way in which Shklovsky's thought sits at the core of one of the major ways in which contemporary literary critics have attempted to "do" world literature in the twenty-first century—the quantitative analysis of literary texts spearheaded by Franco Moretti and his methodology of "distant reading." Described by Jonathan Arac as a "formalism without close reading," Moretti's methodology of distant reading is shown to rest on the Shklovskian belief that plot is the fundamental unit of literary analysis, and that such analysis has the potential to create "models" of literary texts that have the potential to allow one to see the underlying structures of complex objects like literary texts. The chapter concludes by stating that because of such visionary work in the quantitative analysis of world literature conducted by critics such as Franco Moretti, the legacy of Shklovsky's work is likely to be felt in the field of world literature for many more decades to come.

In chapter 11 Steven Mills considers how Viktor Shklovsky altered the direction and substance of literary theory by arguing that art casts a vision of the mundane in new contexts and perspectives. This paradox forces the spectator to behold an object as if for the first time and compels her to appreciate and engage the object with renewed value. His essay, focusing on Rosa

Montero's novel *Tears in the Rain*, proposes a new vision for Shklovsky's theory of *defamiliarization*: novels that make social issues strange intend the reader to face these problems afresh, and the works shift away from literary art and become social art. As conversations toward social change continually address the topics of racism and bigotry, they also face the danger of weakening by over discussion. *Tears*, suggests Mills, distances the individual from the social comfort zone to effect change as it forces the reader to see anew problems that were once hidden. The essay suggests that *defamiliarization* and *shklovskian* thought have shifted from literary theory to social actions as kindling to reignite the discussion of equality.

Chapter 12 written by Eric Naiman explores the influence of Shklovsky's most famous article, "Art as Device," on the writing of Laura Mulvey's extremely influential "Visual Pleasure and Narrative Cinema." Essentially, this article's methodology is one of comparative deconstruction; and as the author considers the meaning of the term "feminist formalism," he uses each article to explore the way in which dynamics of gender trouble the argument in the other. Naiman suggests that Shklovsky's article has a misogynistic tenor that has rarely been explored, while Mulvey's approach to gender is internally inconsistent: a manifesto for feminist filmmaking and film-watching unfolds by attacking the image of woman. Is this because Mulvey's article founders as a result of its reliance on Shklovsky's canonical critical text? In responding to this question, the author considers the textology of both articles: the changes in the works in the course of their publication and republication reveal the way in which potentially disruptive forces were repressed and smoothed over. Naiman notes that there has been very little attention to Shklovsky's article as a single work; likewise, Mulvey's manifesto has been considered for its ideas, but not for the rhetoric of their expression.

In chapter 13 Annie van den Oever brings to our attention an essay by Maxim Gorky "In the Kingdom of Shadows" that suggested that the Lumière's cinematograph proved to be a machine that created distortions and disproportions in the representation of people and things, making them *look strange* if not *grotesque*. The author argues that for Gorky, the images created by the new cinema machine had an abundant and often hilarious expressive potential—the potential that soon was unleashed to the fullest by the Futurist performances adding to the already existing "craze" of the early film shows.

Consequently, her essay argues that Viktor Shklovsky's modern art theory of the 1910s, revolving around the famous key term *ostranenie* ("making strange" or estrangement) and focusing on the *estranging* techniques used in the arts and their evident effects, must be understood in relation to the ways the new cinema machine made humans and things *look strange* if not *grotesque*, as Gorky had aptly argued in 1896. The *strangeness* of the early film shows as understood by Gorky and the *craze* celebrated in the avant-garde performances by Shklovsky and his Futurist friends form the basis of this key text founding Russian Formalism. In essence, this chapter presents a radical critique on the dominant readings of this modern art theory and the foundational text by Shklovsky as "Russian Formalist," and to support its claim, the essay revisits the "Art as a Technique" within the historical context of the effects of the new cinema machine and what it really "did" to make Maxim Gorky label it as a "grotesque creation."

Chapter 14 presents us an essay written by Alexander Markov who talks about how the leaders of Russian formalism distanced themselves from philosophical discussions, considering their radical criticism of the preceding aesthetic as sufficient solution of philosophical problems. He argues that the case of Shklovsky, who introduced philosophical modes of argumentation not only for polemical purposes, but for better interdisciplinary studies of art, is the most important. Therefore, he aims to reconstruct this positive argumentation, often unclear due to the declarative style of Shklovsky's writings. The author proves that deep inspection of art as a psychological fact among facts and acts of consciousness allowed Shklovsky to reintroduce the most influential philosophical traditions, not as an intellectual fashion, but as a framework for reassembling art criticism as both subjective and objective. In conclusion, Markov suggests that the appeal to the semiotic project of Leibniz that tends to explain odd transitions between grammar, rhetoric, and poetics in Russian formalism, as well as Nietzsche's doctrine of subjective risks of the progress, and Buecher's explanation of the origin of art from rhythmic work—are all relevant for the formalist notion of device. Shklovsky's uniqueness is in combining all three philosophies in his cinema theory: the frame was understood in Leibniz's mood, the cinema plot came closer to Nietzsche's doctrine of tragedy, and film reception was arranged according to Buecher's naturalistic approach to art. The essay suggests that the major achievements of Shklovsky's analysis were an integral part of Russian philosophy, seminal for discussions on the social mission of philosophers and writers and on poetics as program of rational argumentation in the world of creative decisions.

Chapter 15 by Ilya Kalinin explores one particular and unexpected intellectual substrate of Shklovsky's ideas by referring to the figure of Nikolay Fyodorov (1829–1903) and his radical, controversial and utopian "Philosophy of Common Task." Having influenced many figures of the Russian avant-garde, including Vladimir Mayakovsky and Velimir Khlebnikov, Pavel Filonov and Andrey Platonov, the teachings of Fydorov were suppressed in the 1930s, along with the utopianism of early revolutionary culture. The author asserts that Viktor Shklovsky, who had assumed the status of one of the most prominent literary critics in the USSR from the 1930s and had emerged most forcefully at the center of cultural life in the Khrushchev era of the "Thaw" (1953–1959), still had his roots in the avant-garde origins of Soviet culture that endowed him with additional symbolic weight. Thus, the author tries to demonstrate that practically all early works of Shklovsky were rooted in the avant-garde culture where the name of Fydorov was completely absent. However, as Kalinin argues in the essay, in today's revealed *fedorovian* stratum one may find the echo of Russian cosmism in Shklovsky's early works that deal with the poetic language.

In chapter 16 Holger Pötzsch highlights a certain ambivalence in the thinking of Viktor Shklovsky that seems to oscillate between an arguably reductive art-for-art's-sake position where attention to literariness and estrangement merely reveals a play of form apparently without connections to an extra-literary or extra-artistic reality, and a deeply contextualizing approach that perceives art's main function as challenging and renewing a reader's or onlooker's view onto, and therefore, being in the world. In this chapter, the author will argue that this *doubleness* is not something emerging at a late stage of Shklovsky's career but has been a decisive feature in his thinking from the very beginning. Consequently, this chapter traces this ambiguity with reference to the mixed origins and legacies of Shklovsky's key term of *ostranenie*. Then, through a comparison with Brecht's V-effect, it will highlight important differences between the two thinkers and point to political implications of these. The essay will argue in favor of a contextual understanding of *ostranenie* as directed toward the world, yet as still different from Brecht's dialectical understanding. Finally, the chapter will present illustrative examples from applications of the concept of *ostranenie* in the study of computer games and highlight a senso-motoric understanding of the concept that is specific for this "new" medium.

This is the book that we are pleased to offer to your attention.

Part I

Shklovsky's Heritage in Literature

Chapter One

Thinking in Images, Differently

Shklovsky, Yakubinsky, and the Power of Evidence

Michael Eskin

I

To begin with, Viktor Shklovsky was neither the first to dispute that "art is thinking in images," thus co-founding the movement—Russian Formalism—he has virtually become synonymous with; nor was he the first to suggest that poetry and art in general aim at *defamiliarizing* the familiar, thus giving the movement its central conceptual-methodological tool: "defamiliarization" ("ostranenie").[1] It is worth remembering (1) that Henri Bergson for instance had already used the term "defamiliarize" ("déshabituer") in reference to the goal of art in 1889, twenty-eight years before Shklovsky's own 1917 trailblazer "Iskusstvo, kak priem"—"Art as Device"—in which both of the above arguments were presented; and (2) that the supreme rule of the image in poetry and art in general (going back to Horace's *ut pictura poesis*) had already been explicitly disavowed for instance by the romantics and Pre-Raphaelites. Thus, Bergson observed that "the arts . . . make it such that our faculty of perception . . . defamiliarizes itself [se déshabitue] from . . . everyday life," while Ludwig Tieck and Walter Pater elevated music to the status of supreme aesthetic-artistic model and 'metric'—as most famously expressed in Pater's dictum "All art constantly aspires toward the condition of music" and in Tieck's verse "Love (read: poetry) *thinks* in sweet tones" (rather than *images*, that is).[2]

This is not at all to diminish Shklovsky's role as one of the founders of one of the most influential modern literary-critical schools. But it is to suggest that his literary-historical significance might well be sought in places other than his stark opposition to the Ukrainian philosopher-linguist Aleksandr Potebnya (1835–1891), whose insistence on the intrinsic necessity of images in poetry and "poetic thinking" Shklovsky argued against in particular, or in his claim that art works primarily through *defamiliarization*, whereby we get to *see*, *perceive*, and *feel* the familiar in a fresh, *unfamiliar* way.[3] For if the repudiation of imagery as the conduit for the effectiveness of art and poetry in particular, as well as the foregrounding of art's ability to defamiliarize the familiar were Shklovsky's claims to critical innovation, then he would owe replies to the following queries:

1. How come, then, he himself not only admits that there is "poetic imagery" but welcomes it as "one of the means" of "intensifying our impressions" and "sensation of things," of "giving us back the sensation of life"?[4]
2. How is his notion of defamiliarization—the power of art precisely to "intensify our impressions" and "sensation of things," and "give us back the sensation of life"—different *in essence* from traditional aesthetic approaches (including Bergson's) going back to Aristotle and Longinus and hinging on the notion that art, and poetry in particular, transcends the familiar through the deployment of particular artistic devices?[5]
3. Finally, how is his notion of defamiliarization as a means of enabling us to *see* and *feel* things in their very *aliveness* different in principle from other contemporaneous attempts—such as the Acmeists'—to "experience the world as alive" through poetry?[6]

Or is it perhaps Shklovsky's opposition to the view that poetry is *"thinking* in images" rather than some other activity employing imagery—in other words, is it his claim that "there is an entire realm of art which is not a means of thinking [sposob myshleniia], lyric poetry [lirika] being one such art," that marks his singular contribution to modern poetics?[7] My sense is that here, too, he might find himself in conceptual dire straits on at least two counts:

1. The importance of arguing that poetry is *not* a form of thinking is squarely tied to Shklovsky's opposition to Potebnya, who characterizes both poetry and prose (understood as non-artistic language in general) as modes thinking.[8] But what does it matter *what* we call, or *how* we refer to the creative mental activity that produces poetry (or other forms of art)—whether as "thinking" or by another name—as long as we recognize it *as* some sort of mental-creative process? This question is especially apposite given that Shklovsky's distinction between poetic/artistic and prosaic/non-artistic language is premised on the notion that both, paradoxically, *do employ imagery*—to wit: metaphor and metonymy, respectively:

Thinking in Images, Differently 13

> I am walking down the street, Shklovsky writes by way of example, and notice that the guy in front of me has dropped a package. Since he is wearing a hat, I call out to him, "Hey, Mr. Hat [shliapa], you dropped something!" That's an example of an image—strictly a prosaic trope [primer obraza—tropa chisto prozaicheskogo]. Here's another example. There are several people standing in formation. The attending officer notices that one of them is not standing straight, and says to him: "Hey, you old hat [shliapa], watch your posture!"— This image is a poetic trope [obraz—trop poeticheskii]. In one instance the word "hat" is a metonymy, in the other it is a metaphor.[9]

Why the "thinking" happening in the first example should be any different from the second remains utterly unclear: Both use imagery, and insofar as the first example—being an instance of prose—is "thinking in images," the second must necessarily must be as well, given that it too employs a trope.

2. As I have demonstrated elsewhere, the very compound "thought image," as it emerged in Holland in the seventeenth century—"Denkbeelden"—as more or less synonymous with "idea," doesn't necessarily allow for a conceptual separation between its nominal components—something Shklovsky's entire opposition to Potebnya appears to be predicated on, insofar as it implies that there can be a mental-verbal use of imagery that would *not* be a form of thinking.[10] Not only is this dubious on an axiomatic level, but it opens an entire can of worms concerning the question of the nature of mind, mental processes, and thought in general, which one would best steer clear of . . .

Where, then, to locate what I perceive as the uniqueness and specificity of Shklovsky's vision? For novelty indeed there is, as all would agree—and not simply in the gust of fresh air that the verve and sheer chutzpah of his irreverent style blew into the staid and arid discourse of Russian academe at the time; or in his radical aim to put paid to any form of "psychologism" or "metaphysical" striving (esp. Symbolism) in the name of the concrete work of art embedded in our concrete world—an aim he shared with a number of other contemporary artistic and literary schools and movements (e.g., Acmeism and Futurism).

I would like to sweep all of these "objections" aside, given that Shklovsky's stature as a literary-critical giant remains—deservedly, as I hope to illustrate—comfortably intact, and explore the import of Shklovsky's singularity by revisiting the early history of Russian Formalism and by paying special attention to what I would like to call, for lack of a better term, the *evidentiary tenor* of Shklovsky's seminal early work. Enter Lev Petrovich Yakubinsky.

II

Reminiscing on the beginnings of Russian Formalism, Shklovsky writes in late 1920s: "The best year of my life [luchshii god moei zhizni]—was the year when I spoke to Lev Yakubinsky on the phone for an hour or two each day. We would draw up small tables next to our telephones."[11] Given the central significance for the quality of his life Shklovsky explicitly assigns to his work, we must assume that by the "best year of his life" he also means to say that it must have been a, if not *the*, most *productive* and *creative* period in his life.[12] And since his contribution to Russian Formalism may well be considered his most productive-*qua*-innovative-and-path-breaking *personal-professional* achievement, it behooves us to look deeper into Yakubinsky's contribution to Shklovsky's *annus mirabilis*.

While Yakubinsky's role as an early Formalist has certainly been noted in critical literature, to the best of my knowledge there is no single study devoted to Yakubinsky's impact on and significance for Shklovsky in particular, or, put differently, to Shklovsky's specific dialogue with Yakubinsky.[13]

Let me, therefore, first remind the reader that, as Shklovsky's friend and fellow Formalist Boris Eikhenbaum has pointed out, it was none other than Yakubinsky who laid the groundwork for and initiated Russian Formalism by introducing a *categorial functional, goal-oriented* distinction between "poetic" and "practical" language: This distinction, which "was elaborated in Yakubinsky's articles in the first collections of OPOYAZ"—the *Society of the Study of Poetic Language* the Formalists had formed in the first half of the 1910s—"served as the foundational principle [posluzhivshee iskhodnym printsipom] for all of the Formalists' work on the basic problems of poetics."[14] The articles Eikhenbaum is referring to in particular are "On the Sounds in Poetic Language," in which the distinction between "poetic" and "practical" speech was first elaborated, and the much shorter and more technical "The Accumulation of Liquids in Practical and Poetic Language," in which the distinction was further demonstrated by way of concrete examples from poetry and practical speech. Both pieces were published, respectively, in OPOYAZ's *Collections on the Theory of Poetic Language I* and *II* in 1916 and 1917—the first thus appearing a year *before* Shklovsky's "Art, as Device," and the second in the same year and venue as the latter.[15] Not surprisingly, Shklovsky, too, acknowledges Yakubinsky's pioneering role in the creation of the new movement, citing his early work in the OPOYAZ collections multiple times in "Art, as Device."[16]

Let us then take a closer look at Yakubinsky's two essays and reread Shklovsky's own early Formalist work—"Art, as Device" (1917) and its two predecessors "The Resurrection of the Word" (1914) and "Potebnya" (1916)—in connection with the former, with particular attention to "On the Sounds in Poetic Language" and "Art as Device," given their chronological succession and given that by the time Shklovsky wrote "Art as Device," his critical position had solidified into the Formalist approach he is known for today.

III

This is what Shklovsky has to say about Yakubinsky in "Art, as Device":

> Yakubinsky's article, which states . . . that in poetic language . . . hard-to-pronounce sound combinations are possible is one of the first scientifically sound indications of the opposition . . . between poetic and practical language.
>
> As far as the laws of perception are concerned, we see that routine actions become automatic . . . retreat into the realm of the unconscious and automatic. You will agree if you remember the feeling you had when holding a pen or speaking a foreign language for the first time and compare it to the feeling you have when doing it for the umpteenth time. It's the automatization process that explains the laws of prosaic speech. . . . In quick practical speech words are not fully spoken; the mind only registers their initial sounds. . . . This algebraic way of thinking takes in things by counting and spatializing them; we don't *see* them but *recognize* them . . . Perceived in this way, things dry up, first in experience, and then their very making begins to suffer; due to this kind of perception, prosaic speech is never fully heard (cf. Yakubinsky's article) and therefore never fully spoken. . . . That's how life is reduced to nothing and gradually vanishes. Automatization devours things, clothes, furniture, your wife, and the fear of war.
>
> In his article, Yakubinsky proved the law of phonetic difficulty in poetic language, using the example of sound repetition. The language of poetry is difficult and laborious, which slows down perception. In some particular cases, the language of poetry approximates the language of prose, but this doesn't violate the law of difficulty.

The article by Yakubinsky Shklovsky has specifically in mind is the "The Accumulation of Liquids in Practical and Poetic Language" (1917). As already mentioned, in this short, technical piece, which explicitly refers back to and expands on the foundations laid and insights gained in the much longer "On the Sounds in Poetic Language" (1916), Yakubinsky considers the concrete workings of language in poetry and prose/practical speech, respectively, with special attention to the substitution or dropping of difficult-to-pronounce letter sequences involving liquids (e.g., "r" and "l") in everyday speech, as opposed to their retention in poetry—the reason being, "as explained in my essay in the first *Collection on the Theory of Poetic Language*, that in practical language sounds do not focus the speaker's attention on themselves [and that] the accumulation of liquids breaks the automatism which is the hallmark of practical language."[17] In poetic language, Yakubinsky notes (anticipating Jakobson's "aesthetic" and "poetic function," respectively), "the situation is reversed: we do become consciously aware of the material texture of words, we are enjoined to focus on their sounds above all," thus breaking the automatism of everyday speech.[18]

Focusing our attention on the sounds and material texture of words themselves, however, doesn't mean much—unless we are engaged in phonic, statistical or other forms "algebraic" analysis—and is certainly not the reason that we listen to, read and cherish poetry. And it is precisely Yakubinsky's additional conceptual-descriptive move, elaborated throughout "On the Sounds in Poetic Language" in particular, that is, I argue, of special relevance to Shklovsky's critical approach. The move consists in adding the component of *emotion* to the element of *attention*. For poetic language not only focuses our attention on its phonic and material texture, but it also produces or triggers an "emotional relation" to it within us:

> Focusing on the sounds of speech goes hand in hand with a specific emotional relation to them [emotsional'noe k nim otnoshenie] . . . exposing the phonetic aspects of words is also often accompanied by an emotional experience of their sounds . . . Poetic language . . . reveals our emotional relation to its sounds by dint of its ability to draw our attention to its phonic texture.[19]

Our emotional relation, however, is not limited to the sounds and material texture of poetry, as Yakubinsky further observes:

> As noted earlier, poetic language is characterized by our emotional relation to its sound texture . . . Whereby emotions triggered by the sounds of poetry ought not to run counter to the emotions triggered by its content, and *vice versa*. And if that's the case, then this means that poetry's content and sound texture, are emotionally interdependent. Consequently, poets select sounds and sound sequences based on their perceived emotional suitability to the imagery at hand, and *vice versa* . . . the interdependence of sound and sense in poetry provide a certain theoretical foundation for many a poet's testimony . . . on the unity of form and content in poetry.[20]

Yakubinsky's emphasis on poetry's ability to draw and keep our attention focused on itself both in terms of its 'form' and in terms of its 'content' is yet another crucial step in my attempt to trace Shklovsky's dialogue with Yakubinsky.

The question of the (im)possibility of separating 'form' and 'content' aside, Yakubinsky's expansion of our poetic focus to poetry's semantic-referential layers means that poetry puts us in direct contact with and focuses our attention on the extra-poetic, the world and life itself, as it were—at least to the extent that the meanings of words (of most nouns and their accompanying predicates anyway) do refer to our world in one way or another. Yakubinsky illustrates this point by citing two short passages from Mikhail Kuzmin's 1910 novel *Gentle Joseph*:

> "'Rome'? How beautiful: rounded, dome-like . . . Joseph walked over to the window, and looking at the vanishing line of roofs and buildings . . . at the wide-open sky, he began repeating: "Rome, Rome, Rome . . ." until the sounds had lost their meaning and his soul was filled with a vastness resembling the sky or the dome of a cathedral.
>
> How wondrous: you will understand everything in a word once you start repeating it, once it enters your soul. Look at the flower . . . and repeat its name a hundred times, and you will understand what the flower means, and you will see how it lives . . . but you won't be able tell us about it.[21]

What these two passages palpably illustrate is how intently focusing on the word for a thing or any extra-linguistic entity, how zeroing in on the word's phonic, material, *and* semantic texture—be it "Rome" or "flower," or any another logically proper name—enables us—our "soul"—to get in touch with and enhances our experience of its very being and aliveness: we literally "see how it lives . . ."—whereby "it" may refer to both the thing *and* the word. Both word *and* world come alive in and thanks to poetry's ability to focus our attention in its own specific way.

IV

Which brings us right back to Shklovsky, whose critical approach boils down to the following summary provided in "Art, as Device":

> And so this thing we call art exists so that it may restore the sensation of life [oshchushchenie zhizni], so that it may allow us to feel and experience things [pochuvstvovat' veshchi], so that it may make a stone a stone. The aim of art is to afford the sensation of seeing [videnie], rather than merely recognizing [uznavanie], things; the device of art is the "defamiliarization" [ostranenie] of things and the complication of form. This increases the duration and difficulty of perception [vospriiatiia], since in art the act of perception [vosprinimatel'nii protses] is an end in itself and needs to be extended.

Clearly, in the immediate context of the early days of Russian Formalism, Shklovsky's emphasis on *seeing, feeling, perceiving*, things, the world, and life itself anew and afresh through the intermediary of art and poetry can be traced back directly to Yakubinsky's "On the Sounds of Poetic Language." An investigative result valuable in itself as far as the micro-history of the beginnings of Russian Formalism is concerned.

This, however, is not to suggest that Shklovsky simply "took" these ideas from Yakubinsky—he did not. Much of what Yakubinsky writes about in terms of poetry's ability to put us in touch with and allow us to experience the very aliveness of the world and of *life* itself was very much "in the air" at the time—as attested to, for instance, by Osip Mandelstam's 1913 manifesto

"The Morning of Acmeism," which, as I mentioned earlier, speaks of the necessity of "experiencing the world as alive" through poetry, or by the popularity of the vitalist, *life*-as-opposed-to-*mortifying thought*-oriented philosophy of Henri Bergson, both of which Shklovsky and the other Formalists were familiar with.[22] (As an aside, mark Shklovsky's tongue-in-cheek nod of appreciation to Mandelstam's 1913 collection *Stone*—"to make a stone a stone"—in the above summary paragraph from "Art, as Device.") More importantly, Shklovsky himself had already touched upon all of the themes that would consolidate into their classical formulation in "Art, as Device" in his own earlier essays "Potebnya" and "The Resurrection of the Word," where we find him preoccupied, throughout and in no particular order, with "sensation," "palpability," "experience," and "feeling the world," with "seeing" as opposed to "recognizing," with a "thirst for concreteness" and the need to bring the world and things, which "have died," to life again—all in connection with the "acoustic, or articulatory, or semantic side of the word."[23]

And yet—Eikhenbaum's assessment of Yakubinsky's role as the putative founder of Russian Formalism remains correct, I believe, insofar as "On the Sounds of Poetic Language" and "The Accumulation of Liquids in Practical and Poetic Language" can be said to have brought together, streamlined, linguistically (i.e., scientifically) undergirded, and articulated in a cohesive line of argument some of those core thoughts that we associate with "Art, as Device" today. But only some.

And this is where I would like to revisit Shklovsky's opposition to the view of poetry as a mode of thinking and situate his approach in yet another conceptual-historical context.

V

There is a sense, an indubitable feeling of moral, philosophical, existential apodicticity in "Art, as Device" utterly absent from Yakubinsky's essays—an apodicticity that is not reducible to the style of the manifesto as a genre. Shklovsky *knows* that "it is so," as it were, and it is important that "it be so." That art and poetry make us *see, perceive*, and *feel* things in their very aliveness. I believe that it is crucial to be attuned to this dimension of Shklovsky's early work in order fully grasp its sheer power of effect as well as its staying power—above and beyond its purely historical significance.

Why is it important that "*it be so*," we need to ask Shklovsky?—And, lo and behold, he does indeed provide an explicit answer on at least two occasions—an answer that bears on our very existence.

Diagnosing the state of the world and humanity in 1914, Shklovsky writes: "things have died [veshchi umerli]—we have lost our sensation of the world [oshchushchenie mira] . . . Only the creation of new forms of art can return to humanity its experience [perezhivanie] of the world, resurrect things, and kill pessimism [ubit' pessimism]." Clearly—and this is where Shklovsky and Yakubinsky part company—Shklovsky's critical project was, at heart and from the very beginning, an *ethical-philosophical* one taking the route of aesthetics, whereas the early Yakubinsky's was a literary-linguistic one, occasionally touching upon ethical-philosophical issues. And not only was Shklovsky's project ethical-philosophical in general, but it was specifically concerned with the very survival of humanity, as his invective against pessimism attests to, and as might not be at all surprising given the year in which "The Resurrection of the Word" was written and published: 1914, as the world was getting ready to literally destroy itself and the things in it.

A similar ethical-philosophical note is struck in "Art, as Device" (—and we should keep in mind that the latter was written at the height of World War I, among other social upheavals . . .). In an almost ironic-sounding, yet dead-serious quip against the mortifying, deadening effect of "automatization" and the "prosaic," "algebraic way of thinking," Shklovsky writes: "That's how life is reduced to nothing and gradually vanishes. Automatization [avtomatizatsiia] devours things, clothes, furniture, your wife, and the fear of war." A statement that, although couched in an ostensibly poetological manifesto, is not even marginally aesthetic or poetological, but squarely *ethical-philosophical*—which is underscored by the fact that it is immediately followed by a philosophical quote from Tolstoy—"If the entire, complicated life of many people passes by unconsciously [that is, in an automated way], then it's as if this life never happened"—which in turn cannot help invoking Socrates' "the unexamined life is not worth living."[24]

It is obvious that an entire metaphysical-existential dimension opens up in Shklovsky's text, which catapults it out of the narrow confines of literary or aesthetic criticism and into the realm of those intellectual milestones of humanity—be they short or long—that have managed to capture something important to us all, something above and beyond their putative subject matter, in a way that transcends their own particular historical moment. For what Shklovsky advocates in his all-in-all "inconspicuous"—in the big scheme of things—aesthetic manifesto is nothing less than an existentially all-encompassing, *ethics of anti-automatization* whose basic postulates might go something like this: 1. Wake up and be mindful, *see* and *feel* things. 2. Allow the world and things to thrive, rather destroying them. 3. Attend to your existence and those around you, *see*, *perceive*, pay *attention* to your spouse; 4. Learn to fear war again, then you will think twice about engaging in it, be a pacifist . . .

Of course, you might argue, there is nothing new about the fact that criticism harbors an ethical-philosophical dimension. And indeed, as I have shown at length elsewhere, you would certainly be right.[25] But the point is that we don't typically think of the early Shklovsky as a profoundly *ethical* and *existential* thinker. And I think we should. For it is, I believe, his blend of aesthetic-critical acumen and verve of style coupled with a profound ethical-existential agenda that makes "Art, as Device" such a unique, historically significant, and idiosyncratically innovative text: contracting the critic's attention to the operative minutiae of the literary text and away from history and psychology on the on hand; and, on the other hand, expanding the critic's reach to the ethical-metaphysical confines of human existence as such. And, most importantly, he is simply ethically *right*. For we would all agree, I imagine, that the ethics of loving attention he advocates is a good one, is the right one. We know so in particular because Shklovsky's anti-automatist, mindfulness-advocating followers—from Charlie Chaplin to Iris Murdoch and beyond—have never failed to strike a chord with more than some of us.[26]

But there is an additional aspect to Shklovsky's essay that I would like to address by way of concluding my own essay at trying to understand just what makes this remarkable thinker and his most famous work—"Art, as Device"—so unique in my view.

Let me address this additional aspect by asking: How *does* he know? How does he know that *'it is so'*? How does he know that *'it must be so'*? How can he be so sure?

As my questions indicate, there is a squarely *cognitive, epistemological* dimension to Shklovsky's approach. Of course, you might say, he is a critic, after all!—But I don't mean that. I mean that his critical, *reasoned* approach to the work and specific power of art implies that the very dynamic unfolding between the perceiver of art, the reader of poetry, and the work of art itself is premised on, involves, and happens though a process of *knowing* on the part of the perceiver, reader, etc. In other words, poetry and art in general work in such a way as to make us *know* that the specific work of art we are engaged with at a given moment brings or has brought back to life the world and things, has made us *see* and *feel* them "as they really are," to quote Iris Murdoch.[27] For that is what poetry and art in general are supposed to be able to do, according to Shklovsky: "make a stone a stone" again, allow us to *see* and *feel*, and thus also *know* (that we see and feel) the stone (read: things and the world at large) *as it really is*, in its *living truth*.

Now, we know that Shklovsky is strictly opposed to considering poetry and art in general as modes of *thinking*—by which he means syllogistic, logical *reasoning, ratiocination*, comparative, "algebraic" reasoning involving "recognition," etc. However art achieves its goals, it doesn't do so by reasoning. It makes us *see* and *feel*, and thus know. But *how* does it do it? How does it do it such that Shklovsky can be apodictically sure that "*it is so*"? What kind of "thinking," then, is operative in poetry and art in general?

Here, in a final move, I would like once more to attend to the ubiquity of the motifs of "seeing," "perceiving," and "feeling" in Shklovsky's early work and in particular in "Art, as Device." Verbs and their corresponding actions and experiences within us that guarantee, Shklovsky suggests, both the truth of art and the truth it conveys to us about the world. Let me reiterate this point in more detail: Shklovsky's entire argument is based on the notion that we simply *see*, *feel*, and *perceive* things "as they really are" in response to (certain) works of art *because* these works are such that they speak the truth, tell us the truth about the world—"make a stone a stone"—and must thus themselves be true. If we accept this as Shklovsky's underlying, implicit logical-philosophical premise, then his essay would appear to reveal itself as deeply flawed in that it opens itself up to the charge of subjectivism or relativism ("I see what I see, and you see what you see")—not to mention the circularity of the argument ("because I see it as true it must be true, and *vice versa*").

I suggest giving Shklovsky the benefit of the doubt, however, and reading his reliance on the truth-bearing power of *vision*, *perception*, and *feeling* as part of a long tradition going back to classical rhetoric, subsequently wending its way into philosophy, and trending heavily in Russia and elsewhere precisely during Shklovsky's formative and early professional years; a tradition that locates truth and the perception of truth *not* in argument or logical reasoning but in truth's own, spontaneous 'self-verification' from within itself, as it were: I am referring to the philosophical tradition of *evidence* as the guarantor of truth.

"Evidentia," a term Cicero introduced into philosophy as a translation of the Greek *enargeia* and as synonymous with "perspicuitas"—'clarity,' 'vividness,' perspicuousness,' etc.—is something that, as Cicero explains, "bears the mark of a *true* impression beyond true or false."[28] It is apodictically "*felt* by the mind," as David Hume notes, without requiring or being capable of further—scientific, empirical, or logical—proof.[29] As its very name suggests, it simply "illuminates itself from within itself and brings itself to light."[30]

Nowhere do the workings of *evidence* come to the fore as vividly as in the philosophical founding documents of the modern era: Descartes's *Discourse on Method* and *Meditations*. Famously, Descartes defines the cornerstone of his method for seeking the "truth" as "never accepting anything as true that I don't recognize as such in an *evidentiary* [évidemment] manner, [and] that doesn't present itself to my mind with such clarity and distinction that I couldn't possible doubt it." The "I think, therefore I am" reveals itself to Descartes as precisely such a "truth," "solid and certain"—"most certain and most evident," in fact, as Descartes emphatically reiterates, before moving on to specifying how this *evidentiary certitude* works, namely, owing to the power of the so-called natural light: "What I am capable of perceiving [mihi ostenduntur] thanks to the natural light—for instance that because I doubt [and, hence, think] I must also exist—cannot be doubted, for there cannot be any other power that I trust more than this light."[31] Four centuries later, German philosopher and founder of phenomenology Edmund Husserl, whose impact on the Russian academy at the beginning of the twentieth century is well documented,[32] will use almost the same words as Descartes to talk about the validity and truth of philosophical insight: "Not only the 'I am' is evident, but countless other judgments . . . , insofar as I do not merely opine them but possess the certainty of evidence [Evidenz] that what I perceive is actually given to me as that which I perceive it to be; that I myself grasp it as what it actually is."[33] (We have to remember that Husserl's philosophical method gained early recognition in Russia owing to the lively cultural-philosophical exchange between Germany and Russia in the early 1900s, including the translation into Russian of *Logical Investigations* [1900] as early as 1909, followed, in 1911, by the simultaneous publication in Russian and German of his programmatic essay "Philosophy as a Rigorous Science."[34])

In the present context, Husserl is not only important as a stark proponent of the truth and power of evidence as a mode of engaging with the self and the world, but also because his battle cry in the name of the aliveness of *things themselves* reverberated all across Europe and beyond when it was issued in *Logical Investigations* in 1900: "We want to return to the 'things themselves,'" Husserl proclaimed, and the phenomenological method with *evidence* as its linchpin and supreme arbiter of the truth of things "as they really are" would be the royal road to them.[35]

In light of the above—and without delving any deeper into Husserlian phenomenology at this point, or further discussing his concept of "things themselves" as designating *phenomena*, that is, things *as we perceive them* in the evidentiary light of our "completely developed intuition"—Shklovsky's reliance on his own vision, perception, and feeling for *knowing* what makes a stone a stone, for what things really are *as intuited through the medium of poetry* appears anything but relativist or subjectivist.[36] Like Descartes, Hume, Husserl and others before and after him, Shklovsky can be said to be availing himself of the *ethical-philosophical* right, as it were, to rely on the "great clearness and evidence" of his own "mind" and "senses"—to quote yet another proponent of the power of evidence, George Berkeley—in engaging with the world.[37]

Unlike the philosophers and proponents of the power of evidence mentioned, who looked solely within themselves for truth, however, Shklovsky steps outside of himself, as it were, and interposes the medium of poetry between what he sees, feels, and perceives and the world and things perceived. In other words, Shklovsky's *evidence* will have always already been mediated by art, and the evidentiary work being done in the seeing, perceiving, and feeling he advocates and describes in "Art, as Device" must, consequently, be a dialogical endeavor involving two and taking place somewhere between the poem and the reader, between the work of art and the viewer: Thus, while it might not be *"thinking* in images," poetry reveals itself as very much tasked with some form of thinking by Shklovsky—let's call it *evidentiary thinking* on the borderline between person and work. Certain, though, of his evidentiary knowledge Shklovsky can certainly be—at least as certain as Descartes, Berkeley, Hume, Husserl, and others. And whoever needs more evidence that the world is ever in need of being kept alive?

NOTES

1. Unless otherwise indicated, throughout this essay all translations are my own. On the history of the moniker "Formalism"/"Formalists," see, e.g., Eskin, "Translator's Introduction," 245n1.

2. Bergson, *Essai*, 11–12; Pater, "The School of Giorgione" (1877), cited in *The Renaissance*, 111; Tieck's line ("Liebe denkt in süßen Tönen"), from the 1799 poem "Love," cited in Frühwald, *Gedichte der Romantik*, 51; Horace, "Art Poetica," l. 361, cited in *Satires, Epistles, and Ars Poetica*, 480). See also Curtis, "Bergson." Concerning the equation of "love" and "poetry" in Tieck's poem, suffice it to note that it is based on the romantics'—especially the German romantics'—valorization of *heart/emotion/passion* over *head/mind/reason* (think of Johann Jakob Breitinger's battle cry for a new "heart-stirring writing style [herzrührende Schreibart]"), with *love* rising to the rank of supreme romantic emotion and poetic articulation (Breitinger, *Critische Dichtkunst*, vol. 2, 353–354).

3. Potebnya, *Iz zapisok*, 83 ("Bez obraza net iskusstva, v chastnosti poezii [Without the image, there is no art, and no poetry in particular]"), 97 ("Esli smotret' na poeziiu . . . kak na . . . sposob myshleniia i poznaniia, to takzhe nuzhno budet smotret' i na prozu [If we view poetry . . . as a mode of thinking and cognition, then we have to view prose in the same way]"). Shklovsky quotes both passages in "Iskusstvo."

4. Shklovsky, "Iskusstvo" ("obraz poeticheskii . . . sredstvo usileniia vpechetleniia . . . uvelicheniia oshchushcheniia veshchi . . . vernut' oshchushchenie zhizni"); "Potebnya" ("poetichekii obraz . . . od[in] iz sredstv").

5. "Excellence," in poetry, Aristotle notes, means avoiding the "banality" of "standard terms [kuriôn onomátôn]" and reaching "beyond the familiar [exallátousa]" through the use of unfamiliar, "exotic [xenikoîs]" devices, such as "loan words, metaphors, lengthenings, and all divergence from the standard" (*Poetics*, 109 [1458a17–21]). "[i]t is always the unfamiliar that wins our wonder," which is why the poet should aspire, according to Longinus, to "distinction of language" so as to "amaze us" (*On the Sublime*, 163, 277). See also Attridge, *Peculiar Language*.

6. "oshchushchenie mira kak zhivogo" (Mandel'shtam, "Utro Akmeizma" [1913], in *Sobraniye Sochinenii*, vol. 1, 180).

7. Shklovsky, "Iskusstvo."

8. Potebnya, *Iz zapisok*, 97 ("If we view poetry . . . as a means of thinking [sposob myshleniia] . . . then we have to view prose in the same way").

9. Shklovsky, "Iskusstvo."

10. See Eskin, "Denkbilder." The Dutch term "Denkbeelden" was coined by Willem Goerree in 1668 (see Goerree); see also Kirst, "Walter Benjamin's *Denkbild*," and Schulz, "Zum Wort, Denkbild.'"

11. Shklovsky, *Gamburgskii schët*, 423.

12. Shklovsky's single-minded focus on the life-quality-value of his work comes to the fore most saliently and poignantly in the following lines about Roman Jakobson, which immediately follow his nostalgic memories of Yakubinsky: "I am convinced that Roman Jakobson's departure for Prague is a great tragedy for my and his work [bol'shoe neshchast'e dlia moei i dlia ego raboty]. I am convinced that those who belong to the same literary formation or group [liudi odnoi literaturnoi gruppirovki] must think of each other's work first, and must alter their

personal destinies for each other [dolzhny schitat'sia v svoei rabote drug s drugom, dolzhny dlia drug druga izmeniat' lichnuiu sud'bu]" (*Gamburgskii schët*, 423).

13. See, for instance, Erlich, *Russian Formalism*, 73–79; Steiner, *Russian Formalism*, 140–167; Bartling, *Beyond Language*, 26, 266; Flack, *The Expressiveness*, 118–127; Berlina, "Translating," 156.

14. Eikhenbaum, "Teoriia formal 'nogo metoda,'" 380.

15. Yakubinsky, "O zvukakh" and "Skoplenie," both, respectively, in *Sborniki po teorii poeticheskogo iazyka I* and *II* (St. Peterburg, 1916/1917).

16. For Yakubinsky's essays in English, see Yakubinsky, *On Language and Poetry*.

17. Yakubinsky, "Skoplenie," 177.

18. Yakubinsky, "On the Sounds" 33 / "O zvukakh," 164; Jakobson, *Language*, 43, 69.

19. Ibid., 38, 41, 44 / 167, 169, 170.

20. Ibid., 45–46 / 170.

21. Ibid., 42–43 / 169.

22. Mandelstam, *Sobraniye Sochineny*, vol. 1, 180 ("oshchushchenie mira kak zhivogo"); Bergson, *L'évolution créatrice*, v–xi ("parenté de la pensée logique avec la matière inerte . . . poussée vitale . . . dépasser le point de vue de l'entendement [au nom] de la vie"). See also Curtis, "Bergson," 109–110, Erlich, *Russian Formalism*, 51ff.

23. Shklovsky, "Voskreshenie" ("My ne perezhivaem privychnoe, ne vidim ego a uznaem . . . zhazhda konkretnosti . . . zhivogo poeticheskogo chut'ia . . . veshchi umerli—My poteriali oshchushchenie mira . . . Neobkhodimo sozdanie novogo . . . na videnie, a ne na uznavanie passchitannogo iazyka"; "Potebnya" ("oshchutimost'iu . . . sozdat' oshchutimoe, perezhivaemoe v samoi svoei tkani, postroenie . . . ili akusticheskaia, ili proiznositel'naia, ili zhe semasiologicheskaia storona slova").

24. Tolstoy, diary entry of March 1, 1897 (not referenced in the 1917 version of "Art, as Device"), cited in Shklovsky, *Gamburgskii schët*, 63. Plato, *Apology*, 133 [38a5–6].

25. Eskin, "Answerable Criticism."

26. I am thinking of Chaplin's 1936 movie *Modern Times* in particular. Iris Murdoch has famously philosophized in the name of a close "attention . . . towards the great surprising variety of the world" (*The Sovereignty*, 27, 65), in the name of a "true vision . . . which reveals to us all things as they really are" (ibid., 64, 68).

27. Murdoch, *The Sovereignty*, 68.

28. Cicero, *The Academy (Lucullus)*, bk. 2, ch. 6, 34 ("ἐναργείαι—ut Graeci, perspicuitatem aut evidentiam nos si placet nominemus"), bk. 2, ch. 11, 43 ("sed propria veri non communi veri et falsi nota").

29. Hume, *A Treatise*, vol. 3, 628–629 ("this different feeling I endeavour to explain by calling it a superior *force*, or *vivacity*, or *solidity*, or *firmness*, or *steadiness* . . . [I]n philosophy we can go no farther, than assert, that it is something *felt* by the mind").

30. Heidegger, *Zur Sache des Denkens*, 73 ("Evidentia . . . meint das, was in sich selber aus sich selber her leuchtet und sich ins Licht bringt"). "Evidentia" is morphologically constructed from the prefix "ex-" (Lat.: "out of," "from") and "videntia" the nominalized form of the present active participle "videns" (Lat.: "seeing," "perceiving," "appearing"), derived from the verb "videre" (Lat.: "to see," "to seem," "to appear"). Thus, "evidentia" could be rendered, literally, as: "appearing out from within itself."

31. Descartes, *Discours*, 18, 32; *Meditationes*, 25, 38–39.

32. Bykova, "On the Phenomenological"; Haardt, *Husserl*; Flack, *The Expressiveness*, 2; Bartling, *Beyond Language*, 18, 22.

33. Husserl, *Logische Untersuchungen*, 357.

34. Husserl, "Philosophie als strenge Wissenschaft." Concerning the Russian-German cultural exchange, think for instance of Boris Pasternak's sojourn in Marburg in 1910, Mandel'shtam's in Heidelberg in 1909, and Gustav Shpet's in Göttingen in 1912–1913, where Husserl was teaching at the time.

35. "Wir wollen auf die 'Sachen selbst' zurückgehen" (Husserl, *Logische Untersuchungen*, 6). Concerning the ripple effect of Husserl's "return to 'things themselves,'" see, for instance, Mandel'shtam, "Utro Akmeizma" (see note 6) and Ezra Pound's 1912 precept that poetry

should engage in the "direct treatment of the thing" (*Literary Essays*, 5). On Pound and Husserl, see Eskin, "Denken in Bildern," 1; Wilhelm, *Ezra Pound*, 72–73.

36. "An vollentwickelten Anschauungen wollen wir uns zur Evidenz bringen" (Husserl, *Logische Untersuchungen*, 6).

37. Berkeley, *A Treatise*, 1.

WORKS CITED

Aristotle. *Poetics.* Translated by Stephen Halliwell. Cambridge, MA: Harvard University Press, 1995.

Attridge, Derek. *Peculiar Language: Literature as Difference from the Renaissance to James Joyce*. Ithaca, NY: Cornell University Press, 1988.

Bartling, Scott. *Beyond Language: Viktor Shklovsky, Estrangement, and the Search for Meaning in Art.* PhD diss., Stanford University, 2015.

Bergson, Henri. *Essai sur les donnés immédiates de la conscience* (1889). Paris: Quadrige/PUF, 1993.

———. *L'évolution créatrice* (1907). Paris: Quadrige/PUF, 1986.

Berkeley, George. *A Treatise Concerning the Principles of Human Knowledge* (1710). London: Jacob Tonton, 1734.

Berlina, Alexandra. "Translating 'Art as Device.'" *Poetics Today* 36.3 (2015): 151–156.

Breitinger, Johan Jakob. *Critische Dichtkunst* (1740). 2 vols. Stuttgart: Metzler, 1966.

Bykova, Marina F. "On the Phenomenological Philosophy in Russia." *Russian Studies in Philosophy* 54.1 (2016): 1–7.

Cicero, Marcus Tullius. *The Academy.* Edited by James Reid. London: Macmillan, 1874.

Curtis, James. "Bergson and Russian Formalism." *Comparative Literature* 28.2 (Spring 1976): 109–121.

Descartes, René. *Discours de la méthode* (1637). Edited by Charles Adam and Paul Tannery. Paris: Léopold Cerf, 1902.

———. *Meditationes de Prima Philosophia* (1641). Edited by Charles Adam and Paul Tannery. Paris: Léopold Cerf, 1904.

Eikhenbaum, Boris. "Teoriia formal'nogo metoda" (1926). *O Literature: Raboty raznykh let.* Moscow: Sovetskii pisatel', 1987. 375–408.

Erlich, Victor. *Russian Formalism: History and Doctrine*. The Hague, Paris, New York: Mouton Publishers, 1955.

Eskin, Michael. "Answerable Criticism: Reading Celan Reading Mandel'shtam." *Arcadia* 35.1 (2000): 66–80.

———. "Denkbilder: Zu einem Motiv bei Durs Grünbein." In *Bildlichkeit im Werk Durs Grünbeins*. Edited by Christoph auf der Horst and Miriam Seidler. Berlin, Boston: de Gruyter, 2015. 141–162.

———. "Translator's Introduction to Yakubinsky's *On Dialogic Speech*." *PMLA* 112.2 (1997): 243–248.

Flack, Patrick. *The Expressiveness of Experience: A Structural and Phenomenological Account of the Russian Formalists' "Aesthetics of Estrangement."* PhD diss., Karl University, Prague, 2010.

Frühwald, Wolfgang (ed.). *Gedichte der Romantik*. Stuttgart: Reclam, 1993.

Goeree, Willem. *Inleydinge Tot de Al-gehmeene Teycken-konst [Manual for the General Art of Drafting]* (1668). Leiden: Primavera Press, 1998.

Haardt, Alexander. *Husserl in Rußland: Phänomenologie der Sprache und Kunst bei Gustav Spet und Aleksj Losev*. Munich: Wilhelm Fink, 1993

Heidegger, Martin. *Zur Sache des Denkens*. Tübingen: Niemeyer, 1988.

Horace [Quintus Horatius Flaccus]. *Satires, Epistles and Ars Poetica*. Translated by H. Rushton Fairclough. London: Heinemann; Cambridge, MA: Harvard University Press, 1942.

Hume, David. *A Treatise on Human Nature* (1739/1740). 3 vols. Oxford: Clarendon Press, 1888.

Husserl, Edmund. *Logische Untersuchungen: Untersuchungen zur Phänomenologie und Theorie der Erkenntnis* (1900). Vol. 2/1. Tübingen: Niemeyer, 1993.

———. "Philosophie als strenge Wissenschaft." *Logos: Inernationale Zeitschrift für Philosophie I* (1910/1911): 289–341.

Jakobson, Roman. *Language in Literature*. Edited by Krystyna Pomorska and Stephen Rudy. Cambridge, MA: The Belknap Press, 1987.

Kirst, Karoline. "Walter Benjamin's *Denkbild*: Emblematic Historiography of the Recent Past." *Monatshefte* 86.4 (1994): 514–524.

Longinus. *On the Sublime*. Translated by W. H. Fyfe. Cambridge, MA: Harvard University Press, 1995.

Mandelstam, Osip. *Sobranie Sochinenii*. Edited by Pavel Nerler et al. Mandelstam Society edition. 4 vols. Moscow: Art-Biznes-Tsentr, 1993–1997.

Murdoch, Iris. *The Sovereignty of Good*. London: Routledge, 2001.

Pater, Walter. *The Renaissance: Studies in Art and Poetry*. New York: Modern Library, 1950.

Plato. *Euthyphro, Apology, Crito, Phaedo, Phaedrus*. Translated by Harold North Fowler. Cambridge, MA: Harvard University Press, 1914.

Potebnya, Aleksandr. *Iz zapisok po teorii slovesnosti: Poeziia i proza. Tropy i figury. Myshlenie poeticheskoe i mificheskoe. Prilozheniia*. Edited by Maria V. Potebnya. Kharkov: Parovaia Litografiia i Tipografiia M. Sil'berberg i S-v''ia, 1905.

Schulz, Eberhard Wilhelm. "Zum Wort, Denkbild.'" *Wort und Zeit: Aufsätze und Vorträge zur Literaturgeschichte*. Edited by Erich Trunz. Neumünster: Wachholtz, 1968. 218–252.

Shklovsky, Viktor. *Gamburgskii schët: Stat'i, vospominaniia, esse* (1928). Moskva: Sovetskii pisatel', 1990. http://lib.co.ua/memoir/shklovskiyvictor/gamburgskiy-schet.jsp.

———. "Iskusstvo, kak priëm." *Sborniki po teorii poeticheskogo iazyka II*. St. Peterburg: 18-aia gosudarstvennaia tipographiia, 1917. 3–14. http://www.opojaz.ru/manifests/kakpriem.html#Anchor-%1F%3EMB%3E%3C-17504.

———. "Potebnya." *Birzhevye vedomosti, utrennii vypusk*, No. 16010 (December 30, 1916). http://www.opojaz.ru/shklovsky/potebnya.html.

———. *Voskreshenie slova*. St. Peterburg: Tipografiia Z. Sokolinskogo, 1914. http://philolog.petrsu.ru/filolog/shklov.htm.

Steiner, Peter. *Russian Formalism: A Metapoetics*. Ithaca: Cornell University Press, 1984.

Wilhelm, James J. *Ezra Pound in London and Paris 1908–1925*. College Park: Pennsylvania State University Press, 1990.

Yakubinsky, Lev. *Izbrannye raboty: Iazyk i ego funktsionirovanie*. Edited by A. A. Leont'ev. Moscow: Nauka, 1986.

———. "O zvukakh stikhotvornogo iazyka." *Sborniki po teorii poeticheskogo iazyka I*. St. Peterburg: 18-aia gosudarstvennaia tipographiia, 1916. 6–30. In Yakubinsky, *Izbrannye raboty*, 163–175.

———. *On Language and Poetry: Three Essays*. Translated from the Russian by Michael Eskin. New York: Upper West Side Philosophers, 2018.

———. "On the Sounds in Poetic Language." In Yakubinsky, *On Language and Poetry*. 31–53.

———. "Skoplenie odinakovykh plavnykh v prakticheskom i poeticheskom iazykakh." *Sborniki po teorii poeticheskogo yazyka II*. St. Peterburg: 18-aia gosudarstvennaia tipographiia, 1917. 15–23. In Yakubinsky, *Izbrannye raboty*, 176–182.

Chapter Two

The Odyssey of Viktor Shklovsky

Life after Formalism

Basil Lvoff

More than anyone, Shklovsky's greatest adversary is Shklovsky. Particular ideas of his may be discredited, and they have been (e.g., by the Bakhtin circle);[1] nonetheless, the overall vision of literature that Shklovsky and his fellow Formalists advanced is incontestable—as any worldview, especially when rooted in empirical, personal, inferences about *how art is made*.[2] Yet, measured by his own yardstick—that of defamiliarization and recalcitrance to trade-offs—Shklovsky appears guilty of apostasy, defeated.

He is charged with betrayal of his legacy (culminating in a public recantation of Formalism in 1930) and then accused of a slavish and apologetic imitation of his early works (the latter, in such nostalgic books as 1964 *Once Upon a Time* [Zhili-byli]) and in "remakes." Some examples include the somewhat sanitized editions of *Zoo, or Letters Not about Love* (originally published in 1923), or the 1983 revised and expanded edition of *Theory of Prose* (originally published in 1925 and 1929).

Because of this, Shklovsky's fifty-year-long journey after Formalism has been held in ill repute, with such masterpieces as *Bowstring: On the Dissimilarity of the Similar* (1970) or *Letters to a Grandson* (published in 2002) overshadowed by his earlier writings. Meanwhile, Shklovsky's post-Formalist oeuvre is immense,[3] spanning the period between 1930 and 1984 (the year of his death), and all this short chapter can do is invite the reader to foray into this insufficiently explored territory.

THE MATTER AT HAND

The case of *Shklovsky v. Shklovsky* resembles that of perhaps his favorite literary personage, Don Quixote. In the second volume of the novel, the legendary hidalgo has to confront himself, on two levels. "It is most interesting," Shklovsky commented, "that in the second part Don Quixote knows about the first part and at the same time argues with the second part, which is forged."[4] The forged second part, of course, was not merely a figment of Cervantes' imagination. Before the second part of his novel saw the light of day, an unauthorized sequel by a certain Avellaneda (the falsifier's real name is unknown) had already been published (a practical illustration of the law of alienation in art), while in the novel itself, the real Don Quixote met his impostor. Cervantes admitted: "[F]rom countless directions I have been goaded into sending him [the Don Quixote of the second volume] out, in order to purge the disgust and the nausea caused by another Don Quixote who has been roaming through the world masquerading as the second part."[5]

Likewise, Shklovsky embraced confrontation, in a truly quixotic spirit; "my article," Shklovsky once wrote, "is published in the same way by which I live—by way of dispute."[6] Early on, disputatiousness earned Shklovsky a reputation for being a troublemaker, a brawler, a *skandalist*, as Veniamin Kaverin titled his eponymous novel with Shklovsky as a prototype for one of the main characters.[7] Disputatiousness, this bared dialectic, remained an aesthetic principle of Shklovsky's—only now, after Formalism, he argued less with his former opponents among the impressionistic, philosophy-oriented, or Marxist critics, and more with the doctrine that he and his friends, including Roman Jakobson,[8] were developing in the 1910s and 1920s. Shklovsky's former students, such as Kaverin or Arkady Belinkov,[9] believed, not entirely without reason, that he was untrue to himself.

However, it would be simplistic to regard his every disagreement with his earlier ideas as a retreat—after all, above all else, Shklovsky and his fellow Formalists prized the ability to change, hence their fondness for Leo Tolstoy as an artist who kept evolving all his life.[10] Besides, the evolution of Russian Formalism itself had already been under way in the 1920s—from the model in which art and socioeconomic reality were seen as perfectly separate in their development (see Shklovsky's 1923 book *A Knight's Move*), to the model in which they interacted (see Shklovsky's 1928 book *Material and Style in Leo Tolstoy's Novel "War and Peace"*).[11]

To Shklovsky, the ability to "swerve" from oneself was vital,[12] and self-contradiction was not only self-propelling—it was a source of reality, as evidenced by his remark that, thanks to the conflict between *Don Quixote*'s first and second parts (genuine and counterfeit), "the novel's protagonist feels real as such and is not imitating the sensation of authenticity [*zhiznennost'*]."[13] Shklovsky understood well that, as long as he was vigorously disputed, he was real, and the fact that he has been, up to the present,[14] speaks louder than words. Like Cervantes with Don Quixote, Shklovsky put attacks on his main hero, Viktor Shklovsky,[15] to good use and did not mind the imposters; however, like Cervantes again, there was one thing that he must have resented.

In the preface to the second volume, Cervantes reprimanded the author of the fake *Quixote* who, to scoff at Cervantes' writing skills, made puns about the hand Cervantes had lost in the Battle of Lepanto. "What I cannot help resenting," Cervantes wrote, "is that he charges me with being old and maimed, as if it had been in my power to halt the passage of time, as if the loss of my hand had occurred in some tavern and not on the greatest occasion that present, past, or future ages have ever seen."[16] Shklovsky could have addressed these words to those who, like Kaverin, also called him to account for losing an arm, as it were.

Shklovsky gave his right arm for his most cherished possession: his craft. It would be best to call it the craft of *siuzhetoslozhenie*, plot-construction (after Shklovsky's "The Relationship between Devices of Plot Construction and General Devices of Style," a cornerstone essay in *Theory of Prose*). *Siuzhet* was more than a technique for Shklovsky; derived from the French *sujet*, it implied subjectivity and selfhood, and the art of *siuzhetoslozhenie* was indeed synonymous with life—genuine, defamiliarized, self-authored life (*bytie*), opposed to its automated, depersonalized and desensitized, simulacrum (*byt*). *Siuzhetoslozhenie* was a literal and literary realization of the modernist principles of *zhiznetvorchestvo* (life-creation) and *zhisnestroitel'stvo* (life-building),[17] which explains why Shklovsky writes in *A Sentimental Journey* that, in the face of death, it was his (work on) *siuzhet* that he thought about: when a bomb exploded in his hands (1920) and on the eve of a duel (1921). Shklovsky survived this and other dangers of World War I and the Civil War, having preserved his craft (that of authoring art, its theory, and his own life).

Soon, however, in 1922, he had to save himself by fleeing from the Bolshevik government that was trying to arrest him as a former Socialist Revolutionary. Shklovsky found himself in Berlin, and even though he wrote there what is considered one of his finest books, *Zoo, or Letters Not about Love*, he felt that he was suffocating, deserted in a foreign country whose language (like any other but Russian) he did not speak. Neither could Shklovsky console himself with his émigré compatriots, looking to the past and not the future, cut off from tumultuous Russia, where "human flesh could be eaten" but at the same time "universities work[ed]" and "theaters [were] full."[18] Living in Berlin meant more personal safety, even comfort, but in Russia, where the revolutionary vortex had not yet subsided, one could still feel "wind resistance," as Shklovsky, an avid automobilist, put it.[19] Shklovsky wanted to return home, not knowing that already in the 1930s the dead calm of Stalinism would envelop his country. It was there, in Berlin, in the last letter of the documentary novel *Zoo*, that Shklovsky declared: "I raise my arm and surrender"—asking the Soviet government's permission to return.[20] The permission was granted, and miraculously, unlike so many others, Shklovsky survived (a contemporary likened him to a tilting doll);[21] he survived in spite of the cautionary story (expunged from the subsequent pre-perestroika editions of *Zoo*) that he told in the same letter, about the Askers (Turkish soldiers) in World War I, found dead with their right arms stretched—their gesture signifying surrender.

For some time, Shklovsky was able to carry on with his work in Soviet Russia, even defying Marxist literary critics in open debates.[22] Meanwhile, he shunned ideological clashes and in 1924 declared that he "solemnly resigned his rank and title of a member of the Russian intelligentsia," averring: "I am accountable to no one and know nothing, save a few devices of my craft [*masterstvo*]."[23] Yet this did not suffice, and two years later Shklovsky fell back again in *The Third Factory*, one of his saddest and most ironic books,[24] about "the writer's unfreedom."[25] Shklovsky declared: "We [the Formalists] love the wind of revolution. . . . When an automobile slows down . . . , the pressure drops. It is unbearable. The emptiness sucks you in. Let me speed up."[26] But at the same time, he wrote as though in favor of this unfreedom: "In all of Pushkin's life, perhaps only the bullet of d'Anthès wasn't necessary. / But fear and oppression are necessary."[27] This sounds somewhat deterministic; determinism was widespread among the Russian intelligentsia of Stalin's time.[28] However, rather than despair, Shklovsky was hoping that, eventually, his craft, and all the values it stood for, would outsmart the circumstances: "My craft is cleverer than I."[29]

Today, there are grounds to believe that it did. Yet back then, for all his irony—often inaccessible to his opponents who mistrusted him nonetheless, and justly so—in 1930 he had to recant the very thing for whose sake he had made all these sacrifices: his craft, or, to be more precise, the theory, the worldview that became known as Russian Formalism. Shklovsky had no choice but to proclaim his brainchild "a monument to a scientific error," as the title of the eponymous article had it. Yet, though this surrender was "ostensible" (as Richard Sheldon has demonstrated)[30] and though it allowed Shklovsky's survival, when, after Stalin's death, Shklovsky returned to his old plot, he found himself in the shade of that arm he had stretched in 1922 and then again in 1930.

SHKLOVSKY'S HOMECOMING, OR Δ FOR ΔEFAMILIARIZATION

It was the phrase "I raise my arm and surrender" that Kaverin took for an essay about Shklovsky's life, written in 1973 and posthumously published in 1989 as "the last shot in their literary duel."[31] Kaverin may have well titled his essay "*J'accuse!*" even though at the end of it he mercifully says that Shklovsky "is not to blame for being forced to raise his arm fifty years ago."[32] Many of Kaverin's accusations are personal, involving people with whom both Kaverin and Shklovsky were close. However, rather than tread on this shaky ground and discuss who betrayed whom (Shklovsky also leveled his accusations), it is more important to focus, in this chapter devoted to Shklovsky's legacy, on what Kaverin says about Shklovsky's craft.

According to Kaverin, Shklovsky, once an intrepid theorist and writer, forfeited his talent (his *siuzhet*) to compromise: "Shklovsky wrote at least sixty books and about one and a half thousand articles. But these are not (or at least not entirely) the kind of books and articles that he could and wanted to have written."[33] This is a heavy blow given the fact that "to be a writer who knows . . . how to write . . . mattered more to Shklovsky than any theory," as Jan Levchenko justly remarks.[34] Kaverin calls Shklovsky's books from the late 1920s on "unsuccessful," including among others *Matvei Komarov: The Dweller of Moscow* (1929), *The Life of the Artist Fedotov* (1936), and *Marco Polo* (1936).[35] Kaverin maintains that in them, because of them, Shklovsky lost the ability to make bold, broad, brilliant generalizations about literary history, "drawn to exceptionality—the trait that is not typical of a true historian."[36] Shklovsky's "characters," Kaverin continues, "did not come out well, . . . like museum pieces, they had no language of their own."[37] Meanwhile, for Shklovsky, Kaverin, and the people of their circle, connected with Russian Futurism, a museum was a symbol of dead culture excluded from history.

There is some truth in Kaverin's words. Shklovsky's books of the Stalin period were indeed an escape to the exotic: the lives of the lesser-known figures of eighteenth-and nineteenth-century Russia; the olden times (as with the unoriginally patriotic and, in all honesty, not very memorable 1940 book *Minin and Pozharsky*); the legendary travels of Marco Polo,[38] etc. Of course, each of these books deserves a separate discussion, and there is a world of difference, for example, between *Minin and Pozharsky* and the book on *Matvei Komarov*, which, for all its flaws, was a pioneering study of Russian eighteenth-century mass literature.[39] Nevertheless, those reading Shklovsky from approximately 1930 to 1953 will probably agree that it was getting harder and harder for him to speak his mind. "Between 1948 and 1953" especially, Sheldon observes, "almost nothing written by Shklovsky appeared in print," and in 1953 "[h]e reached the nadir of his existence as critic and writer . . . with the book *Remarks on the Prose of the Russian Classics* [*Zametki o proze russkikh klassikov*], a dismal product of this difficult period."[40] Levchenko's evaluation of this period in Shklovsky's life is both disenchanted and admiring. On the one hand, commenting on Shklovsky's 1933 book *Chulkov and Levshin*, he calls Shklovsky's "drifting towards Marxism" "superficial, not going beyond ritual references to economic and social factors' influence on the literary process."[41] Yet, on the other hand, Levchenko says: "A brilliant stylist and master of definitions, Viktor Shklovsky managed to cache . . . the capital of the Formal method in the clusters of manuals, collections of essays, film scripts and potboiler literature [*belletristika*], even children's literature."[42]

For this alone, Shklovsky should be given credit—"caching" his innermost ideas during a time when he felt "like a silver fox in a furrier's shop,"[43] having been a former opponent of the Bolsheviks and having lost all his siblings to the Civil War and the Gulag. Moreover, however bad the book about the artist Fedotov, for example, was, it clearly stated, written in Aesopian language (this second, unofficial language of the Soviet Union), that genuine art always outlives the despot (see the scene before Fedotov's death, when the artist is talking to his loved ones).[44] This book may very well be regarded as the squeak of a toy elephant (Shklovsky's self-comparison from *The Third Factory*), but squeaking seems preferable to muteness.

Furthermore, the *siuzhet* of Shklovsky's oeuvre provides an alternative to Kaverin's hardline view according to which he abandoned his cause to write about museum pieces. It is possible to maintain that writing about the minutiae of seventeenth-, eighteenth-, or nineteenth-century everyday life, writing about *things*, Shklovsky carried out the mission of saving them from oblivion. This is already the leitmotif of his famed essay "Art as Device" (1917): "Automatization eats away at things, clothes, furniture, one's wife, and the fear of war."[45] With the advent of Stalinism, however, the perennial attempt to hold on to the things of this world, constantly trying to slip away from us, reached Orwellian proportions, when nothing was stable and no one was certain any longer how much two and two made. Mikhail Iampolski describes this era in his review of Aleksei German's masterwork about Stalinism, the film *Khrustalyov, My Car!* The motion picture begins with the narrator "complaining about the poor memory of eyewitnesses who do not even remember the Persian lilac that once grew in 'our street.'"[46] The logic here is the same as that of Shklovsky: when we drop our guard and stop noticing the most obvious and smallest things—trees, furniture, etc.—it may end up in our getting used to war or the vanishing of thousands and millions of people around us, as happened so often in the last century.

Iampolski writes that German's film (as confusing, I might add, as the late books of Shklovsky) shows "memory work, pulling out various details [and] attaching grotesque significance to what appears to be perfectly insignificant."[47] Iampolski's words also unlock Shklovsky's style, with its constant digressions from the main theme to trivia and with its repetitions. Albeit some of these repetitions may have been unintentional (later in his life, Shklovsky dictated his texts), it would be simplistic to think that about all of them. If we turn to Shklovsky's 1963 *Leo Tolstoy*, the book that he was proud of, we will see that repetitions function like a camera zooming in on an object from various angles (multiple shots of the same object from unexpected angles are present in Abram Room's film *Bed and Sofa* [*Tret'ia Meshchanskaia*], based on Shklovsky's script).

This can be seen already in the first section of the Tolstoy book, "About the Green Sofa that Was Later Upholstered in Black Oilcloth": instead of describing the sofa in one compact paragraph, Shklovsky starts it again and again, as it were, in paragraphs two–six and eight (the latter repeats paragraph four, from a slightly different "angle"). It is noteworthy, moreover, that the sofa about which Shklovsky wrote in 1963 also featured in "Art as Device." To explain automatization and the need for defamiliarization, Shklovsky quoted Tolstoy, who wrote in his diary that, wiping dust in his room one day, he suddenly could not remember whether he had dusted off the sofa or not.

"I'm not writing a guidebook. I'm simply remembering the rooms in which Tolstoy lived"—this sentence from the 1963 book is more meaningful than it may look.[48] At first blush, old Shklovsky is wandering in Tolstoy's rooms as well as in the works of Russian and world literature, pointlessly so, jumping from one topic to another without much reason. This manner has already been partly justified, or *motivated* as the Formalists would say, by Iampolski's description of memory work, with its seemingly random and incommensurate details, narrative inconsistencies, and non sequiturs. However, there is more to this style of writing if we see it for what it is—essayism.

The essay is a performative genre; akin to a poem, it is lost in summaries. The very etymology of the term "essay" goes beyond "attempt" and "trial" to a Proto-Indo-European root meaning "to drive out, move." The essay is indeed always on the move, its "means of unfolding the plot" hidden in the intervals, *promezhutki*, between the paragraphs.[49] Each indentation is like a notch, a scar for every twist and turn in the thought's odyssey. Shklovsky's reader has to make these deliberate mental leaps with the author. Thus, a reader of *Bowstring* may turn to the section "New Petrograd and 'The Overcoat'" and try to "connect the dots" between the last four paragraphs. Shklovsky's essays put into practice the bowstring and lyre theory that he borrowed from Heraclitus and elaborated. Compared to the stick, the bow is a new principle of unity; deviating from itself, bent, the bow (its shape resembles Δ, the mathematical symbol of change) meets itself and confirms its identity, akin to Odysseus, who had to leave home in order to return and become himself. Thus, rupture—between the paragraphs of an essay or in the *siuzhet* of one's life—turns out to be the necessary condition of discovering and redeeming one's identity.[50]

The bowstring principle also explains Shklovsky's polemic against Structuralism—much better than saying that he was simply trying to get even with former allies such as Jakobson. Shklovsky was against, in his own words, "extrapolating the laws of grammar to the field of art"; "do not analyze and judge Dostoyevsky's characters by the laws of syntax and etymology," he wrote.[51] In *Bowstring*, Shklovsky devoted a whole chapter to Structuralism ("Language and Poetry"). He acknowledged the Structuralists' achievements and the fact that he needed to catch up with their theory. Yet he considered such articles as Jakobson's "Poetry of Grammar and Grammar of Poetry" a step backwards, in the direction of "old rhetoric," which can classify types of speech and explain the use or absence of personal pronouns in a poem but disregards the main thing about the work it analyzes.[52] "The main thing in analyzing art," Shklovsky said, "is not to lose the sensation [*oshchushchenie*] of art, the touch [*osiazanie*] of it, because otherwise the very object of study will become meaningless, nonexistent."[53] In refusing to see language as the ultimate point of reference for understanding art, Shklovsky overcame, rather than departed from, the language-centered perspective of early Russian Formalism. This was exactly the case that Aage A. Hansen-Löve describes as "the transition of the verbal into the semiotic" in the evolution of modernism.[54]

There was a time when Shklovsky wrote: "A literary work is pure form; it is not a thing, nor material, but a relationship of materials [*otnoshenie materialov*]."[55] Subsequently, Shklovsky lost the desire to hew to the old hyperbole about pure form; instead, he emphasized the "relationship of materials," saying: "Today, I proceed from the conviction that the very fact of perception contains the juxtaposition [*sopostavlenie*] of the work with the world."[56] Key to Shklovsky's thinking, as Serguei Oushakine remarks,[57] was the principle of montage, which Shklovsky, concurring with Eisenstein, considered a meaning-making contradiction rather than a peaceful assembly of parts. That is precisely what Shklovsky calls "the dissimilarity of the similar"—the subtitle of *Bowstring*. In fact, the whole composition of *Bowstring* is montage-like; in its chapters, Shklovsky confronts fellow Formalists Tynyanov and Eikhenbaum, the Structuralists, and many others. He also confronts Bakhtin, and it is Bakhtin's concept of *sobytie*, event, literally translated as co-being, that comes to mind, for contradiction—stemming from Old Latin *com* ("with," "together"), so that "speaking against" could also be seen as "speaking towards"—contradiction, too, is a form of event, a type of dialogue.

Returning to themes of his youth[58] and clashing with them, Shklovsky's late books complete the arc of his *siuzhetoslozhenie*. His early and late works—1929 and 1983 *Theory of Prose*, free verse poems from the 1914 collection *Leaden Lot* [*Svintsovyi zhrebii*] and bracingly poetic *Letters to a Grandson*—stand in dialectical unity with one another. In 1983 *Theory of Prose*, the last published book of his lifetime, Shklovsky tells the ending to his film script of *Don Quixote*. Don Quixote is dead; Dulcinea approaches his body and puts a book under his head. The book is *Don Quixote*. At this moment, the people who have been watching all along begin to whisper; they are whispering the man's real, nonliterary, name: Alonso Quixano. As always with Shklovsky, this is a parable, a parable about stepping out of your own shadow and regaining your authenticity. This is also the best description of Shklovsky's odyssey and perhaps the most important, practical lesson of his legacy for us to learn.

NOTES

1. See Bakhtin, Mikhail, and Pavel Medvedev, *The Formal Method in Literary Scholarship: A Critical Introduction to Sociological Poetics*, trans. Albert J. Wehrle (Baltimore: Johns Hopkins University Press, 1991).

2. See Shklovsky, Viktor, *Tekhnika pisatel'skogo remesla* (Moscow and Leningrad: Molodaia Gvardiia, 1927).

3. See Sheldon, Richard, *Viktor Shklovsky: An International Bibliography of Works by and about Him* (Ann Arbor: Ardis, 1977).

4. Shklovsky, Viktor, *O teorii prozy* (Moscow: Federatsiia, 1929), 115. Hereafter abbreviated *OTP*. In this chapter, preference is given to the Russian editions of Shklovsky's work as the history of his original publications is at issue. All translations from Russian are mine, unless indicated otherwise.

5. Cervantes, Miguel de, *Don Quixote*, trans. Walter Starkie (New York: Signet Classics, 2001), 524.

6. Shklovsky, Viktor, *Gamburgskii shchet: Stat'i—vospominaniia—esse (1914–1933)* (Moscow: Sovetskii pisatel',' 1990), 106. Hereafter abbreviated *GS*. To read more about the implicit values of Shklovsky's disputatiosness, see Lvoff, Basil [Lvov, Vasily], "V diskussionnom poriadke," *Voprosy Literatury* 2 (2012).

7. See Chudakova, Marietta, and Evgeny Toddes, "Prototipy odnogo romana," in *Al'manakh bibliofila. Vypusk X* (Moscow: Kniga, 1981).

8. See Galushkin, Alexander, ed., "Viktor Shklovsky i Roman Jakobson. Perepiska (1922–1956)" and "Eshchë raz o prichinakh razryva V. B. Shklovskogo i R. O. Jakobsona," *Roman Jakobson: Teksty, dokumenty, issledovaniia*, ed. Henryk Baran (Moscow: Rossiiskii gosudarstvennyi gumanitarnyi universitet, 1999). Also see *Viktor Shklovsky i Roman Jakobson. Zhizn' kak roman*. Directed by Vladimir Nepevny. Moscow: Telekompaniia "Gamaiun," 2009.

9. See Belinkov, Arkady, and Natalia Belinkova, *Raspria s vekom (v dva golosa)* (Moscow: Novoe literaturnoe obozrenie, 2008), chapter 8. See Berlina, Alexandra, "The Poker of Russian Formalism: Shklovsky as Protagonist," in *Viktor Shklovsky: A Reader*, ed. Alexandra Berlina (New York: Bloomsbury, 2017).

10. See Shklovsky, Viktor, *Energiia zabluzhdeniia: Kniga o siuzhete* (Moscow: Sovetskii pisatel',' 1981).

11. See Levchenko, Jan, "Poslevkusie formalizma: Proliferatsiia teorii v tekstakh Viktora Shklovskogo 1930-kh godov," *Novoe literaturnoe obozrenie* 4 (2014). See Lvoff, Basil, "When Theory Entered the Market: The Russian Formalists' Non-Marxian Approach to Mass Culture," *Ulbandus Review, A Culture of Institutions / Institutions of Culture* 17 (2016). Hereafter abbreviated *WT*.

12. The use of the word "swerve" (canonized in Harold Bloom's literary theory of the anxiety of influence) is deliberate here—see Lvoff, Basil [Lvov, Vasily], "Literaturnyi kanon i

poniatie strannosti: Russkii formalizm i Kherold Blum," *Zhurnalistika i kul'tura russkoi rechi* 2 (2012).

13. *OTP*, 115.

14. See Smirnov, Igor, "Formalizm i nigilizm," *Zvezda* 2 (2014).

15. That Shklovsky treated his own life as a book is known to everyone who has read him—see Kalinin, Ilya, "Viktor Shklovsky kak priëm," in *Sistemy*, ed. Serguei A. Oushakine, vol. 1 of *Formal'nyi metod: Antologiia russkogo modernizma*, ed. Serguei A. Oushakine (Moscow: Kabinetnyi uchënyi, 2016). Also see Razumova, Angelina, "Put' formalistov k khudozhestvennoi proze," *Voprosy literatury* 3 (2004).

16. Cervantes, 525–526.

17. See Ioffe, Denis, "Zhiznetvorchestvo russkogo modernizma sub specie semioticae. Istoriograficheskie zametki k voprosu tipologicheskoi rekonstruktsii zhizn'—tekst," *Kritika i semiotika* 8 (2005).

18. *GS*, 74.

19. Shklovsky, Viktor, "Zoo, ili Pis'ma ne o liubvi, ili tret'ia Eloiza," in *Iu. N. Tynyanov. V. B. Shklovsky. Proza*, ed. Vladimir Novikov (Moscow: SLOVO/SLOVO, 2001), 693.

20. Ibid., 698.

21. Zelinsky, Kornelii, "Kak sdelan Viktor Shklovsky," *Zhizn' iskusstva* 14 (1924).

22. See Tihanov, Galin, "Marxism and Formalism Revisited: Notes on the 1927 Leningrad Dispute," *Literary Research/Recherche Littéraire* 37–38 (2002).

23. *GS*, 187.

24. See Steiner, Peter, "The Praxis of Irony: Viktor Shklovsky's Zoo," in *Russian Formalism: A Retrospective Glance: A Festschrift in Honor of Victor Erlich*, eds. Robert Louis Jackson and Stephen Rudy (New Haven: Yale Center for International and Area Studies, 1985). See Grits, Teodor, *Tvorchestvo Viktora Shklovskogo (O "Tret'ei fabrike")* (Baku: Tipografiia OMZAKa, 1927).

25. Shklovsky, Viktor, *Tret'ia fabrika* (Moscow: Artel' pisatelei "Krug," 1926), 67. Hereafter abbreviated *TF*.

26. Ibid., 17.

27. Ibid., 85.

28. See Mandelstam, Nadezhda, *Hope Against Hope: A Memoir*, trans. Max Hayward (New York: Atheneum, 1983), 44: "We had really been persuaded that we had entered a new era, and that we had no choice but to submit to historical inevitability . . . Propaganda for historical determinism had deprived us of our will and the power to make our own judgments. . . . The usual line was to denounce history as such: it had always been the same, mankind had never known anything but violence and tyranny."

29. *TF*, 97.

30. Sheldon, Richard, "Viktor Shklovsky and the Device of Ostensible Surrender," *Slavic Review* 34 (1975). Hereafter abbreviated *VK*.

31. Novikov, Vladimir, "Poetika skandala," *Roman s literaturoi* (Moscow: Intrada, 2007), 77.

32. Kaverin, Veniamin, *Epilog* (Moscow: Vagrius, 2006), 55.

33. Ibid., 51.

34. Levchenko, 131–132.

35. Kaverin, 50.

36. Ibid.

37. Ibid.

38. Kaverin argued that Shklovsky's main reason for writing about Marco Polo was to use as an allegory the story of the traveler whom nobody believed when he returned home.

39. See *WT*.

40. *VK*, 108.

41. Levchenko, 143.

42. Ibid. To read Shklovsky on children's literature, see Shklovsky, Viktor, *Staroe i novoe* (Moscow: Detskaia literatura, 1966).

43. Shklovskaya-Kordi, Varvara, ed., "K 100-letiiu Viktora Shklovskogo. Izium iz bulki," *Voprosy literatury* 1 (1993), 322.

44. Nicholas I is that despot in the book, but it could easily be any other tyrant given the allegorical nature of Shklovsky's writing. Besides, *The Death of Vazir-Mukhtar*, the novel of Shklovsky's friend and ally Yuri Tynyanov, had already been written; in its prologue, the free and fearless people of the '20s are juxtaposed with their direct opposite, the people of the '30s, when Nicholas was emperor; what Tynyanov wrote about the '20s and '30s in the nineteenth century easily applied to the twentieth.

45. *OTP*, 13.

46. Iampolski, Mikhail, "Ischeznovenie kak forma sushchestvovaniia," *Kinovedcheskie zapiski* 44 (1999). Retrieved from http://www.kinozapiski.ru/ru/print/sendvalues/656/.

47. Ibid.

48. Shklovsky, Viktor, *Lev Tolstoi* (Moscow: Zhizn' zamechatel'nykh liudei, 1963), 9.

49. *OTP*, 91.

50. For an illuminating study of this sort of rupture, from Kant to the Russian Formalists and Bakhtin, see Holquist, Michael, and Ilya Kliger, "Minding the Gap: Toward a Historical Poetics of Estrangement," *Poetics Today* 26:4 (2005).

51. Garzonio, Stefano, "Viktor Shklovsky i Dzhovanni Bokkachcho: Ob istorii odnoi maloizvestnoi stat'i Shklovskogo," in *Epokha "ostraneniia." Russkii formalizm i sovremennoe gumanitarnoe znanie: Kollektivnaia monografiia*, eds. Jan Levchenko and Igor Pilshchikov (Moscow: Novoe literaturnoe obozrenie, 2017). Retrieved from https://play.google.com/books/reader?id=myMrDwAAQBAJ&pg=GBS.PR20-IA11.w.2.0.39.

52. Shklovsky, Viktor, *Tetiva: O neskhodstve skhodnogo* (Moscow: Sovetskii pisatel,' 1970), 238. Hereafter abbreviated *Tetiva*.

53. Ibid., 231.

54. Hansen-Löve, Aage A., "Perspektivy russkogo formalizma: Logotsentrizm vchera i segodnia," in *Epokha "ostraneniia." Russkii formalizm i sovremennoe gumanitarnoe znanie: Kollektivnaia monografiia*, eds. Jan Levchenko and Igor Pilshchikov (Moscow: Novoe literaturnoe obozrenie, 2017). Retrieved from https://play.google.com/books/reader?id=myMrDwAAQBAJ&pg=GBS.PP53.

Hansen-Löve also mentions Marshall McLuhan as an example of this shift in modernism. Shklovsky's essays, especially later ones, contain striking resemblances to McLuhan's theory, as well as that of Bruno Latour (Serguei Oushakine's observation), as a case of what can be called relational agency. This agency does not belong to one system; it is intermediated: people shape their tools (including language) and vice versa. People and things, perceptions and sensations, the word and the world determine each other. To read more about it, see Lvoff, Basil, "Viktor Shklovsky and Marshall McLuhan: Beyond Common Sense," *New Zealand Slavonic Journal* 49–50 (2015–2016 [2018]).

55. *OTP*, 226.

56. *Tetiva*, 230.

57. See Oushakine, Serguei, "'Ne vzletevshie samolëty mechty': O pokolenii formal'nogo metoda," in *Sistemy*, ed. Serguei A. Oushakine, vol. 1 of *Formal'nyi metod: Antologiia russkogo modernizma*, ed. Serguei A. Oushakine (Moscow: Kabinetnyi uchënyi, 2016), 52.

58. Salman, Marina, "Molodoi Shklovsky. (Po arkhivnym materialam)," in *Vienna Slavic Yearbook. 5*, ed. Stefan Michael Newerkla and Fedor B. Poljakov (Wiesbaden: Harrassowitz Verlag, 2017).

WORKS CITED

Bakhtin, Mikhail, and Pavel Medvedev. *The Formal Method in Literary Scholarship: A Critical Introduction to Sociological Poetics*. Translated by Albert J. Wehrle. Baltimore: Johns Hopkins University Press, 1991.

Belinkov, Arkady, and Natal'ia Belinkova. *Raspria s vekom (v dva golosa)*. Moskva: Novoe literaturnoe obozrenie, 2008 (in Russian).

Berlina, Alexandra. "The Poker of Russian Formalism: Shklovsky as Protagonist." In *Viktor Shklovsky: A Reader*, edited by Alexandra Berlina, 30–44. New York: Bloomsbury, 2017.

Cervantes, Miguel de. *Don Quixote*. Translated by Walter Starkie. New York: Signet Classics, 2001.
Chudakova, Marietta, and Evgeny Toddes. "Prototipy odnogo romana." In *Al'manakh bibliofila. Vypusk X*, 172–190. Moskva: Kniga, 1981 (in Russian).
Galushkin, Alexander. "Eschë raz o prichinakh razryva V. B. Shklovskogo i R. O. Jakobsona." In *Roman Jakobson: Teksty, dokumenty, issledovaniia*, edited by Henryk Baran, 136–143. Moskva: Rossiiskii gosudarstvennyi gumanitarnyi universitet, 1999 (in Russian).
———. "Viktor Shklovsky i Roman Jakobson. Perepiska (1922–1956)." In *Roman Jakobson: Teksty, dokumenty, issledovaniia*, edited by Henryk Baran, 104–135. Moskva: Rossiiskii gosudarstvennyi gumanitarnyi universitet, 1999 (in Russian).
Garzonio, Stefano. "Viktor Shklovsky i Dzhovanni Bokkachcho: Ob istorii odnoi maloizvestnoi stat'i Shklovskogo." In *Epokha "ostraneniia." Russkii formalizm i sovremennoe gumanitarnoe znanie: Kollektivnaia monografiia*, edited by Ian Levchenko and Igor Pilshchikov. Moskva: Novoe literaturnoe obozrenie, 2017 (in Russian).
Grits, Teodor. *Tvorchestvo Viktora Shklovskogo (O "Tret'ei fabrike")*. Baku: Tipografiia OMZAKa, 1927 (in Russian).
Hansen-Löve, Aage A. "Perspektivy russkogo formalizma: Logotsentrizm vchera i segodnia." In *Epokha "ostraneniia." Russkii formalizm i sovremennoe gumanitarnoe znanie: Kollektivnaia monografiia*, edited by Ian Levchenko and Igor Pilshchikov. Moskva: Novoe literaturnoe obozrenie, 2017. Retrieved from https://play.google.com/books/reader?id=myMrDwAAQBAJ&pg=GBS.PP53 (in Russian).
Iampolski, Mikhail. "Ischeznovenie kak forma suschestvovaniia." *Kinovedcheskie zapiski* 44 (1999). Retrieved from http://www.kinozapiski.ru/ru/print/sendvalues/656/ (in Russian).
Ioffe, Denis. "Zhiznetvorchestvo russkogo modernizma sub specie semioticae. Istoriograficheskie zametki k voprosu tipologicheskoi rekonstruktsii zhizn' —tekst." *Kritika i semiotika* 8 (2005): 126–179 (in Russian).
Kalinin, Ilya. "Viktor Shklovsky kak priëm." In *Sistemy*, edited by Serguei A. Oushakine, vol. 1. *Formal'ny metod: Antologiia russkogo modernizma*, edited by Serguei A. Oushakine, 63–106. Moskva: Kabinetnyi uchënyi, 2016 (in Russian).
Kaverin, Veniamin. *Epilog*. Moskva: Vagrius, 2006 (in Russian).
———. *Skandalist, ili Vechera na Vasil'evskom ostrove*. Moskva: Gosudarstvennoe izdatel'stvo khudozhestvennoi literatury, 1963 (in Russian).
Levchenko, Ian. "Poslevkusie formalizma: Proliferatsiia teorii v tekstakh Viktora Shklovskogo 1930-kh godov." *Novoe literaturnoe obozrenie* 4 (2014): 125–143 (in Russian).
Lvoff, Basil [Lvov, Vasily]. "Literaturny kanon i poniatie strannosti: Russkii formalizm i Kherold Blum." *Zhurnalistika i kul'tura russkoy rechi* 2 (2012): 86–103 (in Russian).
———. "V diskussionnom poriadke." *Voprosy literatury* 2 (2012): 1–21 (in Russian).
Mandelstam, Nadezhda. *Hope Against Hope: A Memoir*. Translated by Max Hayward. New York: Atheneum, 1983.
Novikov, Vladimir. "Poetika skandala." In *Roman s literaturoi*, 76–85. Moskva: Intrada, 2007 (in Russian).
Oushakine, Serguei. "'Ne vzletevshie samolëty mechty': O pokolenii formal'nogo metoda." In *Sistemy*, edited by Serguei A. Oushakine, vol. 1. *Formal'ny metod: Antologiia russkogo modernizma*, edited by Serguei A. Oushakine, 9–60. Moskva: Kabinetnyi uchënyi, 2016 (in Russian).
Razumova, Angelina. "Put' formalistov k khudozhestvennoi proze." *Voprosy literatury* 3 (2004): 131–150 (in Russian).
Salman, Marina. "Molodoi Shklovsky. (Po arkhivnym materialam.)" In *Vienna Slavic Yearbook*. 5, edited by Stefan Michael Newerkla and Fedor B. Poljakov, 148–167. Wiesbaden: Harrassowitz Verlag, 2017 (in Russian).
Sheldon, Richard. "Viktor Shklovsky and the Device of Ostensible Surrender." *Slavic Review* 34 (1975): 86–108.
———. *Viktor Shklovsky: An International Bibliography of Works by and about Him*. Ann Arbor: Ardis, 1977.
Shklovskaya-Kordi, Varvara, ed. "K 100-letiiu Viktora Shklovskogo. Izium iz bulki." *Voprosy literatury* 1 (1993): 322–330 (in Russian).

Shklovsky, Viktor. "Pis'ma vnuku." *Voprosy literatury* 4 (2002): 264–300 (in Russian).
―――. "Sentimental'noe puteshestvie." In *Yu. N. Tynyanov. V. B. Shklovsky. Proza*, edited by Vladimir Novikov, 430–641. Moskva: SLOVO/SLOVO, 2001 (in Russian).
―――. "Zoo, ili Pis'ma ne o liubvi, ili tret'ia Eloiza." In *Yu. N. Tynyanov. V. B. Shklovsky. Proza*, edited by Vladimir Novikov, 642–698. Moskva: SLOVO/SLOVO, 2001 (in Russian).
―――. *Chulkov i Levshin*. Leningrad: Izdatel'stvo pisatelei v Leningrade, 1933 (in Russian).
―――. *Energiia zabluzhdeniia: Kniga o siuzhete*. Moskva: Sovetskii pisatel,' 1981 (in Russian).
―――. *Gamburgskii schët: Stat'i—vospominaniia—esse (1914–1933)*. Moskva: Sovetskii pisatel', 1990 (in Russian).
―――. *Khod konia*. Moskva and Berlin: Gelikon. 1923 (in Russian).
―――. *Lev Tolstoy*. Moskva: Molodaya Gvaridiia (Zhizn' zamechatel'nykh liudei), 1963 (in Russian).
―――. *Marko Polo*. Moskva: Zhurnal'no-gazetnoe ob'edinenie, 1936 (in Russian).
―――. *Material i stil' v romane L'va Tolstogo "Voina i mir."* Moskva: Federatsiia, 1928 (in Russian).
―――. *Matvei Komarov. Zhitel' goroda Moskvy*. Leningrad: Priboi, 1929 (in Russian).
―――. *Minin i Pozharskii*. Moskva: Sovetskii pisatel', 1940 (in Russian).
―――. *O teorii prozy*. Moskva: Federatsiia, 1929 (in Russian).
―――. *O teorii prozy*. Moskva: Sovetskii pisatel', 1983 (in Russian).
―――. *Staroe i novoe*. Moskva: Detskaia literatura, 1966 (in Russian).
―――. *Svintsovyi zhrebii: Dar Viktora Shklovskogo Lazaretu deiatelei iskusstv*. Sankt-Peterburg: Tip. Z. Sokolinskogo, 1914 (in Russian).
―――. *Tekhnika pisatel'skogo remesla*. Moskva—Leningrad: Molodaia Gvardiia, 1927 (in Russian).
―――. *Tetiva: O neskhodstve skhodnogo*. Moskva: Sovetskii pisatel,' 1970 (in Russian).
―――. *Tret'ia fabrika*. Moskva: Artel' pisatelei "Krug," 1926 (in Russian).
―――. *Zametki o proze russkikh klassikov: O proizvedeniiakh Pushkina, Gogolia, Lermontova, Turgeneva, Goncharova, Tolstogo, Chekhova*. Moskva: Sovetskii pisatel,' 1953 (in Russian).
―――. *Zhili-byli*. Moskva: Sovetskii pisatel', 1964 (in Russian).
―――. *Zhizn' khudozhnika Fedotova*. Moskva: Izdatel'stvo detskoi literatury, 1936 (in Russian).
Smirnov, Igor. "Formalizm i nigilizm." *Zvezda* 2 (2014). Retrieved from https://zvezdaspb.ru/index.php?page=8&nput=2243 (in Russian).
Steiner, Peter. "The Praxis of Irony: Viktor Shklovsky's *Zoo*." *Russian Formalism: A Retrospective Glance: A Festschrift in Honor of Victor Erlich*, edited by Robert Louis Jackson and Stephen Rudy, 27–43. New Haven: Yale Center for International and Area Studies, 1985.
Tihanov, Galin. "Marxism and Formalism Revisited: Notes on the 1927 Leningrad Dispute." *Literary Research/Recherche Littéraire* 37–38 (2002): 69–77.
Tynyanov, Yuri. *Kiukhlia. Smert' Vazir-Mukhtara*. Moskva: Kniga, 1981 (in Russian).
Viktor Shklovsky i Roman Jakobson. Zhizn' kak roman. Directed by Vladimir Nepevny. Moskva: Telekompaniia "Gamayun," 2009, https://vimeo.com/154703239 (in Russian).
Zelinsky, Kornelii. "Kak sdelan Viktor Shklovsky." *Zhizn' iskusstva* 14 (1924): 13–14 (in Russian).

Chapter Three

The Eternal Wonderer or Who Was Viktor Shklovsky?

Slav N. Gratchev

In December 1913, in the "Stray Dog" café[1] located in St. Petersburg, then the capital of the vast Russian Empire, Viktor Shklovsky made his first appearance as a literary critic. He could not know that for the next seventy-five years he would continue a career that would be constantly shifting between scholar and writer. In 1982 he would leave us wondering and debating the same question: who was Viktor Shklovsky?

It is always invaluable for scholars to find uncensored, unclipped evidence that will support our investigations. Such evidence has been lying in the basement of the Moscow State University Library since 1982, when the former university professor, Victor Duvakin, deposited his collection of tapes on the shelves. He knew that no one would be interested in them until the next century, and he was right.

The early 1980s were turbulent: Leonid Brezhnev[2] died in 1982, and the new leader of the USSR became the unpredictable Yuri Andropov.[3] With this former Head of the KGB, freedom could easily have had an even tighter grip on its throat; obviously, no one was interested in Duvakin's collection of memories. Then the famous perestroika came.[4] It brought us a longed-for freedom, but it also brought us a desperate poverty. So, it took another ten years for people to finally start to think again about the future and not just about today. The "great time" of Duvakin's collection finally knocked on the door of the library: the collection was retrieved from the shelves, and the old bobbins of magnetic tapes started to be re-played again, and this time they would be digitized. There was so much of everything in this unusual collection: voices of people with international fame, like Dmitri Shostakovich[5] and

Roman Jakobson. There were real gems—like 12 hours of conversations with Mikhail Bakhtin and 3.5 hours with Viktor Shklovsky.

Today, for those of us who are trying to establish the historic truth, these "memories of the survivors" as I call them, are more precious than diamonds. Today, in the twenty-first century we, all of a sudden, have an opportunity to hear the voices of these live legends—people with whom oral interviews were recorded by the Soviet philologist and sheer enthusiast, Victor Duvakin, in 1967 and 1968. It is precisely these interviews that, while I was translating them from Russian to English, helped me answer this question[6]—once and for all.

Shklovsky, in fact, became a writer long before he made his academic debut in the "Stray Dog": in 1907 his first short story was published in one of the futuristic magazines *Vesna* ["The Spring"], which, coincidentally, I think, had the same title: *The Spring*. Next, when, in 1982, Shklovsky finished (another coincidence?) his last academic book *O teorii prozy* ["About the Theory of Prose"], the circle of his career was closed; clearly, his career as a writer had ended with his career as an academician.

Today, when all the discussions about Formalists are over, people often do not remember why Shklovsky, and others with him, many years ago received the derogatory nickname—formalists. Yet, the fact is that they, for the first time in literary scholarship, did exactly what they are still remembered for today; they shifted their attention to the *form* of the artifact instead of collecting numerous, and often useless, facts. Why is *Don Quixote* a novel and not a poem? Why is *Childe Harold's Pilgrimage* a poem and not novel? Those seemingly simple questions require quite difficult answers. Then the second set of questions comes: How were *Don Quixote* and *Childe Harold* made? And at this moment, those "formalists" (as they were called initially by the retrogrades) all of a sudden became The Formalists. Why? Because they, for the first time ever, were able to offer answers to these burning and very important questions. Thus, the nickname, coined to offend, had turned into a brand. The brand soon become known all over the world (even though there was no internet or email!), and numerous linguistic schools in different parts of the world started to get inspiration from those few Russian scholars locked in the vast spaces of the "most free land," in which, after the first days of the Revolution, the "Iron Curtain" was painstakingly erected so that even a bird would not be able to leave the country without written permission from the Communist Party.

Very soon this "curtain" would separate the country from the outside world, and, in the darkness of the night, mass arrests would start. People—and most often the best people, the cream of the crop of the country—were arrested in the middle of the night and taken away for interrogation, and nobody would ever see them again. At this time, Shklovsky also found out that he was on the list to be arrested, and he decided to run, just in time. In the middle of a cold winter in 1922 he crossed, on ice, the Finland bay to land in Finland, and he asked for refuge there. Then he moved to Germany where all Russian intellectuals, blown away by the winds of the ruthless Bolshevik revolution, gathered together to continue to serve their country, to the best of their limited abilities.

In a year and a half, Shklovsky, drawn by never-ending nostalgia, returned to the USSR where he reunited with his family and resumed his academic activities. It was not an easy thing to do in the totalitarian country; by 1929 all liberal and independent journals that did not reflect the ideas and goals of the Communist party were shut down. In 1930, to save himself and his family from inevitable prosecution, Shklovsky had to publish an article titled "Monument of the scientific error" where he admitted that Formalism was a mistake. By then, the leaders of the former Formalist School had taken different roads. Roman Jakobson[7] went to the United States. Tomashevsky[8] maintained a low profile, although he was still not able to escape constant and severe criticism. Eikhenbaum[9] (one of the most respected Tolstoy scholars) had to comply with nonsense to save his life. Osip Brik left this world at the age of 47, and Yury Tynyanov[10] died during the Leningrad Siege[11] from poor nutrition. Shklovsky survived them all but not because he was a conformist (as some scholars claimed he was) but because he was simply fortunate not to fall between a hammer and an anvil. In fact, the Soviet system was hammering blindly, and those who managed to hide at the moment of attack saved their lives. The hammer was too busy to return and rather continued its destruction in other places.

For two difficult decades (1933–1953), Shklovsky worked on writing screenplays, historical novels, and essays. Studying history was safe at this time of total terror. Being a screenplay writer was also quite innocent; every screenplay was ordered and approved by the Communist party anyway. Freelance artistic activity was frozen: to become a writer one had to become a member of the Union of Soviet Writers.[12] Without this membership, no publishing house would ever publish one's work. So, for many years, Shklovsky, in order to continue publishing, had to maintain a prudent balance between what he loved and what he needed to write. We do not believe that anyone should condemn him for that; when you live under totalitarian regime, there is only so much you can do and say, or you could be crashed by that merciless and powerful totalitarian machine.

Real scholarship was defeated by the "only right point of view"—of Marx and Lenin. Scholars sheltered themselves in niches like preparing complete works of Russian and European classics, translating and preparing comments for some special editions. Those comments, of course, had to be scrutinized by the censors first, who were on guard to dismantle any "erroneous Western theory." What kind of discussion or disagreement could there be with the Communist party whose leaders knew "absolutely everything" and could easily give recommendations to Pablo Picasso (if he happened to live in the USSR, of course) on how to mix paints!

On one beautiful morning, on March 5 of 1953, "the Father of all nations"—as Stalin was called in the USSR—finally died. Nikita Khrushchev[13] declared the "anti-Stalin" crusade, and scholars got a breath of fresh air. Shklovsky responded with a brilliant book about Fyodor Dostoevsky—the first serious study written about the greatest Russian writer in the last 30 years. Dostoevsky was forbidden in the USSR, and his books were removed from all libraries because in one of his novels[14] he "dared" to warn that the Socialists, with their crazy and, essentially, terroristic ideas about revolution and society, would destroy Russia, its culture, and ultimately its people.

It is unfortunate that Shklovsky's former best friend, Roman Jakobson, living in the United States, heavily criticized this book. Jakobson, being on a high house and teaching egalitarian courses at Massachusetts Institute of Technology naturally assumed that the principle of social justice could prevail in any society, as in the United States, and he could not understand the bleak Soviet reality Shklovsky was living through. His former friend, colleague, and compatriot, Jakobson could not now comprehend that even writing such a book was a heroic deed that only the bravest could have done.

Khrushchev's thaw did not last for long, and people soon realized that "Soviet freedom" was no more than an illusion that never existed and never will. The difference now was that people were not arrested so easily, but the soviet oppressive machine was as powerful as ever. Boris Pasternak,[15] who published *Doctor Zhivago*[16] in Italy after being turned down by all the domestic publishers, was defamed, deprived of work, and consigned to oblivion. His heart did not take it lightly, and Pasternak died in about one year, in complete solitude. Only a few of his old friends attended the funeral, those who did not fear the regime and declared that Russia had lost one of its greatest writers and poets. Shklovsky was one of those who came to the funeral of his good old friend.

The life story of any remarkable person will inevitably become a source of valuable information about his era. That is why memoirs eventually become an invaluable document for those who study that person's works or the era he/she lived in. The only problem with memoirs is that not everything can be trusted to paper, especially in a society that does not enjoy freedom. Professor Victor Duvakin, for example, experienced the "gratitude' of his government, when, after 40 years of dedicated service to the university, he was dismissed merely because he expressed doubts that his former student, Andrey Sinyavsky,[17] should be reproached so heavily for publishing his book in the West. The next day Duvakin lost his job.

Yet, as the Spanish proverb says, "No hay mal que por bien no venga" [there is nothing bad that can come without bringing some benefits]. Together with the painful dismissal, Duvakin received a long-desired freedom to do what he had been planning to do for the longest time: interview people who were around when the most dramatic events and changes were happening in our country—the Revolution, the terror, World War II.

First of all, Duvakin made a list of those he would love to visit—more than 300 people. Unfortunately, some of them died while Duvakin was interviewing others, but the total number of those with whom he held interviews is impressive—295. One of them was Viktor Shklovsky.

His voice is the real reflection of a history that he saw through the eyes of the philistine and not of the scientist; he does not exaggerate anything for the sake of political conjuncture but wants to convey to us images of people once dear to him. He is simply talking about things that he thinks are interesting or important. He mentions many names he assumes you should know; he expresses his emotions. He is just a real person, relaxed and happy to share his memories.

The importance of his recollections is obvious: a scholar who would try to write today about the dramatic relationship between Mayakovsky and Lilya Brik[18] could not know the *exact* context when such and such an event or conversation took place and what *exactly* was said. Shklovsky often does. Because he was there. He was present when the bullet was taken out of Mayakovsky's head. He truly walked with Alexander Blok[19] in St. Petersburg for two entire nights. He was a friend of Sergei Yesenin[20] and his first wife, Zinaida,[21] who later became the wife of Vsevolod Meyerhold.[22] He was a personal friend of Maxim Gorky.[23] He attended Lenin's speech three times[24] and was the close friend of Sergei Eisenstein.[25]

In these dialogues, Shklovsky gives us a slice of Russian micro-history—when the most dramatic events of the twentieth century took place in Russia and the USSR—and proves once again that his first call—the call of the writer—was for him, certainly, the most important one. Despite international recognition as a scholar, Shklovsky always remained, for himself, a writer who not only liked to create stories but also liked to find out how stories were made.

As Eva Thomson noted, Shklovsky was so much an ichthyologist that he eventually turned into a fish.[26] It is not often that a scientist merges with the subject of his study and does it so successfully.

NOTES

1. The "Stray Dog" café was a cult art cabaret located in downtown St. Petersburg. The café became famous when the most notable Silver Age poets (Anna Akhmatova, Osip Mandelstam, Nikolay Gumilev, Vladimir Mayakovsky, Vsevolod Meyerhold, and Velimir Khlebnikov, among others) became frequent visitors there. The café existed from late December 1911 until March 1915, when it closed, supposedly due to World War I.

2. Leonid Brezhnev (1907– 1982) was a political leader of the USSR for eighteen years (1964–1982). By skillfully dismissing Nikita Khrushchev, Brezhnev assumed power and, in the

beginning, demonstrated the good qualities of a truly progressive leader. In 1972 he met with American President Richard Nixon, and the end of Cold War started to loom on the horizon. However, later Brezhnev became obsessed with political intrigues, family difficulties, and his personal health, and the USSR gradually slipped into a deep depression known as an era of *zastoi* ["stagnation"].

3. Yuri Andropov (1914–1984) was, perhaps, the most controversial leader of the USSR. Being a very intelligent and educated person, Andropov understood that socialism in the USSR was living its last years. To save the country from collapse, drastic economic and political reforms were necessary, and this is what Andropov focused on. During the fifteen months of his rule, Andropov did more than all the other Communist Party leaders combined ever dreamed of accomplishing, but his health deteriorated rapidly. Despite the massive anti-Soviet propaganda and a time of the most antagonistic relations with the West, Andropov was declared The Man of the Year by *Time* (1983).

4. Perestroika (1985–1991) was the massive re-organization of the USSR's economic and political life, initiated by Mikhail Gorbachev. The results of perestroika have definitely been positive for the world's political stability and predictability; the Cold War between the West and the USSR was over. By the same token, perestroika and its repercussions for the country and its ordinary citizens were far from perfect, or expected; devaluation of the national currency, devastation of the economy, food stamps for essential goods like sugar, oil, soap, etc. are just a few negatives that impacted the lives of Russians who, in general, condemned perestroika.

5. Dmitry Shostakovich (1906–1975) was one of the greatest composers of the twentieth century. He is the author of 15 symphonies, 3 operas, and 3 ballets. He was a close friend of Igor Stravinsky and Sergey Prokofiev and worked as a Professor at the Petersburg Conservatory.

6. I make a reference here to a book recently translated and published: *Dialogues with Shklovsky: The Duvakin Interviews, 1967–1968*. Eds. Slav N. Gratchev and Irina Evdokimova (Lanham: Lexington books, 2019).

7. Roman Jakobson (1896–1982) was one of the most influential linguists and literary theorists of the twentieth century. After immigrating to the United States (1942), Jakobson lectured at Columbia University, Harvard, and MIT. During Khrushchev's political "thaw" and Brezhnev's time, Jakobson frequently visited the USSR, giving lectures and participating at different conferences.

8. Boris Tomashevsky (1890–1957) was one of the prominent Soviet literary scholars. He prepared the first edition of Alexander Pushkin's complete works and participated in the preparation of academic editions of Fyodor Dostoevsky and Anton Chekhov. All his life, Tomashevsky tried to stay away from politics as much as possible, focusing exclusively on academic activities.

9. Boris Eikhenbaum (1886–1959) was one of the key figures of OPOYAZ and one of the most prominent Tolstoy scholars. A man of brilliant education and incredible intelligence (he spoke all European languages fluently), Eikhenbaum managed to avoid persecution for a long time, but in 1949 he was fired from the university for "cosmopolitism." Only after Stalin's death was he able to return to academic activities.

10. Yuri Tynyanov (1894–1943) was one of the most influential Soviet literary critics, translators, poets, and playwrights. He was one of the most esteemed exponents of Russian Formalism. His last years were overshadowed by a progressing, serious disease that eventually brought him to a premature grave at the age of 49.

11. The Siege of Leningrad (often called the Leningrad Blockade) by the German Nazis started on September 8, 1941, and lasted until January 27, 1944, or exactly 900 days. When the siege began, the city had very little food stored, so the famine started almost immediately. More than 1,000,000 civilians would die from it in the next 900 days. Leningrad never surrendered to the Germans and strove to maintain its cultural life despite everything: the 7th Symphony of Shostakovich was born at the time. The continuous air strikes did not prevent the Leningrad libraries from remaining open during the entire siege. The city factories also continued to produce tanks that were immediately shipped to the front.

12. The Union of Soviet Writers was created by the Bolsheviks in 1934 as a vehicle of state control and censorship. Becoming a member of the Union meant gaining permission to publish books and earn money by writing. The Union also supported its members in "good" standing financially (by giving them nice apartments, country cottages, excellent medical service, and money). To lose one's Union membership usually spelled disaster: the unfortunate writer would never be able to publish anything in the USSR and would also lose any previous benefits, including, at times, their apartment. In 1934, the Union consisted of 1,500 writers; in 1991 (the year when the Union was dissolved) it had about 10,000 members.

13. Nikita Khrushchev is among the most well-known Soviet leaders. He served as First Secretary of the Communist Party from 1953 to 1964 and as Premier from 1958 to 1964. This time was marked with the end of repressions, a political "thaw" in the country, and the revival of cultural life. A very impulsive and stubborn person, Khrushchev created significant tensions with many Western leaders and almost brought the world to the brink of a nuclear war. Still, the USSR's economic progress under his leadership is undeniable.

14. The reference here is to *The Demons* (1871), the sixth novel of Fyodor Dostoevsky. Being disturbed by the wave of terrorism that swept over the Russian Empire, Dostoevsky wrote this highly politically charged novel that was soon called "the novel-prediction," "the novel-warning," and now is considered as one of his best novels, along with *The Brothers Karamazov* and *Crime and Punishment*.

15. Boris Pasternak (1890–1960) was, perhaps, one of the most significant Soviet poets, but he is also one of the most important twentieth century writers. For his great novel, *Doctor Zhivago* (1957), Pasternak received the Nobel Prize and became the second Russian writer awarded this prestigious award (after Ivan Bunin). During Stalin's reign, to save his life and to support the family, Pasternak focused on translation. His translations of Shakespeare, Goethe, Shiller, and Calderon are still among the very best. The publication of *Doctor Zhivago* in 1957 in Italy (because it was rejected by all publishers in the USSR) brought universal fame to Pasternak but created serious problems for him in his own country. The atmosphere of open animosity displayed by the official authorities ended up destroying Pasternak's health and contributing to his premature death in 1960.

16. *Doctor Zhivago* (1956) is a novel of the Russian poet Boris Pasternak. In the USSR the novel was immediately rejected for publication, and Pasternak sent the monograph to the Italian publisher Feltrinelli, who became famous for the first publication of one of the best novels of the twentieth century. In 1958 Pasternak received the Nobel Prize in Literature, but in the USSR Pasternak became a literary outcast. It is terrifying to admit, but not a single person in the USSR dared to raise his voice in support of this genius, who died alone in his house one year later, humiliated and crushed by his own country and his own people.

17. Andrei Sinyavsky (1925–1997) was a prominent Soviet writer, literary critic, and dissident who had to leave his country because of the publication in the West of his novels, which were prohibited to be published in the USSR. When the publication was discovered, Sinyavsky was arrested and sentenced for seven years. After his return, he emigrated to France where he became a professor of Russian literature in Sorbonne. His radical views on the "Jew question" in Russia provoked a very negative reaction from Alexander Solzhenitsyn, the Literature Nobel Prize Laureate.

18. Lilya Brik (b. Kagan) (1891–1978), known as "The Muse of the Russian Avant-garde," hosted one of the most famous literary salons of the twentieth century. Mayakovsky's "A Cloud in Trousers" was dedicated to her. Until her very last day, Brik maintained close contacts with some of the most interesting people of the twentieth century: Alexander Solzhenitsyn, Mstislav Rostropovich, Pablo Neruda, Phillipe and Polina Rothschild, and Yves Saint Laurent, to name a few. At the age of 87, after breaking her hip, Lilya could not continue the active lifestyle she was accustomed to, and she committed suicide in Moscow.

19. Alexander Blok (1880–1921) was one of the most celebrated Russian poets of the twentieth century. Born to an aristocratic family, Blok accepted the Bolshevik Revolution in 1917, a move that surprised many of his admirers and friends. In 1921 he became ill and needed treatment abroad, but permission to leave Russia was not issued to him until three days after his death.

20. Sergey Yesenin (1895–1925) was one of the most prominent Russian poets of the early twentieth century. A peasant by birth, he was able to get a decent education, then moved to St. Petersburg where he was welcomed by the artistic bohemia. In 1921 he married Isadora Duncan and traveled with her to Europe and the United States. He returned very disappointed with his family life and what he saw in the West, but the NKVD never forgave Yesenin this trip abroad. In 1925 he was forced into a psychiatric clinic, from which he escaped to Leningrad. A few days later, he was found dead in a room in the hotel Astoria. Many scholars believe that Yesenin was murdered by the NKVD, but the official version is that the poet committed suicide.

21. Zinaida Reich (1894–1939) was the wife of Vsevolod Meyerhold, who was also a brilliant actress and played in his theatre. In 1934, after staging the famous *The Lady with the Camellias*, which met with Stalin's disapproval, Meyerhold's theatre was closed. Zinaida wrote a letter to Stalin where she explicitly told him that had no taste or understanding of the theatre. Soon Meyerhold was arrested, and 24 days later two individuals broke into Meyerhold's apartment and brutally murdered Zinaida Reich. Historians believe that all of this was staged by the NKVD, as the murderers were never found. A few days later, Meyerhold was sentenced to death and shot.

22. Vsevolod Meyerhold (1874–1940) was one of the most remarkable Russian actors and theatre directors of all times. Starting on the stage of the Moscow Art Theatre, he soon founded his own theater (Meyerhold Theater). After the revolution, he had a chance to defect while on tour in France, but he did not and instead returned to the USSR. After staging the famous *The Lady with the Camellias*, which met with Stalin's disapproval, his theatre was closed, and Meyerhold was arrested and sentenced to death.

23. Maxim Gorky (b. Aleksey Peshkov) (1868–1936) was a major Russian and Soviet writer, often described as the founder of Socialist Realism. He was also a political activist and did much to save the lives of many fellow writers. In 1921, because of an increasingly repressive climate for intellectuals, Gorky left the USSR for Italy. After a personal invitation from Stalin in 1931, Gorky returned to the USSR, but his relationship with Stalin soured after 1934. In 1936 he was "hospitalized" and never returned home. Some scholars insist that Gorky was poisoned on Stalin's orders.

24. Vladimir Lenin (b. Ulyanov, 1870–1924) was the leader of the Bolshevik party and its successful coup in October 1917. A man of exceptional intelligence (he spoke five European languages fluently), titanic energy, mesmerizing oration, and prolific writing, Lenin was also an extremely cruel man ready to shed the blood of thousands of people to achieve his personal goal. The repressions he started right after the Revolution were unprecedented in Russian history: the extermination of the Romanov family, including children and servants; the starting of a Civil War that cost Russia 3,000,000 lives; hunger and the epidemic of typhus that cost another 5,000,000 human lives; and the exodus of 3,000,000 intellectuals from Russia. This is perhaps not even a full list of the repercussions of his rule. Lenin died at the age of 54, after a second stroke.

25. Sergei Eisenstein (1898–1948) was one of the most influential cinema directors of all times. His *Battleship Potemkin* (1925) was applauded not only in the USSR but also in the West. Right after that, Eisenstein was invited to work for Paramount Pictures, but something did not work out. At the same time, Eisenstein received a personal invitation from Stalin to return to the USSR. In his home country, Eisenstein, due to his enormous international prestige, survived the repressions and was able to make two extraordinary films: *Alexander Nevsky* (1938) and *Ivan the Terrible* (1945, remained unfinished). All those years Eisenstein was productively teaching and writing about the theory of film. He died young from a heart attack at 50, at his desk, while working on an essay titled *The Colored Film*.

26. Eva Thompson. "Victor Shklovsky, or Fish Turned Ichthyologist," *Books Abroad*, Winter 1973 v. 47, no. 1, 79–82.

WORKS CITED

Dialogues with Shklovsky: The Duvakin Interviews, 1967–1968. Eds. Slav N. Gratchev and Irina Evdokimova. Lanham: Lexington Books, 2019.
Dostoevsky, Fyodor. *Prestuplenie i nakazanie.* Vol. 6. Leningrad: Nauka, 1972.
_____. *Besy.* Vol. 10. Leningrad: Nauka, 1974.
_____. *Bratia Karamazovy.* Vols. 14–15. Leningrad: Nauka, 1976.
Pasternak, Boris. *Doktor Zhivago.* Moskva: Agentsvo FTM, 2014.
Thompson, Eva. "Victor Shklovsky, or Fish Turned Ichthyologist." *Books Abroad.* Winter 1973, v. 47, no. 1, 79–82.

Chapter Four

Defamiliarization in Translating Lewis Carroll's *Wonderland*

Victor Fet and Michael Everson

VIKTOR SHKLOVSKY AND THE STRANGE LANDS

"Art is thinking in images," begins Shklovsky's seminal essay "Art as a device" (1917),[1] echoing the first page of the most famous children's book: "And what is the use of a book, thought Alice, without pictures or conversations?" Shklovsky, whose early work is based on important British authors, especially Lawrence Sterne, was well aware of *the* most iconic, imaginary *strange* world in English literature: Lewis Carroll's books *Alice's Adventures in Wonderland* (1865; below, *AAIW*) and *Through the Looking-Glass and What Alice Saw There* (1871; below, *TTLG*).

There are numerous connections—conceptual, historical, and biographical, many just of one or two degrees of separation—between Carroll and Shklovsky, which are worth tracing. There is a direct connection between the English classical nonsense and the Shklovskian estrangement in Futurist poetry.[2] Already in his first brief essay "Resurrecting the word" (1914), twenty-one-year-old Shklovsky calls for a new language.[3] He wrote: "The 'arbitrary' and 'derived' words of Futurists are born . . . the language of poetry is not comprehensible but semi-comprehensible . . . folk songs are often sung not in dialect but in a 'heightened' language. . . . Aristotle in his *Poetics* recommends making language sound foreign. . . . There is a need for creation of new, 'tight' language (Kruchenykh's expression), aimed at seeing instead of recognizing. . . . Not theorists but artists will be the first to travel these paths."[4] These words echo another abrasive linguist philosopher: "'When I use a word,' Humpty Dumpty said, in rather a scornful tone, 'it means just what I choose it to mean—neither more nor less.' 'The question is,' said Alice, 'whether you can make words mean so many different things.' 'The question is,' said Humpty Dumpty, 'which is to be master—that's all.'"

An iconoclast in his attitude toward language, art, culture and its expansion into all realms of life, Viktor Shklovsky had many predecessors in much quainter times, and we claim Lewis Carroll as one of these early figures. Shklovsky formulated *defamiliarization* (Russ. *ostranenie*) or *estrangement* —literally, it means *making strange*—as the fundamental law of art in 1917, the year of very strange events in Shklovsky's native Russia. Strange worlds were created and explored by the *avant-garde* (Futurists, Surrealists, Dadaists, Expressionists) all across Europe before and after the Great War. To explore strangeness in art and language, Shklovsky relied heavily on folklore and children's literature.[5]

Shklovsky (1893–1984) was five years old when Lewis Carroll died. At this age, Shklovsky's younger compatriot Vladimir Nabokov (1899–1977), a future translator of *AAIW*, was reading Lewis Carroll in English, raised in an affluent Anglophone Russian family. That was, however, rare in Russia where English was not the preferred foreign language. When Carroll himself was alerted, around 1870, that a young lady in Russia, a "Ms Timiryazeff," wants to translate *AAIW*, he arranged to send her French and German translations. The first Russian translation (1879) was heavily domesticated, and published without Carroll's or translator's name. There is a high possibility that the translator was Ekaterina Boratynskaya (née Timiryazeva), a friend of Leo Tolstoy—and the first teacher of an eight-year-old Boris Pasternak.[6]

Name-dropping comes easily as one unravels a tapestry of this network of Russian intellectuals, writers, and poets, which emerged after the Great Reforms of Alexander II, through the 1870s–1910s. This fragile world fell apart in 1917, with the downfall of the Russian Empire and a short-lived Russian Republic. Its demise has briefly generated the early Soviet *avant-garde*, a natural extension of the Silver Age that involved its younger generation, both the Futurist poets—such as Vladimir Mayakovsky, Velimir Khlebnikov, and (in his early years) Boris Pasternak, and the Formalist scholars who studied the new language of poetry—such as Shklovsky, Roman Jakobson, and Boris Eikhenbaum. As millions of other Russians, they were decimated by early death (Khlebnikov), suicide (Mayakovsky), emigration (Jakobson), and imprisonment. A few—like Pasternak or Shklovsky—were survivors and witnesses.

Earlier in a still peaceful Russia, the Symbolist poet Poliksena Solovyova (1867–1924), who wrote under a pen name Allegro, published her own Russian translation of *AAIW* (1909).[7] Solovyova ran a wonderful biweekly children's journal, *Tropinka* (A Little Path) (1906–1912), read mostly by the children of St. Petersburg literary and artistic elite. The journal, where Allegro's translation was serialized in 1909, became an "unofficial organ" of the Symbolist Movement. It published such great Silver Age figures as Alexander Blok, Konstantin Balmont, Alexei Remizov, Zinaida Gippius, Dmitri Merezhkovsky, and others.[8] Most of those listed above had to leave Russia after the 1917 Bolshevik Revolution—or died soon, like Blok or Solovyova.

In the ensuing anarchy of the Civil War (1917–1920), Shklovsky's world became strange and deformed; his two brothers were killed; he himself fled abroad as a Socialist-Revolutionary; returned to the Soviet Union in 1923 during a brief spell of New Economic Policy; witnessed, and actively promoted, a brief burst of creativity—which was over by 1930, the year of Mayakovsky's suicide and Shklovsky's repentance.

Mayakovsky, arguably the most important figure in Shklovsky's life, could have been familiar with Lewis Carroll in an early Russian translation, as Miron Petrovsky suggests.[9] If this is correct, some of Mayakovsky's surrealistic, cosmic imagery (the 100-mile telescoping neck of the poet himself!) in his 1922 Communist propaganda poem *Piatyi Internatsional* [The Fifth International] might be based on Alice's neck extension (*AAIW*, Ch. 4).

The lives of Mayakovsky and Shklovsky are forever connected to two Kagan sisters (Lili Brik and Elsa Triolet). Triolet's husband Louis Aragon (they met in 1928) happened to be the first French translator, in 1929, of Carroll's *The Hunting of the Snark* (1876), which many consider the first Surrealist poem. This was, as Martin Gardner noted, "shortly before he [Aragon] completed his transition from Snarxism to Marxism."[10] The first Surrealist manifesto published in 1924 by André Breton claimed Carroll as their own; and in 1931, Aragon claimed that Carroll's nonsense writings were a disguised protest against the Victorian bourgeois morality and hypocrisy.

More than once, Shklovsky mentions Carroll's works. In *The Theory of Prose* he wrote: "In a strange book, *Alice in Wonderland*, people are put on trial before the crime is committed, and are sentenced. A common thing sounds like a fairytale. For a fairytale, it is too sad."[11] As it often happens, Shklovsky confuses *AAIW* and *TTLG*; in *AAIW* the Knave of Heart is given a sentence before the verdict, but it is in *TTLG* where time is reversed, and the Anglo-Saxon messenger Hatta is sentenced before committing a crime.

Shklovsky clearly knew the 1924 Russian translation of *TTLG* (the first and only until 1967)[12] since he uses, more than once, a wonderful neologism that appears in its Russian title, *Zazerkal'e*.[13] Vladimir Ashkenazi (pen name "V. Azov") will be remembered by this single Russian word that he invented. Translatable as Transmirroria or Transmirrorland, *Zazerkal'e* assigns a potent toponym to Carroll's unnamed chess-world country behind the Looking-Glass. Ashkenazi (who emigrated to Paris in 1926) modeled this world on Russian toponyms which imply that the geographic area in question is located "on the other side." The boundary could be a mountain range (*Zakavkaz'e* ['Transcaucasia']), a river (*Zamoskvorech'e* ['Trans-Moskva-River']), or a lake (*Zabaikal'e* ['Transbaikalia']), all well-known and widely used toponyms. Azov's great neologism is firmly rooted today in Russian. Both Anna

Akhmatova and Ariadna Efron (daughter of Marina Tsvetaeva) compared their life in the USSR with the world of *Zazerkal'e*. As the literary scholar and translator Evgeny Vitkovsky recently wrote: "We were told that we lived in Wonderland, but it was a demagogical lie: for almost the entire twentieth century we lived Behind the Looking-Glass."[14] In Shklovsky's work, *zazerkal'e* is an important concept. In *The Energy of Delusion*, he says about literature: "Great people are greatly lost in front of life. They try to find the land of *Zazerkal'e*, they touch the mirror with their hands, but it does not let them through."[15] Shklovsky places this term in the title of part 2 of his *The Theory of Prose* ("The rhyme of poetry, the rhyme of prose. Structuralism and zazerkal'e").[16]

Starting from the 1920s, the best children's poets in Russia—Samuil Marshak and Korney Chukovsky—were Anglophiles who played a crucial role in translating and adapting English folklore and literature. Protected by Marshak's authority, the brilliant 1930s poets of the Oberiu (Ob''edinenie real'nogo iskusstva, or the Real Art Group)—Daniil Kharms, Alexander Vvedensky, Nikolay Zabolotsky, Nikolay Oleinikov—for a short while carried the torch of the 1920s Futurism before disappearing in the meat-grinder of the Communist dictatorship (only Zabolotsky survived). The strange worlds of the *oberiuts* connect to the Futurism and Formalism and to the later European absurdist tradition. It is not by chance that many of these names—such as Kharms—are known today mainly as children's poets. Among Kharms's unpublished works we find the attempted Russian translation of the first lines of the Hatter's song from *AAIW* ("Twinkle, twinkle, little bat").

Thus, amid the strangest circumstances, Lewis Carroll's works kept coming to Shklovsky's native Russia. Unable to speak out under the Soviet regime, the world of literature shrunk; in the 1930s, much of the Russian language and its evolution in the USSR has retreated into the nursery and into translation.

TRANSLATING THE WONDERLAND

Lewis Carroll's *AAIW* is one of the most translated literary texts (over 200 languages and dialects). In 2015, celebrating the 150th anniversary of the book, a three-volume collection of bibliography and scholarly papers was published, titled *Alice in a World of Wonderlands*.[17]

In 1917, Shklovsky wrote: "Russian literary language, originally alien to Russia, has penetrated into the human masses so deeply as to level many dialectical varieties. Literature, meanwhile, began to care for dialects . . . and barbarisms."[18] The language issues become "curiouser and curiouser" when languages collide and cohabit, and translation is an ultimate test and joy of this collision. Shklovsky's compatriot Mikhail Bakhtin assigned an important role to *polyglossia*, or coexistence of different languages—maintained that "language first becomes aware of itself through contact with other languages."[19]

Shklovsky's *defamiliarization*, or estrangement in literature and art (Russ. остранение [*ostranenie*]) has been adopted recently as a strategy in literary translation. There is always a degree of defamiliarization in translation, discussed as *domestication* versus *foreignization*, in the terminology of Venuti.[20] From a complete adaptation ("domestication," where a translator is very "visible," and largely takes over) to "foreignization" (where a translator pretends to be "invisible"), many approaches and traditions exist, bearing on the target language and culture in their relationship to the foreign ones.

"If literature is an exclusively linguistic phenomenon, it becomes impossible to understand how the translation of literary works is possible,"—mused Shklovsky.[21] In the case of Lewis Carroll's playful texts, any attempt to translate his "untranslatable wordplay" faces the issue of handling defamiliarization. Two conflicting approaches are possible. One (a foreignization) is to remain true to the original as much as possible and to produce an "academic" text often at the expense of losing author's humor or even meaning. Another is a more interesting, playful approach, which includes domestication: a tactful replacement of the text's specific elements (names, speech features, puns, parodies, etc.) by their linguistic and cultural equivalents. The latter approach was favored by Lewis Carroll himself, who in his note to the first German translation (by Antonie Zimmermann in 1869) praised the translator in the following words: "The author wishes to express his indebtedness to the translator, who has replaced certain occasional parodies of English childhood poetry—understandably unfamiliar to German children—by comparable parodies of well-known German poems. Similarly, certain untranslatable English puns have been replaced by suitable material which the book owes solely to the adroitness of the translator" (transl. from German by W. Weaver).

Recently, Evertype (formerly in Ireland, now in Dundee, Scotland) has emerged as the leading Carrollian publisher of today, with over 100 books published in a decade. The Evertype editions focus especially on translations of Lewis Carroll's books into new and rare languages. Some of the newest (2015–2018) translators (e.g., Bashkir, Kyrgyz, Romani, Shor, Yakut) were advised to engage in playful domestication strategies in applying local content as they create their Wonderlands; this refers specifically to parody and wordplay. A number of recommendations has been suggested, among them various devices of domestication that can be interpreted as Shklovskian defamiliarization.

WILLIAM THE CONQUEROR, DOMESTICATED

Already less than a year after the *AAIW* book first appeared in print, on October 24, 1866, Lewis Carroll wrote to his publisher, Macmillan: "Friends here seem to think that the book is untranslatable in either French or German, the puns and songs being chief obstacles." Indeed, any translator of the Alice books faces inevitable difficulties in *translating the untranslatable*, first of all numerous puns and parodies.[22]

Many playful translators of the past choose to replace the "dry" history lecture by Carroll's Mouse about William the Conqueror and his Normans. In 1923, Vladimir Nabokov (Sirin) carefully led his Ania/Alice and her readers across abysses separating tongues and cultures.[23] In the "dry lecture" on medieval Russian history, Nabokov's Mouse explains how "after Monomakh's death, Kiev passed not to his brothers but to his sons, and became therefore a family property of Monomakhovichs. . . . While they lived in friendship, their power in Kiev was strong; but when their relationships worsened . . . , the Ol'govich princes rose against them, and took Kiev by force more than once. . . . But the Monomakhovichs, in their turn."[24] This text was taken by Nabokov verbatim from a famous textbook of Russian history by Sergey Platonov (1860–1933).[25] A prominent historian, Platonov was arrested in 1930 and accused of plotting with Germany for "restoration to the Russian throne of his former student, Grand Duke Andrei Vladimirovich"; he was exiled to Samara and died there. For the emigré children who read Nabokov's translation in 1923, the textbook words about Kievan struggles were not at all dry—they bore a fresh echo of Russian Civil War, at the same time pictured by Bulgakov in his *White Guard* (1924)—where Viktor Shklovsky, an active fighter, was a prototype of a demonic Mikhail Shpoliansky.

In Evertype translations to rare languages, we offer an opportunity of Mouse's "dry lecture" replacement as a window into translator's own history. A purist may argue that this is not a Lewis Carroll's text; but we have Carroll himself on record recommending replacement. Some (but not all) translators accept his game, in order to make Wonderland more accessible to the children in their culture.[26] Here, a translator needs certain tact and sensitivity toward the national history and its recognizable characters. The first example of an Evertype domestication of this type is in Nicholas Williams's Irish translation, where the Mouse reads text from Keating's seventeenth-century genealogies—dry stuff indeed.[27] Another example of such cultural, playful replacement is given below for the first Bashkir translation of *AAIW* (2017) by Güzäl Sitdykova:[28] she decided to remind the reader about the Bashkir history of the sixteenth century, as chronicled by Pëtr Rychkov in the eighteenth century. Here is this text in a back-translation, a wonderful example of Shklovskian defamiliarization:

"Ahem!" said the Mouse with an important air. "Are you all ready? This is the driest thing I know. Silence all round, if you please! '—After the fragmentation of the Golden Horde, the Bashkir territories were divided between the Siberian and the Kazan Khanates, as well as the Nogay Horde, whose rulers aimed to seize the Bashkir lands. Upon his defeat of the Kazan, Ivan the Terrible called on the Bashkir people to voluntarily become his royal subjects. The Russian government guaranteed protection to the Bashkir—'"

"Ugh!" said the Parrot, with a shiver.

"I beg your pardon!" said the Mouse, frowning, but very politely. "Did you speak?"

"Not I!" said the Parrot, hastily.

"I thought you did," said the Mouse. "I proceed. '—protection to the Bashkir against the advances of the Nogay and Siberian khans and from other enemy invasions. The Moscow Tsar retained with the Bashkir the patrimonial rights to their lands—'"

"Retained *what*?" said the Duck.

"The patrimonial rights to their lands," the Mouse replied: "of course you know what 'land' means."

"I know what 'land' [=soil, ground] means well enough; when *I* dig in it and retain something for my ducklings," said the Duck: "it's generally a worm. The question is, what did Ivan the Terrible retain?"

The Mouse did not notice this question, but hurriedly went on: '. . . the Bashkirs, in turn, undertook to carry out military service at their own expense and pay the *yasak* tax to the crown. Thus, Moscow made serious concessions to the Bashkirs, which, naturally, met its global interests—' How are you getting on now, my dear?" it continued, turning to Alice as it spoke."[29]

A RUSSIAN HUMPTY DUMPTY

"You seem very clever at explaining words, Sir," said Alice to Humpty Dumpty. We single out this character—the language philosopher from *TTLG*, which cuts an iconic figure not unlike a friendly cartoon of Shklovsky himself—to illustrate defamiliarization in its complex context of the Russian translations of Lewis Carroll.

"Shaltay-Boltay," the traditional Russian rendering for Humpty Dumpy (an example of a duplicating, rhymed nursery-rhyme name) fits well the Shklovskian interest in language expansion through colloquial dialecticisms and 'Barbarisms' and happens to be the a product of the same milieu that generated early Soviet *avant-garde*. In fact, the name's choice itself happens to be contemporary with Shklovsky's and Jakobson circle's studies of the expanding language, in the context of translations of children's literature.

This name was first applied to Humpty Dumpy by Samuil Marshak (1887–1964)—the future leading Russian children's poet and, like Shklovsky, one of the survivors of the Stalin's dictatorship—in 1923 in his Russian translation of the *Humpty Dumpty* nursery rhyme.[30] Shaltay-Boltay is one of the main characters in *TTLG*, and Marshak's translation was later adopted by Nina Demurova in her 1967 *TTLG* translation.[31]

Shaltay-Boltay is clearly a defamiliarizing (foreignizing) name. While not English-sounding as would be a simple transliteration "Khampti-Dampti," it is still only vaguely recognizable by a Russian ear: *boltay* (a form of *boltat'*) means both "to babble" and "to shake." It can reflect the egg nature of the character since a derived word *boltun'ia* means "an omelette." *Shaltay* has no Russian translation. The expression *shaltay-boltay* (or *shaltay-baltay*) exists in Russian dictionaries; it first appeared in literature in 1856, originally meaning a special artificial slang (of the Kuban Cossacks) used to communicate with the Adyghes (non-Russian natives of the North Caucasus).[32] In the North Caucasus, the expression came to mean "foreign speech." In Siberian and Orenburg dialects, according to the Dahl dictionary, it means "babble, empty talk." It was used in this meaning in some Russian classical literature before 1923, e.g., in the stories by Anton Chekhov and Maxim Gorky (in the latter, it is used by a non-Russian Muslim ethnic characters). The choice of the name Shaltay-Boltay, which includes a potent rhyme and reduplication common to the Turkisms in Russian, was possibly affected by a Turkic-influenced Russian dialect of the North Caucasus (Ekaterinodar, Kuban'), where Marshak lived in the early 1920s.

We found *shaltay-baltay* right in the middle of the Shklovskian world, in Velimir Khlebnikov's long poem *Tiran bez T* (1922). There, this expression meaning "empty talk" is used by a Persian character who mentions Leo Tolstoy (whose biography will be published by Shklovsky in 1963) as a Russian holy man (a "dervish") and a prophet (Zardesht, i.e., Zarathustra). This "barbaric," intentionally accented passage is worth quoting:

> Russki ne znai—plyokho!
> shaltay-baltay ne nado, zachem? Plyokho!
> Uchitel', davay
> (50 let)—stol'ko pal'tsev i stol'ko—
> Aziya russkaya.
> Rossiya pervaya, uchitel'—kharyasho.
> Tolstoy bol'shoy chelovek, da, da, russkiy dervish!
> A! Zardesht, a! Kharyasho!
>
> (Know no Russian–bad!
> Don't shaltay-baltay, why? Bad!
> Teacher, give that many and that many fingers—(in 50 years)
> Asia [will be] Russian.
> Russia is the first; teacher, good.
> Tolstoy big man, yes, yes, Russian dervish.
> Ha! Zardesht, ha! Good!)[33]

Khlebnikov went to Persia in 1921 as an unlikely, dervish-like figure with the Red Army attempt to establish the Soviet regime at the Gilyan Province on the Caspian Sea. This "colonial" trip mirrored Shklovsky's own earlier military experience, also in Persia, but with the Tsarist troops in 1917. The tradition to borrow Turkic words in Russian is a classical one, starting especially with Lermontov's poetry and Tolstoy's prose all related to Russian conquest of the Caucasus in the nineteenth century. Both Shklovsky and Khlebnikov appear as the very late heirs to the same Oriental tradition, very important for Russian culture, expanding Russian language in a way similar to British appropriation of Indian words into English.

This type of paired, rhymed words was specifically noted by Jakobson in the commentary to his early (1921) article about Khlebnikov; Jakobson listed *shaltay-baltay* among others.[34] Shklovsky also often discussed similar repeated structures in folklore in his early work.[35]

In discussing defamiliarization, Shklovsky always paid a special attention to dialects, colloquialisms, use of foreign languages, and other forms of language heterogeneity, which Mikhail Bakhtin, a few years later, named *heteroglossia*. Shaltay-Boltay a good example of Bakhtinian heteroglossia,[36] originally defined as presence of elements of another language or dialect creating linguistic diversity. A classic example given by Bakhtin was of a Russian peasant addressing God in Church Slavonic rather than in modern Russian, which he speaks to his family. One can argue that Carroll's "Jabberwocky," an obvious predecessor of the Futurist "zaumnyi iazyk" (a transsense language) and Oberiu absurdist poetry, is a "mock heteroglossic" defamiliarization where an invented language needs to be interpreted by a skilled linguist, Shaltay-Boltay.

DEFAMILIARIZED ILLUSTRATIONS

Again, "what is the use of a book without pictures?" Hundreds of great artists have labored for 150 years on illustrating Wonderland, an enormously diverse and extensive tradition. In Evertype's practice as the Carrollian publisher of new translations, we prefer to reproduce John Tenniel's imagery as much as possible in reverence to the first illustrator who was supervised by Lewis Carroll himself. Using Tenniel is a tool of defamiliarization (foreignization) is a direct reference to the familiar, classical Victorian imagery. At the same time, a degree of domestication is needed in cases when the text itself has been considerably changed in a translation, and its characters do not fit Carroll's images anymore.

An Irish translation of *AAIW* by Pádraig Ó Cadhla (1875–1948) was first published in 1922, with illustrations by K. Verschoyle. For the new 2015 edition of this "hibernicized" version.[37] The classical Tenniel pictures were used with masterful domestications by Byron W. Sewell. Every illustration featuring Eibhlís (Alice) was re-drawn so she could wear an Irish costume;

the animal and bird illustrations made use of the Irish fauna—since Ó Cadhla made them all native to Ireland—rather than those of Tenniel (which were probably based on animals that could be seen in the London Zoo). One of the most interesting decisions was in the depiction of the Mock Turtle. Tenniel's illustration famously shows a hybrid creature with a sea turtle's body and a calf's head, hind legs, and tail. Verschoyle's illustration showed an ordinary calf with a turtle shell tied to its back. In the 2015 edition, Everson and Sewell gave a nod to Verschoyle, as their Mock Turtle is also a calf wearing a turtle shell.

When the first Russian 1879 translation was reprinted by Evertype in 2017,[38] we asked Byron W. Sewell to redraw some of the classical Tenniel pictures to fit the text. In this translation, Sonia (Alice) does not hold a flamingo when she is approached by the Duchess; instead, she left her crane (which replaces the flamingo) behind but kept the hedgehog, carrying it in her headscarf. Accordingly, the Duchess is afraid of the prickly hedgehog, rather than of a potentially biting flamingo.

Evertype promotes Carrollian translation even to languages which have passed out of use. This is also an old Carrollian tradition; "Jabberwocky" appeared in Latin very soon after *TTLG* was published. For the first translation of *AAIW* recently done in Old English by Peter Baker,[39] Tenniel-inspired illustrations were meticulously created by Sewell to modify costumes and objects accordingly—as he had done previously with Brian Lee's translation of *Alice* into Middle English verse.[40] There, the White Hare (as there were no rabbits in the England of the Béowulf's) carries an astrolabe (there were no pocket-watches yet), and the Mad Tea-Party becomes a Mad Beer one (there was no tea either). Even further back in time, a Gothic translation was created by David Alexander Carlton, with "domesticated" illustrations to reflect the barbarians that sacked Rome.[41]

In such playful, estranging approaches, images, languages and cultures collide, evolve, hybridize and cross-fertilize, to the ultimate joy of a reader, following the spirit of both Lewis Carroll and Viktor Shklovsky.

ACKNOWLEDGMENTS

VF is grateful to Nina Demurova who has brought both of Lewis Carroll's *Alice* books to his generation in Russia, enhanced by charming poetry of Samuil Marshak, Dina Orlovskaya, and Olga Sedakova. We are grateful to Byron W. Sewell for his meticulous illustrating labor and profound interest to all things Carrollian.

We thank many Carrollian scholars and enthusiasts, and especially translators into lesser-used languages, for the fascinating experience we have both enjoyed in editing and publishing their works with Evertype. Slav Gratchev kindly invited us to contribute to this volume. VF is grateful to Galina Fet for her support.

NOTES

1. Viktor Shklovsky, "Art as Device," in *Viktor Shklovsky: A Reader*. Edited and translated by Alexandra Berlina (New York: Bloomsbury Academic, 2017), 73.
2. Grigory L. Tulchinsky, "L′iuis Keroll: nonsens kak predposylka istiny" [Lewis Carroll: Nonsense as a preliminary condition of truth], *Rossiia i Britaniia v epokhu prosveshcheniia. Opyt filosofskoi i kul'turnoi komparativistiki. Chast' 1. Filosofskii vek.* [Russia and Great Britain in the Age of Enlightenment. Philosophical and Cultural Comparative Studies. Part I. The Age of Philosophy]. Almanakh 19 (Sankt-Peterburg: SPb Tsentr istorii idei [Center for the History of Ideas], 2002), 130.
3. Viktor Shklovsky, "Resurrecting the Word," in *Viktor Shklovsky: A Reader*. Edited and translated by Alexandra Berlina (New York: Bloomsbury Academic, 2017), 73.
4. Translation by Alexandra Berlina.
5. Viktor Shklovsky, *O teorii prozy* [On the Theory of Prose] (Moskva: Federatisia, 1929), 64–66. Translation by Victor Fet.
6. Victor Fet, "Around *Sonja*: On the First Russian Translation," *Knight Letter*, Vol. II, 37, no. 97(Fall 2016): 25–34.
7. [Lewis Carroll] L′iuis Kérroll. *Prikliucheniia Alisy v' stranie chudes'* [Alice's Adventures in Wonderland]. Translated by Allegro [P.S. Solovyova]. Illustrations by John Tenniel (Sankt-Peterburg: Tropinka, 1909).
8. Victor Fet, "Three Early Russian Translations," *Knight Letter*, II, 28, 98 (Spring 2017), 16–17.
9. Miron S. Petrovsky, "Vladimir Mayakovsky i L′iuis Keroll," [Vladimir Mayakovsky and Lewis Carroll] in Kerroll, L. *Dnevnik puteshestviia v Rossiiu v 1867 g., ili Russkii dnevnik. Stat'i i ésse o L'iuise Kérolle.* [Carroll, L. Journal of a tour in Russia in 1867. Articles and Essays about Lewis Carroll] (Chelyabinsk: Entsiklopediia; Sankt-Peterburg: Krriga, 2013), 306–309.
10. Lewis Carroll, *The Annotated Hunting of the Snark*. Edited with notes by Martin Gardner, illustrations by Henry Holiday and others, introduction by Adam Gopnik. ("Definitive Edition" ed.) (W. W. Norton, 2006), 117.
11. Viktor Shklovsky, *O teorii prozy* (Moskva: Sovetskii pisatel',' 1983), 246. Translation by Victor Fet.
12. [Lewis Carroll] Karroll, L′iuis, *Alisa v Zazerkal'i* [Alice in Transmirroria]. Translated by V. Azov [V.A. Ashkenazi]. Poems translated by T.L. Shchepkina-Kupernik. Illustrations by John Tenniel (Moskva-Petrograd: L.D. Frenkel′, 1924).
13. Viktor Shklovsky, *Zhili-byli* [Once there lived . . .] (Moskva: Sovetskii pisatel′, 1966), 368; *Energiia zabluzhdeniia* [The Energy of Delusion] (Moscow: Sovetskii pisatel′, 1981), 330; *O teorii prozy* (1983), 98, 235. Translation by Victor Fet.
14. Victor Fet, "Beheading First: On Nabokov's Translation of Lewis Carroll," *The Nabokovian* 63(2009), 62–63. Quote from E. Vitkovsky translated by Victor Fet.
15. Shklovsky, *Energiia zabluzhdeniia*, 330. Translation by Victor Fet.
16. Shklovsky, *O teorii prozy* (1983), 98. Translation by Victor Fet.
17. Jon Lindseth and Allan Tannenbaum (eds.), *Alice in a World of Wonderlands*, Vols. 1–3. (New Castle, DE: Oak Knoll Press, 2015.)
18. Shklovsky, "Art as Device," 95. Translation by Alexandra Berlina.
19. Victor Fet, "Russian Translations of Lewis Carroll's *Alice* Books: A Bakhtinian Reaccentuation," in *Mikhail Bakhtin's Heritage in Literature, Arts and Psychology: Art and Answerability*. Ed. Slav N. Gratchev and Howard Mancing (Lanham, MD: Lexington Books, 2018), 63.
20. Lawrence Venuti, *Translator's Invisibility: A History of Translation* (New York: Routledge, 1995), 100.

21. Serena Vitale, *Shklovsky: Witness to an Era* (Champaign: Dalkey Archive Press, 2012), 80
22. Nina M. Demurova, "Alice speaks Russian: The Russian translations of *Alice's Adventures in Wonderland* and *Through the Looking-Glass*," *Harvard Library Bulletin* 5(1994–1995), no. 4, 11–29.
23. [Lewis Carroll] Karrol, L[iuis], *Ania v' stranie chudes* [Ania in Wonderland]. Translated by V. Sirin [V.V. Nabokov]. Illustrations by Sergey Zalshupin (Berlin: Gamaiun, 1923).
24. Back-translation from Russian by Victor Fet, based on the parodied text of Lewis Carroll.
25. Fet, "Beheading first," 54.
26. Liubov′ Arbaçakova and Victor Fet, "The First Translation of *Wonderland* into Shor," *Knight Letter*, II, 28, 98(Spring 2017), 21.
27. Lewis Carroll, *Eachtra Eibhlíse i dTír na nIontas. Alice's Adventures in Wonderland* in Irish. Translated into Irish by Nicholas Williams. Illustrations by John Tenniel (Cathair na Mart: Evertype, 2007).
28. [Lewis Carroll] L'iuis Kerroll, *Älisänen Säyerstandağı majaraları. Alice's Adventures in Wonderland* in Bashkir. Translated into Bashkir by Güzäl Sitdykova. Illustrations by John Tenniel. (Portlaoise: Evertype, 2017).
29. Translation from Russian by Victor Fet.
30. Samuil Marshak, *Dom, kotoryi postroil Dzhek* [A House That Jack Built]. Illustrated by V. Konashevich (Peterburg-Moskva: Vsemirnaya literatura, Gosizdat, 1923).
31. [Lewis Carroll] L'iuis Kerroll, *Prikliucheniia Alisy v strane chudes. Alisa v Zazerkal'e* [Alice's Adventures in Wonderland. Through the Looking-Glass, and What Alice Found There]. Translated by N.M. Demurova. Poems translated by S.Ia. Marshak and D.I. Orlovskaia. Introduction by N.M. Demurova. Illustrations by Petar Chuklev (Sofia: Izdatelstvo literatury na inostrannykh iazykakh, 1967)
32. Fet, "Russian Translations of Lewis Carroll's *Alice* Books," 68.
33. Translation by Victor Fet.
34. Roman Jakobson, *Raboty po poetike* (Moskva: Progress, 1987), 315.
35. Shklovsky, *O teorii prozy* (1929), 34. Translation by Victor Fet.
36. Fet, "Russian translations of Lewis Carroll's *Alice* books," 68.
37. Lewis Carroll, *Eachtra Eibhlíse i dTír na nIontas. Alice's Adventures in Wonderland* in Irish. Translated into Irish by Pádraig Ó Cadhla. Illustrations by Byron W. Sewell and John Tenniel (Portlaoise: Evertype, 2015).
38. [Lewis Carroll], *Sonia v tsarstve diva* [Sonia in a Kingdom of Wonder]. The first Russian translation of *Alice's Adventures in Wonderland* [Translated by E.I. Boratynskaya (?).] Illustrations by John Tenniel and Byron W. Sewell. Introduction and notes by Victor Fet. (Portlaoise: Evertype, 2017).
39. [Lewis Carroll] Hlóðwíg Carroll, *Æðelgýðe Ellendǽda on Wundorlande. Alice's Adventures in Wonderland* in Old English. Translated into Old English by Peter S. Baker. Illustrations by Byron W. Sewell (Portlaoise: Evertype, 2015).
40. Lewis Carroll, *The Aventures of Alys in Wondyr Lond. Alice's Adventures in Wonderland* in Middle English verse. Translated into Middle English verse by Brian S. Lee. Illustrations by Byron W. Sewell (Cathair na Mart: Evertype, 2013).
41. Lewis Carroll, *Balþos Gadedeis Aþalhaidais in Sildaleikalanda. Alice's Adventures in Wonderland*. Translated into Gothic by David Alexander Carlton. Illustrations by Byron W. Sewell (Portlaoise: Evertype, 2015).

WORKS CITED

Arbaçakova, Liubov′ and Victor Fet. "The First Translation of *Wonderland* into Shor." *Knight Letter*, II, 28, 98(Spring 2017): 20–22.
Carroll, Lewis. Kerroll, L'iuis. *Prikliucheniia Alisy v' stranie chudes* [Alice's Adventures in Wonderland]. Translated by Allegro [P.S. Solovyova]. Illustrations by John Tenniel. Sankt-Peterburg: Tropinka, 1909 (in Russian).

———. Karrol, L[iuis]. *Ania v stranie chudes* [Ania in Wonderland]. Translated by V. Sirin [V.V. Nabokov]. Illustrations by Sergey Zalshupin. Berlin: Gamaiun, 1923 (in Russian).
———. Karroll, L'iuis. *Alisa v Zazerkal'i* [Alice in Transmirroria]. Translated by V. Azov [V.A. Ashkenazi]. Poems translated by T.L. Shchepkina-Kupernik. Illustrations by John Tenniel. Moskva-Petrograd: L.D. Frenkel', 1924 (in Russian).
———. Kérroll, L'iuis. *Prikliucheniia Alisy v strane chudes. Alisa v Zazerkal'e* [Alice's Adventures in Wonderland. Through the Looking-Glass, and What Alice Found There]. Translated by N.M. Demurova. Poems translated by S.Ia. Marshak and D.I. Orlovskaia. Introduction by N.M. Demurova. Illustrations by Petar Chuklev. Sofia: Izdatel'stvo literatury na inostrannykh iazykakh, 1967 (in Russian).
———. *The Annotated Hunting of the Snark*. Edited with notes by Martin Gardner, illustrations by Henry Holiday and others, introduction by Adam Gopnik. ("Definitive Edition" ed.). New York: W. W. Norton, 2006.
———. *Eachtra Eibhlíse i dTír na nIontas. Alice's Adventures in Wonderland* in Irish. Translated into Irish by Nicholas Williams. Illustrations by John Tenniel. Cathair na Mart: Evertype, 2007 (in Irish).
———. *The Aventures of Alys in Wondyr Lond. Alice's Adventures in Wonderland* in Middle English verse. Translated into Middle English verse by Brian S. Lee. Illustrations by Byron W. Sewell. Cathair na Mart: Evertype, 2013 (in Middle English).
———. Carroll, Hlóðwíg. *Æðelgýðe Ellendǽda on Wundorlande. Alice's Adventures in Wonderland* in Old English. Translated into Old English by Peter S. Baker. Illustrations by Byron W. Sewell. Portlaoise: Evertype, 2015 (in Old English).
———. *Eachtra Eibhlíse i dTír na nIontas. Alice's Adventures in Wonderland* in Irish. Translated into Irish by Pádraig Ó Cadhla. Illustrations by Byron W. Sewell and John Tenniel. Portlaoise: Evertype, 2015 (in Irish).
———. *Balþos Gadedeis Aþalhaidais in Sildaleikalanda. Alice's Adventures in Wonderland*. Translated into Gothic by David Alexander Carlton. Illustrations by Byron W. Sewell. Portlaoise: Evertype, 2015 (in Gothic).
———. Kérroll, L'iuis. *Älisänen Säyerstandağı majaraları. Alice's Adventures in Wonderland* in Bashkir. Translated into Bashkir by Güzäl Sitdykova. Illustrations by John Tenniel. Portlaoise: Evertype, 2017 (in Bashkir).
———. *Sonia v tsarstve diva* [Sonia in a Kingdom of Wonder]. The first Russian translation of *Alice's Adventures in Wonderland*. [Translated by E.I. Boratynskaya (?).] Illustrations by John Tenniel and Byron W. Sewell. Introduction and notes by Victor Fet. Portlaoise: Evertype, 2017 (in Russian).
Demurova, Nina M. "Alice Speaks Russian: The Russian Translations of *Alice's Adventures in Wonderland* and *Through the Looking-Glass*." *Harvard Library Bulletin* 5(1994–1995) no. 4: 11–29.
Fet, Victor. "Beheading First: On Nabokov's Translation of Lewis Carroll." *The Nabokovian* 63(2009): 52–63.
———. "Around *Sonja*: On the First Russian Translation." *Knight Letter*, Vol. II, 37, no. 97(Fall 2016): 25–34.
———. "Three Early Russian Translations." *Knight Letter*, II, 28, 98(Spring 2017): 16–17.
———. "Russian Translations of Lewis Carroll's *Alice* Books: A Bakhtinian Re-accentuation." In *Mikhail Bakhtin's Heritage in Literature, Arts and Psychology: Art and Answerability*. Ed. Slav N. Gratchev and Howard Mancing, 63–83. Lanham, MD: Lexington Books, 2018.
Jakobson, Roman. *Raboty po poetike* [Works on Poetics]. Moscow: Progress, 1987 (in Russian).
Lindseth, Jon and Allan Tannenbaum (eds.). *Alice in a World of Wonderlands*, Vols. 1–3. New Castle, DE: Oak Knoll Press, 2015.
Marshak, Samuil. *Dom, kotoryi postroil Dzhek* [A House That Jack Built]. Illustrated by Vladimir Konashevich. Peterburg-Moskva: Vsemirnaia literatura, Gosizdat, 1923 (in Russian).
Petrovsky, Miron S. "Vladimir Mayakovsky i L'iuis Kerroll." [Vladimir Mayakovsky and Lewis Carroll]. In Kerroll, L. *Dnevnik puteshestviia v Rossiiu v 1867 g., ili Russkii dnevnik. Stat'i i esse o L'iuise Kérolle.* [Carroll, L. Journal of a tour in Russia in 1867. Articles and

Essays about Lewis Carroll], 297–310. Cheliabinsk: Entsiklopediia; Sankt-Peterburg: Kniga, 2013 (in Russian).

Shklovsky, Viktor. *O teorii prozy* [On the Theory of Prose]. Moskva: Federatsiia, 1929 (in Russian).

———. *Zhili-byli* [Once there lived . . .]. Moskva: Sovetskii pisatel', 1966 (in Russian).

———. *Energiia zabluzhdeniia* [The Energy of Delusion]. Moskva: Sovetskii pisatel', 1981 (in Russian).

———. *O teorii prozy* [On the Theory of Prose]. Moskva: Sovetskii pisatel', 1983 (in Russian).

———. "Resurrecting the Word." In *Viktor Shklovsky: A Reader*. Edited and translated by Alexandra Berlina, 63–72. New York: Bloomsbury Academic, 2017 (first published 1914).

———. "Art as a Device" In *Viktor Shklovsky: A Reader*. Edited and translated by Alexandra Berlina, 73–96. New York: Bloomsbury Academic, 2017 (first published 1917).

Tulchinsky, Grigory L. 2002. "L'iuis Kerroll: nonsens kak predposylka istiny" [Lewis Carroll: nonsense as a preliminary condition of truth]. In *Rossiia i Britaniia v epokhu prosveshcheniia. Opyt filosofskoi i kul'turnoi komparativistiki. Chast' 1. Filosofskii vek.* [Russia and Great Britain in the Age of Enlightenment. Philosophical and Cultural Comparative Studies. Part I. The Age of Philosophy]. Almanakh 19. Sankt-Peterburg: SPb Tsentr istorii idei [Center for the History of Ideas], 2002: 130–150 (in Russian).

Venuti, Lawrence. *Translator's Invisibility: A History of Translation.* New York: Routledge, 1995.

Vitale, Serena. *Shklovsky: Witness to an Era.* Translated by Jamie Richards. Champaign: Dalkey Archive Press, 2012.

Chapter Five

Shklovsky and Narrative Theory

David Gorman

By broad consent, Viktor Shklovsky is recognized as an ancestor of modern narratology. He developed his ideas about narrative as part of his work with the Society for the Study of Poetic Language (OPOYAZ), that is, in the course of his involvement in what is known today, somewhat misleadingly, as the Russian Formalist school.[1] This essay attempts a survey of Shklovsky's distinctive ideas about narrative art. The text of reference will be his *Theory of Prose*, in the English translation of the enlarged edition of 1929 (the first appeared in 1925). A number of Shklovsky's other works from the 1920s add to our understanding of his views on stories and storytelling.

I speak deliberately in referring to Shklovsky as an ancestor of narratology, rather than calling him a narratologist outright. While he may have been an inspiration for the new discipline that arose in the 1960s and 1970s, the adaptations involved were quite selective. Moreover, we today must beware of reading narratological ideas wholesale back into Shklovsky—beware above all of ascribing to him the very idea of a comprehensive or systematic conception of narrative. Because the term "theory" now carries this connotation in the academic humanities, the title *Theory of Prose* may be misleading. In general, Shklovsky was not a systematic thinker. His work on narrative displays a distinctive attitude toward the topic, in the frame of which he developed certain methods and introduced some technical terms. One may aim to elucidate this approach, as I do in what follows—but the result will not be a set of concepts that could be expounded in a textbook chapter. Uncertainty arises here because of the most obvious feature of Shklovsky's work, his writing style, staccato and digressive. Perhaps it obscures a system of thought? This is certainly possible: I do find that Shklovsky had the beginnings of a theory (in the contemporary sense) about literary history, a topic touched upon in *Theory of Prose* at least as frequently as that of narrative composition, a theory further elaborated by the most systematic thinker among the OPOYAZ group, Yury Tynyanov. Even if it meets anyone's definition of a theory, however, Shklovsky's thought about literary evolution still needs to be to be reconstituted from remarks scattered through his writings. But I do not find this to be the case with his ideas on story and plot, an impression confirmed by Shklovsky's later writings on narrative, which are now becoming available in English, and will be considered briefly at the end of this essay.

The unsystematic nature of Shklovsky's thought and writing, though disconcerting to an academic student of narrative, is appropriate to this author. The very loose formation of individuals whom we now refer to as Russian Formalists included many academics (notably Roman Jakobson, Boris Eikhenbaum, Vladimir Propp, Boris Tomashevsky, and Tynyanov), but non-academics like Osip Brik also played important roles. Shklovsky belongs to the second type: journalist, memoirist, autobiographer, novelist, publicist of new trends in art and literature, he did not write for an academic audience. The studies collected in *Theory of Prose* represent his only forays into academic territory, and they are tentative at best. Throughout his career, Shklovsky worked as what used to be called a man of letters, not a scholar. This is not the place to go into the problem of reading Shklovsky, but it is imperative to note that you cannot expect an organized exposition in any of Shklovsky's publications. He not only gives the appearance of dropping the thread of what he says, he actually does regularly seem to lose track of what he is discussing. His constant asides and digressions often convey his most important points. Shklovsky's ideas must be assembled like a mosaic.

Before considering the specifics of Shklovsky's approach to narrative, a few observations should be made concerning *Theory of Prose*. The first is this: in addition to literary evolution and narrative, many subjects arise in this rich, chaotic book. It also touches, often extensively, on matters related to literary art (or art in general), including genre, style, parody, and defamiliarization. This chapter, focused as it is on Shklovsky's ideas about stories, attempts to steer clear of these other matters. A second thing worth noting is the inclusiveness of the literary corpus that Shklovsky surveys. *Theory of Prose* deals with every kind of narrative, from primitive folktales to contemporary fiction, and from popular culture to high art, with side comments on poetry, painting, and film. Examples from Russian literature and culture are especially prominent, but Shklovsky is a truly cosmopolitan critic. A third point is the most important one for what follows: as a student of narrative, Shklovsky is very much an eclectic. He does not propose to subsume or sweep away all previous approaches to the subject in a completely renovated account of storytelling; on the contrary, he helps himself to traditional terms and concepts, many of which go back to Aristotle: aside from plot itself, he frequently mentions unity, peripeteia (reversal), recognition, and denouement; from folklore studies he adopts motif and theme, and in the later chapters, from cinematography, montage. Of course he also introduces new vocabulary, to be discussed further; but these terms form part of a mix.

CONCERNING *FABULA* AND *SUJET*

If one judged by reference works, textbooks, and what comes up in Internet searches, Shklovsky's major contribution to the analysis of narrative would be the distinction between *fabula* and *sujet*. And this difference, as every introduction to narratology explains, has to do with the sequence of occurrences in a narrative, the *fabula* being the series considered in their inherent chronological order, and the *sujet* the way that these occurrences are narrated in a composition, which may not be sequentially. But while Shklovsky is indeed concerned, throughout *Theory of Prose*, as well as in *Literature and Cinematography* (1923), with distinguishing *sujet* from *fabula*, this is not the contrast he intended. What has become the textbook account, standardly attributed to Shklovsky, in fact originates with Tomashevsky, in the chapter of his *Theory of Literature* on "Thematics" (1925).[2]

Tomashevsky's adaptation provides a fine example of how academic critics have tried to recuperate insights from Shklovsky's fertile, chaotic writings for purposes of establishing teachable doctrine. In this case, Tomashevsky seems to have picked up on the first part of a passage in Shklovsky's chapter on *Tristram Shandy*: "The concept of plot (*sujet*) is too often confused with a description of the events in the novel, with what I'd tentatively call the story line (*fabula*)."[3] In the context, however, late in this essay on Sterne's technique, it is obvious that this is not a formulation, on Shklovsky's part, of a thesis about the poetics of narrative, but something much more characteristic of him, an aside, an incidental remark in which he notes the possible relevance of his general notion of *fabula* and *sujet*, which comes out in the qualification that follows this "tentative" remark in the next sentence: "As a matter of fact, though, the story line [*fabula*] is nothing more than material for plot [*sujet*] formation."

In drawing this distinction, Shklovsky contrasts material with form, making us wonder whether "material" is just a substitute for the notion of content, traditionally contrasted with form. But this would be a misunderstanding: "The fairy tale, the novella, the novel are combinations of motifs," he explains in chapter 2 of *Theory*; "the song is a combination of stylistic motifs; therefore the *syuzhet* and the *syuzhet* potential are the same form as rhyme. When we analyze a work of art, from the point of view of *syuzhet* potential, we have no need of the term 'content.' Therefore one must understand form as a law of *syuzhet*-structure."[4] He adds in chapter 9 that, as opposed to considering form as "a kind of covering which we must penetrate" to get to the content, we must understand that a "literary work is pure form. It is neither thing nor material, but a relationship of materials."[5] Ironically, then, Shklovsky proposed the *fabula/sujet* dichotomy to make a point about art generally, not specifically about narrative—though the distinction applies there as well, because storytelling is after all a form of art.[6]

Although the interpretation of *sujet* and *fabula* as relating to the sequence of narrative incidents was a post-Shklovskyan development, I do not suggest that we abandon this application, which has been so useful to the development of modern narratology, where it often serves as the first lesson in narrative analysis. I simply think that the invocation of Shklovsky's name in connection with what has become the standard pedagogical practice of introducing *fabula* and *sujet* is an example of mythology. As for the distinction between a series of occurrences in their inherent sequence and the order in which they are presented in the work, ironically, Shklovsky noticed that difference as well, and returns to it more than once in *Theory of Prose*—which likely influenced Tomashevsky's redefinition—but discussed it under a different heading entirely. I will return to this; but here I will quote a passage from *The Hamburg Score* (1928) that not only shows how Shklovsky distinguished form and material, but also that he was aware of the possibility of transposing story sequence as a narrative technique. He is discussing film narrative here, in which, he observes, "The basic construction of plot is reduced to [an] arrangement of semantic elements. We take two contradictory everyday life situations and resolve them with a third one, or we take two semantic elements and create a parallelism, or we take several semantic elements and arrange them in a stepped order. But the typical foundation of the plot is the *fabula*, an everyday life situation, though the everyday life situation is only a particular instance of semantic construction, and we can create a mystery novel out of any novel not by changing the *fabula* but merely by rearranging its constituent parts: by moving the end to the beginning, or a more complex rearrangement of the parts."[7]

COMPOSITION

For those of us interested in narrative specifically, the place to start in *Theory of Prose* is not the first chapter (the celebrated "Art as Device") but the second, dealing with devices of *sujet* construction as one set of cases of literary ("stylistic") devices. In fact, the two chapters have a parallel design. In "Art as Device" Shklovsky begins with a doctrine about poetry that he aims to refute: the claim that the essence of poetry is imagery. This doctrine is generally associated with the Symbolist movement, but he quotes the influential critic and theorist Aleksandr Potebnya to represent this view, which Shklovsky criticizes as reductive. On the Symbolist account, poetry becomes a secondary phenomenon, a symptom of the psychological events that generate images and in terms of which poetry is to be explained. For Shklovsky however, the key notion is not image, but device. He emphasizes the compositional dimension of poems—and indeed artworks generally—as arrangements of devices for an expressive purpose.

Likewise, the chapter on plot devices begins by identifying a school of critical thought (in this case about folktales) the reductive tendencies of which Shklovsky aims to expose. And likewise, he chooses an individual to represent this style of analysis, Aleksandr Veselovsky. Members of "ethnographic" school, as he calls them, have the idea that folk narratives should be decomposed into elements, "motifs," which should be explained piecemeal in causal terms, for example as relics of customs or rituals. To Shklovsky, this treatment eliminates what is specific to folktales, and what makes them a part of literature: their plot structure. The ethnographic approach, Shklovsky argues, "focuses exceptional attention on the motifs, only casually questioning the significance of the influence of one narrative scheme on another and having absolutely no interest in the laws of *syuzhet* construction."[8] A story is a unity, not a patchwork; once again, the notion Shklovsky urges is that of artistic composition.

Undercutting the causal account of folklore is the existence, ubiquitous among folktales, of what Shklovsky calls "nomadic plots," which he also calls "roving anecdotes." The very same situations, characters, outcomes, and other story elements appear over and over in stories in folklore traditions across the world. Faced with this phenomenon, ethnographic analysts must resort to claiming, implausibly, that this must be the result of either borrowings or coincidences; but it can be explained, Shklovsky holds, "only by the existence of special laws of *syuzhet* construction."[9] There is background assumption here, which is aesthetic: literary art is not the exclusive product of high culture: it arises in popular culture, which is why literary critics have such a good resource in folklore studies—provided they reject its reductive aspect. Folklorists like Veselovsky (according to Shklovsky) want to explain tales in historical, socio-economic terms, for instance as evidence for some archaic custom; but a better explanation lies to hand, in "a conventionality which lies at the heart of every literary work, in that situations are freed from their everyday interrelation and influence each other according to the laws of the given artistic web."[10]

This methodological error is not limited to folkloristics, as Shklovsky notes: "during the period of 'Sturm und Drang' in Germany, for the duration of five years, the vast majority of dramas were based on the *syuzhet* of fratricides"; but "this is not proof that at this moment in Germany fratricide occurred on a massive scale."[11] This phenomenon in high culture is not to be understood in documentary terms, but in terms of literary conventions. It happens that Shklovsky is criticizing ethnography in this chapter of *Theory of Prose*, but this is not the only discipline that lends itself to reductionism, as he points out in *Knight's Move* (1923). "There are critics who think that one can make judgments about the behavior of the heroes in a work of art not on the foundation of laws of art but on the foundations of the laws of psychology. These critics are, of course, interested in the question regarding the nature of King Lear's madness and are even looking for a suitable medical term in Latin."[12]

Once we grasp that Shklovsky's focus is on the compositional aspect of literary narrative, rather than the material that it shapes—be it social, psychological, or ideological—the other tendencies in his analyses fall into place as part of a connected account, the outlines of which are made hard to discern by his digressive, montaged style of presentation. Even reconstructed, his approach to narrative may fall short of constituting a "theory of prose"; but he certainly has a method.

FUNCTION

The most distinctive feature of Shklovsky's approach is his functionalism. Here is a good specimen, from the second chapter of *Theory*, concerning adventure novels:

> The hero is not killed immediately, since he still proves useful for recognition. If they wish to eliminate him, then he is carried off somewhere.
>
> Very often these episodes, with theft and flights and other futile endeavors, are complicated by the fact that the victims are in love with each other and strive toward their goal by the longest path. The successive episodes differ insignificantly one from the other and in adventure novels play the same role of retardation as the task or fabulous ritual in fairy-tales, or a parallelism and retardation in songs. Shipwreck, kidnapping by pirates, etc., have been selected for the *syuzhet*, not for domestic, but for artistic and technical reasons. There is no more of domestic life here, than there is Indian domestic life in the King of a chess game.[13]

The lessons implied here are put to work in every chapter of Shklovsky's book: the feature of narrative requiring attention is not realism or the lack of it—a point to which we will return—but such compositional features as recognition, delay, parallelism, and so forth. Do not, Shklovsky in effect says, reduce narratives to historical documents by asking, like the ethnographic analysts, after the origin of each element; instead, the thing to ask about any story element is what its role is in the totality of interacting elements that make up the narrative.

This maxim is illustrated in the chapter on *Don Quixote*, in an aside on the inn that is the setting for most of the action in Part One of Cervantes's novel. Alonso Quijano fancies himself a wandering knight, of course, and he travels a considerable distance during these chapters, for example into the Sierra Morena. Nevertheless, during roughly a quarter of this narrative, Don Quixote is ensconced at a single inn, to which he returns and at which other characters he has met eventually congregate. Cervantes is entirely unconcerned with rendering these coincidences plausible, and what matters about the inn for narrative analysis is what Shklovsky calls its "compositional" function.[14]

Functional analysis applies not only at the micro-level, of understanding the contribution of story elements to the plot, but at the macro-level, of perceiving the configuration of motifs that characterize a group of narratives. A genre would be one sort of grouping, and in the remarks quoted above, Shklovsky is speaking casually about distinctive features of adventure novels. In chapter 5 of *Theory*, he provides a much more detailed analysis of another kind of group, the corpus of stories that make up the Sherlock Holmes mysteries.[15] Although the passage is too long to quote, even if we subtract the asides inevitable in Shklovsky,[16] he lists a sequence of occurrences beginning with discussions of previous cases and ending with the explanation of the facts in the present case given by Holmes, with such intermediate episodes as the initial misinterpretation of the clues by Watson and the false solution given by a detective. Shklovsky does not claim that every element listed must occur in every Sherlock Holmes story; however he is doing more than identifying the kinds of thing that happen in the stories of this corpus. He is giving a morphological analysis: in other words, he sets out the pattern of occurrences that distinguishes a Holmes story. Shklovsky's analysis of Holmes stories presumably inspired Propp's *Morphology of the Folktale* (1927); but in any case, it certainly influenced narrative studies before and after Propp—among other examples one must cite Boris Eikhenbaum's "O. Henry and the Theory of the Short Story" (1925) and Tzvetan Todorov's *Grammaire du Décameron*, and the tradition of story-grammars that followed from that.

Perhaps the best-known bit of functional analysis in contemporary narrative theory concerns "Chekhov's gun": the idea, attributed to Chekhov, that if a gun is described in the first scene of a play hanging on a wall, it will necessarily go off in some later scene. The more thoroughly functionalist Shklovsky notes that there is an exception to this narratological cliché, which has to do with genre. "In a mystery . . . the gun that hangs on the wall does not fire. Another gun shoots instead."[17] All the other features of Shklovsky's work on recounting stories can be seen as corollaries of his functionalism.

DEVICE AND MOTIVATION

In his functionalist approach to narrative, Shklovsky introduced several new ideas. The most promising of these, I believe, is the idea that plot devices may be motivated—or not. Although he uses device/motivation analysis throughout *Theory of Prose*, Shklovsky treats the method as something already understood. For help understanding it, we might turn to the preface of his epistolary novel *Zoo* (1923), where he explains that using a collection of letters to constitute a narrative work, as he has, constitutes a device, and he has motivated the device by means of a love affair, in accordance with a literary convention: "in an epistolary novel, the essential thing is motivation—precisely why should these people be writing to each other? The usual motivation is love and partings."[18] A more diffuse example is provided by Tolstoy's story "Strider" (*Kholstomer*), discussed in the first essay in *Theory of Prose*, and further in chapter 3.[19] The device governing it is estrangement: Tolstoy gives an alienated description of life among Russian high society, motivated by the use of a horse as the focal consciousness. To this analysis Shklovsky adds a fascinating observation: although the horse dies before the end of the story, the estranged description continues. In other words, a device can continue to function even when no longer motivated. Conversely, as Shklovsky goes on to discuss (or rather presupposes that his readers already grasp), devices can be "laid bare": the narrative can self-consciously undercut the motivation of its devices so that they stand out.

It is worth trying to explain the basis of this approach, if only because Shklovsky nowhere does. In the first place, it seems that we are only talking about narrative compositions. Besides novels and tales, Shklovsky uses these terms with drama, film, and narrative verse, and it is hard to see how they would apply to non-narrative. In any case, a device is a compositional element in narrative: the *sujet* consists of a set of devices. The purpose of motivating devices is to conceal their compositional nature, to make an artwork pass as something natural, spontaneously occurring rather than constructed. The source of material for motivation is simply the non-literary world. Not all authors need have this goal; another artistic effect can be achieved by laying bare the device, foregrounding the composed nature of the narrative composition. Tentative summary: if devices are *literary*, motivation is *non-literary*, and laying a device bare is *meta-literary*.

Of course, Shklovsky provides no criteria for identifying devices and forms of motivation; but this would be worth considering. As for devices, he sometimes characterizes them in very general terms, as in the list of "*syuzhet* devices" included in chapter 2: "tautology, tautological parallelism, psychological parallelism, retardation, epic repetitions, [and] narrative rituals (peripeteia)";[20] at other times, he gives concrete examples, as when in chapter 3, he states that the following motifs are all devices: father versus son, brother versus brother-in-law, husband at his wife's wedding, "the elusive criminal," and "the innocent criminal."[21] As for motivation, Shklovsky introduces the notion very diffusely throughout his second chapter, on folktales. The kind of thing he has in mind—here I give one example in place of trying to cite many—would be the use of friendly ants or birds as motivation for the device of the successful resolution of a seemingly impossible task—sorting a mixed pile of seeds in one night. In the next chapter, Shklovsky shows how this carries over to literary narratives: for example, in a quest story, of having one character serve as a protagonist to connect the episodes constitutes the device (a technique Shklovsky calls "threading," discussed further below), the motivation will be a journey.[22] Analysis in term of device and motivation carries over to high literature as well: among other examples given in later chapters, Shklovsky notes how, in *Don Quixote*, the primary motivation for the action shifts between Part One and Part Two of the novel, where "Don Quixote is no longer deluded so much as he is a victim of hoaxes."[23]

By contrast, Shklovsky did far better explaining the notion of laying bare devices, famously in his chapter on *Tristram Shandy*; but the phenomenon is illustrated elsewhere as well, for instance when in the second part of *Don Quixote*, the speeches Sancho makes as governor "differ radically from what we have been accustomed to hear from" this character, and "Cervantes himself points out the incongruity and thus lays bare the device."[24]

This way of thinking about narrative still awaits development. To my knowledge, only Gérard Genette has attempted to follow up on the concept of motivation, and only in one essay.[25]

ANTI-MIMETICISM

"Why is it that King Lear does not recognize Kent?" Shklovsky cites Tolstoy as asking, "Why do Kent and Lear not recognize Edgar?"[26] The answer to this, as Tolstoy knew very well, is literary convention. Clark Kent's glasses keep anyone from recognizing that he is Superman—speaking of Kents—because otherwise we could not get on with the story: "the unreality [of a literary work] disturbed Shakespeare no more than the question 'Why cannot a Knight move straight?' disturbs a chess player."[27] A less obvious consequence of Shklovsky's functionalism, which saturates his work in a way that there is no room here to explore at length, involves a demotion of mimeticism in narrative art, where it becomes one option among others. A helpful exposition of this kind of conventionalism is Jakobson's essay "On Realism in Art" (1921), which is written in a very Shklovskyan spirit, and can be read as another example of an academic trying to sort out and set forth in an organized manner (as Tomashevsky, Tynyanov, and Propp also attempted to do) ideas that swirl inchoately in *Theory of Prose*. The critique of verisimilitude as a literary value would become a touchstone for Roland Barthes and other Structuralist and Post-structuralist critics, who follow Shklovsky in emphasizing the deliberate and often self-conscious aspect of narrative and other forms of art. "A poet often renounces verse in verse, while a novelist renounces fiction in fiction. Even in cinema a hero will reply on screen (I myself have seen this), 'How beautiful! Just like in the movies.' The creation of an illusion, its consolidation, and its dismantling are all devices of art."[28]

SOME TERMS AND CONCEPTS

Throughout *Theory of Prose* (and elsewhere), Shklovsky offers comments on narrative design which, while unsystematic in nature, draw on a set of terms that he coined for narrative techniques, structures, and types, terms that he seems to use fairly consistently. He nowhere defines these terms, or attempts to set them out in a way that shows their relationship. One might attempt a catalog, however.

A fairly intuitive device that Shklovsky highlights, threading, was mentioned previously. The idea is that a single element, present continuously in the narrative, acts as a thread on which episodes and material can be hung: for instance, a hero on a quest. The question arises whether only characters can serve as threads, though Shklovsky does not address it. Characters are however the only examples he uses for this device. The fact that this is the only connection in which such a basic concept of narrative analysis arises in *Theory of Prose* is a symptom of the demotion of the category of character in "formalist" (or it would be better to call it functionalist) narrative study.[29]

A term that, by contrast, has likely puzzled readers of Shklovsky is "stepped construction." It is easy to conclude that this means parallel design in a narrative, especially when Shklovsky describes "progressive" construction as the "simplest form of plot construction"[30]; but parallelism is only one feature. There must also be difference, as in, "Someone's been sleeping in my bed' . . . 'And someone's been sleeping in my bed'; . . . And someone's been sleeping in my bed—and there she is!'" This is not only a device of folk narrative; Shklovsky gives many examples of it, and repeatedly argues that "step-by-step construction" is a basic element in Tolstoy's literary art.

Another device on which Shklovsky focuses is that of framing one narrative within another. The second half of his chapter on *Don Quixote* is taken up with Cervantes's use of this technique to incorporate material into his novel; and in the preceding chapter, on structures in fiction, he emphasizes its role not only in Boccaccio's *Decameron*, but in other story collections and in narratives like T*he Golden Ass*.

Delay, deceleration, retardation—these are terms that Shklovsky uses for a function basic to narrative, which many devices can fulfill, in ways that he surveys throughout *Theory of Prose*. The thought is that the point of a fictional story would be lost if it concluded too quickly—if the detective guessed the criminal's identity right away: "the fundamental law of peripeteia is that of retardation . . . That which should be revealed immediately and that which is already clear to the audience is slowly discovered by the hero."[31] As he points out, with sufficient ingenuity, an author can delay the finale indefinitely, as in many adventure stories and romances.

Finally, Shklovsky was well aware of the possibility of disordering the story sequence to produce a narrative effect (even though it is a misunderstanding to think that he used the terms *sujet* and *fabula* in this context). As he explains, recounting effects before their causes is one way of producing a mystery—but, on the one hand, mysteries can be constructed in a completely different way,[32] and, on the other, this device does not necessarily have this function: *Tristram Shandy* is full of sequence-reversals, yet with no mysterious effect.

LATER WRITINGS

Shklovsky survived the Stalinist era and, after the Thaw, he continued to write—copiously—about literature in general and narrative in particular. *Bowstring* (1970) and *Energy of Delusion* (1981, subtitled *A Book on Plot*) are available now in English translations, as well as the selections included in *Viktor Shklovsky: A Reader* from *Tales about Prose* (1966) and *On the Theory of Prose* (1983). A detailed comparison of his later writings on narrative to his writings from the 1920s would be interesting, but not feasible here. I will conclude, however, with a few preliminary remarks.

Overall, continuity greatly outweighs difference, in terms not only of Shklovsky's ideas about stories but also of his style. He continued to write as a man of letters rather than a scholar throughout. His trademark writing technique, in which a subject is inconsequently dropped after a few paragraphs but restlessly picked back up again after several pages, is still in evidence. The literary corpus he cites remains much the same, with its touchstones of fairy tales, the *Decameron, Don Quixote*, Pushkin, and above all Tolstoy still very much in place (he seems to have spent the Freeze rereading rather than reading much new). If Shklovsky had had a systematic theory of narrative—or if, perhaps, he had brought one to completion during the Stalinist interval—then he had ample opportunity to set it out in these late writings. However, there is no evidence of that. Just as if he had never left off after the second edition of *Theory of Prose*, Shklovsky still refers to narrative under the heading of "prose," and he continues to focus on *sujet* (plot), particularly chapters 4, 5, and 20 in *Energy* and in the seventh chapter (titled "On the Functions of Plot") of *Bowstring*.

A review of these and other late writings on narrative finds Shklovsky discussing his perennial topics with regard to narrative composition: coincidence, deceleration and impediments in narrative; devices motivated and laid bare; exposition and denouement; montage; motifs and their function; mysteries and riddles (erotic and otherwise); nomadic (or "traveling") plots and the absurdity of searching for their origins; parallel and stepped construction; reversal; and the unity of narrative works. This observation is not a criticism: the fertility of Shklovsky's ideas guarantees that there was always more he could say about the phenomena he observed, and even his repetitions seem worthwhile. Toward the end of *Energy*, he says about his quest for the essence of *sujet*, "Throughout my life and until this day I still don't have a clear idea of what plot really is";[33] but anyone feeling dismayed by this confession should also keep in mind a previous remark, which perhaps identifies the true status of these writings: "my life is not eternal and this is my attempt to leave behind at least some notes as a keepsake."[34]

NOTES

1. That it was neither formalist nor a school I argue in "Russian Formalism," in *A Companion to Literary Theory*, edited by David H. Richter (Oxford: Wiley, 2018): 37–47, to which this essay is a sequel.

2. Published in English translation as if it was an essay.

3. Shklovsky, *Theory of Prose*, translated by Benjamin Sher (Elmwood Park, IL: Dalkey Archive Press, 1990): 170.

4. Shklovsky, "On the Connection between Devices of *Syuzhet* Construction and General Stylistic Devices," translated by Jane Knox, in *Russian Formalism*, edited by Stephen Bann and John E. Bowlt (New York: Barnes & Noble, 1973): 71. I have Americanized spellings in this alternate version of the second chapter in *Theory of Prose*; note the alternate transliteration of *sujet*.

5. Shklovsky, *Theory of Prose*, 189.

6. Shklovsky's most extended discussion of dichotomy in opening chapters of his *Literature and Cinematography*, translated by Irina Masinovsky (Elmwood Park, IL: Dalkey Archive Press, 2008): 1–23. Wolf Schmid provides an authoritative discussion of the matter in his *Narratology* (2003): see 175–185.

7. Shklovsky, *The Hamburg Score*, translated by Shushan Avagyan (Elmwood Park, IL: Dalkey Archive Press, 2017): 159–160. The essay quoted is "Poetry and Prose in Cinematography."

8. Shklovsky, "On the Connection," 51.

9. Ibid., 50.

10. Ibid., 51.

11. Ibid., 66.

12. Shklovsky, *Knight's Move*, translated by Richard Sheldon (Elmwood Park, IL: Dalkey Archive Press, 2005): 94.

13. Shklovsky, "On the Connection," 63–64.

14. Ibid., 87.

15. Shklovsky, *Theory of Prose*, 115.

16. The translation that Shklovsky used includes some apocryphal stories, which is unproblematic, since authorship is irrelevant to this kind of analysis.

17. Ibid., 110.

18. Shklovsky, *Zoo*, translated by. Richard Sheldon (Elmwood Park, IL: Dalkey Archive Press, 2001): 3.
19. Shklovsky, *Theory of Prose*, 63, 70–71.
20. Ibid., 54; see also *Theory of Prose*, 108, where he adds puns and coincidences to the list.
21. Ibid., 54.
22. Ibid., 68–69.
23. Ibid., 91.
24. Ibid., 98; and see 95; in chapter 3, Shklovsky discusses how Chekhov motivates his story devices (53, 60).
25. See my translation of "*Vraisemblance* and Motivation" (1968), in *Narrative* 9.1 (2001): 239–258.
26. Shklovsky, "On the Connection," 48.
27. Ibid., 65.
28. Shklovsky, *Theory of Prose*, 185.
29. Shklovsky's functionalism is laid bare in this comment on Lesage's protagonist: "Gil Blas is not a human being at all. He is a *thread* . . . by means of which all the episodes of the novel are woven together" (ibid., 66); see chapters 3 and 4 throughout.
30. Ibid., 118.
31. "On the Connection," 66–67
32. Shklovsky, *Theory of Prose*, 101–103.
33. Shklovsky, *Energy of Delusion*, translated by Shushan Avagyan (Elmwood Park, IL: Dalkey Archive Press, 2007): 414.
34. Ibid., 119.

WORKS CITED

Berlina, Alexandra, ed. and trans. *Viktor Shklovsky: A Reader*. New York: Bloomsbury Academic, 2016.

Eikhenbaum, Boris. "O. Henry and the Theory of the Short Story." Trans. I. R. Titunik. In *Readings in Russian Poetics, Formalist and Structuralist Views*. Ed. Ladislav Matejka and Krystyna Pomorska (1971). Rpt. Champaign, IL: Dalkey Archive Press, 2002. 227–270.

Genette, Gérard. "*Vraisemblance* and Motivation." Trans. David Gorman. *Narrative* 9.1 (2001): 239–258.

Gorman, David. "Russian Formalism." In *A Companion to Literary Theory*. Ed. David H. Richter. Oxford: Wiley, 2018. 37–47.

Jakobson, Roman. "On Realism in Art." Trans. Karol Magassy. In *Language in Literature*. Ed. Krystyna Pomorska and Stephen Rudy. Cambridge: Harvard University Press, 1987. 19–29.

Propp, Vladimir. *Morphology of the Folktale*. Trans. Laurence Scott (1958), rev. Louis A. Wagner. Austin: University of Texas Press, 1968.

Schmid, Wolf. *Narratology: An Introduction*. Trans. Alexander Starritt. De Gruyter, 2010.

Shklovsky, Viktor. *Bowstring: On the Dissimilarity of the Similar*. Trans. Shushan Avagyan. Elmwood Park, IL: Dalkey Archive Press, 2011.

Shklovsky, Viktor. *Energy of Delusion: A Book on Plot*. Trans. Shushan Avagyan. Elmwood Park, IL: Dalkey Archive Press, 2007.

Shklovsky, Viktor. *The Hamburg Score*. Trans. Shushan Avagyan. Elmwood Park, IL: Dalkey Archive Press, 2017.

Shklovsky, Viktor. *Knight's Move*. Trans. Richard Sheldon. Elmwood Park, IL: Dalkey Archive Press, 2005.

Shklovsky, Viktor. *Literature and Cinematography*. Trans. Irina Masinovsky. Elmwood Park, IL: Dalkey Archive Press, 2008.

Shklovsky, Viktor. "On the Connection between Devices of *Syuzhet* Construction and General Stylistic Devices." Trans. Jane Knox. *Russian Formalism*. Ed. Stephen Bann and John E. Bowlt. New York: Barnes & Noble, 1973. 48–72.

Shklovsky, Viktor. *Theory of Prose*. Trans. Benjamin Sher. Elmwood Park, IL: Dalkey Archive Press, 1990.

Shklovsky, Viktor. *Zoo, or Letters Not about Love*. Trans. Richard Sheldon (1971). Rpt. Elmwood Park, IL: Dalkey Archive Press, 2001.
Todorov, Tzvetan. *Grammaire du Décameron*. The Hague: Mouton, 1969.
Tomashevsky, Boris. "Thematics." *Russian Formalist Criticism: Four Essays*. Ed. and trans. Lee T. Lemon and Marion J. Reis. Lincoln: University of Nebraska Press, 1965. 62–95.

Chapter Six

Ostranenie and Genre

Semiotic Subversions in The Crying of Lot 49 *and "Death and the Compass"*

Melissa Garr

There is an ages-old debate (most prevalent among math teachers and their students) about whether process or product is more important. The argument for process is that without the process, there would be no product, whereas without the product, the process would be meaningless. Detective fiction already goes a long way toward dispelling the need for a process-product dichotomy, because in detective fiction it is the following of a meticulous process that leads to a highly desirable product—the imposition of order upon chaos. This order can only be achieved through a particular kind of process that is intimately and intricately linked to it. The challenge for detective fiction authors is to maintain the novelty of the plot without the reader becoming inured to the question itself by erasing both parts.

If, as Viktor Shklovsky contends, poetic speech is formed speech, then literary genres such as detective fiction could be conceived as a formed speech act consisting of a set of formulae and expectations readily identifiable to the reader. These can, however, serve to lull the reader into passive consumption of novelistic genres rather than conscious engagement with them, particularly in detective fiction, as imposing order through the resolution of a mystery is accomplished by a carefully crafted labyrinth of clues that lead readers to a single exit.

In Thomas Pynchon's *The Crying of Lot 49* and Jorge Luis Borges's "Death and the Compass," however, the authors deliberately enstrange (or defamiliarize)[1] the genre itself by using symbols to lure the main characters into fake mysteries that end ambiguously in the middle of the labyrinth of clues, with no way out. The investigators actively create mysteries that are in themselves red herrings, or semiotic subversion of the genre's tropes and expectations. In each story, a final resolution is denied to the reader, but the process has still resulted in a meaningful artistic product which is fully recognized by the reader, through *ostranenie*.

Viktor Shklovsky's idea of *ostranenie*, variously translated as "defamiliarization" and "enstrangement," is initially presented in "Resurrecting the Word" and "Art as Device" through discussions of poetic language and poetic imagery; as opposed to prosaic language and imagery, which registers with the mind automatically and nearly unconsciously, poetic language and imagery draws attention to its artistic and constructive devices. For Shklovsky, then, the purpose of art is to complicate or enstrange the process of perception itself, such that art becomes "a means of experiencing the process of creativity" regardless of the nature of the artifact.[2] The artistic process is laid bare by complicating both objects and forms. His initial discussion of the devices by which this is accomplished begins with the image; for example, since riddles couch their subjects in unfamiliar terms or plays on words with the purpose of obfuscating them, *ostranenie* is "the foundation of all riddles."[3] Thus, *ostranenie* is a useful critical framework for examining the complex symbols that undergird the mysteries in *The Crying of Lot 49*, such as the ubiquitous muted post-horn of Tristero, and "Death and the Compass," with its oft-examined repetitions of threes and fours, rhomboid geometric figures, and labyrinths. These signs and their signifiers are unraveled multiple times in both narratives, obfuscating their role in the resolution of the riddles the investigators seek to solve.

Shklovsky's discussion of *ostranenie*, however, does not stop with language and the image; he is also concerned with artistic forms and the context that governs our artistic experience of them. In the second chapter of *Theory of Prose*, for example, he discusses plot and motif and the importance of understanding these forms against a background of other literary forms that existed before. New forms, according to Shklovsky, appear "not in order to express a new content, but rather, to replace an old form that has already outlived its artistic usefulness."[4] The discussion during the remainder of that chapter focuses on structural devices that affect the plot itself (which we could call the artifact, here, as Shklovsky previously described with respect to the creative process), such as framing and deceleration devices, that lead into a general discussion of fictive structures. These structures are accumulations of images and language into systemic wholes that govern the artistic organization of the content of the artistic work, or, in the case of a novel, the way in which the story is organized and told. It is precisely in these systemic organizing structures that the effects of *ostranenie* are most likely to be produced on the scale of the whole work, as well as in its component images. By any reasonable definition, coherent and regular systems of plot construction and organization of motifs are classified as "genres." Thus, Shklovsky spends the bulk of the *Theory of Prose* examining motifs and plot construction devices across various genres, as they enstrange the stories and content themselves. He begins, for example, with a fairly thorough examination of Don Quixote's unique transformative expression of conventional adventure and chivalry motifs in his speeches, and how Don Quixote's presence as a conscious "reader" affects the ways in which interpolated stories in various genres are told and interpreted (and, sometimes, embodied). He also spends fully two chapters discussing detective and mystery stories and novels, as they expand on his earlier discussion of the enstranging effect of riddles and their images. The mystery genre (of which Shklovsky includes detective fiction as a subset) avails itself of many narrative devices that reframe the "mystery" that readers of adventure novels had become accustomed to as a matter of course—the intervention of a narrative sidekick (i.e., Watson) to whom the process must be explained, for example, which both retards the narrative and creates the possibility of two or more lines of action to be pursued by the reader.[5] Mystery stories by Dickens also utilize structures like parallelism, displacement and error in order to complicate readers' perceptions and lay bare the device of the text. Readers engaged in these stories are aware that they are responsible for a metacognitive process of engagement with the author, in addition to enjoying/consuming the story itself. Shklovsky advises anyone interested in seeing Russian literature and its plot structures in a new light should look to the ways in which motifs are structured in detective stories such as Conan Doyle's.

Although Shklovsky clearly demonstrates that the detective and mystery genres are exemplary of structural *ostranenie*, detective fiction has developed significantly since 1925. Indeed, Shklovsky's book was written during the interwar "Golden Age" of detective fiction, which featured such prolific practitioners as Agatha Christie, S.S. Van Dine and Dorothy L. Sayers. During this period, detective fiction authors famously sought to create "rules" for detective fiction, such as S.S. Van Dine's oft-cited list of 20 conventions, published in 1928 in *The American Magazine*.[6] In this way, detective fiction, which once enstranged adventure stories and perceptions of law and order, went through a process described by Shklovsky in "Resurrecting the Word": the conventions began to "fossilize" (Mikhail Bakhtin might say "ossify"), at least in the *intentions* of its practitioners to codify its process of creation, which consequently affected reader expectations. Classic detective works became "covered with the glass armor of familiarity—we remember them too well, we've heard them as children,[7] we've read them in books, we've quoted them in passing,[8] and now we have calluses on our souls—we no longer experience them."[9] Detective novels, featuring a Holmes-type detective engaging in what Edgar Allan Poe called a process of "ratiocination" are popularly now known as "cozy" detective novels. Raymond Chandler famously took issue with this fossilization of the genre in his 1944 essay "The Simple Art of Murder," in which he argues that detective fiction needed to be concerned again about being art, rather than a crossword puzzle loosely disguised by a plot.[10] He pointed to Dashiell Hammett's model of the private eye as a rejuvenation of the genre, and Chandler himself practiced this model by writing the Philip Marlowe series. Chandler credited Hammett for giving "murder back to the kind of people that commit it for reasons."[11] Chandler and Hammett's model estranged the genre primarily by modifying the expected motifs, rather than the structural devices. For example, they removed the detective from the parlor-room and placed him on urban streets; and they made the detective a hardened man as prone to use his fists as his intellect, but adhering to an internally consistent moral code (often juxtaposed with corruption in the official police forces). What remains is the investigative process that imposes rational order onto the chaos of criminality embodied in the murder, the multiple plot structures in which the timelines of the crime and the investigation unfold in different directions simultaneously, and the riddle challenge for the reader, but these elements were seen in a new light given their change in context and frame. By the mid-1960s, however, these so-called hard-boiled detective stories had also become products of unquestioning and comfortable consumption in print and in film. The enstranged version of the cozy novels of the past were likewise "seen and not recognized."[12]

The 1942 story "Death and the Compass" by Jorge Luis Borges and the 1966 Thomas Pynchon novel *The Crying of Lot 49* fulfill the artistic need for *ostranenie* outlined by Shklovsky—that "the creation of new art forms can restore to man the experience of the world, can resurrect things and kill pessimism"[13]—for both the cozy and hard-boiled variants of the detective story. Each of them exemplifies conventions of the detective story that Shklovsky described in detail (the "Story Based on Error," in the case of "Death and the Compass," and the "Story Based on Parallelism" in *The Crying of Lot 49*), but as these conventions had become fairly "fossilized" and "seen but not recognized" in the cozy and hard-boiled detective stories by the time of each story's publication, each utilizes a complex language of signs (in the semiotic sense) to enstrange detective fiction conventions and draw the reader's attention once again explicitly to the *mystery* of the story and foreground its contingent artistic representation of the world. They serve as examples of the progression of later twentieth-century detective fiction into unconventional directions, and also highlight that *ostranenie* is an artistic *process* that continually and intentionally removes the artifact "from the domain of automatized perception."[14] The great dilemma of the detective genre is, according to Devin Fromm, is that although "the genre may move in directions of metaphysical detection, where the story shifts from epistemological engagement to ontological doubt . . . it remains a literary object to be consumed like anything else."[15] Conditioning the *way* in which it is consumed, automatically or with purposeful and conscious recognition, is the artistic task of the detective fiction author.

Shklovsky's description of the "Story Based on Error" in his chapter on Dickens and the mystery novel is particularly applicable to the structural elements that undergird the plot of "Death and the Compass." In this story, a Talmudic scholar is found murdered in a hotel room on the third of December. On his typewriter is found a page with the line "La primera letra del Nombre ha sido articulada"[16] ("The first letter of the Name has been uttered"). Supposing that this clue indicates a "rabbinic" turn to the crime, the main character, a private detective named Erik Lönnrot, takes it upon himself to investigate the Tetragrammaton and the Kabbalah, although his colleague Treviranus suggests that it was likely an attempted robbery in which the murderer accidentally came into the wrong room. A second murder occurs on January third, and a third on February third, each with a message declaring that another letter in the Name has been uttered. A map sent to Treviranus shows that each murder's location corresponds to the points of an equilateral triangle, which superficially appears to wrap up the case, but Lönnrot knows the Tetragrammaton has four letters and goes alone to the spot on the map that represents a fourth location, creating a perfect rhombus. At that location, his criminal nemesis Red Scharlach is waiting to kill him; the first murder was indeed a robbery gone awry, but Scharlach uses Lönnrot's investigative focus and rationality to entrap him.

David A. Boruchoff notes the similarities in this story to Shklovsky's depiction of the detective genre: the "manipulation of false and true solutions, simultaneous actions and parallel intrigues, and the device of inversion."[17] The inversion primarily occurs in the respective investigative tracks of the two detectives—classically, the private detective's "interesting" intellectual puzzle is correct while the official police can't figure it out, whereas the opposite is true in "Death and the Compass"—and in the resolution of the crime. Lönnrot, to his credit, does correctly follow the clues laid out for him by the criminal; however, the culmination of his investigation leads to his own demise and underscores the failure of his pure, detectivesque rationality. This is, as Julia Kushigian points out, "unsettling for the reader who demands the codification of what is or isn't permissible in a detective story"—those readers conditioned and automatized by familiarity with Christie, Sayers, Chesterton, Doyle and Van Dine. Borges does not allow this to go unchallenged; he "recognizes this anxiety in the reader but does not grant him sympathy."[18] The order established at the end through the geometry superimposed on the story's setting and the rationality of the investigation stems from the chaos of criminality rather than the justice typically provided by the detective; on the other hand, both solutions are the product of two highly rational and purposeful minds. The essential conflict in the story is between "a stylized, literary universe and a stylized, literary convention,"[19] and the struggle between them is a significant way in which *ostranenie* is achieved. The effect of *ostranenie* in the reader is mirrored in Lönnrot's bewildered response to finding Scharlach waiting for him at the villa: "Scharlach ¿usted busca el Nombre Secreto?"[20] ("Scharlach, are you also seeking the Secret Name?") This utterance indicates that Lönnrot has become so invested in the Kabbalistic aspects of his investigation that he has apparently forgotten that he is supposed to be there to prevent a crime.

Shklovsky further notes in "Story Based on Error" that the simplest plot form is step-by-step construction, which often forms a circular structure.[21] "Death and the Compass" begins with a discussion of the ending, how Lönnrot foresaw the final crime even though he was unable to prevent it. Subsequently, the crimes are set up sequentially and based on an apparent numerical and geometric pattern—superficially based on the number three, as the crimes all occur on the third of the months in question, the last of the three notes indicates that the "última de las letras del Nombre ha sido articulada"[22] ("the last of the letters of the Name has been uttered"), and the locations occur at the points of a geographical equilateral triangle. The savvy reader of detective fiction, accustomed to finding hidden clues and discarding the obvious trails as red herrings, catches that the Tetragrammaton has four letters instead of three, indicating that the many threes in the text are a false trail. In the error-type story, according to Shklovsky, "the confusion of two given concepts is motivated by an external resemblance in circumstance that involves an ambiguous interpretation."[23] The three is *ostensibly* right in the context of the tale, especially when one considers that Treviranus' name points to the number three, and his solution to the crime was the correct one; but as many critics have pointed out, they are really both right, since the number 4 and its associated symbols in the story contain the number three and its symbols. The rhombus contains the triangle, the number four contains the number three, and the Tetragrammaton, although it consists of 4 characters (JHVH), really only contains the individual letters J, V, and H.[24] Both sets of signs lead to the same mastermind, but it is not a liberating sense of order that is imparted by this knowledge, but rather the consciousness of the "limitations of genre."[25] Lönnrot's response to this awareness of his own medium's limitations is to posit to Scharlach the possibility of meeting him as an adversary in another "avatar," in a different kind of labyrinth, a single line where his adversary could never reach him, because he'd have to traverse an infinite number of points in between. In this avatar Lönnrot "creates a new world, the world in which his linear labyrinth would make him the victor—not victim of the criminal."[26] This could certainly be a more comfortable and familiar denouement in the detective genre, but that sense is undermined by the inability of such a labyrinth to be mapped onto the rational world of the conventional detective story. The bullet fired from Scharlach's gun, for example, must also traverse a line between the gun and Lönnrot's body; geometrically, this may mean that it has to traverse infinite points before it reaches him, but the pure geometrical logic of this will not prevent the bullet from tearing through him anyway.

Symbolic language does not supersede the *ostranenie* of the Word in "Death and the Compass," by any means. Whereas Lönnrot seeks absolutes in the mystery of the Names of God, his investigation forces him to "enfrentarse a la falibilidad del lenguaje y su incapacidad de garantizar significados absolutos"[27] ("to confront the fallibility of language and its incapacity to guarantee absolute meanings"). This linguistic fallibility is highlighted in the ways in which Borges tortures the Spanish language in the story, using orthographic markers and phonemic groupings that don't exist in Spanish and render many significant words nearly unpronounceable by a native Spanish speaker. Katherine Brown notes that this forces the reader to concentrate minutely on the language of the story itself and how letters and symbols combine to create words and meaning.[28] Each time a Spanish-speaking reader encounters the name of the protagonist, Lönnrot, it jars them into awareness of how arbitrarily these linguistic signifiers are tied to the concepts they signify; in this case, a foreign name represents a particular type of detective also foreign in origin to Borges's Argentina, whose logic is foreign to the world upon which it attempts to impose order. The strangeness of the classic detective isn't a new convention (Sherlock Holmes is quite erratic and requires the mediation of Watson), but his failure to resolve the fundamental mystery of the text and to connect signifiers and signified into any meaningful symbolic language enstranges the reader's experience of the detective story.

The Crying of Lot 49, by contrast, uses techniques consistent with what Shklovsky calls the "Story Based on Parallelism." In this novel, a housewife named Oedipa Maas is named as executrix of the will of her wealthy former lover, Pierce Inverarity. During the course of her investigations into his assets and holdings, she begins to come across a symbol that looks like a muted horn. It appears connected to an underground mail system called W.A.S.T.E. and, later, to a sinister, shadowy organization known as Tristero, which historically challenged the hegemony of the European Thurn and Taxis postal monopoly and, in the U.S., appears to challenge postal systems such as Wells Fargo, Pony Express and USPS. After finding that Inverarity owned an entire collection of adulterated stamps and encountering the muted horn symbol with increasing and alarming frequency, Oedipa ultimately becomes uncertain whether the investigation she is pursuing is a product of her mind imposing meaning on things she perceives, or an objective pattern of information suggesting meaning to her. An auction of Inverarity's unusual stamps unearths a mysterious buyer, so she attends the auction, hoping to find verification that any of it is real during the eponymous crying of lot 49. The novel ends, however, at the beginning of the auction, and we are not given any resolution to Oedipa's anxieties. Kristin L. Matthews notes that any liberation on the part of Oedipa or her American readers "depends upon the defamiliarization of conventional processes of reading and interpretation";[29] this is achieved by the lack of expected resolution to the mystery.[30]

Shklovsky describes a story based on parallelism as a comparison between two objects, developed in "two independent stories . . . united often only by the presence of a single narrator or by the place of action." He goes on to specify that mystery novels, on the other hand, deal "not with a comparison of objects but with the displacement of one object by another."[31] Parallel stories form a significant part of the novel's overall structure. One of these is the repeated story of the bones. This first appears in the story of a claim made on the Inverarity estate by a mob boss for the provision of bones to one of Inverarity's companies. The bones belonged to American GIs who were stranded by a lake in Italy during the Second World War. Ultimately, they all died, and their bodies were unceremoniously dumped into an adjacent lake, from which years later their bones were pulled out and sold to American companies. The tale is paralleled, as a secondary character points out, by a similar tale within the play *The Courier's Tragedy*, in which the villainous Duke has a squadron of another country's finest knights slaughtered and their bodies thrown into a lake. He later exhumes the bones and grinds them down to make ink, which he uses in all his communications to that nation as a sick personal joke. This story is the motivation for Oedipa seeing the play in the first place, and encountering mention of Tristero for the first time. Later on, it is revealed that the lake at which Oedipa hears the first version of this tale was in 1853 the setting for a massacre of Wells Fargo riders by mysterious black-clad men (whom readers at this point associate with Tristero). Later, Oedipa finds yet another version of the tale in a book given to her by Professor Emory Bortz, in which Torre and Tassis postal riders were attacked by a lake and slaughtered by black-clad men claiming to be from "Trystero." In these latter two versions, instead of bones, a witness is allowed to survive and tell the tale, echoing the communicative function of the bones in the version from *The Courier's Tragedy*. The bones are also connected by Mr. Thoth's story, who describes how "Indians who weren't Indians" would slaughter Pony Express riders and burn and grind their bones to blacken their trademark feathers. This particular tale's recurrence illustrates that what is dead does not stay dead, but is regurgitated and used in new and often irreverent forms; in Oedipa's world, information such as this story cycles incestuously and "is a feedback loop of sorts, it demands of readers new interpretive practices."[32]

The play itself also appears as a parallel story whose recurrence exposes the text's artifice by turning the protagonist into a theatrical spectator. Driblette's performance of the play is "an adapted copy of an apocryphal copy of a manuscript whose originality cannot be attested."[33] The line in the play that first references Tristero ("no hallowed skein of stars can ward, I trow / Who's once been set his tryst with Trystero"[34]) appears, unlike the story of the bones in the lake, only once in the entire novel; the sign "Tristero" is established as central to the mystery by its treatment in that individual performance, during which, when the actual word is avoided, a "gentle chill, an ambiguity, begins to creep in among the words."[35] The actual naming of Tristero, paradoxically, does nothing to dispel the ambiguity, but rather increases the sense of mystery surrounding it, propelling Oedipa to begin her investigation by seeking out variant editions of the work in other places. The director Driblette himself has no script and offers no explanation for the inclusion of the line, but rather admonishes Oedipa for being "hung up on words," when the reality of the play resides entirely in the mind of its director. She finds other editions from a used book store, the Berkeley library, and a college professor at the local university in San Narciso; the only indication she receives that this line exists anywhere outside the individual performance she watched is a hint from Professor Bortz that there is a possibly similar line in a pornographic variant of the play, sealed in the Vatican archives. The reader cannot help but be aware that the entirety of the mystery surrounding Oedipa hinges upon two signs—the word Tristero and the muted post horn symbol—and she is propelled forward in her investigation of both as much by random coincidence as she is by any deliberate, logical investigative action on her part. The role of coincidence enstranges the experience of reading detective fiction, in which a reader expects tight plotting and purposeful, rational, linear movement toward concrete resolution.

Coincidence is foregrounded in the novel's fulcrum point, which highlights parallelism between the novel's first and second halves. This fulcrum point is the night Oedipa spends in San Francisco, a place far removed from Pierce Inverarity and the almost incestuously hermetic city of San Narciso; it is a large metropolitan area in which it is unlikely for personal patterns to emerge, as large urban centers tend to foster anonymity (and are typical of the hard-boiled detective subgenre). She encounters the post horn in a gay bar, in the window of a Chinese apothecary shop, in a children's game in chalk on the sidewalk, on an old anarcho-syndicalist newspaper, stitched on the jackets of a street gang, scratched onto a bus seat, on a laundromat bulletin board, being drawn by a Mexican girl in the fog of her breath on a bus window, in a poker-player's notebook at the airport, in a bathroom stall, being referred to by a young man French kissing his mother goodbye, tattooed on a man's hand, and attached to a number of other marginalized people.[36] The locations and frequency of the appearance of the "Tristero horn" sow doubt that this could be a hoax, as it would be impossible to predict her movements or to involve as many people as she sees associated with this sign. On the other hand, Oedipa's vision itself is the common denominator, and she is the creator of meaning with respect to this particular sign via her investigations. She wonders if the prevalence of the mediated clues were supposed to "make up for her having lost the direct, epileptic Word,"[37] and later reflects that because she has grown to expect to see the horn associated with certain kinds of people and situations, "perhaps she did not see it quite as often as she later was to remember seeing it"[38]—even though a few pages earlier she confidently believes that *"she was meant to remember."*[39] The detective novel's prescribed expectation that a search for clues would follow a linear, progressive path is enstranged by the seemingly random, coincidental turns of Oedipa's investigation, which instead of taking her to a solution, lead her only to four possibilities: that the horn and Tristero's subversive attacks on communication are real, that she is having a psychological breakdown and hallucinating the clues, that the entire thing is an elaborate hoax set up by Inverarity before his death, or that she is masochistically fantasizing a plot against herself. As these four options lie open before her, the auction of the stamps appears as a possible indicator of which way to take that might be "a real alternative to the exitlessness, to the absence of surprise to life" that is plaguing her.[40] Unfortunately, both she and the reader are left trapped in the infinitely recursive reflective sequencing of the novel (described by Francisco Collado-Rodríguez as a *maze*[41]), without either an exit or even a clear direction to follow.

Indeed, in both tales, the labyrinth is the sign that embodies the greatest part of *ostranenie* with respect to the detective genre. A labyrinth, on the one hand, is typically the creation of an ordered, rational mind, which an equally rational mind can solve and for which there is exists one solution; this is consistent with expected conventions of detective stories. The labyrinths in "Death and the Compass" and *The Crying of Lot 49*, on the other hand, encompass infinite and ever-changing pathways leading to destinations unknown, but never to an exit or a reward. The rhomboid labyrinth co-created by Lönnrot and Scharlach provides the solution to the two murders only incidentally, and does not lead to the Word (the Name of God) that Lönnrot is seeking; the fourth letter is never uttered. Oedipa's disclosures are likewise each "a new signifier in search of a signified that multiplies itself into more signifiers, an endless chain."[42] Like the alternative labyrinth that Lönnrot imagines for himself as a salvation (a single, unbroken line of infinite points), Oedipa's experience of endlessly bifurcating clues offers no hope of meaningful movement in the process of investigation toward a meaningful conclusion. Terry Fairchild argues that in *The Crying of Lot 49* "it is not a question of meaningless versus meaningfulness. It is a matter of endless possibilities that can accommodate both extremes."[43] This is true in both works. In traditional detective fiction, the *process* of investigation is supposed to tend toward meaning in the product of a significant resolution, but it is the *product* of the investigation that typically bears that meaning and imposes it retroactively across the entire text (such that the reader may want to read the story again consciously and look for clues s/he missed the first time). In the two works examined here, neither the process nor the product stands out as meaning-bearing in itself, nor can the combination of the two allow a reader to create some sort of definitive meaning upon finalizing the story. In this way, the absurdity of existence itself is highlighted by the artistic construction of the texts, to which the reader's consciousness is explicitly directed by the enstranging effects codified into the stories' structure and plot motifs, in order to subvert the reader's expectations of an otherwise familiar, "cozy" genre.

NOTES

1. Benjamin Sher makes a case for the neologism "enstrangement" as a translation for the Russian остранение, or *ostranenie* (which he spells *ostraniene*), because the more common term "defamiliarization" implies that the process transforms the known into the unknown, when in fact Shklovsky's actual concept initiates with something known and almost thoughtlessly recognized, that becomes more fully and consciously *seen* or perceived. He avoids the existing English word "estrangement" due to connotations from other disciplines. *Ostranenie* is itself a neologism in Russian, thus Sher produces a parallel word in English to embody both the concept and its irregular spelling. Alexandra Berlina, while acknowledging the value of Sher's neologism, notes that it is frequently misread and even misquoted by critics as "estrangement" and argues in favor of using the Russian transliteration *ostranenie* when it refers to a noun, and "enstrange"/"enstranged" in English for verb and adjective, respectively. Though not a native speaker of Russian myself, I will, with the reader's indulgence, presume to follow Berlina's example and use *ostranenie* when a noun is required.
2. Viktor Shklovsky, *Theory of Prose* (Champaign: Dakey Archives Press, 2015), 6.
3. Shklovsky, *Prose*, 11.
4. Shklovsky, *Prose*, 20.
5. Shklovsky, *Prose*, 140.
6. It is worth noting that many of Van Dine's well-established contemporaries violated most of these conventions at one time or another, regardless.
7. For example, the *Encyclopedia Brown* series specifically marketed to children.
8. "Elementary, my dear Watson!"—a phrase which, incidentally, Sherlock Holmes never actually said.
9. Alexandra Berlina, *Viktor Shklovsky: A Reader* (New York: Bloomsbury, 2018), 67.
10. Raymond Chandler, "The Simple Art of Murder," in *The Art of the Mystery Story: A Collection of Critical Essays*, ed. Howard Haycraft (New York: Simon and Schuster, 1946), 222–237.
11. Chandler, "Murder," 234.
12. Berlina, *Shklovsky*, 70.
13. Berlina, *Shklovsky*, 70. I will point out here that although "Death and the Compass" and *The Crying of Lot 49* are *thematically* and *existentially* pessimistic, their enstranging devices renew the genre, thereby dispelling *artistic* pessimism (i.e., the idea that there is nothing new under the sun).
14. Shklovsky, *Prose*, 12.
15. Devin Fromm, "In Search of No Thing: Latin American Detection, Irreal Investigations, and the Politics of Noncoincidence," *Clues: A Journal of Detection* 33:1 (2015), 73.
16. Jorge Luis Borges, "La muerte y la brújula," in *Ficciones* (Madrid: Alianza, 2003), 156.
17. David A. Boruchoff, "In Pursuit of the Detective Genre: 'La muerte y la brújula' of J.L. Borges," *Inti: Revista de literatura hispánica* 1:21 (1985): http://digitalcommons.providence.edu/inti/vol1/iss21/24.

18. Julia A. Kushigian, "The Detective Story Genre in Poe and Borges," *Latin American Literary Review*, 11:22 (1983): 34.
19. Boruchoff, "Pursuit," n.p.
20. Borges, "Muerte," 167.
21. Shklovsky, *Prose*, 118.
22. Borges, "Muerte," 161.
23. Shklovsky, *Prose*, 120.
24. Nadine Bornholt, "Numbers in Jorge Luis Borges' 'Death and the Compass,'" *CiberLetras: revista de crítica literaria y de cultura* 22 (2009): www.lehman.cuny.edu/ciberletras/v22/bornholt.html.
25. Boruchoff, "Pursuit," n.p.
26. Robert Carroll, "Borges and Bruno: The Geometry of Infinity in 'La muerte y la brújula," *Modern Language Notes* 94:2 (1979): 328.
27. Katherine L. Brown, "En busca del 'inefable Nombre de Dios': El Tetragrámaton, el lenguaje y la creación literaria en 'La muerte y la brújula,'" *Bulletin of Hispanic Studies* 94 (2017): 666.
28. Brown, "Nombre," 658.
29. Kristin L. Matthews, "Reading America Reading in Thomas Pynchon's *The Crying of Lot 49*," *Arizona Quarterly* 68:2 (2012): 93.
30. Tore Rye Anderson's detailed examination of the paratext of the many editions of *The Crying of Lot 49* refers to how the 1966 Lippincott edition confused the reader even more with respect to the novel's lack of resolution, by including 9 blank pages at the end of the text. A reader, arriving at the concluding lines in which Oedipa settles down to await the beginning of the auction of the Tristero stamps, eagerly turns to what looks like the next chapter, and is confounded to find nine additional pages of nothing instead of the anticipated denouement. Tore Rye Anderson, "Distorted Transmissions: Towards a Material Reading of Thomas Pynchon's *The Crying of Lot 49*," *Orbis Litterarum* 68:2 (2013): 110–142.
31. Shklovsky, *Prose*, 120.
32. Matthews, "Reading," 90.
33. Francisco Collado-Rodríguez, "Meaning Deferral, Jungian Symbolism, and the Quest for V. in Thomas Pynchon's *The Crying of Lot 49*" *Critique: Studies in Contemporary Fiction*, 56:3 (2015): 263, doi: 10.1080/00111619.2014.888047.
34. Thomas Pynchon, *The Crying of Lot 49* (New York: HarperCollins, 2006), 58.
35. Pynchon, *Lot 49*, 55.
36. Tore Anderson notes the prevalence of racial marginalization in the book and Oedipa's relative blindness to it while she is relentlessly pursuing her muted post horn symbol (121).
37. Pynchon, *Lot 49*, 95.
38. Pynchon, *Lot 49*, 100.
39. Pynchon, *Lot 49*, 95, original emphasis.
40. Pynchon, *Lot 49*, 141.
41. Collado-Rodríguez, "Meaning," 260.
42. Terry Fairchild, "Infinite Correlation in Pynchon's *The Crying of Lot 49*," *Consciousness, Literature and the Arts* 10:1 (2009): www.dmd27.org/fairchild2009.html.
43. Fairchild, "Correlation," n.p.

WORKS CITED

Andersen, Tore Rye. 2013. "Distorted Transmissions: Towards a Material Reading of Thomas Pynchon's *The Crying of Lot 49*." *Orbis Litterarum* 68 (2): 110–142.
Berlina, Alexandra. 2018. *Viktor Shklovsky: A Reader.* New York: Bloomsbury.
Borges, Jorge Luis. 2003. "La muerte y la brújula." In *Ficciones*, 153–72. Madrid: Alianza.
Bornholt, Nadine. 2009. "Numbers in Jorge Luis Borges 'Death and the Compass.'" *CiberLetras: revista de crítica literaria y cultura* 22. www.lehman.cuny.edu/ciberletras/v22/bornholt.html.

Boruchoff, David A. 1985. "In Pursuit of the Detective Genre: 'La muerte y la brújula' of J.L. Borges." *Inti: Revista de literatura hispánica* 1 (21). http://digitalcommons.providence.edu/inti/vol1/iss21/24.

Brown, Katherine L. 2017. "En busca del 'inefable Nombre de Dios': El Tetragrámaton, el lenguaje y la creación literaria en 'La muerte y la brújula.'" *Bulletin of Hispanic Studies* 94: 657–675.

Carroll, Robert. 1979. "Borges and Bruno: The Geometry of Infinity in 'La muerte y la brújula.'" *Modern Language Notes* 94 (2): 321–342. https://jstor.org/stable/2906749.

Chandler, Raymond. 1946. "The Simple Art of Murder." In *The Art of the Mystery Story: A Collection of Critical Essays*, by Howard Haycraft, 222–37. New York: Simon and Schuster.

Collado-Rodríguez, Francisco. 2015. "Meaning Deferral, Jungian Symbolism, and the Quest for V. in Thomas Pynchon's The Crying of Lot 49." *Critique: Studies in Contemporary Fiction* 56 (3): 255–269.

Fairchild, Terry. 2009. "Infinite Correlation in Pynchon's The Crying of Lot 49." *Consciousness, Literature and the Arts* 10 (1). www.dmd27.org/fairchild2009.html.

Fromm, Devin. 2015. "In Search of No Thing: Latin American Detection, Irreal Investigations, and the Politics of Noncoincidence." *Clues: A Journal of Detection* 33 (1): 72–81.

Kushigian, Julia A. 1983. "The Detective Story Genre in Poe and Borges." *Latin American Literary Review* 11 (22): 27–39.

Matthews, Kristin L. 2012. "Reading American Reading in Thomas Pynchon's The Crying of Lot 49." *Arizona Quarterly* 68 (2): 89–122.

Pynchon, Thomas. 2006. *The Crying of Lot 49*. New York: HarperCollins.

Shklovsky, Viktor. 2015. *Theory of Prose*. Champaign: Dalkey Archive Press.

Chapter Seven

Shklovsky and Things, or Why Tolstoy's Sofa Should Matter

Serguei Alex. Oushakine

It's useful to begin by going against the tradition.

—Vsevolod Meyerhold[1]

Yuri Tynianov's *Literary Evolution* (1927) begins with a striking critical assessment of the state of literary studies in early Soviet Russia. As Tynianov put it, "Among other cultural disciplines, the position of the history of literature could be compared to the position of a colonial state."[2] This dominated status was mainly a result of two key factors. On the one hand, "the individualistic psychologism" completely took over the history of literature, producing a situation in which "inquiries about literature" had been replaced "by inquiries about the psychology of the author," while the study of literary evolution was overshadowed by the interests in the origin of literary phenomena.[3] On the other hand, Tynianov emphasized, the approach to the *literary* field was informed mostly by non-literary methods, which were shaped by various *social* fields (politics, ideology, everyday life, etc.).[4] As a result, the subaltern, colonial literary studies were forced to express themselves in a "foreign" language; they were pushed to rely on alien formats and forms; they were destined to realize themselves through mimicry and borrowings. Moreover, the studying of literature was often amounted either to studying peripheral and marginal literary phenomena, or literature was perceived as a foil for studying non-literary processes (politics, ethnography, etc.).

The decolonizing solution that Tynianov offered is well known. Today, we would call it a version of the identity politics. Namely, the subaltern literary studies could acquire their own language of expression if—*and only if*—they would realize and recognize themselves as an independent subject. Or, to use Tynianov's own words, "the building of the literary science (*literaturnaia nauka*)" could be possible only when a literary product (*proizvedenie*) is perceived as an independent "system," in which elements are interconnected with each other, and with the system as a whole.[5]

Tynianov's position is important in many aspects, but I want to follow only one problem that he identified: his persistent and consistent methodological rejection of psychologism in studies of literature. Crucially, Tynianov was not alone in this. Roman Jakobson expressed the same concern but framed it in a more caustic way. If for Tynyanov, the psychologizing of literary studies was a form of epistemic violence, then, for Jakobson the attempt to reduce literature to its emotional effects was a manifestation of a fundamental absence of *any epistemology* at all. As Jakobson framed it already in his very first major essay on new Russian poetry, "references to the world of emotions are one of the most ubiquitous justifications for the use of the poetic language. This world of emotions is a storage closet of sorts. It is a dumping ground for anything that could not be otherwise justified, practically used, or rationally explained."[6] Explaining through emotions, in other words, was perceived as an attempt to hide a lack of an explanatory framework. Shklovsky, in his *Literature and Cinematography* pointed to the core of this problem by juxtaposing poetics and psychology. "In literature,"—he writes,—"everything is a material: be it fire, hunger, or grief. In a fairytale, to roll downhill in a barrel full of sticking nails is not cruel. In art, blood is not bloody."[7]

And yet: despite these multiple statements (and their number could be easily expanded), for almost a century the academic perception of Formalism has been curiously framed within the language of psychology of perception. I will cite only three symptomatic examples.

In 1919, Victor Shklovsky published in the Kiev journal *Hermes* a compilation of his main ideas under the title *Philological Commonplaces of the Contemporary Studies of Poetry*. The text contained a now famous line: "dance is a walk that is being felt." I will return to this line a bit later, here I just want to show how Shklovsky's original idea about de-automatization of perception was received at the time of its publication. Vladimir Makkoveisky, the editor of the journal, accompanied the essay with a series of his own footnotes, turning Shklovsky's "philological commonplaces" into psychological clichés:

> A finger makes itself know by creating pain. It is through this pain, through this act of falling out of the usual automatic harmony of the consciousness, that the finger juxtaposes its own individuality as something that is objective, as

something that does not need to depend on the consciousness, as something that protests against this necessity to depend.[8]

The estranging de-automatization of the usually harmonic consciousness re-emerges in the editor's comment as an analogue of illness. This pathologizing (and psychologizing) reading of the Formal method is perhaps the most extreme here; yet the logic of this approach is rather standard. In 1929, Nikolai Efimov, a rather supportive reader of Formalism, in his study pronounced the following verdict: "at the core of the Formalists' understanding of the development of literature, there is a theory of perception. . . . The whole field of literature is turned into a stimulant, into an agent of subjective psychophysical conditions. . . . In a sense, the Formalist model of literary evolution offers a simple psychological genesis of a new form from the psychophysiological conditions of perception."[9] Efimov did not reject the independence of the literary field; rather, he saw in Formalism no other possibility of working with this field outside the framework of the psychology of perception.

Fifty years later, another major scholar of Russian Formalism would follow the same path. Aage Hansen-Löve in his detailed monograph from 1978 slightly transformed the model already articulated by Efimov by translating the "psychophysical stimulants" into categories of aesthetic perception: "The key idea of early Formalism about aging and fossilization of linguistic devices,—as well as of the thought structures and behavioral patterns more generally,—could be traced back to the aesthetics of perception."[10] Basically equating Potebnya and Shklovsky, Hansen-Löve claimed, "For Potebnya, image is an act of consciousness that makes meaningful the "material" side of the word. It is exactly this "physical," sensuous visual appeal that guarantees the aesthetic efficacy of the word, and prevents us from approaching the word only as a "sign of a thought" which has lost its [material] form."[11] And in a footnote that follows this passage, Hansen-Löve tells us that "there is exactly the same ideas in Shklovsky's *Resurrection of the Word*, and in his essay on Potebnya."[12]

What we have here is a clear assumption that for the Formalists, the physical, sensuous aspect of the word (or, rather, of the signifier)—is a condition of its aesthetic efficiency. Formalism is seen not simply as a colony of psychology, but also as an example of colonial mimicry: the active appropriation of psychological methods (the aesthetics of perception) is perceived as a way of creating its own,—*proper*—methods of literary analysis. The empathic relation to the material (*vchustvovavnie,* the sensuous identification),[13] emerges as a particular aspect of an aesthetic experience and as the epistemology of the Formal method as such.

Basically, Formalism has been turned into an endless sentimental journey. It has been framed as a continuous return to the true feeling of the form. The point of the Formal analysis—we've been told decades after decades—is to revive our senses by overcoming the dullness of our perceptions. We know it when we *feel* it. Or, to flip it around, it is only when we feel something, we become certain that something exists.

In what follows, I want to offer a different reading of the Formal method. I show that Formalists' contribution cannot be reduced to the attempt to re-install the perceiving individual at the center of the literary analysis. Rather, the Formalists revolutionized literary scholarship by offering us a strikingly post-humanist and post-social picture of the world, in which things and humans are entangled in heterogenous assemblages. Against the highly ideological environment, they insisted on paying a close attention to the material, basically offering us a non-Marxist version of historical materialism.

In his earlier work, Homi Bhabha usefully pointed out that colonial mimicry does not have to be just an exercise in mimesis that equates a dominant model with the normative one. Reproduction, Bhabha, reminds us could be also a form of parody—with its double vision and the uncanny dissolution of the parodying subject.[14] In the colonial psychologism of the Formal method, I want to trace precisely this dual effect of the parodic approach. Tynianov's understanding of "the process of the parodic engagement with an object" productively expands Bhabha's idea about the destabilizing effect of parody.[15] In Tynianov's theory of parody, the act of parodic reproduction exploits the original in two ways. Performatively, it reveals the fossilization of the form, its routinization; parody ridicules something that has become a cliché. Structurally, the parodic act relies on this mechanized routine in order to organize—to smuggle in, indeed—a new substance.[16] To be effective parody has to introduce a new material through the constraints of the old form.

What kind of material could it be in Formalists' case? How did they transform the language of perception from within? In what directions could they traverse the "dumping ground" of emotionally driven literary studies? Let me go back to Shklovsky's *Philological Commonplaces*, in which he usefully highlighted the nature of this new material:

The task of art is the creation of tangible things.
Dance is a walk that is being felt.
The task of instrumentation is to produce a ballet of articulating organs and the feeling of discourse.
Let your feet feel the path that they travel on.[17]

In the rest of my essay, I focus precisely on the "road that affords the foot the feeling of the stones."[18] Following Bruno Latour, in my reading of Formalists, I also want to ask: "When we act, who else is acting?"[19] I am interested in the independently existing tangible things that the Formalists tried to organize with the help of the old psychological form. Feelings in their case were a way of getting to things; they were a tool for mapping out the things' constellations.

In their work, the Formalists forcefully drew our attention to the autonomous life of matter, and to the active participation of material objects in the formation of those emotions and feelings that scholars of Formalism like to isolate so much. The dominant anthropocentric focus on perception, the traditional desire to split "the walk that is being perceived" from the stony road, which makes this walk possible in the first place, does not simply separate the walk from its material foundation. Also, and maybe more important, this approach turns this solipsistic walk without a road into a movement without any direction.

When reading Formalists—Shklovsky and Tynyanov first of all, but also Jakobson and Boris Eikhenbaum—it is hard to miss their consistent attempt to transform the social optics in order to demonstrate how the human being emerges as "a relation of things," to use Shklovsky's description.[20] The Formalist thing is not just a metaphor or a backdrop for events. The Formalist thing is an active participant of these events. It is an inalienable part of the individual. And, at the same time, it is an active agent of change.

It is striking to see how in his *Introductory Letter* in *Zoo*, Shklovsky delineates an important methodological shift: things are not simply screens for projecting human needs and desires. Instead, things are an independent material force that is able to generate an appropriate version of the human being. Let me read this part closely.

Shklovsky starts rather predictably. A montage of a few sentences gives us a familiar picture in which things are utilitarian objects, expanding the capacities of the individual: "A tool does not just extend the arm of an individual; it also expands itself into the individual. Apparently, a blind person localizes his/her sense of tactility on the tip of his/her walking stick."[21] A tool is nothing more than a prosthetic extension of the human; a stick is an underdeveloped hand. Things are objects that did not succeed in becoming humans. Hence a logical conclusion: "I experience a little attachment to my shoes; yet they are my extension; they are a part of me."[22] But suddenly, Shklovsky makes his classical knight move, and his logic begins to develop in a very different direction. Things start to show their own, uncontrollable intentionality. Things can constrain people. Or even take them hostage:

Even a walking cane was capable of changing gymnasium students, and therefore they were not allowed to use it.
A monkey on a tree twig seems to be more sincere; but the twig also has an impact on psychology.
And the psychology of a cow on a slippery ice has become proverbial by now.[23]

Materials afford and determine possibilities. Psychology emerges as a direct continuation, or even as a consequence of the road that is not only perceived by the feet but that also puts these feet (hooves?) in a state of direct (and unpredictable) dependency on the road. Right after that, Shklovsky formulates his overall conclusion, radically changing his discursive position in order to present the point of view of the thing:

> Machines change the human being in the most radical way.
> Machine-gunners and contrabass-players are the continuation of their instruments.
> Weapons make a person braver.
> A horse turns him into a cavalryman.
> Things do with the person what he makes out of them.[24]

The contrabass makes out of a human being a contrabassist who is capable of utilizing the contrabass. The thing demands a person who is trained to actualize the potentialities of the thing. From this point of view, the thing, then, is far from being an ossified, passive matter. Nor is it a software that defines the protocol of the person's actions (or cow's movement on ice). The thing emerges as a means of formation, as a method of specification and individuation that turns a human, say, into a cavalryman.

In fact, what Shklovsky offers us in this passage is a brief summary of the transition that took place in social sciences and humanities in the last two decades—from the semiotically driven studies of material culture (that is perceived as an extension of the human)—to New Materialisms that view technological and natural substances as actors, whose "vitality, trajectories, and power" cannot be reduced to the meanings, intensions, and symbolic significance imposed on them by the humans.[25] Almost one hundred years before Bruno Latour, things in Shklovsky's writings "authorize, allow, afford, encourage, permit, suggest, influence, block, render possible, forbid, and so on," as Latour would describe it in 2005.[26] Or, to use Shklovsky's own rhetoric from 1923, "Things rule the human being. Things reformatted the human being. . . . Things walk around the earth. How could we make them work for us? And should we?"[27]

Why did the Formalists allow the thing "to straddle their broad back," as Ivanov-Razumnik put it in his essay on futurism?[28] For Latour, as we know, the postsocial turn toward objects and things was a chance to demonstrate that "social relations," "social forces," and "social actions" were never limited to the relations among people only. By emphasizing the "power of objects,"[29] he expanded the meaning of such key sociological notions as "activity" and "agency." What Latour calls *actant* is "anything that modifies a state of affairs by making a difference."[30]

Despite multiple similarities and similar sensibilities in their regard to things, Shklovsky is not a proto-Latour. In his later work on Vertov, Shklovsky expressed this difference clearly: "the word is either not quite a thing yet or it is *not* a thing already. The word is a generalization of . . . different things; it is an act of dividing them into groups."[31] Why, then, there is this 'orientation toward the material," as Shklovsky called it.[32] What was the purpose of this object-oriented ontology, as we would call it today? I will describe only one moment that I think is crucial for understanding the purpose and function of the Formalist thing: the role of the thing in revealing the convention-driven nature (*uslovsnost*) of discursive production; the ability of things to undermine the perceived mimetic correspondence between the world of objects and the world of their representations.

The material autonomy of the thing helped to reveal the fundamental discordance (*neviazka*), as Tynyanov called it, between the signifier and the referent.[33] The parodic discordance between the material *and* literary worlds documented and exposed the insufficiency of existing means of expression. Moreover, this discordance drew attention to the process of dissimilation (*raspodoblenie*), which normally takes place during the translation of the material substances and practices into the language of literary forms. As a result, literariness emerged as a series of actions aimed to flatten and simplify things—optically as well as discursively. To show how this was achieved in Shklovsky's work, I quote from his *Techniques of the Writer* (1930).

The book was intended as a manual for amateur writers, but instead of trying to professionalize their art of writing, Shklovsky encouraged his readers not to give up their non-literary profession. As he explained, "A writer should have a second profession not to avoid a death from starvation but in order to be able to create literary things. He should not let this second profession fall into oblivion. He should be practicing it by being a blacksmith, or a doctor, or an astronomer. He should not leave it behind, when he enters the field of literature, as if it were galoshes, forgotten in a hallway."[34] Immediately after that, Shklovsky switches to the opposite example:

> I knew one blacksmith who brought me his poems, in which he "shutters with his hammer the cast iron of rails." I pointed out to him that, first of all, rails are not forged with hammer; they are rolled. Secondly, they are not from cast iron but from steel. Thirdly, when you strike metal with hammer, the goal is not to shutter it but to forge it. And, fourthly, since he is a blacksmith himself, he ought to know all that more than anyone else. His response was: But this is just a poem![35]

What I find important in this critique of literary dissimilation is, again, the formative role of the thing. Shklovsky approaches the materiality of the thing as an invitation to renew the vocabulary of expressive means, to change stagnated devices and conventions of description, and, in the final analysis, to revisit the ways "to concatenate thoughts (*stseplenie myslei*)."[36] As he claimed elsewhere, "Instead of stealing materials from technology once in a while, we should live in it permanently. It is because of this non-literary work that we could create a new literary form."[37]

Symptomatically, Shklovsky found little use in the montage of the everyday in the factorgraphic accounts (*ocherki*) of Sergei Tretiakov or in the documentary films of Dziga Vertov's *kinoki*, with their self-proclaimed direct, non-mediated access to reality.[38] The disagreement, I believe, was caused precisely by the unwillingness of these authors to recognize differential dimensions of the system of representations and the system of material things, which Shklovsky was so aware of. In his famous letter to Tynyanov, Shklovsky wrote in 1925: "Art relies on affordances of things (*kachestvo predmetov*) to generate an experience of the form. The difficulty that the proletarian writers encounter has to do with their attempts to fit things into the screen without changing their dimensions."[39]

In other words, "fitting" things into a cinematic or a literary framework required their transmedial adjustment; therefore, claims about their "unmediated" appearance on screen or their "factographic" representations in text signaled the ignoring of the nature of the artistic process as well as of the nature of material objects. "Shadows in painting,—Shklovsky explained in his *Semantics of Cinema* (1925),—"are a convention, but they could be replaced only by another convention."[40] Without an aesthetic device, "cinematic things in the films of the *kinoks*, are disconnected from each other; they are not turned on; they are not presented. . . . Things are impoverished, because there is no tendentious—in the artistic sense of this word,—*attitude* toward things."[41]

The dissimilation (*raspodoblenie*) of the material world was used in Shklovsky's work to transform the unacknowledged *discursive position* (that people like Tretiakov or Vertov would deem transparent) into a *discursive pose,* that is to say, into a consciously deployed rhetorical convention.[42] Correspondingly, the task of the author, then, was to reveal these conventions, i.e., to objectify the authorial position 1) by seeing things as if they "have never been described yet," and 2) by placing them in "the relations that have never been described before."[43] Objectual metaphors (*veshchnye metaphory*)[44] allowed Shklovsky to construct his texts as a delicate balance between materialization and dematerialization. By linking two different rows—the objectal and the human—he emphasized the produced and montaged nature of the literariness of the artistic text. This enchaining, this concatenation simultaneously fastened things together and broke them apart.[45] The world that he presents is the same world that Latour would describe later as the world "made of concatenations of mediators," where each point, each conjunction could generate a new action, and could pivot the overall movement in a different direction.[46] For instance, in Shklovsky's *Zoo,* the assembling of different rows—what Eisenstein called "a montage of real artificialities"[47] becomes the main organizing principle of the narrative.

The saddest thing of all, is to ride in a car with an electric engine. It has no heartbeat, it is filled with heavy batteries and they are charged. But the plates will lose their charge and the engine will stop.
How do you start a car that has no heart? No crank to turn?
Poor Russian emigration!
It has no heartbeat.
Like a car with an electric engine whose batteries went dead, cruise around town, without noise and without hope. Our batteries were charged in Russia. Here, we keep going around in circles, and soon we will grind to a halt. The lead battery plates will turn into nothing but sheer weight.[48]

Metaphors are linked here with metonyms; things—with symbols; humans—with machines, creating in the end a grotesque assemblage: a man as a dead car, which, nonetheless, is cruising around town, with a false engine.

It is instructive to approach Shklovsky's attempts to bring together materiality of things and literariness of discourse through the optics of another pioneer of the Formal method: the theater director Vsevolod Meyerhold. The link between Shklovsky and Meyerhold is not surprising (though rarely explored). They both started roughly at the same time by insisting that the goal of art is not to imitate and reproduce life but to organize it in a particular way, to twist it—through the lens of artistic devices and styles. Already in 1913, in his *Balagan*, Meyerhold wrote:

> Viewers come to a theater to see the art of humans. But when the actor simply walks around the stage, all by himself, this is hardly an art. The audience expects imagination, play, mastery. Instead, the audience gets either life as is, or its slavish imitation. . . . The art of staging is all about . . . picking a right mask, or an ornament, or a costume. It is about demonstrating the brilliance of the actor's technique in front of the audience. . . . We watch life not in order to replicate these observations with the photographic precision in our work ("in our play"). Rather, we use these observations as materials that would help us develop our technique.[49]

The discrepancy of the similar, the dissimilation of the world of things in cinema and literature, that Shklovsky advocated in his writings, would be articulated by Meyerhold first as a "striving toward the simulated unlikelihood (*uslovnoe nepravdopodobie*)" in 1913, and would evolve by 1933 into "simulated realism."[50] By relying on masks, bodies, and stage-sets, Meyerhold would forefront the conditional nature of theater—its theatricality. His biomechanics—"the art of plastic forms within the spatial limits of the stage"[51]—could be seen as the perfect realization of Shklovsky's dance-walk in real life. Biomechanics was a movement that was felt; but also it was a movement that "felt" its own road.

The grotesque of the mask, the overemphasized structure of the biomechanical gesture, the whimsicality of stage props were all deployed to reveal and parody at the same time the constructive principles of theatrical production. As Meyerhold explained it to leaders of amateur theaters in 1933:

> We are not scared by the fact that in *The Government Inspector* the stage was filled up with a big screen that has eleven doors. We do not want to mimic reality, and we do not want our viewers to do this, either—because life cannot be recreated on stage. Because the stage is constructed in such a way that it cannot encompass life.[52]

This emphasis on conventions—together with a resolute rejection of mimesis—blocked the psychological identification of the viewer with what s/he saw on stage, forcing the audience to assume an analytical (and distanced) position. Explaining his production of the play *I want a baby* by Sergei Tretiakov, Meyerhold described how he was going to compensate the schematic quality of the play characters by the active involvement of the audience *during* the performance:

> I will bring the audience on stage. And the performance will be interrupted by discussions. . . . The characters won't hide the fact that they are only schemes. . . . This would guarantee us that all the crooked or unresolved questions that the playwright suggested, would not be resolved in a wrong manner.
> We would even provide the audience with provocative remarks to read . . . and we will ask Tretiakov to come out on stage (once in a while) and to tell the actor that he pronounces his lines wrongly.
> And on the poster for the performance, we will not write First Performance. Or Second. Or Third. Instead, we will say: discussion number one, two, or three.[53]

"The road of art,—Shklovsky writes in an article,—is a crooked road that brings us back."[54] For Meyerhold, the dissimilation of life, the translation of reality into schemes, masks, and stage props, was a similarly crooked way of getting back to vitally important questions. But this circular path was not a simple loop. Tools of dissimilation allowed the practitioners of the Formal method to ask and express vitally important questions through artistic means, without having to borrow languages and conventions from other fields.

In their parodic engagement with artistic conventions *and* the world of materials, both, Meyerhold and Shklovsky tried to expose their artistic devices. Both formalized the form, so to speak, in order to reveal the presence of the author in the text/stage. To a large degree, this desire to bare the device came from a general striving to expose again and again the non-transparency of the medium of expression, to show its material quality, and its objectified nature. But also, this baring displayed the non-correspondence between the available form and its material content, like Meyerhold's characters, formal structures refused to "hide the fact that they are only schemes," i.e., dissimilated and parodic indices of reality.

And this brings me to my last point. For the century of its existence, the Formalist concept of art as a way of estranging things has become a common place. Yet, the emphasis on the role of the material that I have tried to foreground today allows us to recall the origin of estrangement that gets routinely obfuscated by the anthropocentric obsession with human feelings and perception.

Given the Formalists' interest in materiality, it is hardly a surprise that the biography of the Formal method began with a thing. More precisely, with Tolstoy's sofa. In his *Art as Device*, Shklovsky famously quotes an entry from Tolstoy's diary: "As I was walking around, dusting off in my room, I came to the sofa. For the life of me, I couldn't recall whether I had already dusted it off or not. Since these movements are habitual and unconscious, I felt that it was already impossible to remember it. If I had in fact dusted the sofa and forgotten that I had done so, i.e., if I had acted unconsciously, then this is tantamount to not having done it at all."[55]

Furniture that unexpectedly emerged on the path of the writer, suddenly produced a small-scale actor-network formation, which generated a chain of synchronic relations between the sofa and the writer (*What should I do with this sofa now? Should I dust it off or not?*). But also, this encounter of the man and a thing demanded a particular diachronic reconstruction of the recent past (*Did I dust it off already or not?*). This process of individualizing the previously undifferentiated furniture—or to reverse it, this insistence of the sofa on being taken seriously (and autonomously)—results in Shklovsky's seminal idea about recovering the sense of life by recovering the sense of a thing. That is to say, by "making stone—stony."[56] The goal of art, in other words, is to transform the unconscious, petrifying sclerosis of the human into the real tangibility of the thing.

That initial stone would generate a chain of milestones in Shklovsky's work, demarcating key moments in the unfolding of the Formal method. The stone would reappear in *A Sentimental Journey*. The second part of the book starts with a canonical description of self-petrification:

> When you fall like a stone, you don't need to think;
> When you think, you don't need to fall.
> I confused these two occupations.
> The forces moving me were external to me....
> I am only a falling stone.
> A stone that falls and can, at the same time, light a lantern to observe its own course.[57]

Most likely, borrowed from Spinoza, this stony stone observing its own movement is an interesting realization of the desire to experience the thing, articulated in the *Art as Device*. In *A Sentimental Journey*, the stoniness of the thing is hardly doubted. But just as clear is another aspect, too: namely, a lack of correspondence between the *trajectory* of the course and *the intention* of the falling stone. The motivation for the movement has nothing to do with the materiality of the moving object, even though the experience of the movement is completely synchronized with the experience of the road.

Later on, in his *Once Upon a Time*, Shklovsky perfected this conflation of the road and the thing, of structure and material. Speaking about his life in Persia, he mentioned that in "this country, my heart was battered down in the same way as a harsh road is battered down by the furry feet of camels. . . . I feel like a camel and the road at the same time."[58] The distinction between the object and the subject is about to disappear here, creating a hybrid and dynamic entanglement that brings together the matter and the directionality of the road, as well as the reflexivity of the man who experiences the materiality of this congealed space-and-time.

The third, and seemingly, the last time, the stone emerges in Shklovsky's essay *A Conversation with Friends* (1936). Speaking about the history of Formalism, he revisits Tolstoy:

> Leo Tolstoy described how he could not understand movements of a man who was doing something with stones. He came closer to the man. It turned out, the man was sharpening his knife with a stone. The man did not need the stone; he needed the sharpness of the knife.[59]

The materiality, that proverbial stoniness of the stone, did not return the feeling of life here. But it made possible the renewal of the lost efficiency of the instrument: a new quality (sharpness) emerged in the process of a forced bonding of things (stone and knife).

To map out the crooked trajectory of Shklovsky's road: from furniture to a concrete sofa; from the sofa to stoniness; from stoniness to the stone itself, and finally—to the sharpness of the knife, affected by the stone. Or slightly differently: from the material world—to a distinct thing; from a thing—to the perception that it generates, and, in the end—to the ability of things to influence—*to shape and form*—qualities of other things in the act of their connectedness.

What seems to be critical in this movement is the following. The sharpness of the knife—just as the path of the falling stone—emerged here as a consequence of a certain lack of freedom. The quality (of feeling) and the dynamic (of movement) are determined *externally*, from the outside. To put it differently, the desire for autonomy and sovereignty of the literary field, with which I began this essay, remained just that: a desire. The sharpness of feelings required a stone, revealing the constitutive dependency on external material fields and external material factors.

This dependency certainly could result in its own reification: for instance, in the production of various colonial formations within the field of literary studies that Tynyanov criticized. Unlike Tynyanov, Shklovsky did not lament this colonial dependency on external forces, rows, and fields, though. Nor did he relapse into some kinds of phantasy about building totally autonomous (literary) realms. Instead, in his typical idiosyncratic move, he flattened the verticality of these asymmetric relations of power, and presented the colonial subalternity as a form of distributive agency: a stone fused with a knife in order to create a sense of sharpness.

Stones of dependency, in other words, do not have to end up as building blocks of colonial (or anti-colonial) architecture. Rather, they could be seen as material conditions for very different processes—be it a pavement for a continuous movement or a tool for sharpening sensations.

No doubt, the centennial life of estrangement has produced a lot of historical and contextual reasons for seeing traces of psychologism and sensualism in the Formalist deployment of "feelings" and other "emotional experiences." I tried to suggest a different trajectory of reading, taking the Formalists' rejection of the imperial domination of "the individualist psychologism" as my starting point. This re-focusing, as I tried to show, produces an unexpected shift: by moving away from usual feelings and emotions, it reveals what Shklovsky called "the continuous fractality of things,"[60] without which all those feelings and emotions would not be possible.

NOTES

All translations from the Russian language are mine unless it is indicated otherwise.

1. Vsevolod Meyerhold, "O paradoksal'nom podkhode v reshenii obraza i stseny" in Vsevolod Meyerhold, *Stat'i. Pis'ma. Rechi. Besedy. Chast' vtoraia, 1917–1939* (Moskva: Iskusstvo, 1968), 490.
2. Yury Tynyanov, "O literaturnoi evoluitsii" in Yuri Tynyanov, *Arkhaisty i novatory* (Leningrad: Priboi, 1929), 32.
3. Tynyanov, "O literaturnoi evoluitsii," 32.
4. Tynyanov, "O literaturnoi evoluitsii," 33.
5. Tynyanov, "O literaturnoi evoluitsii," 33.
6. Roman Jakobson, "Noveishaia russkaia poezia. Nabrosok pervyi: podstupy k Khlebnikovu" in *Formal'nyi metod: Antologiia russkogo modernizma*. Vol. 3. Edited by Serguei Oushakine (Ekaterinburg-Moscow: Kabinetnyi uchenyi, 2016), 139–140. (Hereafter, I will cite this collection in an abbreviated form—as *FM*—indicating a volume and a page.)
7. Viktor Shklovsky, *Literatura i kinematograf* (Berlin: Russkoe universal'noe izdatel'stvo, 1923), 58.
8. See Viktor Shklovsky, "Iz filologicheskikh ochevidnostei sovremennoi nauki o stikhe," *Germes* 1 (1919), 70, ft. 4.
9. Nikolai Efimov, *Formalizm v russkom literaturovedenii* (Smolensk, 1929), 84–85.
10. Aage Hansen-Löve, *Russkii formalizm. Metodologicheskaia rekonstruktsiia razvitiia na osnove printsipa ostraneniia*. Trans. S. A. Romashko (Moskva: Iazyki russkoi kul'tury, 2001), 41.
11. Hansen-Löve, *Russkii formalizm*, 42.
12. Hansen-Löve, *Russkii formalizm*, 42.

13. Hansen-Löve, *Russkii formalizm*, 70, 156.
14. Homi Bhabha, "Of Mimicry and Man: The Ambivalence of Colonial Discourse," *October* 28 (Spring 1984), 125–133.
15. Yury Tynyanov, "O parodii" in *FM*, 1: 611.
16. Yury Tynyanov, "Dostoevskii i Gogol, (k teorii parodii)" in *FM*, 1: 543.
17. Shklovsky, "Iz filologicheckikh," 70.
18. Viktor Shklovsky, "Sviaz' priëmov siuzhetoslozheniia s obshchimi priëmami stilia" in *FM* 1: 147.
19. Bruno Latour, *Reassembling the Social: An Introduction to Actor-Network-Theory* (Oxford: Oxford University Press, 2005), 43.
20. Viktor Shklovsky, "Sergei Eisenstein" in Viktor Shklovsky, *Zhili-byli* (Moskva: Sovetskii pisatel, 1966), 485.
21. Viktor Shklovsky, "Zoo, ili Pis'ma ne o liubvi" in Shklovsky, *Zhili-byli*, 175–76.
22. Shklovsky, "Zoo", 176.
23. Shklovsky, "Zoo", 177–8.
24. Shklovsky, "Zoo", 177–8.
25. Jane Bennett, "A Vitalist Stopover on the Way to a New Materialism" in *New Materialisms: Ontology, Agency, and Politics* (Durham: Duke University Press, 2010), 47.
26. Latour, *Reassembling the Social*, 72.
27. Shklovsky, "Zoo", 195.
28. R. F. Ivanov-Razumnik, "Futurizm i 'Veshch'." *Kniga i revoliutsiia*, 8–9 (1921), 23.
29. Latour, *Reassembling the Social*, 83.
30. Latour, *Reassembling the Social*, 71.
31. Shklovsky, Viktor. "O Dzige Vertove" in *FM*, 1: 253.
32. Shklovsky, Viktor. "Bor'ba za formu" in *FM*, 1: 223.
33. Tynyanov, "Dostoevskii i Gogol'," 530.
34. Viktor Shklovsky, *Tekhnika pisatel'skogo remesla* (Moskva: Molodaia gvardiia, 1930), 6.
35. Shklovsky, *Tekhnika pisatel'skogo*, 6.
36. Shklovsky, *Literatura i kinematograph*,16.
37. Shklovsky, "Bor'ba za formu," 225.
38. For more details, see Viktor Shklovsky, "Kuda shagaet Dziga Vertov" in *FM*, 1: 245–47. See also: Sergei Tretiakov, "The Biography of the Object," *October* 118 (Fall 2006): 57–62.
39. V. Shklovsky V.—Yu. Tynianovy in Viktor Shklovsky, *Gamburgskii schët. Stat'i—Vospominaniia—Esse (1914–1933)*, edited by A. Galushkin and A. Chudakov (Moskva: Sovetskii pisatel, 1990), 303.
40. Viktor Shklovsky, "Semantika kino" in *FM*, 1: 243.
41. Shklovsky, "Bor'ba za formu," 225.
42. Tynyanov, "O parodii," 623.
43. Shklovsky, *Tekhnika pisatelskogo*, 10, 18.
44. Tynyanov, "Dostoevskii i Gogol," 538.
45. Viktor Shklovsky, *Podënshchina* (Leningrad: Izdatel'svo leningradskikh pisatelei, 1930), 7.
46. For more detail, see: Latour, *Reassembling the Social*, 59.
47. Sergei Eisenstein, "Montazh attraktsionov" in *FM*, 1: 339.
48. Shklovsky, Zoo, 244–45.
49. Vsevolod Meyerhold, "Balagan" in *FM*, 3: 534.
50. Vsevolod Meyerhold, "Ideologiia i tekhnologiia v teatre" in *FM*, 3: 587.
51. Vsevolod Meyerhold, "Aktër budushchego" in *FM*, 3: 569.
52. Meyerhold, "Ideologiia i tekhnologiia," 587.
53. Vsevolod Meyerhold, "Doklad o plane postanovki p'esy S.M.Tretiakova 'Khochy rebënka'" in *FM*, 3: 700.
54. Shklovsky, "Sviaz' priëmov," 147.
55. Viktor Shklovsky, "Iskusstvo kak priëm" in *FM*, 1: 136.
56. Shklovsky, "Iskusstvo kak priëm," 136.

57. Viktor Shklovsky, "Sentimental'noe puteshestvie" in Viktor Shklovsky, *Eshchë nichego ne konchilos.'* (Moskva: Propaganda, 2002), 142.
58. Shklovsky, *Zhili-byli*, 126.
59. Viktor Shklovsky, "Razgovor s druz'iami" in *FM*, 1: 281.
60. Shklovsky, "Razgovor s druz'iami," 226.

WORKS CITED

Bennett, Jane. "A Vitalist Stopover on the Way to a New Materialism" in *New Materialisms: Ontology, Agency, and Politics*. Durham: Duke University Press, 2010, 47–69.
Bhabha, Homi. "Of Mimicry and Man: The Ambivalence of Colonial Discourse." October 28 (Spring 1984): 125–133.
Efimov, Nikolai. *Formalizm v russkom literaturovedenii*. Smolensk, 1929 (in Russian).
Eisenstein, Sergei. "Montazh attraktsionov" in Oushakine, *Formal'nyi metod*, Vol.1: 337–341 (in Russian).
Hansen-Löve, Aage. *Russkii formalizm. Metodologicheskaia rekonstruktsia razvitiia na osnove printsipa ostraneniia*. Trans. S. A. Romashko. Moskva: Iazyki russkoi kul'tury, 2001 (in Russian).
Ivanov-Razumnik, R. F. "Futurizm" i "Veshch'" *Kniga i revoliutsiia*, 8–9 (1921): 22–27 (in Russian).
Jakobson, Roman. "Noveishaia russkaia poezia. Nabrosok pervyi: podstupy k Khlebnikovu" in Oushakine, *Formal'nyi metod*, Vol.3: 246–304 (in Russian).
Latour, Bruno. *Reassembling the Social: An Introduction to Actor-Network-Theory*. Oxford: Oxford University Press, 2005.
Meyerhold, Vsevolod. "Doklad o plane postanovki p'esy S. M. Tret'iakova 'Khochy rebënka' in Oushakine, *Formal'nyi metod*, Vol.3: 700–701 (in Russian).
———. "Balagan" in Oushakine, *Formal'nyi metod*, Vol.3: 522–547 (in Russian).
———. "Ideologiia i technologiia v teatre" in Oushakine, *Formal'nyi metod*, Vol.3: 580–597 (in Russian).
———. "Aktër budushchego" in Oushakine, *Formal'nyi metod*, Vol.3: 566–571 (in Russian).
———. "O paradoksal'nom podkhode v reshenii obraza i steny" in Vsevolod Meyerhold, *Stat'i. Pis'ma. Rechi. Besedy. Chast' vtoraia, 1917–1939*. Moskva: Iskusstvo, 1968, 490–491 (in Russian).
Oushakine, Serguei, ed. *Formal'nyi metod: Antologiya russkogo modernizma*. 3 Vols. Moskva–Ekaterinburg: Kabinetnyi uchënyi, 2016 (in Russian).
Shklovsky, Viktor. "Iz filologicheskikh ochevidnostei sovremennoi nauki o stikhe." *Germes* 1 (1919): 67–72 (in Russian).
———. *Literatura i kinematograf*. Berlin: Russkoe universal'noe izdatelstvo, 1923 (in Russian).
———. *Tekhnika pisatel'skogo remesla*. Moskva: Molodaia gvardiia, 1930 (in Russian).
———. *Podënshchina*. Leningrad: Izdatel'svo leningradskikh pisatelei, 1930 (in Russian).
———. *Zhili-byli*. Moskva: Sovetskii pisatel, 1966 (in Russian).
———. "Sergei Eisenstein" in Shklovsky, *Zhili-byli*, 466–514 (in Russian).
———. "Zoo, ili Pis'ma ne o liubvi" in Shklovsky, *Zhili-byli*, 165–226 (in Russian).
———. Yu. Tynianovu in Shklovsky, V. *Gamburgskii schët. Stat'i—Vospominaniia—Esse* (1914–1933), edited by A. Galushkin and A. Chudakov. Moskva: Sovetskii pisatel, 1990, 302–303 (in Russian).
———. "Sentimental'noe puteshestvie" in Shklovsky, V. *Eshchë nichego ne konchilos.'* Moskva: Propaganda, 2002, 15–266 (in Russian).
———. "Sviaz' priëmov siuzhetoslozheniia s obshchimi priëmami stilia" in Oushakine, *Formal'nyi metod*, Vol.1: 147–181 (in Russian).
———. "O Dzige Vertove" in Oushakine, *Formal'nyi metod*, Vol.1: 248–261 (in Russian).
———. "Bor'ba za formu" in Oushakine, *Formal'nyi metod*, Vol.1: 222–225 (in Russian).
———. "Semantika kino" in Oushakine, *Formal'nyi metod*, Vol.1: 242–244 (in Russian).

———. "Kuda shagaet Dziga Vertov" in Oushakine, *Formal'nyi metod*, Vol.1: 245–247 (in Russian).
Tretiakov, Sergei. "The Biography of the Object," *October* 118 (Fall 2006): 57–62.
Tynyanov, Yury. "O literaturnoi evoliutsii" in Yury Tynyanov, *Arkhaisty i novatory*. Leningrad: Priboi, 1929, 30–47 (in Russian).
———. "O parodii" in Oushakine, *Formal'nyi metod*, Vol.1: 603–631 (in Russian).
———. "Dostoevsky i Gogol (k teorii parodii)" in Oushakine, *Formal'nyi metod*, Vol.1: 530–561 (in Russian).

Chapter Eight

The Motherland Will Notice Her Terrible Mistake*

Paradox of Futurism in Jasienski, Mayakovsky and Shklovsky

Norbert Francis

Russian Futurism surprised readers and writers alike during the years of social ferment leading up the 1917 Revolution. In particular, the participants in the movement themselves had no idea what events would have in store for them. Three among them, Bruno Jasienski, Vladimir Mayakovsky, and Viktor Shklovsky, are representative of the literary upheaval, explosion of creativity, and of the difficult decisions, writers came to face. Taken together for comparison, a study of their work also gives us a sense of the confusion of the time, how outcomes often seemed strangely arbitrary, and how events took unexpected turns. On another level, the route taken by each writer, nevertheless, is consistent with the overall direction of art and culture during the Soviet era. Paradoxically perhaps it was the writer who most directly challenged the assumptions of early Socialist Realism (more precisely its precursors) who survived to later reflect on the history. An interesting aspect of this history is the relationship between the Futurists and Russian Formalism. The discussion of their work will turn on three important historical studies that trace the course of the revolution (the broader context) and the course of parallel literary currents.

I

Futurism emerged during the Silver Age in the wake of the 1905 Revolution along with conjugate avant-garde movements in literature (e.g., led by Sergei Yesenin, by Anna Akhmatova and Nikolai Gumilev). Inspired by the eruption in creativity in the modern plastic arts, Cubism in particular, poets were sometimes leading creators in both fields. Allied as they came to be, modern painting and the transformation in poetics, a common cause was envisioned in a new philosophy of art.[1] Far from a coherent theory of aesthetics, among the writers for their part, the unifying objective at first consisting in a vague rejection of all tradition.[2] As Futurism evolved, the internal tendencies diverged widely, sometimes in contrary directions. Nevertheless, in its early development Futurist poets tended to coincide in their aesthetic point of view with the central theoretical orientation of Formalism: that the new poetry would not depend on the expression of thoughts or feelings or on a given content but on experimentation on the patterns of language itself. The task of Futurism was to free language from its traditional subservience to meaning.[3] The word, "as such," as the object of art, in poetry, would be liberated from its prosaic communicative function. On one level or another, this had always been true of poetic language in general; Futurists and Formalists now deliberately took up this concept to try to consider its logical implications, and if possible, carry it as far as they could. The revolutionary upheaval of the time that enveloped Futurist artists suggested to many (probably most) of them a direction that also may have contributed to the eventual dispersal of the movement, as it plausibly contradicted the "word as such" perspective: that the innovation in art would not, in reality, be independent of meaning and content, but would contribute to changing the very human condition, help create the "new man." On this view, new art would actually be capable of doing this. Two of the writers featured in the present chapter came to be representative of this point of view.

Initially, the overriding and guiding conception that would overturn art in language was the self-sufficiency of poetry; that writers would be set free by coming to see that expression and creativity in this domain obey their own laws. Unlike in the domain of prosaic language, the connection between the sign and the object had to be revealed "slowly," then disrupted, showing itself to be "inadequate," thus intensifying our perception. The effect is evident even in everyday examples as when we listen in our mind's ear to the street hawker's specialized discourse style.[4] Here, Jakobson was thinking both as a partisan of Futurism and as a linguist, trying at the same time to keep these observations and reflections separate. Within a few years the experiments took writers in different and unexpected directions as events moved quickly.

II

In May 1929, as Bruno Jasienski was given a hero's welcome arriving in Leningrad (by June 1930 elected to the Secretariat of Moscow Association of Proletarian Writers), Mayakovsky was at his rope's end, shunned by the influential literary circles that he had tried so hard to please in his last years. But within months of his arrival there seemed to be nothing that Jasienski could do to save himself either. Kolesnikoff traces the compelling story of the Russian edition of his most celebrated narrative work, the editing of the translation of *I Burn Paris* coming to be a paradigm example of the method of Socialist Realism. The first translation (1928, with a subsequent edition published in 1930) portrayed the ushering in of the new era of the Workers Commune, utopia born in the aftermath of a peculiar plague in which all the inhabitants of the Gomorrah of bourgeois decadence perish, all except the proletarians. While the first reviews looked the other way from aspects of the Futurist design effectively displayed by Jasienski thanks to the ideological clarity of the content, the novel soon came under scathing criticism, prompting dutiful and loyal rewrite for a corrected edition (appearing in 1934). Remarkable and revealing were the required revisions as by all measure the author had complied with his objective of creating for the front of the arts a "weapon of the class struggle." On the plague motif: its spread needed to be the work of the "government" instead of a desperate individual as in the original. The recourse of the prisoners having been the first to be spared (they drank from a different aqueduct system) was deleted, to be replaced by the participation of a more historically progressive social force, in the same way as the correction of a number of the figures and devices because for the editors the required content needed to be presented even more unambiguously, without all the metaphor (83–85).[5] For the reviewers the grotesque and fantastic *Mannequin's Ball*, set again in decadent Paris, while politically acceptable, may have suffered from the same defect of literary figure, original impulse of imagination and innovation carried over from his early years of experimentation.[6]

Following the consolidation of one-party rule in January 1918, Mayakovsky's writing gives the appearance of evolving such that it can be judged to be somewhat less servile to the regime than that of his Polish comrade. *The Bathhouse* (1930), for example, touched on the sensitive theme of bureaucracy. Comparing objectively, however, we should admit that during the period beginning in 1918 the parallels with Jasienski are more substantive than occasional, both poets publicly renouncing Futurism on schedule in response to official disfavor. Mayakovsky's poems, his non-commissioned work of great artistic merit aside, become as stilted and propagandistic as those of his RAPP colleagues—granting, to be fair, that overall his mastery of the propaganda-poem genre should be estimated as displaying the most advanced compositional and creative skill, perhaps deserving the highest recognition within this genre above any other twentieth-century poet. Despite continuing criticism of his work by party members and officials, his loyalty was beyond question, eager as he was to demonstrate this devotion in the denunciation of enemies of the state. "The Saboteur" was published the day following the death-sentence convictions of the Shakhty show-trial in *Komsomolskaya Pravda*, the same year (1927) of "Dzerzhinsky's Soldiers," personal poetic tribute to the OGPU. In "Our Attitude" (1929) Mayakovsky actively participated in the RAPP sponsored campaign of vilification against Boris Pilnyak and Yevgeny Zamyatin.[7]

III

The second part of Shklovsky's story begins where Jasnieski and Mayakovsky leave off. Many years later, the historic interview given to Serena Vitale in Moscow deserves our close reading. None of the other protagonists from the years of intense study and experimentation, under conditions upon Vitale's visit of the censorship still in force (sixty years in force by 1978), ever came to have the same opportunity of an interview. When she asked why young Russians considered him "a writer, so to speak, of the establishment,"[8] in a fury, Shklovsky ordered to her leave his apartment, that same evening calling to ask forgiveness. The question was unfair (and we don't know if such was acknowledged by her the next day); but she did the field of Russian literature a service by posing it (and not editing it out), to give us the opportunity to go back to the historical record and trace the evolution of the turn of century literary movements and the emergence of the constraints and controls that cut them short.

While Jasnieski and Mayakovsky represent the cases of violent demise, Shklovsky remained behind to continue working, part of the generation that rejected exile. How it was possible that he and many of his colleagues were able to survive the Red Terror of the 1920s and the Great Purge of the 1930s is as perplexing as Jasnieski's apparently most bizarre fall from favor.[9] About the writers who didn't or couldn't take the option of living abroad we often ask Vitale's question. Then, conversely, the temptation arises to try to see more in their later public reflections than we should. But our assessment, today, should follow from the merits of the work from each moment in time, the actual words or the refusal or inability to pronounce them, and what we know of the conditions that constrained them from one moment to the next. Sheldon, probably the most perceptive of Shklovsky's critics and editors, may perhaps have set the tone for the temptation to overstate, see too much, with the suggestion that "Monument to a Scientific Error" (1930) was an "ostensible surrender," a "device" (ix–xxii).[10]

The wave of executions following the dissolution of the Constituent Assembly,

deportation of the writers and academics to Western Europe (in 1922 Shklovsky escapes to Berlin), and the full-fledged attack on OPOYAZ initiated by Trotsky in 1924 (*Literature and Revolution*), followed by Lunacharsky, to become unanimous and unquestioned among the remaining party spokespersons on literary questions, all set the stage for official state policy to be announced in 1934 at the Congress of Soviet Writers.[11] By 1929 Formalism had been routed and banished (serious discussion already essentially over by 1926), more likely to be cited in the transcript of a police interrogation than a thoughtful book review.

With the stage set for the second wave of repression, judgements and their implementation become more and more arbitrary. The Shklovskys's decision, at great risk to themselves during the years of the Great Purge, to take in Nadezhda and Osip Mandelstam (the year prior to his arrest) testifies to the aura of disarray and fatalism of the time, provoking both fear and recklessness. For Viktor Shklovsky, having them close again, must have brought him back to the productive years of twenty years prior, and the first waves of repression that obliged him to join the exile in Western Europe, and then to the pre-revolution roots of the Futurist and Acmeist artists. The Formalist analysts, even in their early affinity with Futurism, wanted to study all of the new developments coming forward in the midst of the great ferment of the time.

Having as house guest the soon to be fugitive poet and his wife provoked again many questions. In her memoir, Nadezhda Mandelstam asked why the war against the Acmeist poets was one of annihilation, from the very beginning. Critiques from all sides in the debate, of course, were to be expected. On the one hand, with writers who still identified with the pre-revolutionary Symbolist tradition, the discussion of differences continued along the same lines that had marked the separation. But for the rapidly growing proliferation of politically inspired pro-regime factions (Proletcult and like-minded groups), the Acmeist poets became part of the problem for not signing up for the solution. From the early years the regime itself was surprisingly ruthless, culminating in the 1921 execution of Gumilev.[12] Upon the officialization of overt Socialist Realism, scores are settled with the death in concentration camp of Osip Mandelstam (1937), and the unrelenting persecution of Akhmatova. With her son, Lev, held hostage, the forced verses of adoration could not ever have been exacted from her any other way. One afternoon, young Nikita Shklovsky let slip an observation to the visitors, sensing that it was safe to share it.

Nadezhda retold the legend of Lenin's telegram. Gorky, according to versions, had promised to intervene on Gumilev's behalf. But by all evidence the sentence was carried out immediately upon conclusion of the trial proceedings. Another version of the legend claimed that the mother of Larisa Reisner had pressed Lenin for a stay. But no record of the mythical order has ever been located in archives, as of the publication of the account in Nadezhda's memoir.[13] Mayakovsky insisted in conversations that he had seen it, promising to show her the copy.

The lively debate with the Futurists, forming with them part of the broad movement for a new poetics in the years prior to the revolution was interesting because Futurists and Acmeists had branched off from the same common trunk. The paths of exploration took different directions, and at the same time converged partially on shared ideas about literature and creativity. On any assessment of the discussion, it is important to draw an important distinction that often found itself entangled in the heat of polemic. On the one hand, Futurist and Acmeist creative writers, for example, debated questions of aesthetic principle and artistic merit. On the other hand, students of literary language, aligned with the school of Formalism (often not active poets themselves), tried, so to speak, to stand above the debates among creators. They did this in order to study the underlying substrates, what all poetic tendencies and movements share, even if personally they might come to sympathize with one side or another. If they were also poets they would actively promote one or the other aesthetic posture over the other. But modern and historical tendencies and even ancient traditions were of similar interest for their research program.

For the Acmeists, the shift from the nineteenth-century prescriptions consisted in a change of perspective away from the artist's world view toward a deeper reflection on the work of art itself (not to imply that, previously, writers did not study poetic language). About the reality of the world the Guild of Poets "smiled," for there was the endlessly more convincing reality of art, in its own words. Language in art, according to them, was not for the mechanical and efficient transmission of thoughts. Rather, all the elements of the word (including its conscious sense) needed to be drawn into the work of creation. Here there appeared a profound complexity—a "more virgin and denser forest . . . the boundless complexity of our dark organism." They called on writers to "love the existence of the thing more than the thing itself, . . . [their] own existence more than [themselves]." This reflection required the "ability to feel the surprise . . . to be continually amazed."[14] The sense of autonomy of the artist found reflection in the celebration of the deeply personal and intimate. In part for this reason, *Tristia* (1921), similarly as with the poems of his colleagues, must have flew in the face of the verse-slogan of the day. Despite the difference of viewpoint with the Futurists, Eikhenbaum in particular (among the Formalists) was able to appreciate important points of contact with the conceptions of the Acmeist poets.

IV

The decade was perhaps the longest ever for Russia. Then surprisingly, in a chapter of *Mayakovsky and His Circle* (1940), Shklovsky reviewed the contributions of OPOYAZ,[15] and paid the price (Avagyan, viii–ix).[16] The stern recrimination was swift in coming, especially regarding the accounts of Mayakovsky's early participation in the soon to be proscribed literary movements. Subsequent references by Shklovsky to the Formalists' seminal work, in reality spanning fewer years of productive work than is usually recognized, return to the official assessment of how his theory was "incorrect."

Shklovsky's self-criticisms prompt us today to go back to the original documents. We must, because to accept the retractions at face value or try to put the best spin on them distracts us from studying the true contributions of the Formalists from the period when they were able to work uncensored. The distraction and lack of clarity about this problem risks miseducating the young generation of scholars who are taking another look at the upheavals of modern literature at the turn of the nineteenth century to the twentieth.

The first rescue and recovery of Shklovsky's theory of art and literature that we need to undertake comes from the *Monument of a Scientific Error* itself—the self-criticism of his perhaps most memorable call for artistic autonomy in "Regarding Art and Revolution": in response to the "clamor . . . for a new art that will correspond to the new-class ideology, . . . we have emancipated art from daily life." The "color of the flag that flies over the city fortress" cannot dictate theme or style for any field of poetry, music, sculpture or painting.[17] Obviously referring to the essential core properties of art (not the success of rulers across history to impose their ideology upon the work of artists), the claim is hardly controversial. But in *Monument* (1930), and again 14 years into Brezhnev's application of the Zhdanov doctrine, to Serena Vitale, the proposition of autonomous (from government policy) literature he declared as wrong.[18]

Looking back to the first twenty-five years of the twentieth century for purposes of contrast, the approach that is being proposed in this chapter is that, fundamentally, Shklovsky's rectifications from 1930 on deserve the same credibility as Akhmatova's ode to Stalin.[19] That year, there was no dishonor in the surrender. Jakobson and Tynyanov had already hinted at a dissociation from previous positions, in a vague ("self")-criticism published in *New LEF*,[20] repudiating "scholastic Formalism," quoted at length by Shklovsky in *Monument*. The definitive party line had been given in *Literature and Revolution* already five years previously.[21] There was nothing to explain during the interview with the Italian scholar that afternoon in Moscow forty-eight years later.

Contrary to the induced rectification, the essays collected in *Knight's Move* stand as one of the clearest calls of attention to the impending state management of art and literature. The antecedents for the policy of Socialist Realism were already in place, early warnings made previously by Gorky, among others, in *Novaya Zhizn*. Shklovsky's warning come forward in part from his collaboration with young independent writers, given impulse, in turn, from the February Revolution and the artistic movements of the new century.[22] To avoid further confusion, it is important to point out that the polemic surrounding the essays was not really about problems of aesthetics, the impending virulence testimony to larger imperatives.

The polarization also gave way to hasty formulation, difficult to defend. The idea of freedom from the outside world, reflected in the same guiding principle applied by the Supremacist painters, is straight forward and easy to understand for any unbiased observer.[23] But what did not follow from this concept was the negation of the influence of historical factors or the rejection of a materialist approach to the study of art. On this point Shklovsky could not win the argument against his Marxist critics. In the long run the superficially correct position of official cultural policy could not be sustained either, for different reasons (for one, because the debater's point was scored based on a narrow, politically motivated, line of argument). In the meanwhile, the youthful and inexperienced Formalists had set their own trap, on this question. The error was curious because they themselves had on previous occasions proposed a model for the scientific study of poetic language. This linguistic study would eventually be informed by research on the material underpinnings of verbal art in all its different presentations across history and culture (the "verbal" coming to be the core notion). One of the founding objectives for modern research on literary creation, that we can indeed trace to this period, was to make the concept of estrangement more precise, an aspect of Shklovsky's hypothesis that could not be reduced to historical and materialist factors, especially in the tendentious way his critics presented these factors. How the process of making strange helps define our aesthetic apperception of poetry, for example, actually *should* be studied by means of focused observation and analysis on immediately relevant linguistic and sonorous patterns, independent of non-relevant factors (in the "outside world," related to the "color of the flag," etc.). This approach to the study of literature of course does not imply in any way that scholars shouldn't study, for example, the ideological aspects of literature, or even that such an approach is inherently less interesting or unimportant. In the same way, the Formalist approach to research, strictly speaking, passes no judgement on the motivation of creative writers who find inspiration in one or another ideology, nor evaluates the content, per se, of their work.

In the end, the OPOYAZ and Moscow Linguistic Circle view on historical and material factors actually showed itself to be on the right track in most respects (even as it was formulated inexactly). Conversely, the party line on revolutionary art and literature, has failed to provide a coherent theory for understanding art and creative writing. Again, one can argue that on this last question the predecessors of the Union of Soviet Writers and the China National Literature Workers Association did not have this purpose in mind in first place. Why for them was the debate so important as to deserve the attention of the highest officials of the Soviet regime? When Shklovsky and his colleagues declared the independence of art "from life," the idea was that for studying its essential properties it was necessary, for analytical purposes, to separate the patterns and structures out (away from) the content, the meaning. For creators themselves (as opposed to the theorists), the related idea was that art needed to be driven by the imagination, free from the didactic manual, and free from what Mayakovsky, in a different context, called *byt*.[24] What was it about this method of research, and the related but separate approach to creative writing, that the Marxists of 1920 found so scandalous? Trotsky considered the Formalist approach to studying poetry to be "reactionary." Perhaps it wasn't so much about the proposal that considerations of meaning, and message, could be set aside for purposes of analysis. Rather, content now appeared to be an essential criterion because what could not be left to chance were certain meanings and messages, in particular. The standard applied with greater force, presumably, to the work of writers than to the research of analysts. Interestingly, still today a version, or new installment, of this debate attracts considerable attention in literary theory and criticism, topic for another occasion.

V

In later years, Shklovsky minimized his contribution to the discussion on the short-lived initiative of *zaum* verse (81).[25] But his "On poetry and trans-sense language" is actually the sharpest analysis of this avant-garde experiment, of invaluable implications for research on poetics today. Thus, again, we need to follow the path of self-criticism, unraveling it, back to the original. His goal in the trans-sense paper (1916) was to explore the function of language that is independent of the expression and understanding of meaning, drawing on the tonal and rhythmic patterns that set it apart. This dimension of language, deliberately manipulated in creative settings, specialized for one or another genre of verbal art, underlies poetic forms spanning centuries and cultures, including modern popular styles of wide-reaching audience (for example in vocal performances by jazz musicians in the North American tradition).[26] The article traces the study of the use of the sound patterns of language historically through to late nineteenth-century experiments on resonance in typical speech, comparing and contrasting these patterns to those in poetry and music. Recent experimental work on this connection has been carried forward by researchers led by psychologist Dale Purves, among a number of other research groups, representing an important vindication of the Formalists' citation of the early scientific work on the psychoacoustics of voice. The sonorous patterns themselves evoke affective responses, for example, associated with the "sensual tonality" in the sounds of language, feelings brought forth, emotions evoked, independently of the conceptual structure associated with the words.[27] These same principles underlying the scientific study of sound patterning in literature have been taken up by writers themselves, Tzvetan Todorov and Octavio Paz perhaps being among the most prominent, as they have reflected upon what appears to be an essential feature of poetic language. Shklovsky then points to what is one of the main take-away conclusions: that the trans-sense form, the vocal "sounds [striving] to be language,"[28] appears "covertly" in poetry, generally: "[concealing] itself under the mask of some often deceptive content . . . poets themselves have to admit that they do not understand the content of their own verses."[29] The translators of the article quote N. Mandelstam, referring to the process of composing by Osip: as converting "a ringing in the ears" into a "silent mouthing, then into whispering, then the inner music" (in chapter 39 of her memoir "Moving lips").[30] In another context, Mandelstam describes the translation as "[returning] word into music." Thus, this fleeting avant-garde genre suggested reflection on one of the fundamentals of art in language, no less.

Eikhenbaum, among the Formalists, most explicitly pointed to the "melodic principles of verse": the altered syntax of poetry is shaped to conform to the rhythmic patterns of verses, with the parallel contours of intonation to form the phrasing of the poem.[31] According to this view, the "melodic principles" consist of the patterns of contour, a proposal that was taken up and elaborated upon years later by musicologist F. Lerdahl. In short, we could say that the intonational contour subsumes all the aspects of prosodic structure then linked to the component of rhythm. Minus the fixed pitches and intervals of musical melody, per se, the poem is recited (as in "spoken word"), as opposed to performed musically. Language set to music (with all of its typically required components, including the pitches of a scale) is "song," and by definition becomes poetry. Poetry can be either sung or recited. Precisely, one of the questions that OPOYAZ asked, and had made the first tentative attempt to answer, was: in what way is verse different from prosaic discourse? What seems apparent so far from this review is that the work on the sound patterning of poetry (its musical features) is linked in some way to the concept of estrangement.

Trans-sense writing inspired a group of modern poets who formed the Union of Real Art, Daniil Kharms, author of *Today I Wrote Nothing*, among the most celebrated in later years (after 1960, manuscripts recovered by his sister and a musicologist friend published in samizdat). Arrested and exiled in the early 1930s for his experimental work, surrealist and absurdist, he reportedly saved himself from execution on subsequent arrest by feigning mental illness. Interestingly, testimony perhaps to the appeal of his works for children, he received an early posthumous rehabilitation and public recognition, decades before Glasnost. See Jakovljevic's study for a review of his work and account of his influence today, living inheritance of this current of Russian Futurism.

VI

According to the final edited version from the chapter on "Language and poetry" in *Bowstring*—published six years into the Brezhnev era—the proposal for future research in "Art as Device" (1916) was a rash declaration.[32] To the contrary, together with Eikhenbaum's "Theory of the Formal Method," it forms part of the foundation, in two short programmatic documents, of the modern scientific study of poetic language. The decision to focus attention on the figures, implements and designs of art language, during the few years they would have to work on the problem, promised a better understanding of what defamiliarization and estrangement meant. "Art as Device" gives several examples of creating the *special perception* (particular or peculiar) by means of the technique of singularization, setting the object of perception apart and distinguishing it. The effect is one of distortion, making the object appear as if for the first time, no longer familiar and automatic. One is reminded, here, of the use of the diminutive in colloquial everyday discourse, to suggest beauty or to express endearment. This example of "peculiarization" in some languages is associated with the caring and affection sense of the diminutive in one of the meanings of the word "detail"—*detalle* (Sp.), *dettaglio* (It.), *detalhes* (Pt., plural) as in the 1971 Roberto Carlos song. What singularizing does is to compel in us a sensation of the patterns of language, the new sense attained by the implementation of the artistic means of the poet. This cognizance or affect (typically not subject to our awareness unless we study it) involves a kind of prolongation and "difficulty." Studying it, for Shklovsky, held out the possibility of finally understanding the difference between prose exposition and poetic language. He and his co-workers already had rejected the seemingly easy solution, that poetry could be reduced to emotive expression, although this element of musical/poetic perception appears to play some role.

Briefly, to return to the problem of meaning: the Formalists clearly did not dismiss all consideration of this aspect of literary language. Where the interesting question resided, for them, is in *how* meaning is expressed in poetry, in the *patterns* of meaning. The overall idea of defamiliarization should apply to this domain as well. How in the semantic patterns are the expected associations, sequences, all the various conceptual frames, and so forth, distorted or violated? What is the difference between the ubiquitous everyday prosaic metaphor and artistic metaphor? In narrative forms, how does the artist flout the expectations of how events, time and space are represented, in an aesthetic way (as opposed to a random and plainly incoherent way)?

True enough, members of OPOYAZ took the idea of estrangement and defamiliarization and tried to apply it too broadly, reaching too far, in presenting it, for example, as the factor that accounts for historical development in art. In fairness, part of the explanation for change is probably related to system-destabilizing movement spurred by habituation; and to also be fair, this debate was neither decisive for the theory of the Formalists nor, in all honesty, very interesting. But for one last time regarding the history and the material of the artistic genres, as the examples in "Art as Device" show, narrators and especially poets already knew about defamiliarization, long before even Aristotle alluded to it indirectly in *Poetics*. OPOYAZ just gave the concept a name and laid out the rough sketches of a program of research for the humanities to try to better understand it. This program starts, as the Formalists were beginning to conceive it, with studying what we can recover from the traditions of verbal art long before even the first invention of writing.

NOTES

* Final verse line from a poem written in 1937 by Bruno Jasienski in Butyrki prison prior to his trial and conviction.

1. Martov, Vladimir, *Russian Futurism: A History* (Berkeley: University of California Press, 1968), 2–13.
2. Burliuk, David et al., "Slap in the Face of Public Taste." *Words in Revolution: Russian Futurist Manifestos 1912–1928* (Washington, DC: New Academia, 2004[1912]), 51–52.
3. Kolesnikoff, Nina, *Bruno Jasienski: His Evolution from Futurism to Socialist Realism* (Waterloo: Wilfrid Laurier University Press, 1982), 20.
4. Jakobson, Roman, *My Futurist Years* (New York: Marsilio Publishers, 1992), 66–152.
5. Kolesnikoff, 83–85.
6. Jasienski, Bruno, *The Mannequin's Ball* (Amsterdam: Harwood Academic Publishers, 2000).
7. Jangfeldt, Bengt, *Mayakovsky: A Biography* (Chicago: University of Chicago Press, 2014), 263–467. In 1930, perhaps out of desperation, Mayakovsky applied for membership in RAPP and was accepted.
8. Vitale, Serena, *Shklovsky: Witness to an Era* (Champaign: Dalkey Archive Press, 2012), 28–29.
9. Mayakovsky's biographers are correct to avoid speculation about the circumstances of his death, considering the lack of evidence for any direct outside involvement or decisive political break between the poet and the regime. But the case of Jasienski deserves our closer examination. In the first place, given his absolute and unswerving discipline in serving the Party, nothing in his writing suggested anything to the contrary. Early accounts, curiously, denied the execution, alleging rather that he died of typhus while in custody (perhaps such being the official version). To be fair, the complete record may not have been available until

more recently. What all current versions appear to omit, however, is the most obvious reason. The years 1937–1938 witnessed the round up and mass NKVD liquidation of Polish residents in the Soviet Union, (over 110,000 executed among 139,000 sentenced), singling out, pointedly, members of the Polish Communist and Socialist Parties. The story of Jasienski's desperate attempts at denunciation of comrades and friends and his own admission of guilt in response to the typically nonsensical accusations is consistent with purge methods of the time.

10. Sheldon, Richard. "Viktor Shklovsky and the Device of Ostensible Surrender" Introduction to *Third Factory* (Champaign: Dalkey Archive Press, 1977), ix–vlii.

11. Gorky, Maxim et al., *Soviet Writers Congress* (London: Lawrence & Wishart, 1977[1934]).

12. As was discussed in a previous study of the controversy, Francis, N., "The Trotsky-Shklovsky Debate," *International Journal of Russian Studies*, 6.1 (2017): 15–27, it is not in any way a contradiction to point out that the years of the New Economic Policy (1921–1928), inaugurated by the suppression of the Kronstadt rebellion, were marked by both:

- a partial opening in publishing opportunities and for debates in art and literature, *and*
- a continuation of repression against civil society, writers included.

As Jangfeldt (157–185) points out, carrying over the Red Terror practices of 1917–1920 to the period of market reform, for the ruling party, were a necessary measure. Diminished control over the economy needed to be compensated for by greater political control. Nineteen-twenty-one was the year of the Cheka-manufactured Tagenstev conspiracy, the 61 executed writers and intellectuals (rehabilitated in 1991 when the files came to light) being the most notable case, in all, civilian victims numbering in the many thousands. In the same proportion, the Gulag system expanded significantly, during the period 1922–1923, Richard Pipes, "Lenin's Gulag," 141–145.

13. Mandelstam, Nadezhda, *Hope Against Hope: A Memoir* (New York: Atheneum, 1970), 109–110.

14. Mandelstam, Osip, "The Morning of Acmeism.," *The Russian Review*, 24.1 (1965[1919]): 50.

15. Shklovsky, Victor, *Mayakovsky and His Circle* (New York: Dodd, Mead & Company, 1972[1940]), 111–120.

16. Avagyan, Shushan, Preface to *Bowstring: On the Dissimilarity of the Similar* (Champaign: Dalkey Archive Press, 2011[1970]), viii–ix.

17. Shklovsky, Victor, *Knight's Move* (Champaign: Dalkey Archive Press, 2005[1923]), 21–22.

18. Vitale, 100.

19. Yokota-Murakami, Takayujki, in "Thought Censorship . . . and Voice in Mandelstam," *Canadian Review of Comparative Literature*, 41.1 (2014): 46–52, analyzes at length the phenomenon of extorted poetry.

20. Tynyanov, Juri and Jakobson, Roman. "Problems in the Study of Literature and Language." *Readings in Russian Poetics* (Cambridge: MIT Press, 1971[1928]), 79–81.

21. Trotsky, Leon, *Literature and Revolution* (New York: Russell & Russell, 1924[1957]).

22. Lunts, Lev, *In the Wilderness* (Las Cruces: Xenos Books, 2014[1922]), 127–136.

23. Recall that the research method of abstracting from content is taken up in a very specific way by OPOYAZ theory: as a strictly methodological recourse for analysts of literature for the purpose of understanding literariness, not as a suggestion for the work of artists. Because Shklovsky had a foot in both Formalism (the first purpose) and Futurism (during the early years, the second), the two are sometimes confounded, in these instances to his disadvantage in debate.

24. *Byt*: the everyday grind, complacency and mendacity of daily life. "Motionless *byt*." "Slits of *byt* filled with fat and coagulate." "The swamp of *byt* . . . covered over with slime and weeds" (*About This*, 1923). In a recent review appearing in *The Nation*, Ehrenreich summed up what the basic idea was behind the independence-from-life approach: the need to "steal new sets of eyes . . . and unimagined senses." Art narrative (as in the novel) is . . . "a weird box of . . . openness . . . a compact revolution."

25. Shklovsky, Victor, "On Poetry and Trans-Sense Language," *October,* 34 (1985[1916]): 81.

26. The ethnographic study of Wirtz on Santería verse, "Making sense of unintelligible messages," 435–462, points to one example of this dimension of creative language use, arguably one that addresses the question of literariness, in this case, appropriately, from the oral tradition. Along the same lines, Jakobson and Waugh summarized the research on emergent child poetics in *The Sound Shape of Language*, as did Shklovsky in his paper, for another perspective on the problems of understanding the defining qualities of poetic language. The paper quotes Gorky (in *My Childhood*), how "in the boy's memory a poem [was] simultaneously stored in two ways: as words and also as what I call patches of sound." (15). The foundational principles, deep down, of literariness are not found in books, Eikenbaum, "The Illusion of Skaz."

27. Shklovsky, "On Poetry and Trans-Sense Language," 8–12.
28. Shklovsky, "On Poetry and Trans-Sense Language," 22.
29. Shklovsky, "On Poetry and Trans-Sense Language," 16.
30. Mandelstam, N., 186–187.
31. Eikenbaum, Boris. "El Principio Melódico del Verso.," *Antología del Formalismo Ruso: Volumen II, Semiótica del Discurso y Posformalismo Bajtiano* (Madrid: Editorial Fundamentos, 1995[1921]), 37–42.
32. Shklovsky, Victor, *Bowstring: On the Dissimilarity of the Similar* (Champaign: Dalkey Archive Press. 2011[1970]), 285.

WORKS CITED

Avagyan, Shushan. Preface to *Bowstring: On the Dissimilarity of the Similar,* by Victor Shklovsky, vii–xi. Champaign: Dalkey Archive Press, 2011[1970].

Burliuk, David, Alexander Kruchenykh, Vladimir Mayakovsky and Victor Khlebnikov. "Slap in the face of public taste." In *Words in Revolution: Russian Futurist Manifestos 1912–1928,* edited by A. Lawton and H. Eagle, 51–52. Washington, DC: New Academia, 2004[1912].

Ehrenreich, Ben. "Making Strange: On Victor Shklovsky." *The Nation,* February 5, 2013.

Eikenbaum, Boris. "The Illusion of Skaz." In *Anthology of Russian Futurism,* edited by Ellendrea Proffer and Carl Proffer, 233–235. Ann Arbor: Ardis, 1980[1918].

———. "El Principio Melódico del Verso." In *Antología del Formalismo Ruso: Volumen II, Semiótica del Discurso y Posformalismo Bajtiano,* edited by Emil Volek, 37–42. Madrid: Editorial Fundamentos, 1995[1921].

Francis, Norbert. "The Trotsky-Shklovsky Debate: Marxism versus Formalism." *International Journal of Russian Studies* 6, 1 (2017): 15–27.

Gorky, Maxim; Karl Radek, Nikolai Bukharin and Andrei Zhdanov. *Soviet Writers' Congress.* London: Lawrence & Wishart, 1977[1934].

Han, Shui'er, Janini Sundararajan, Daniel Bowling, Jessica Lake and Dale Purves. "Co-variation of Tonality in the Music and Speech of Different Cultures." *PLoS ONE* 6, 5 (2011) 1–5.

Jakobson, Roman. *My Futurist Years.* Compiled and edited by Bengt Jangfeldt and Stephen Rudy. New York: Marsilio Publishers, 1992.

Jakobson, Roman and Linda Waugh. *The Sound Shape of Language.* Bloomington: Indiana University Press, 1979.

Jakovljevic, Branislav. *Eventuations: Daniil Kharms' Mise-en-Page.* PhD diss. New York University, 2002.

Jangfeldt, Bengt. *Mayakovsky: A Biography.* Chicago: University of Chicago Press, 2014.

Jasienski, Bruno. *The Mannequin's Ball.* Amsterdam: Harwood Academic Publishers, 2000.

Kolesnikoff, Nina. *Bruno Jasienski: His Evolution from Futurism to Socialist Realism.* Waterloo: Wilfrid Laurier University Press, 1982.

Lerdahl, Fred. "The Sounds of Poetry Viewed as Music." In *The Cognitive Neuroscience of Music,* edited by Isabelle Peretz and Robert J. Zatorre, 413–429. Oxford: Oxford University Press, 2003.

Lunts, Lev. *In the Wilderness*. Las Cruces: Xenos Books, 2014[1922].
Mandelstam, Nadezhda. *Hope Against Hope: A Memoir*. New York: Atheneum, 1970.
Mandelstam, Osip. "The Morning of Acmeism." *The Russian Review* 24, 1 (1965[1919]): 47–51.
Markov, Vladimir. *Russian Futurism: A History*. Berkeley: University of California Press, 1968.
Paz, Octavio. *El Arco y la Lira*. México DF: Fondo de Cultura Económica, 1956.
Pipes, Richard. "Lenin's Gulag." *International Journal of Political Science and Development* 2, 6 (2014): 140–146.
Sheldon, Richard. Introduction to *Third Factory*, by Victor Shklovsky, ix–vlii. Champaign: Dalkey Archive Press, 1977.
Shklovsky, Viktor. "Art as Technique." In *Russian Formalist Criticism: Four Essays*, edited by Lee T. Lemon and Marion J. Reis, 3–24. Lincoln, NE: University of Nebraska Press, 1965[1917].
———.*Bowstring: On the Dissimilarity of the Similar*. Champaign: Dalkey Archive Press. 2011[1970].
———. *Knight's Move*. Champaign: Dalkey Archive Press, 2005[1923].
———. *Mayakovsky and His Circle*. New York: Dodd, Mead & Company, 1972[1940].
———. "Monument to a Scientific Error: Context No. 24." Translation of "Pamiatnik nauchnoi oshibke," *Literaturnaia Gazeta*, No. 4, January 27, 1930, by Shushan Avagyan. Champaign: Dalkey Archive Press. https://www.dalkeyarchive.com/monument-to-a-scientific-error/.
———."On Poetry and Trans-Sense Language." *October* 34 (1985[1916]): 3–24, translated by Gerald Janecek and Peter Mayer, Cambridge: MIT Press.
Todorov, Tzvetan. *Teoría de la Literatura de los Formalistas Rusos*. México DF: Siglo Veintiuno Editores, 1970.
Trotsky, Leon. *Literature and Revolution*. New York: Russell & Russell, 1924[1957].
Tynyanov, Yury and Roman Jakobson. "Problems in the Study of Literature and Language," In *Readings in Russian Poetics*, edited by Ladislav Matejka and Krystyna Pomorska, 79–81. Cambridge: MIT Press, 1971[1928].
Vitale, Serena. *Shklovsky: Witness to an Era*. Champaign: Dalkey Archive Press, 2012.
Wirtz, Kristina. "Making Sense of Unintelligible Messages in Divine Communication." *Text & Talk* 2, 4 (2007): 435–462.
Yokota-Murakami, Takayuki. "Thought Censorship under Totalitarianism: A Precarious Relationship between Thought and Voice in Mandelstam." *Canadian Review of Comparative Literature* 41, 1 (2014): 43–53.

Chapter Nine

Framing and Threading Non-Literary Discourse into the Structure of Cervantes's *Don Quixote II*

Rachel Schmidt

The characters, themes and episodes that mark Miguel de Cervantes's literary masterpiece, *Don Quixote de la Mancha,* all appear in part I, published in 1605. Here we meet Don Quixote, the impoverished country gentleman who transforms himself into a knight errant, and his illiterate but intelligent squire Sancho Panza. Here Don Quixote, armed with his ancestor's lance, knowledge of chivalric romances and active imagination, turns the dusty countryside of La Mancha into a land populated with giants, and involves all those he meets in his hapless adventures. In the *Don Quixote de la Mancha II* (published in 1615), there are only pseudo-adventures staged by others for Don Quixote, for what really happens in this volume are conversations.[1] Martín Moran describes Cervantes's novel as a lengthy conversation between Don Quixote and Sancho in which they negotiate the codes and the referential frames which give form to all that follows.[2] The protagonists' conversation, instead of detracting from the narrative arc, allows them to relive their past adventures and permits the narrator to reorder the events according to thematic motifs as well as to reconstruct the narrative in a manner such that different events group and regroup.[3] The grouping and regrouping of motifs suggest the model of threading and framing proposed by Viktor Shklovsky. Cervantes used threading and framing to structure *Don Quixote de la Mancha II* according to motifs from the non-literary genres of his period that governed politics, law, economics, dueling, swordsmanship and masculine behavior, thus complicating or estranging them, to use another of Shklovsky's terms.

In his *Theory of Prose* (1990), Viktor Shklovsky expounds upon threading and framing as structural components of fiction. He describes threading as a means of linking one story motif to another through the protagonist, as exemplified by the hero's tale in which the tasks he must accomplish represent a threading device.[4] Cervantes's *Don Quixote de la Mancha* lends itself to analysis according to Shklovsky's formalist approach because of the contrast between madness and wisdom built into the character of Don Quixote as well as the narrative structure in which subplots interlace with the main plot.[5] Although Shklovsky does not consider all of Cervantes's inset tales to be out of place (he regards the tale of Dorotea disguised as Princess Micimicona particularly well-framed), he certainly highlights the estrangement involved in placing wise speeches in the mouth of a madman. In fact, Alonso Quijano, by imagining himself to be the knight errant Don Quixote facing a series of foes, sets himself within a threading composition. Referring to Don Quixote's speeches in part I, Shklovsky states that "Cervantes found that he needed Don Quixote as a unifying thread of wise sayings."[6] When Shklovsky refers to Don Quixote's speech in *Don Quixote de la Mancha I*, chapter 37, on arms vs. letters, he describes it as "essentially out of place."[7] In Shklovsky's terms, this out of placeness, so to speak, would be an estranging technique by which both the old trope of the arms vs. letters and the image of the Don Quixote as the out-of-place knight errant are rendered alien. The references to the non-literary genres in the first chapters of part II are out of place, if one may, and work in a similar fashion, defamiliarizing both the genres (and all they represent) and Don Quixote.

To clarify, placing the wise speech in the mouth of the madman has the effect of making it strange, causing estrangement, if we choose to apply this Shklovskyian term to the phenomenon. Here also enters the concept of framing, related to the Russian Formalist's notion of being in or out of place. Whereas threading runs through the narrative like the warp holding the woof, the frame stands outside a tale to give it context. Thus, Shklovsky writes of interpolated stories such as "Psyche and Cupid" framed within Apuleius's *The Golden Ass*.[8] If an inset story is well-framed, it takes its appropriate place, unlike Don Quixote's incongruous speeches. Don Quixote gives his first "wise" speech, the Ovidian discourse on the lost golden age, to an illiterate group of goatherds; hence, it is for Shklovsky "essentially out of place," not only because a madman speaks it but also because it is spoken to an inappropriate audience.[9] His second speech on the various ends that noble lineages meet is directed to his flabbergasted niece, and followed by a third on glory, which Shklovsky notes is a hodgepodge of remembered quotes.[10] Regarding *Don Quixote de la Mancha II*, published 10 years after part I, in 1615, Shklovsky notes the structural introduction of "small inset anecdotes," often integrating "distinct 'historical words' and actions" into the text."[11] He mentions the "set" episodes such as the brayers in chapters 25–27 and the page in chapter 24, but passes over their significance to focus on Sancho's Barataria episodes, as well as those of Ricote and Roque Guinart, as a "perfect type of threading."[12] We can recuperate from Shklovsky's analysis of *Don Quixote de la Mancha I* the notion of threading as a hermeneutic tool that allows us to distinguish motifs and themes that are related to the words and actions historically unique to Cervantes's time that appear in the first 24 chapters of *Don Quixote de la Mancha II*, many of which are linked to non-literary discourses concerning politics and masculinity. We might now call these historic words related to actions discursive phrases, that is to say, phrasal lexical items that belong to certain non-literary discourses and that signal the presence of the semantic frame of a non-literary discourse.

The first chapter of *Don Quixote de la Mancha II* begins with an examination of our protagonist's sanity testing his ability to engage in political discourse with his friends, the village priest and barber. As the text reads:

> [I]n the course of their conversation they began to discuss what is called reason of state and ways of governing, correcting this abuse and condemning that one, reforming one custom and eliminating another, each one of the three becoming a new legislator, a modern Lycurgus, a latter-day Solon, and they so transformed the nation that it seemed as if they had placed it in the forge and taken out a new one, and Don Quixote spoke with so much intelligence regarding all the subjects they touched upon that his two examiners thought there was no doubt that he was completely well and his sanity restored.[13]

As far as it goes, Don Quixote appears sane, for he is able to hold forth in the political genre of reason of state (*razón de estado*). Part II opens, then, with the same split within the character of its insane/wise protagonist that structured part I, but placing this particular political discourse, known for its adaptation of Machiavellian concepts while at the same time demonizing Machiavelli, in the mouth of a self-proclaimed knight errant has an estranging effect.[14] In a pique of morbid curiosity, Don Quixote's friends test his sanity further, urging him to advise the king concerning the threat of Turkish invasion on Spanish soil. The barber does so by saying that the list of impertinent advice and schemes (*arbitrios*) given by the so-called *arbitristas* to the king are impossible, ridiculous, or harmful.[15] Here Cervantes profiles Don Quixote according to the comic type he created in his exemplary novella, the *Colloquy of the Dogs,* of the *arbitrista,* a type based on Spaniards who petitioned the monarchy with proposed economic and bureaucratic reforms.[16] Don Quixote, who realizes he is being baited, responds that his advice is neither impossible nor crazy, but rather a plan just as just and as easy to accomplish as any proposed by an *arbitrante*.[17] Don Quixote's use of the term *arbitrante* instead of *arbitrista* speaks to his awareness that he is perceived, like the *arbitristas,* as a fool, but that he claims to speak from a position of sanity. Of course, his advice is none other than the ridiculous and completely anachronistic plan that the king should publish a call for all knights errant wandering through Spain to convene upon the court on a given day, their number being sufficient to overwhelm the Turks. As Cascardi states, by beginning part II in this way Cervantes reminds us that "the quixotic project to restore knight-errantry is, in fact, the comical transposition of an underlying political project that has both theoretical and practical dimensions."[18] In this opening episode references to the valorized discourse of reason of state and *arbitrios*, serve both a structural and an estranging purpose. They link part II to part I by threading the dual nature of the insane/wise protagonist across the 10-year gap that separates the two volumes, at the same time that they estrange the political discourse that will appear time and time again as a thread throughout *Don Quixote de la Mancha II*.

The thread of political discourse reappears in chapter 6 when Don Quixote's housekeeper, expressing her dismay at his neighborly visits, exclaims that she must complain to God and the king so that they might correct his behavior. Don Quixote replies that if he were the monarch, he would not respond to the "countless importunate requests presented to me each day."[19] In Spanish, the importunate requests are *memoriales impertinentes*, these being another reference to the work of *arbitristas* or those making out-of-place requests of the king. Diego de Covarrubias defined the term *memorial* in 1611 as a petition (presumably written) given to a king or a superior as a memoir of business or negotiation.[20] *Memoriales* and *arbitrios* were often one and the same, and served purposes other than just presenting ideas or pleas before the monarch. Many of them were not impertinent, but rather addressed serious political and economic problems in need of reform, such as putting an end to the short-term, high-interest loans paid to foreign bankers and used to finance the transport of Spanish troops and goods.[21] Don Quixote, however, aligns *memorialistas* and *arbitristas* with the troublemakers who come to court looking for money, about whom Felipe II complained in 1588.[22] In a petition to the Cortes, the King had written that: "there is a large number of people who spend their lives in court in these chimeras of thinking up schemes, means and novelties ... it seems to them that to speak of making money makes it lawful for them to go about sounding off about means and schemes."[23] To the housekeeper's stunned reply that there must be knights in the king's court, Don Quixote answers with a speech differentiating between courtesans, who would be those excoriated by Felipe II for trumpeting about their schemes, and knights errant. According to our protagonist, courtesans are those who do not leave the safety of the court, who travel only by looking at maps, and who know their enemies only through portraits. They fight in a world of representations and appearances, whereas knights errant suffer in body and confront their enemies in person. This speech can be considered in itself a sort of *arbitrio* insofar as it takes as its starting point an analysis of early modern political and social change. Midway through his apt insights into the artifice of the early modern court, Don Quixote veers into the artificiality of chivalric romance, commenting that the "good knight errant may see ten giants whose heads not only touch the clouds but go above them, each with legs that are two immense towers and whose arms resemble the masts of large and powerful ships, each eye like a huge mill wheel burning hotter than a glass furnace, yet he must not be afraid in the slightest."[24] As his niece aptly replies, Don Quixote has wandered off again into the source of his insanity, the lying fiction of knight errantry. The doubling of Don Quixote's madness and wisdom continues apace, yet what distinguishes part II from part I of *Don Quixote de la Mancha* is that the protagonist's wisdom in the second half will speak more to contemporary issues of politics and masculinity.

Paying attention to the discursive fluctuations in the conversation allows us to hear the tension between old and new social behavior that frames Don Quixote's quest and his relation to Sancho Panza. For example, the thematic material of Don Quixote's *arbitrio*, his desire that knights errant replace courtesans, continues to enter into his discussion with Sancho as they set out on their adventures. Thus, in chapter 8 he discusses the desire for fame that spurred on not only the ancient Romans but also the Spaniards who accompanied the conquistador Cortés. Sancho, who only a few breaths ago declared himself firmly Catholic and an undying enemy of the Jews, manages to derail his master's train of thought from the worldly and pagan topic of fame by asking him where these ancient heroes now lie. Don Quixote imparts his knowledge of ornate tombs in Rome, but will not yield to Sancho's further request that they become saints with tombs adorned by lamps, candles, paintings, crutches and prosthetics. Acknowledging that there are Christian friars who are also highly revered, Don Quixote insists that knight errantry itself is a religion and that sainted knights errant reside in heaven.[25] Moreover, he concedes to Sancho that although there are many errant clerics, there are few who merit the name of knights. The narrator then wryly notes that the pair spend the next day and night in "this and other similar conversations, and nothing worth recounting happened to them, which caused no small sorrow to Don Quixote."[26] When viewed as a mere link between adventures, as Don Quixote might see it, Chapters 6 to 8 seem to contain very little, and thus in chapter 9 Don Quixote sends Sancho out in search of Dulcinea. And yet these conversations, being a sort of extended *arbitrio* in which Don Quixote defends his knight errantry as necessary for the republic, contribute to Sancho's education in such a way that, much to the surprise of Cide Hamete Benengeli and centuries of readers, the squire will be able to govern Barataria. That is to say, this political discourse serves not only to glue distinct actions together but also to cement the relationship of the two protagonists and to render verisimilar some of the most inventive and socially critical episodes in the novel.

In addition, they further Sancho's developing argument for financial gain in his position as squire, which is an important thread linking part I and part II.[27] If we can argue that Don Quixote asserts an argument for the primacy of knights errant over courtesans, an essentially conservative argument that hearkens to a pre-modern time, we can likewise argue that Sancho continuously, if covertly, argues for a modern economic order of wage-based labor. Molho demonstrates that the characterization of Sancho Panza, like Don Quixote, is also based on a duality, which in Sancho's case arises from the folkloric doubling of simplicity and cleverness seen, for example, in the common Sancho proverbs and the carnivalesque Panza figures.[28] Sancho is a reversible figure, whose dual nature of idiocy and knowledge allows him to speak uncomfortable truths to his master. The peasant's doubled nature extends to his multivalent speech, for more than any other character, Sancho, although illiterate, is surprisingly fluent and pragmatic in his use of various discourses. Just as Don Quixote's wisdom is rendered strange by his madness, Sancho's economic cleverness is rendered strange by his illiteracy and simplicity. In what he calls the "drama" of Sancho's salary, Johnson shows how Sancho moves his relationship with his master away from a medieval feudal one toward a modern one through four key moments in part II, the first of which is his petition for a salary. The final three occur in quick succession at the end of the book, when Don Quixote tries unsuccessfully to physically force Sancho to whip himself to disenchant Dulcinea (part II, chapter 60), when he then tries to shame him into resuming the whipping (part II, chapter 68), and when he finally offers him a price per stroke, thus entering into the modern notion of labor as commodity (part II, chapter 71).[29] There are multiple ironies here. Sancho never whips himself too much, but at the end only pretends to whip himself in order to stop his master's pleading and win his good will. Most ironic, of course, is the fact that Sancho, in a stroke of cleverness, "enchants" a peasant girl outside of Toboso into the figure of Dulcinea, thus holding his master hostage to a figment of his own imagination throughout the entire course of part II. Thus, the "enchantment" boomerangs on Don Quixote's own imagined transformation of the peasant Aldonsa Lorenzo into Dulcinea.

In chapter 7, Don Quixote must choose either Sancho Panza or Sansón Carrasco, his somewhat malicious university-educated neighbor, as his squire. As the two pretenders vie for Don Quixote's favor, it is interesting to note how they attempt to sway our protagonist. In his attempt to win his case, Sansón Carrasco only speaks the language of chivalric romance:

> it would weigh heavily on my conscience if I did not convey to this knight and persuade him that the strength of his valiant arm and the virtue of his valorous spirit should tarry and be constrained no more, for delay thwarts the righting of wrongs, the defense of orphans, the honoring of damsels, the favoring of

widows, the protection of married women, and other things of this nature that touch on, relate to, depend on, and are attached to the order of errant chivalry.[30]

The syntax, vocabulary and worldview of this invocation are all deliberately archaic and literary, and, although they please Don Quixote, do not serve Sansón's purpose of convincing the knight to hire him as a squire but only manage to make Sancho's eyes water up at the thought of being replaced by another. Quite the opposite, Sancho uses varied discourses to speak to his master. In so doing, he reveals a more nuanced relationship with Don Quixote. Trying to put his master into a good mood, he starts by stringing together proverbs, to which his master responds that he speaks pearls.[31] Encouraged, Sancho strings together more clichés, this time from the *ars moriendi* discourse.[32] Only then does he introduce the thorny topic of a salary, to which his master replies with the model of knight errantry, saying that he would give him a salary if he could show him the slightest evidence of one in the histories of knight errantry. Although Don Quixote reverts to what he recognizes as the ancient custom of knight errantry, his language is not archaic as he negotiates with his squire. First of all, he asks Sancho to find evidence in the documentary record for salaries. He then considers that squires did receive some sort of recompense, such as an island, title, or sovereignty, and then uses a very modern word, *aditamento*, to invite Sancho back. According to the Corpus Diacrónico de Español, *aditamento,* meaning an addition to a legal agreement, occurs first in 1487, and occurs rarely in literature, usually in a satirical context.[33] Cervantes uses it again in part II, chapter 51, when Sancho Panza, now serving as governor of the Island Barataria, sets forth regulations for providing wine for his jurisdiction, with the *aditamiento* that the place of origin be stated so that the proper price might be given it and that those who would water it down or change its name be executed.[34] That is to say, when discussing Sancho's request for a salary, itself a modern notion, Don Quixote uses modern legal discourse, even though he falls back on the medieval customs of knight errantry. Byrne names this combination of ancient code with new laws "*mos hispanicus,* [which] does not dismiss out of hand the old laws, as did the *mos gallicus.* Nor does it follow *mos italicus* with an automatic assumption of the viability of those earlier codes in a contemporary context."[35] Again, by framing the legal discourse, a discourse threaded throughout part II, within the character of Don Quixote, Cervantes renders it strange through the character's madness, just as the framing of economic discourse is rendered strange by Sancho's simplicity.

Threaded to Don Quixote's initial critique of courtesans, chapters 16 to 22 form a discursive unit based on masculine honor in its various subgenres, including poetic theory, treatises on dueling and swordsmanship and the non-literary treatises on what was called true honor. Critics have often focused on chapters 16 to 18 as a unit, for they recount the pleasant hours Don Quixote spends with Diego Miranda, the so-called Knight of the Green Coat, in whose house he gives his famous defense of poetry (chapter 16). In chapter 17 this highpoint is deflated by the battle with the lion, who merely yawns and turns away from our protagonist's challenge. Aghast at Don Quixote's action, the sedentary gentleman, Diego Miranda, tells Sancho that his master is crazy (*loco*) to which the squire replies that he is reckless (*atrevido*).[36] Diego Miranda then approaches Don Quixote and draws on the discourse of true honor (*verdadera honra*) in an attempt to dissuade him from his attack on the lion: "Señor Knight, knights errant ought to undertake adventures that promise some hope of success, not those that are completely devoid of hope, for the valor that crosses over into temerity has more to do with madness than courage."[37] The true honor discourse, typified by Jerónimo Jiménez de Urrea's *Dialogue of True Military Honor* (*Diálogo de la verdadera honra militar*, 1566), appealed to nobles whose caste identity and purpose was in flux, as their warrior office was replaced by the professional soldier and as their political profession became that of courtesan and bureaucrat. Urrea insisted that it was a mark of a "foolish, insane man" (*loco desatinado*) to follow his "insanity to the damage of one's honor, life and even soul, which is the worst."[38] Indeed, Don Quixote understands that Diego Miranda accuses him of temerity, for he responds by undoing one of the topoi of true honor: "although I knew it was exceedingly reckless, because I know very well what valor means; it is a virtue that occupies a place between two wicked extremes, which are cowardice and temerity, but it is better for the valiant man to touch on and climb to the heights of temerity than to touch on and fall to the depths of cowardice."[39]

Even in the plot, the discourse of true honor plays a central role in Cervantes's creation of the novel. In one of his examples of a case in which a man must act to protect his honor in the face of a challenge, Urrea names a participant *Espejo*, meaning Mirror. Although Urrea insists that human reason must prevail over animal force, he gives many instances in which men must defend their honor for only they are ultimately responsible for the loss of their honor. To that extent, the honorable man must determine whether someone speaks in jest or in sincerity, whether someone is in a position to actually harm his honor, and whether one is of an equal social position, as one beneath him cannot actually harm him. In a crucial part of his argument, Urrea refers to a man whose honor has been challenged as Mirror, and explains how the injury to his honor turns him into a so-called *Actor*. Urrea offers this example: "Don Pedro de Herrero rained blows upon Mirror; it impinged upon Mirror to state that don Pedro had injured him badly, and as a traitor. Don Pedro responded that he lied, such that Mirror was injured and charged as an Actor, obliged to prove that Don Pedro had hit him badly and as a traitor."[40] The thread returns to chapters 12 to 15, in which the Knight of the Woods is revealed to be Don Quixote's rascally neighbor and would-be squire Bachelor Sansón Carrasco. By daylight Sansón's clothes shine like gold because they are adorned with moon-shaped mirrors, leading the narrator to rename him the Knight of the Mirrors (*Espejos*).[41] This knight injures our knight errant with a lie. Before he supposedly knows to whom he speaks, Sansón boasts to Don Quixote of having defeated in battle the famous Don Quixote de la Mancha and having made him confess that his Casildea is more beautiful than Dulcinea. The situation parallels Urrea's example, and thus Don Quixote is obliged to defend his honor in battle as an *Actor*.

Once the Knight of the Woods is defeated and unmasked by our protagonist, he returns to challenge and defeat Don Quixote in Barcelona, this time as the Knight of the White Moon. Sansón justifies this final defeat to Antonio Moreno as an act of charity based on pity for Don Quixote so that he might recover his good judgement lost to the nonsense of knight errantry. Antonio Moreno will not accept Sanson's pious rationalization, condemning him for having performed an injury or *agravio* to the whole world for having cured its most entertaining madman.[42] An *agravio* is, according to Covarrubias, the irrational deed that is done to someone unjustly.[43] In this way, the narrator picks up on the thread of "true honor" already signaled in chapter 14, where reference was made to the mirrors on Sansón Carrasco's clothing and he was called the Knight of the Mirrors. The narrator signals toward a different motivation for the bachelor's pursuit of Don Quixote, as we begin to wonder whether Sansón believes his honor to be injured by our protagonist. The effect of threading the discourse of true honor and dueling throughout this comic conflict is to make strange not only the masculine honor code, but even the social status of the man of learning, who would seem to stand outside the culture of arms. Arms and letters are both estranged.

Throwing light on the transition from a medieval warrior nobility to a modern army, Cervantes also contrasts the ancient and noble weapon, the sword, with the modern and plebeian firearm. In chapter 19, which on the surface appears to be a merely transitional chapter, he satirizes the sword-fighting genre. Merich explored fully the intertextual references to Jerónimo Sánchez de Carranza's *Book of the Philosophy of Arms* (*Libro de filosofía de las armas*, 1582) in *Don Quixote de la Mancha II*, and found it to underlie the ridiculous exchange between the university graduate, who speaks for Carranza's geometrical theory, with the picaresque Corchuelo, who spitefully challenges the academic's scientific angles with his rough, but modern talent.[44] This discourse, known as *destreza de armas*, or talent in arms, threads through Don Quixote's intervention in chapter 27 between the two warring towns in the ass braying adventure and in chapter 32 when Don Quixote explains to the ecclesiastic in the ducal palace the difference between affronts (*afrentas*) and grievances (*agravios*), even leading into the Camacho wedding episode through the assonance of the names Corchuelo and Camacho, which alludes to Basilio's trickery through his use of the sword.[45] The discourses of true honor as well as that of talent in arms were aimed at nobles who sought to distinguish their masculinity, both in conduct and in weaponry, from that of the underclasses. Nonetheless, Cervantes deflates the ideal of the noble swordsman in chapter 24, when Don Quixote meets a poor boy on his way to war, singing: "I'm forced to go to the war / because I'm so poor; / if I had money, believe / me I wouldn't leave."[46] Don Quixote responds to the reality of a professional soldier's poverty and misery with a discourse that is not a pastiche of ideas from chivalric romance, but rather a mélange of phrases praising the death of the soldier, who having left the court, dies in battle. And thus the reader, Sancho and the poor soldier are reminded that there is nothing more honorable than serving God and the king, and that, along the discursive lines of the *arbitrios*, legislation is in the works by which old soldiers will not be allowed to starve. The soldier stands in contrast to the courtesan, and his honor withstands old age, wounds and poverty: "And remember, son, that that the soldier prefers the smell of gunpowder to the scent of musk, and if old age overtakes you in this honorable profession, even if you are full of wounds, and maimed and crippled, at least when it overtakes you, you will not be without honor, an honor that not even poverty can diminish."[47] And so Cervantes picks up the thread of the Don Quixote's *arbitrio* against courtesans and in favor now of old, impoverished soldiers.

As shown here, Viktor Shklovsky's concepts of threading and estrangement are useful interpretive tools not only when applied to narrative elements and literary motifs, but also to discursive and semantic units. They link and thread together seemingly disparate episodes and make apparent themes such as the codes of masculine behavior. Shklovsky himself noticed that Cervantes incorporated historic words and events in *Don Quixote* part II. When we resituate these words within their proper discourses, we can begin to appreciate their framing function; that is to say, they framed Cervantes's narrative fiction within historical problematics and allow us, four centuries later, to glimpse the larger political discourses framing his comic fiction within more serious debates.

NOTES

1. On the pseudo-adventures in part II, see Howard Mancing, *The Chivalric World of Don Quijote. Style, Structure, and Narrative Technique* (Columbia: University of Missouri Press, 1982), 168–169.

2. José Manuel Martín Moran, *Cervantes y el Quijote hacia la novela moderna* (Alcalá de Henares: Centro de Estudios Cervantinos, 2009), 209.

3. José Manuel Martín Moran, "Don Quijote está sanchificado: el des-sanchificado que lo re-quijotice," *Bulletin hispanique* 94:1 (1992): 106.

4. Viktor Shklovsky, *Theory of Prose*, Trans. Benjamin Sher (Elmwood Park, Illinois: Dalkey Archive Press, 1990): 68.

5. Pau Sanmartín Ortí, "Viktor Shklovski, lector del *Quijote*," *Dicenda: Cuaderno de Filología Hispánica* 25 (2007): 226.

6. Shklovsky, *Theory of Prose*, 73.

7. Shklovsky, *Theory of Prose*, 74.

8. Shklovsky, *Theory of Prose*, 69.

9. Shklovsky, *Theory of Prose*, 74.

10. Shklovsky, *Theory of Prose*, 76.

11. Shklovsky, *Theory of Prose*, 92, 94.

12. Shklovsky, *Theory of Prose*, 99.

13. Miguel de Cervantes, *Don Quixote. A New Translation by Edith Grossman* (New York: Harper Collins, 2003), 460. The Spanish reads: "Y en el discurso de su plática vinieron a tratar en esto que llaman razón de estado y modos de gobierno, enmendando este abuso y condenando aquél, reformando una costumbre y desterrando otra, haciéndose cada uno de los tres un nuevo legislador, un Licurgo moderno, o un Solón flamante; y de tal manera renovaron la república, que no pareció sino que la habían puesto en una fragua, y sacado otra de la que pusieron" (Miguel de Cervantes, *Don Quijote de la Mancha II*, Ed. John Jay Allen [Madrid: Cátedra, 2003], 30).

14. Cervantes makes visible the contradictions in the Spanish anti-Machiavellian "reason of state" treatises through highlighting Sancho's concern with his reputation as governor of Barataria (Keith David Howard, "Cervantes's *Don Quijote*, part II, and the Spanish Reason-of-State Tradition," *eHumanista* 31[2015]: 380–83.

15. Cervantes, *Don Quijote de la Mancha II*, 30–31.

16. Jean Vilar, *Literatura y economía. La figura satírica del arbitrista en el siglo de oro* (Madrid: Revista de Occidente, 1973), 69.

17. Cervantes, *Don Quijote de la Mancha II*, 31.

18. Anthony J. Cascardi, *Cervantes, Literature, and the Discourse of Politics* (Toronto: University of Toronto Press, 2012), 50.

19. Cervantes, *Don Quixote. A New Translation*, 491. The Spanish reads: "me escusara de responder a tanta infinidad de memoriales impertinentes como cada día le dan" (Cervantes, *Don Quijote de la Mancha II*, 67).

20. Sebastián de Covarrubias, *Tesoro de la lengua castellana o española* (Barcelona: Editorial Alta Fulla, 2003), 798.

21. For an analysis of Cervantes's incorporation of the this form of loan, called the *asiento*, into his characterization of Carrizales, the protagonist of "El celoso extremeño," see Brian Brewer, "Jealousy and Usury in 'El celoso extremeño,'" *Cervantes: Bulletin of the Cervantes Society of America* 33:1 (Spring 2013): 13–16.

22. Íñigo Ibáñez de Santa Cruz penned an infamous *memorial* in 1599 with the purpose of praising those who sought positions of power, such as the Conde de Miranda, the Duque de Nájera and the Duque de Medina de Sidonia, in the court of Felipe III. It vituperated Felipe II, labeling him an effeminate Flemish watchmaker (José Ignacio Fortea Pérez, "Entre dos servicios: la crisis de la Hacienda Real a finales del siglo XVI. Las alternativas fiscales de una opción política (1590–1601)," *Studia Historica: Historia Moderna* 17([1997]: 64–66).

23. Vilar, *Literatura y economía. La figura satírica del arbitrista en el siglo de oro*, 36–37. The original reads: "ay número grande de gentes que gastan su vida en la Corte en estas quimeras de pensar arbitrios, medios y novedades, . . . pareciendo que por ser plática de sacar dineros les es lícito andar sonando los medios y arbitrios."

24. Cervantes, *Don Quixote. A New Translation*, 492. The Spanish reads: "que el buen caballero andante, aunque vea diez gigantes que con las cabezas no sólo tocan, sino pasan las nubes, y que a cada uno le sirven de piernas dos grandísimas torres, y cada ojo como una gran rueda de molino y más ardiendo que un horno de vidrio, no le han de espantar en manera alguna" (Cervantes, *Don Quijote de la Mancha II*, 68).

25. Cervantes, *Don Quixote. A New Translation*, 508.

26. Cervantes, *Don Quixote. A New Translation*, 508. The original Spanish reads: "semejantes pláticas, sin acontecerles cosa que de contar fuese, de que no poco le pesó a don Quijote" (Cervantes, *Don Quijote de la Mancha II*, 87).

27. On Sancho's salary, see Carroll Johnson, *Cervantes and the Material World* (Urbana: University of Illinois Press, 2000), 15–36, and G. Cory Duclos, "A Squire's Schooling: The Education of Sancho Panza," *Confluencia: Revista Hispánica de Cultura y Literatura* 30:3 (Special Edition 2015): 78–79.

28. Maurice Molho, *Cervantes: Raíces folklóricas* (Madrid: Gredos,1976), 249–261.

29. Johnson, *Cervantes and the Material World*, 29–35.

30. Cervantes, *Don Quixote. A New Translation*, 500. The Spanish reads: "yo encargaría mucho mi conciencia si no intimase y persuadiese a este caballero que no tenga más tiempo encogida y detenida la fuerza de su valeroso brazo y la bondad de su ánimo valentísimo, porque defrauda con su tardanza el derecho de los tuertos, el amparo de los huérfanos, la honra de las doncellas, el favor de las viudas y el arrimo de las casadas, y otras cosas deste jaez, que tocan, atañen, dependen y son anejas a la orden de la caballería andante" (Cervantes, *Don Quijote de la Mancha II*, 78).

31. The proverbs in question, "quien destaja no baraja, más vale un toma que dos te daré," can be translated literally as: "he who cuts doesn't deal, it is better to take than that I give you two" (Cervantes, *Don Quijote de la Mancha II*, 76).

32. Rachel Schmidt, "La praxis y la parodia del discurso del *ars moriendi* en el *Quijote* de 1615," *Anales Cervantinos* 42 (January–December 2010): 125.

33. Real Academia Española, Banco de datos (CORDE) [en línea], *Corpus diacrónico del español*, http://www.rae.es.

34. Cervantes, *Don Quijote de la Mancha II*, 416.

35. Susan Byrne, *Law and History in Cervantes' Don Quixote* (Toronto: University of Toronto Press, 2012), 147.

36. For the English, see Cervantes, *Don Quixote. A New Translation*, 560–561. For the Spanish, see Cervantes, *Don Quijote de la Mancha II*, 147.

37. Cervantes, *Don Quixote. A New Translation*, 561. The Spanish reads: "—Señor caballero, los caballeros andantes han de acometer las aventuras que prometen esperanza de salir bien dellas, y no aquellas que en todo la quitan; porque la valentía que se entra en la jurisdicción de la temeridad, más tiene de locura que de fortaleza" (Cervantes, *Don Quijote de la Mancha II*, 147).

38. The Spanish reads: "en daño de vuestra honra, vida y alma que es lo peor" (Jerónimo Ximénez de Urrea, *Diálogo de la verdadera honra militar* [Zaragoza: Diego Dormer, 1642], 37v).

39. Cervantes, *Don Quixote. A New Translation*, 566. The Spanish reads: "conocí ser temeridad esorbitante, porque bien sé lo que es valentía, que es una virtud que está puesta entre dos estremos viciosos, como son la cobardía y la temeridad; pero menos mal será que el que es valiente toque y suba al punto de temerario que no que baje y toque en el punto de cobarde." (Cervantes, *Don Quijote de la Mancha II*, 154).

40. The Spanish reads: "Don Pedro de Herrera, dio de palos a Espejo: a Espejo le convino dezir, como don Pedro le avia injuriado malamente, y como traydor, Don Pedro le respondió que mentia, de manera, que Espejo injuriado, y cargado, quedó Actor, obligado a provar, como Don Pedro le dio de palos malamente, y como traydor." (Urrea, *Diálogo de la verdadera honra militar*, 50v).

41. Cervantes, *Don Quixote. A New Translation*, 543–544.

42. The Spanish reads: "-¡Oh, señor—dijo don Antonio-, Dios os perdone el agravio que habéis hecho a todo el mundo en querer volver cuerdo al más gracioso loco que hay en él!" (Cervantes, *Don Quijote de la Mancha II*, 522).

43. Covarrubias, *Tesoro de la lengua castellana*, 51.

44. Stefano de Merich, "La presencia del *Libro de la filosofía de las armas* de Carranza en el *Quijote* de 1615," *Cervantes. Bulletin of the Cervantes Society of America*. 27:2 (Fall 2007): 161.

45. Merich, "La presencia del *Libro de la filosofía de las armas* de Carranza en el *Quijote* de 1615," 167, 171, 166–167.

46. Cervantes, *Don Quixote. A New Translation*, 617. The Spanish reads: "A la guerra me lleva / mi necesidad; / si tuviera dineros, / no fuera, en verdad" (Cervantes, *Don Quijote de la Mancha II*, 211).

47. Cervantes, *Don Quixote. A New Translation*, 619. The Spanish reads: "Y advertid, hijo, que al soldado mejor le está el oler a pólvora que a algalia, y que si la vejez os coge en este honroso ejercicio, aunque sea lleno de heridas y estropeado o cojo, a lo menos no os podrá coger sin honra, y tal, que no os la podrá menoscabar la pobreza" (Cervantes, *Don Quijote de la Mancha II*, 213).

WORKS CITED

Brewer, Brian. "Jealousy and Usury in 'El celoso extremeño.'" *Cervantes: Bulletin of the Cervantes Society of America* 33:1 (Spring 2013): 11–43.

Byrne, Susan. *Law and History in Cervantes' Don Quixote*. Toronto: University of Toronto Press, 2012.

Cascardi, Anthony J. *Cervantes, Literature, and the Discourse of Politics*. Toronto: University of Toronto Press, 2012.

Cervantes, Miguel de. *Don Quijote de la Mancha II*. Ed. John Jay Allen. Madrid: Cátedra, 2003.

———. *Don Quixote. A New Translation by Edith Grossman*. New York: HarperCollins, 2003.

Covarrubias, Sebastián de. *Tesoro de la lengua castellana o española*. Barcelona: Editorial Alta Fulla, 2003.

Duclos, G. Cory. "A Squire's Schooling: The Education of Sancho Panza." *Confluencia: Revista Hispánica de Cultura y Literatura* 30:3 (Special Edition 2015): 69–85. Project Muse.

Fortea Pérez, José Ignacio. "Entre dos servicios: la crisis de la Hacienda Real a finales del siglo XVI. Las alternativas fiscales de una opción política (1590–1601)." *Studia Historica: Historia Moderna* 17(1997): 63–90. oaj.org/article/b18a150fc22946ecab8cb9bdac206bc8.

Howard, Keith David. "Cervantes's *Don Quijote*, part II, and the Spanish Reason-of-State Tradition." *eHumanista* 31(2015): 378–389. http://www.ehumanista.ucsb.edu/volumes/31.

Johnson, Carroll B. *Cervantes and the Material World*. Urbana: University of Illinois Press, 2000.

Mancing, Howard. *The Chivalric World of Don Quijote. Style, Structure, and Narrative Technique*. Columbia: University of Missouri Press, 1982.

Martín Moran, José Manuel. *Cervantes y el Quijote hacia la novela moderna*. Alcalá de Henares: Centro de Estudios Cervantinos, 2009.

———. "Don Quijote está sanchificado: el des-sanchificado que lo re-quijotice." *Bulletin hispanique* 94:1 (1992): 75–118.

Merich, Stefano de. "La presencia del *Libro de la filosofía de las armas* de Carranza en el *Quijote* de 1615." *Cervantes. Bulletin of the Cervantes Society of America*. 27:2 (Fall 2007): 155–180.

Molho, Maurice. *Cervantes: raíces folklóricas*. Madrid: Gredos, 1976.

Real Academia Española, Banco de datos (CORDE). *Corpus diacrónico del español*. http://www.rae.es.

Sanmartín Ortí, Pau. "Viktor Shklovski, lector del *Quijote*." *Dicenda: Cuaderno de Filología Hispánica* 25 (2007): 223–244.

Schmidt, Rachel. "La praxis y la parodia del discurso del *ars moriendi* en el *Quijote* de 1615." *Anales cervantinos* 42 (January–December 2010): 117–30.

Shklovsky, Viktor. *Theory of Prose*. Trans. Benjamin Sher. Elmwood Park, IL: Dalkey Archive Press, 1990.

Urrea, Jerónimo Ximénez de. *Diálogo de la verdadera honra militar, que trata cómo se ha de conformar la honra con la conciencia*. 4ª impresión añadida i enmendada. Zaragoza: Diego Dormer, 1642.

Chapter Ten

Shklovsky and World Literature

Grant Hamilton

In 1921, Viktor Shklovsky finished his essay on Laurence Sterne's novel *Tristram Shandy* (1759–1767) with what has become one of the most infamous lines in literary criticism: "*Tristram Shandy* is the most typical novel in world literature."[1] To those unaware of the context in which Shklovsky was writing, it has always seemed a rather curious way to conclude the essay given that it is the first time that the idea of world literature is mentioned. But, for those alive to the fact that Shklovsky was enthralled by, and lecturing at, the translation studio of Maxim Gorky's World Literature Publishing House alongside such luminaries as Konstantin Batyushkov, Alexander Blok, Akim Volynsky, Nikolay Gumilev, Yevgeny Zamyatin, and Boris Eikhenbaum,[2] the statement seems anything but odd. The intellectual climate of Russia in the early 1920s, the period in which the young Shklovsky was finding his critical voice, was one of cultural pluralism and with it, internationalism. For a few precious years, literature was considered "the heart of the world" by both Russia's intelligentsia and politicians,[3] and world literature therefore the means by which a "national one-sidedness and narrow mindedness" could be ended.[4] Understood like this, world literature was positioned as nothing less than "the quintessential literature of modern times,"[5] that which Gorky believed would allow "the Russian people in all its masses ... to know the peculiarities of history, sociology, and psychology of those nations and tribes, with which it aspires to build new forms of social life."[6] And so, when Shklovsky proclaims Sterne's novel the most typical novel in world literature, it is to endorse it as a seminal text among the swirling mass of literature that Gorky and his team were bringing to Saint Petersburg.

For Shklovsky, what makes Sterne's novel such an important text of world literature is that it is the most true-to-type of any literary text. That is to say, it is the most "plotted" and least "storied" of any major novel. Shklovsky spent a life-time explaining that the literary narrative "relies on [a] tension between forward movement and complicating structures"[7] that is not present in the discourse of the everyday. It is, Shklovsky argues, precisely those moments in the literary text that give the reader pause for thought (those "complicating structures") that renders a text "literary." For Shklovsky, such moments belong to the plot (*syuzhet*) of a novel rather than its story (*fabula*), and so if one is to understand the landscape of literature proper one had to understand the form and function of the "plotedness" of a text. As Lee Lemon and Marion Reis explain in their landmark introduction of Russian formalist criticism to the Western world, if the *fabula* can be thought of as "the temporal-causal sequence of narrated events" in the mode of "because of A, then B," then "plot becomes the story as distorted or defamiliarized in the process of telling."[8] Adding a touch more definition to this sense of things, Shklovsky writes,

> Plot is not the incident taking place in a short story or a novel. It is a construction which, through manipulation of events, characters, landscapes, and compression, magnification, or rearrangement of time, creates a certain sensibility, graspable and felt in the way that was intended by the work's author.[9]

Plot, then, is the hallmark of literature (rather than other kinds of discourse), for plot is the means by which the author interferes with the natural (chronological) order of a story and forces the reader to notice things that might otherwise be lost to a haze of the familiar. Indeed, to read literature in terms of the way in which it particularizes the everyday so that it renders the familiar "strange" is arguably Shklovsky's most important contribution to literary criticism. An idea developed in what is perhaps his most widely read essay—the title of which has been translated variously as "Art as Device" and "Art as Technique" (1917)—*ostranenie*, or "defamiliarization," concerns the capacity of literature to combat the habitual way in which one commonly sees and thinks the world. Shklovsky argues that ours is usually (and therefore typically) an automatized passage through life. We are creatures of habit whose behaviors often "retreat into the area of the unconsciously automatic."[10] Such unthinking repetition leads to an habitualization that "devours works, clothes, furniture, one's wife, and the fear of war,"[11] for habit always puts pay to our continuing interest in things. Indeed, if "Art exists," Shklovsky asserts, it is so "that one may recover the sensation of life; it exists to make one feel things, to make the stone *stony*." He continues,

> The purpose of art is to impart the sensation of things as they are perceived and not as they are known. The technique of art is to make objects "unfamiliar," to make forms difficult, to increase the difficulty and length of perception because the process of perception is an aesthetic end in itself and must be pro-

longed. *Art is a way of experiencing the artfulness of an object: the object is not important.*[12]

In other words, the significance of literature is that it has the capacity to interrupt one's interpretative faculty; it has the capacity to interrupt the way in which one regards something and therefore disturb the engine by which perception races toward cognition. For the haze of habit to be broken, for the reader to become aware again of the difference between "holding a pen or speaking a foreign language for the first time [and] performing the action for the ten thousandth time,"[13] the world must be rendered unusual or unfamiliar so that one must pause in order to consciously reflect on what is being said. Indeed, it is precisely in this pause instructed by the process of conscious reflection that Shklovsky says the reader begins to experience the world anew.

However, in the domain of world literature, the quality of defamiliarization that attends the experience of reading (good) literature is not so much a matter of writerly technique as it is a constitutive feature of the literature itself. That is to say, in its escape from the binds of national literature across cultural and linguistic borders, world literature can do no other than present as a literature of defamiliarization,[14] a literature of pause, a literature that requires slow and patient engagement.[15] To all intents and purposes, the very idea of world literature as a body of writing exists in acknowledgement of a stable of literature that inevitably wrenches one away from the familiar and thrusts one into a world of the odd, the strange, or the uncanny. Given this, it is perhaps unsurprising that the work of Shklovsky continues to be influential in contemporary debates in world literature. Yet, it would be wrong to think that such influence arises solely from the continuing relevance of such concepts as estrangement and automatization to the labor of critique. As this chapter demonstrates, much Shklovskian thought is central to one of the major ways in which world literature is theorized and practiced today.

That said, it is perhaps worth beginning by making clear the continuing relevance of *ostranenie* to discussions of world literature. In his important survey of the discipline, Mads Rosendahl Thomsen asserts that "the concept of 'defamiliarization' . . . is still an important implicit or explicit aspect of definitions of literary technique and experience."[16] The reason for this is that "strangeness" marks the writing of the Other, and that engagement with such strangeness seems to allow one to gain access "to new and different layers— of the mind, of the world or of different experiences of reality."[17] Thought like this—as gateway to other ways of thinking and being in the world— "strangeness" continues to be positively figured in literary criticism, especially in that which is brought to bear on world literature. Indeed, when Vilashini Cooppan was re-introducing the notion of world literature to the American classroom at the tail-end of the 1990s in response to the increased interest in the field, uppermost in her mind was developing a strategy of reading and teaching world literature that did not swallow the strangeness of such a literature by unthinkingly concentrating on only what was similar to disparate literatures. She called it "globalized reading" and thought of it not as an "attempt to create an alternative canon so much as to change the prevalent positioning of the canonical and the non-canonical as one another's opposites, with the election of the one appearing to dictate the disappearance of the other."[18] Later in the same essay Cooppan writes,

> the new pedagogy I am sketching is not just a question of recognizing the modern emergence of a transnational, transregional global literature. We must also learn to read older works and older categories of belonging (culture, language, region, nation) in global ways. The "terrains of world literature" are indeed, as Homi K. Bhabha writes, now less those of national traditions than of the colonized, the migrants, the refugees—human products of the changing world-system.[19]

It is a realization that recalls the tenor of the spirit in which Shklovsky and those around him engaged with Gorky's World Literature Publishing House—of recognizing the importance of offering an international vision of worker solidarity in the age of globalization; a vision of the proletariat sublimated from parochial (regional and national) identifications through the pursuit of the broader intellectual territories revealed by events of world-historical import.[20]

Nonetheless, Cooppan's idea of globalized reading was a neat reconciliation of the two dominant but opposing directions in which critics were attempting to "do" world literature. On the one hand was the methodological imperative of close reading associated with David Damrosch's call to unveil the phenomenology (rather than ontology) of world literature.[21] On the other, and the direction in which Cooppan's ideas seemed to be moving toward, was Franco Moretti's contentious call for a "distant reading"[22]—a method for understanding literature not by interrogating particular texts but by gathering together and analyzing massive amounts of data. Indeed, Moretti called for "a maximum of methodological boldness"[23] in an attempt to get to grips with what he says is the 99.5 percent of published novels in the world that remain, to all intents and purposes, unread.[24] On the understanding that the sheer volume of material that any critique of "world literature" (at least, any critique worthy of the name) must address is prohibitively large, Moretti argues that the literary critic must rethink *how* to study literature.[25] Close reading, he claims, simply cannot help those who wish to interrogate world literature because, "at bottom, it's a theological exercise" that concerns the "very solemn treatment of very few texts taken very seriously."[26] Indeed, close reading has always depended on an extremely small canon, and so to do justice to the number and diversity of that which seems to gather under the umbrella of the term "world literature," Moretti suggests that the critic might just have to make "a little pact with the devil."[27] "We know how to read texts," he asserts,

> now let's learn how *not* to read them. Distant reading: where distance, let me repeat it, *is a condition of knowledge*: it allows you to focus on units that are much smaller or much larger than the text: devices, themes, tropes—or genres and systems. And if, between the very small and the very large, the text itself disappears, well, it is one of those cases when one can justifiably say, Less is more.[28]

The justification for such a controversial proposition arrives via Max Weber's observation that "concepts are primarily analytical instruments for the intellectual mastery of empirical data and can be only that"[29]—or, as Moretti puts it, "reality is infinitely rich; concepts are abstract, are poor. But it's precisely this 'poverty' that makes it possible to handle them, and therefore to know."[30] And so, what Moretti proposes is to double-down on conceptualizing literature by turning to a purely quantitative approach to literary criticism. To this end, Moretti's distant reading is a literary criticism composed of graphs, maps, and trees: "graphs" which capture raw numerical data and as such have the potential to falsify existing theoretical explanations of literary trends;[31] "maps" which can disclose patterns obfuscated by the very text(s) from which they emerge;[32] and, (diagrammatic) "trees" which allow one to sketch how far one literature "has moved from another one, or from their common point of origin."[33] The effect of Moretti's distant reading, then, is to make one take a step back from the singular literary text in an attempt to answer grand questions around the nature of literary evolution, the form(s) of literature, and its universal traits.

It is here that one begins to hear the influence of Shklovsky on Moretti's way of thinking about world literature. Talk of literary inheritances, the form of literary narrative, and the universal traits of texts immediately recalls the work of Shklovsky—as it did for Moretti. In fact, over time Moretti came to think and describe his own work as an extension of that carried out by Shklovsky and his contemporaries. In a recent book that Jessica Merrill quite rightly thinks of as an intellectual biography of the notion of distant reading,[34] Moretti refers to Shklovsky as "the critical genius of the age"[35] before reflecting on how his own critical practice is informed by a "formal analysis [that] is the great accomplishment of literary study, and is therefore also what any new approach—quantitative, digital, evolutionary, whatever—must prove itself against."[36] Indeed, the distant reading that Jonathan Arac would later describe as a "formalism without close reading"[37] was a reading process that had the capacity to identify a discrete formal trait in a text and then follow the way in which it changed shape and dimension as it passed through a series of other texts. Nowhere is this strategy more clearly employed than in Moretti's essay "The Slaughterhouse of Literature" (2000), an essay in which Moretti traces the device of "the clue" in detective fiction in an attempt to show that authorial choices of form could be responsible for why some texts continue to be read (canonized) while others are lost to time.

As Moretti acknowledges, Shklovsky had also interrogated the clue in the work of Sherlock Holmes in his seminal work *Theory of Prose* (1925). But where Shklovsky had used it as yet another means of evidencing the claim that the plotted narrative was the hallmark of the literary work (and what better way to demonstrate that than by highlighting the fact that clues in detective fiction must be carefully distributed through a narrative?), Moretti attempted to use the device of the clue as a means of connecting formal analysis to literary history. Why is it Conan Doyle, "him, and not others,"[38] Moretti asks, that the market chooses when they read detective fiction? "Here the economic model has a blind spot . . . It's there, it has to be *there*, or the market wouldn't behave as it does."[39] Moretti's answer is that "what makes readers 'like' this or that book is—form."[40] The hypothesis that emerges from this is that it is the formal choices which an author makes that holds the potential for one text to eradicate its competitors. Yet, while Moretti is honest enough to note that the link between form and (cultural) survivability is at best the grounds for a hypothesis rather than the demonstration of a causal relation,[41] from this point forwards the critic of world literature can no longer in good faith ignore questions of narrative form when examining or proposing (revised) literary histories.

In an attempt to accommodate such questions in his discussion of the evolution of world literature, Moretti abandons the commonly held assumption in literary studies that one generation of writers simply borrows or rejects ideas from those who immediately precede them in favor of an explanatory model drawn from evolutionary theory. What emerges is a picture of literary history that resembles something like a large bush. As Moretti writes, like those of a bush, the branches of literature "coexist and bifurcate . . . overlap and at times obstruct each other—but that, whenever one of them withers away, [the bush is] ready to replace it with an ever thicker and stronger organism."[42] It is a non-linear, discontinuous sense of things that is inherited from Shklovsky's own assertion that "it is not sons who inherit from their fathers, but nephews who inherit from their uncles."[43] In his essay "Literature Beyond 'Plot'" (1921), Shklovsky explains,

> If we line up, say, all the literary saints canonized in Russia between the seventeenth and twentieth century, we won't see a line allowing us to study the history of developing literary forms . . . Nekrasov obviously does not follow Pushkin's tradition. In prose, Tolstoy doesn't descend from Turgenev or Gogol, and Chekhov doesn't come from Tolstoy.[44]

Shklovsky's point here is two-fold. In addition to a certain anxiety of influence that operates on the contemporary writer (an issue explored some 50 years later by Harold Bloom) which acts like a gag to certain modes of expression,[45] it is clear that writers borrow from across adjacent textual forms rather than those in which they sit—"poetry from prose, for instance, or prose from journalism."[46] The charge Moretti sets for himself when thinking world literature is to develop a methodology by which one can trace this incomplete spiraling evolution of literature—a methodology that would allow one to capture the complex evolutionary patterns of a world of literature.

First is to make clear that Shklovsky was right: that plot is the fundamental unit of literary analysis and therefore fundamental to the study of world literature. As Moretti explains in his seminal essay "Conjectures on World Literature" (2000), the typical story told of the rise of the novel form around the world is one of unease. This is because, as Fredric Jameson (and others) had noted, there seemed to be an intrinsic awkwardness between a non-Western reality and its representation through the abstract formal patterns of the Western novel.[47] However, what Jameson read as an antagonism between the dyad of form and content was for Moretti more of an uneasy relationship between three sites: "foreign form, local material—*and local form*" or, put another way, "foreign *plot*; local *characters*; and then, local *narrative voice*."[48] As Moretti continues, it is in fact this third element, the element of the local narrative voice, that makes such novels unstable because it is comment itself that becomes uneasy when the demands of a foreign form makes characters behave in strange ways. Here again the idea of world literature as a literature of estrangement, but this time a literature that is strange even to itself—a literature of cracks and faultiness that run "between story and discourse, world and worldview"[49] that emerges from a "foreignness" that is a complex feature of the text and which necessarily interferes with the very *utterance* of the novel.[50] Understood like this, it is the persistence of the plot that unsettles all, for it is the plot that reveals the unequal dimensions of the circuits of world literature operating *within* the novel form.

Second is to propose a method for the quantitative analysis of plot—something which Moretti outlines explicitly in his essay "Network Theory, Plot Analysis" (2011). Drawing on network theory as that which studies connections within large groups of objects, Moretti creates "models" of literary texts through a process of reduction and abstraction that, he argues, consequently allows one to see "the underlying structures of a complex object."[51] The influence of Shklovsky on Moretti's thinking is palpable here. As Jessica Merrill writes, "Shklovsky's approach is reductionist: his *Theory of Prose* begins with the riddle as his simplest example of narrative and then builds up to fairy tales, novellas, collections of stories (e.g., *The Arabian Nights*), concluding with the novel and modernism."[52] Figured like this, Moretti's reductionism is not quite as naïve as some have supposed it to be.[53]

Indeed, it should not be confused with a trajectory toward the parochial or the pedantic. In fact, precisely the opposite is true. For Moretti, as well as for Shklovsky, such reductionism is the necessary first step in being able to identify universal principles of literature that could, in time, offer a full theory of world literature.

Through the provocative and influential work of Franco Moretti then, the legacy of Shklovsky's work is likely to be felt in the field of world literature for many more decades to come. However, it would be remiss of me to leave one with the impression that it is only through the work of Moretti that Shklovsky's voice is heard in discussion of world literature. Indeed, Shklovsky's work is something like a transcendental force in the field—it is everywhere, even (especially) in its unacknowledged quarters. Those like Dionýz Ďurišin and Itamar Even-Zohar who have worked in one way or another on the literary systems that seem increasingly important to thinking world literature have acknowledged their intellectual debt to Shklovsky and Russian Formalism more generally. But there are a great many more who do not even realize that there is a debt to pay. Perhaps this absent-minded affront to the legacy of Shklovsky will be righted when the digital humanities fully territorializes the terrain of traditional literary and cultural studies, for one will no longer be able to ignore the intimate relationship between the two and the shared desire for a science of literary criticism that is characterized by the production of "a falsifiable criticism."[54] In April 2015, the Stanford Humanities Centre organized an international symposium titled *Russian Formalism and the Digital Humanities*. Reporting on the event, Andrei Ustinov writes that those gathered—including Franco Moretti, Jessica Merrill, Matthew Jockers, Galin Tihanov, and Ilya Kliger—explored the lasting significance of Shklovsky and his contemporaries to an Anglo-American literary theory that is currently unable "to handle the numbers and calculations"[55] necessary to a critique of world literature. With the digital humanities perceived as "a continuation of, rather than return to, the theoretical legacy of the Formalists: Viktor Shklovsky, Yury Tynyanov, Boris Eikhenbaum, Roman Jakobson, Boris Tomashevsky,"[56] the voice of Shklovsky is surely destined to do more than whisper in the ear of those who write on world literature.

NOTES

1. Viktor Shklovsky, "Sterne's *Tristram Shandy*: Stylistic Commentary," in *Russian Formalist Criticism: Four Essays*, ed. and trans. Lee T. Lemon and Marion J. Reis (Lincoln: University of Nebraska Press, 1965), 57.

2. See Maria Khotimsky, "World Literature, Soviet Style: A Forgotten Episode in the History of the Idea," *Ab Imperio* 3 (2013): 149.

3. The phrase is Maxim Gorky's. See Khotimsky, "World Literature, Soviet Style," 120.

4. Such was the claim of Marx and Engels. See Karl Marx and Friedrich Engels, *The Communist Manifesto*, trans. Samuel Moore (London: Penguin, 2002). The full passage to

which I refer here reads: "In place of the old local and national seclusion and self-sufficiency, we have intercourse in every direction, universal inter-dependence of nations . . . National one-sidedness and narrow-mindedness become more and more impossible, and from the numerous national and local literatures, there arises a world literature" (223–24).

5. David Damrosch, *What Is World Literature?* (Princeton: Princeton University Press, 2003), 4.

6. See Khotimsky, "World Literature, Soviet Style," 120.

7. Jessica Merrill, "Distant Reading in Russia: Franco Moretti and the Formalist Tradition," *Eurozine*, 2 May 2018, https://www.eurozine.com/distant-reading-russia-franco-moretti-formalist-tradition/.

8. Lee Lemon and Marion Reis, "Introductory note to Viktor Shklovsky's 'Sterne's *Tristram Shandy*: Stylistic Commentary,'" in *Russian Formalist Criticism: Four Essays*, ed. and trans. Lee T. Lemon and Marion J. Reis (Lincoln: University of Nebraska Press, 1965), 25.

9. Viktor Shklovsky, *Bowstring: On the Dissimilarity of the Similar*, trans. Shushan Avagyan (London: Dalkey Archive Press, 2011), 95.

10. Viktor Shklovsky, "Art as Technique," in *Russian Formalist Criticism: Four Essays*, ed. and trans. Lee T. Lemon and Marion J. Reis (Lincoln: University of Nebraska Press, 1965), 11.

11. Shklovsky, "Art as Technique," 12.

12. Shklovsky, "Art as Technique," 12.

13. Shklovsky, "Art as Technique," 11.

14. Grant Hamilton, "Defamiliarization and the Act of Reading World Literature," in *Deleuze and the Humanities: East and West*, eds. Rosi Braidotti, Kin Yuen Wong, and Amy K.S. Chan (London: Rowman & Littlefield International, 2018), 15.

15. On the notion of "patient reading" see Gayatri Chakravorty Spivak, *Other Asias* (Oxford: Blackwell, 2008), 23.

16. Mads Rosendahl Thomsen, *Mapping World Literature: International Canonization and Transnational Literatures* (London: Continuum, 2008), 99.

17. Thomsen, *Mapping World Literature*, 99.

18. Vilashini Cooppan, "World Literature and Global Theory: Comparative Literature for the New Millennium," *Symploke* 9. 1–2 (2001): 32.

19. Cooppan, "World Literature and Global Theory," 32–33.

20. The language may have been more formal and duty-bound than Gorky's, but even Anatoly Lunacharsky's introduction to the journal *Vestnik inostrannoi literatury* captured this sense of things. He writes, "The Union of Soviet Republics is a unique country . . . However, it does not exist on a continent that is removed from the rest of the world, and neither does it desire to be fenced off from the rest of the world. Conversely, the Union is very interested in participating in the life of the entire world and shaping the life of the world in accordance with the governmental and societal principles that are at the basis of the Union." See Khotimsky, "World Literature, Soviet Style," 125.

21. Damrosch, *What Is World Literature?*, 6.

22. Franco Moretti, "Conjectures on World Literature," *New Left Review* 1 (Jan–Feb 2000): 56.

23. Franco Moretti, "The Slaughterhouse of Literature," *Modern Language Quarterly* 61. 1 (2000): 227.

24. Moretti, "The Slaughterhouse of Literature," 217.

25. Moretti, "Conjectures on World Literature," 54–55.

26. Moretti, "Conjectures on World Literature," 57.

27. Moretti, "Conjectures on World Literature," 57.

28. Moretti, "Conjectures on World Literature," 57.

29. Max Weber, *Methodology of Social Sciences*, ed. and trans. Edward A. Shills and Henry A. Finch (London: Routledge, 2011), 106.

30. Moretti, "Conjectures on World Literature," 57–58.

31. Franco Moretti, *Graphs, Maps, Trees: Abstract Models for Literary History* (London: Verso, 2005), 30.

32. Moretti, *Graphs, Maps, Trees*, 53–54.

33. Moretti, *Graphs, Maps, Trees*, 70.

34. Merrill, "Distant Reading in Russia."
35. Franco Moretti, *Distant Reading* (London: Verso, 2013), 31.
36. Moretti, *Distant Reading*, 204.
37. Jonathan Arac, "Anglo-Globalism?," *New Left Review* 16 (July–August 2002): 38.
38. Moretti, "The Slaughterhouse of Literature," 211.
39. Moretti, "The Slaughterhouse of Literature," 211.
40. Moretti, "The Slaughterhouse of Literature," 211.
41. Moretti, *Distant Reading*, 137–38.
42. Moretti, *Distant Reading*, 18.
43. Alexandra Berlina (ed. and trans.), *Viktor Shklovsky: A Reader* (London: Bloomsbury, 2016), 98.
44. Berlina, *Viktor Shklovsky*, 97.
45. Berlina, *Viktor Shklovsky*, 61–62.
46. Berlina, *Viktor Shklovsky*, 28.
47. See Fredric Jameson, "Foreword: In the Mirror of Alternate Modernities," in *Origins of Modern Japanese Literature* by Karatani Kojin (Durham: Duke University Press, 1993).
48. Moretti, "Conjectures on World Literature," 65.
49. Moretti, "Conjectures on World Literature," 65.
50. Moretti, "Conjectures on World Literature," 66.
51. Franco Moretti, "Network Theory, Plot Analysis," *New Left Review* 68 (Mar–Apr 2011): 84.
52. Merrill, "Distant Reading in Russia."
53. See, for example, Lauren M. E. Goodlad and Andrew Sartori, "The Ends of history: Introduction," *Victorian Studies* 55. 4 (2013): 591–614.
54. Franco Moretti, *Signs Taken for Wonders: On the Sociology of Literary Forms* (London: Verso, 1983), 23.
55. Andrei Ustinov, "The Legacy of Russian Formalism and the Rise of Digital Humanities," *Weiner Slavistiches Jahrbuch* 4 (2016): 288.
56. Ustinov, "The Legacy of Russian Formalism and the Rise of Digital Humanities," 287.

WORKS CITED

Arac, Jonathan. "Anglo-Globalism?" *New Left Review*, 16 (Jul–Aug 2002): 35–45.
Berlina, Alexandra (ed. and trans.). *Viktor Shklovsky: A Reader*. London: Bloomsbury, 2016.
Cooppan, Vilashini. "World Literature and Global Theory: Comparative Literature for the New Millennium." *Symploke*, 9. 1–2 (2001): 15–43.
Damrosch, David. *What Is World Literature?* Princeton: Princeton University Press, 2003.
Goodlad, Lauren M. E. and Andrew Sartori. "The Ends of History: Introduction." *Victorian Studies*, 55. 4 (2013): 591–614.
Hamilton, Grant. "Defamiliarization and the Act of Reading World Literature." In *Deleuze and the Humanities: East and West*, edited by Rosi Braidotti, Kin Yuen Wong, and Amy K.S. Chan, 11–26. London: Rowman & Littlefield International, 2018.
Jameson, Fredric. "Foreword: In the Mirror of Alternate Modernities." In *Origins of Modern Japanese Literature* by Karatani Kojin. Durham: Duke University Press, 1993.
Khotimsky, Maria. "World Literature, Soviet Style: A Forgotten Episode in the History of the Idea." *Ab Imperio*, 3 (2013): 119–154.
Marx, Karl and Friedrich Engels. *The Communist Manifesto*. Translated by Samuel Moore. London: Penguin, 2002.
Merrill, Jessica. "Distant Reading in Russia: Franco Moretti and the Formalist Tradition." *Eurozine*. May 2, 2018. https://www.eurozine.com/distant-reading-russia-franco-moretti-formalist-tradition/.
Moretti, Franco. *Distant Reading*. London: Verso, 2013.
———. "Network Theory, Plot Analysis." *New Left Review*, 68 (Mar–Apr 2011): 80–102.
———. *Graphs, Maps, Trees: Abstract Models for Literary History*. London: Verso, 2005.

———. "The Slaughterhouse of Literature." *Modern Language Quarterly*, 61. 1 (2000): 207–227.

———. "Conjectures on World Literature." *New Left Review*, 1 (Jan–Feb 2000): 54–68.

———. *Signs Taken for Wonders: On the Sociology of Literary Forms*. London: Verso, 1983.

Shklovsky, Viktor. *Bowstring: On the Dissimilarity of the Similar*. Translated by Shushan Avagyan. London: Dalkey Archive Press, 2011.

———. *Third Factory*. Translated by Richard Sheldon. London: Dalkey Archive Press, 2002.

———. *Theory of Prose*. Translated by Benjamin Sher. London: Dalkey Archive Press, 1990.

———. "Art as Technique." In *Russian Formalist Criticism: Four Essays*, edited and translated by Lee T. Lemon and Marion J. Reis, 3–24. Lincoln: University of Nebraska Press, 1965.

———. "Sterne's *Tristram Shandy*: Stylistic Commentary." In *Russian Formalist Criticism: Four Essays*, edited and translated by Lee T. Lemon and Marion J. Reis, 25–57. Lincoln: University of Nebraska Press, 1965.

Spivak, Gayatri Chakravorty. *Other Asias*. Oxford: Blackwell, 2008.

Thomsen, Mads Rosendahl. *Mapping World Literature: International Canonization and Transnational Literatures*. London: Continuum, 2008.

Ustinov, Andrei. "The Legacy of Russian Formalism and the Rise of Digital Humanities." *Weiner Slavistiches Jahrbuch*, 4 (2016): 287–289.

Weber, Max. *Methodology of Social Sciences*, edited and translated by Edward A. Shills and Henry A. Finch. London: Routledge, 2011.

Chapter Eleven

Racism and Robots

Defamiliarizing Social Justice in Rosa Montero's Tears in the Rain *and the Twenty-First Century*

Steven Mills

Literary scholars employ theory and philosophy to interpret and apply literature to life as they examine past and contemporary societies. One school of scholars, Russian theorists, deeply study forms in texts to understand their impact on the reader rather than examining the author, her history, or her story as a part of the text. Viktor Shklovsky, who was part of the Russian formalists, studied defamiliarization, one aspect of artistic form and structure. Defamiliarization is a device that reconnects people with aspects of daily life that have become invisible or unnoteworthy through their constancy (e.g., conversations with family, social conventions of public behavior, and physical surroundings). A writer, using the method of defamiliarization, reproduces elements of daily life in such a way that the reader perceives these elements as unfamiliar, novel, or unexpected: as if seeing it for the first time. This process to discuss defamiliarization—one of Shklovsky's best-known tools of art—began as a method to reconnect observers with life through art. In the twenty-first century, defamiliarization as a device can connect people with their life and society when their interactions have become automated. Bruce Stone claims that for Shklovsky, instead of destroying the sense of life, this recasting to discuss normalcy ultimately renews the viewer's sense of life: "by unhinging our habits of cognition, literature refreshes human perception, renews the experience of being alive."[1] Shklovsky saw that literature and art can deeply move a reader away from a highly automated existence and restore her sense of connectedness to life.

In modern-day society, Shklovsky's theories have stretched beyond the arts and have pushed society to face social issues such as racism and prejudice that, while damaging to its people, also become automatized. For example, psychologists suggest that people fail to recognize their own racism or racist tendencies because they see it as something that society has solved. Psychologists claim that racism has become familiar, automatic, or unseen, and people do not see that they are racist or harbor racist tendencies that, while hidden to their view, loom behind personal and social perspectives and actions. Psychologists' discussion of racism builds on Shklovsky's ideas of defamiliarization in that they argue that to battle what we do not recognize, we must awaken people to what they cannot see. They therefore apply Shklovsky's ideas beyond art and into social arenas in order to raise awareness of racism.

Rosa Montero bridges Shklovsky and psychology as she defamiliarizes humans and racism in her novel *Tears in the Rain*.[2] Robots, humans, aliens, and technologically altered humans all vie for dominance in this science fiction society while they claim supremacy and label other groups as inferior. Montero uses the robots to make humans and their prejudices strange and thereby highlights questions of racism in the reader's society, which turns her gaze to real-world social issues that she otherwise might overlook. Thus, Shklovsky's legacy begins with his project to open literature and examine the structures, the systems, and the tropes behind literature and people's perspective of the world. What Shklovsky introduced as an artistic instrument has evolved into a means of social change, and people of various disciplines look to defamiliarization to restore life to what had become an automatized, partial experience.

SHKLOVSKY VS. FORM

Viktor Shklovsky, recognized as "the father of Russian Formalism,"[3] theorized that the form of poetic language affects the observer independent of a work's content. Consequently, many have argued that for Shklovsky, artfulness depends more on the form and less on the content. According to Sherwood, Shklovsky argued that poetic language is a system "orientated towards a specific function,"[4] and he "altogether denied the influence of life on art, or that he believed that material for art did not originate from non-art sources."[5] Shklovsky saw a distinction, a separation, between art and life, decipherable through its forms within a system. Likewise, Gerald Bruns explains that Shklovsky intended "to foreground the individual text in its formal intelligibility rather than to reconstruct what lies behind the text in the form of an originating expression or rule."[6] If Shklovsky looked to the text to explain the effect and value of art, any connection between art and the viewer's context and history is secondary. Shklovsky and Russian Formalists reduced the world "conceptually, to grasp and contain it within an order of general laws and technological systems, finally to intervene in its operations and to turn it to productive account. To make sense of the world, we must penetrate its incoherent surface and lay bare its deep structures; we must grasp not its hidden meanings but its inner workings."[7] The artist takes the world and exploits the codes that give meaning, which can lead scholars to strip Formalism of any objective aside from exposing forms. Thus, Shklovsky's legacy begins with his project to open literature and examine the structures, the systems, and the tropes behind literature and people's perspective of the world.

However, Shklovsky reaches beyond form and explains that art and poetic language force the reader to see what had become normal and unnoticed. Consequently, she can reconnect with sensation in life lost to automatization. His best-known theory, that of defamiliarization (*ostranenie*), argues that everyday objects, such as a door or a dog, go unnoticed because their mundaneness have made them habitual. Shklovsky argues that as an observer's surroundings become automatic, she loses the richness of life she could enjoy were she to connect completely with her context. As an object or a routine becomes automatic, "all our skills retreat into the unconscious automatic domain."[8] This automatization destroys sensation because without experiencing key elements of life, existence tends toward monotony: "A thing passes us as if packaged; we know of its existence by the space it takes up, but we only see its surface. Perceived in this way, the thing dries up. . . . This is how life becomes nothing and disappears."[9] While the observer can still exist without seeing her commonplace surroundings, this is a cheapened, incomplete existence.

Montero's protagonist, Bruna Husky, witnesses this disconnect in her story world as she observes those who have lost touch with their social and physical surroundings. At one point, she sees others who suffer from total automatization (rather than an automatized environment) through a drug-induced inability to see and connect with their surroundings. The addicts were "passed out, or maybe they were even dead—junkies with their brains fried by drugs."[10] Shortly thereafter, someone focused on getting drugs did not see her and unwittingly bumped into her, to which she nearly reacted with fatal self-defense instincts.[11] The drugs had the same effect as automatization: the consumers failed to notice key elements of their reality such as other people or threats in the vicinity. Their actions were automatized toward getting what they desired and ignoring the subtleties around them. Robinson explains that for Shklovsky, habit is like this drug and forces us to function through automatization, because society suffers from "depersonalization—[a] loss of shared sensation or feeling, [a] breakdown of ideosomatic regulation."[12] Like the druggies in Montero's novels, those who live a daily fixed pattern in life fail to see, to recognize, life and their world. For Shklovsky, "the social world and the aesthetic world have lost the sensation of life (or, to extrapolate a little, that *we* have lost our sensation of life in our experiences of other people and of artworks)."[13] The problem is losing life through normalcy, and Shklovsky observes its effects for a good reason: everyone suffers from this tendency.

Current research in perception and cognition illustrates that we understand and connect with our world by relegating the common to the background, and we notice the new or strange because it is in the foreground. Our brain merges actual perception with expected perception and fills in the gaps between the two to form a model and an understanding of the surrounding world.[14] When the perceived world is consistent with what the brain expects to see, the mind moves on and ignores the rest. Reality is a construct of relevance and cerebral guesses because we do not notice what our brain expects to see. Consequently, we are not fully grasping our reality; much of it is guesswork. Familiarization is the enemy to the rich, lived experiences of engaging our entire context, which is why Shklovsky points to defamiliarization to reconnect people with their world and provide them the ability to restore awareness to life.

SHKLOVSKY VS. SENSATION IN LIFE

Defamiliarization restores vision to the observer along with the sense of sensation that was lost as the world had faded into automatization. An author paints the commonplace door or dog but with a new perspective that makes the object appear strange and forces the reader to notice, or perceive, the object rather than take it for granted.[15] Benjamin Sher explains that Shklovsky's "'seeing' is an active, dynamic act of perception brought into play by the artist's technique which allows us to see what, until then, had not and could not yet come into view."[16] Furthermore, the objective behind defamiliarization goes beyond seeing to reconnecting: "art exists in order to give back the sensation of life, in order to make us feel things, in order to make the stone stony," in order to make people see and not merely recognize.[17] A reader reconnects with life because reading becomes a perceptual experience: art as device estranges and complicates form, which invaluably enhances the duration and complexity of perception given that "the process of perception is its own end in art and must be prolonged."[18] Ultimately, through reading perception "reaches its greatest strength and length, so that the thing is experienced" and the reader rediscovers what had faded through automaticity.[19] Art's objective, more than to force the reader to see her world, is to force her to experience her surroundings, her life, even herself.

Where scholars have seen a focus on form and a disconnect with the world in Shklovsky's writing, defamiliarization draws from a reader's life to connect her with the richness and sensation that she had lost through automatization. Shklovsky claimed that "I am convinced now that the very fact of perception of art depends upon a comparative juxtaposition of a work of art with the world."[20] The artwork and the world must work side by side to restore the reader's sensation she lost through the monotony in life. Shklovsky indicates that defamiliarization restores life in a much broader and richer sense because it forges connections between people and their world, not just the art, but their real context. Given that "*ostranenie* is present almost wherever there is an image,"[21] art enhances reality and lived experience widely through renewed sensation in life. Robinson claims this restoration of perception and vividness is Shklovsky's key focus in defamiliarization: "Shklovsky wants to make the audience *work harder and longer* to perceive things so as to enhance the intensity and therefore the sensuousness of vividness of their perception."[22] He further claims that "a conception of literary works as able to infect readers with the sensation of life, with feeling for matter . . . lies at the heart of Shklovskian formalism. The analysis of literary forms that many readers have taken to be his primary or even sole concern is merely a means to this end, the end of harnessing literature to the old liberal aim of helping people live their lives better."[23] While many link Shklovsky's ideas with form, he argues that art restores the lost richness of life and therefore impacts real people in their real world.

Montero illustrates this restoration of life in *Tears* as Husky experiences a sense of salvation when she connects, as if for the first time, with her greater context and relationship with her universe. Husky's search for identity, a subplot of the novel, hurls her repeatedly into an abyss of loneliness and senselessness stemming from a lack of social or environmental connections. The resolution requires that she recognize her relationship within her world as art does for an observer. Robinson explains: "'at the foundation of art lies a striving to penetrate through life,' specifically by inhibiting sensation on the verge of awareness so as to *intensify* both sensation and awareness, specifically to intensify that awareness (mental mapping) of somatic response that gives us our sense of reality, our feeling of matter, our sense of contact with the material world."[24] Consequently, Husky needed to discover an awareness of her defamiliarized material world to bolster her sense of identity: "Suddenly, Bruna visualized the seat they were sitting on, the circular garden, the city of Madrid, the Iberian Peninsula, the greenish-blue globe of the Earth, the small solar system, the multiarmed galaxy, the vast cosmic darkness dotted with constellations . . . the entire universe. And in the middle of that indescribable immensity, she wanted to believe for just one moment in the consoling illusion that she wasn't alone."[25] As Husky sees, visualizes, perceives her immense social and cosmic context, she feels the sensation of life and restoration to society that she lacked.

DEFAMILIARIZING HUMAN RACE

Rosa Montero focuses estrangement's restoration ability and defamiliarizes humanity in *Tears* in order to reconnect the reader to racism and prejudice in the real world. Montero builds a society in which humanity faces a reassessment of what it means to be human. Humans live alongside individuals representing the Other (androids, aliens, and deformed outcasts) who possess thought, emotions, and self-awareness that once belonged exclusively to the human race. Where humans are no longer unique, the reader faces complex implications and unconventional relationships that question whether she may consider other organisms (synthetic and foreign) as human or if she must redefine human. Because humans traditionally boast a unique level of self-awareness and cognitive abilities, and despite the androids' physiological differences that limit literal equality to humans (e.g., shortened lifespans [10 years] and an identity based on implanted false memories), the robots, who share these abilities, want to be recognized as equals. Nevertheless, the humans resist granting equal status to the replicants and label them as monsters or abominations. This human/android equality debate forces the reader to see her own identity within the tension caused by the synthetic and authentic humans because both possess uniquely human characteristics. This complex AI being defamiliarizes humans because of their similarities: the reader sees her own attributes in the Other—the reps—which forces humanness into a new context and perspective.

Through Bruna Husky and the defamiliarization of humanity, Rosa Montero also defamiliarizes prejudice and the marginalized Other in the real-world context. Furthermore, Montero also defamiliarizes social injustice in real-world society as she juxtaposes racism with arbitrary social classism. Reps think like humans and consider themselves as valuable as humans, yet their equality faces a logical obstacle: they are robots. People relegate them to a lower status because they are quite literally the humans' creations. Thus the humans' position during the replicant wars that, to resolve the conflict, android production "should simply cease."[26] While this logical solution appears plausible given the origin of the androids, the robots themselves oppose such logic: "This possibility is rejected outright by the technos, who view it as genocide: 'What has once existed cannot return to the limbo of nonexistence. . . . We are a new species, and like all living beings, we yearn to continue living.'"[27] Ultimately, the war grants equal rights legally, but the issue is far from resolved given that humans still see androids as inferior objects. This inequality resonates with underrepresented social groups that legally benefit from equal rights but face the reality of bigotry and social injustice.

As Montero estranges the real-world atmosphere of social justice, she forces the reader to pause and consider the robots as a defamiliarized human race who are subject to the same racism and prejudice as the Other. People scorn the androids as inferior machines like many do with those of different color, nationality, or origin. Yet judgment is so common and quick that it can become automatic, and such frequent prejudice undermines any attempt to connect with the Other. This disconnect yields similar results as automatization: namely people fail to see, or experience, Other as a person instead of as a category or a group. Consequently, Montero's juxtaposing humans with robots reorients the gaze toward social injustice. Where the observer faces a weakening awareness of ever-present social construction, defamiliarization can reawaken her to the hidden and overlooked racism in her society. For example, whereas robot discrimination rests on fundamental biological differences in their race, in reality racism is a socially constructed concept void of any real physiological underpinnings. Foundations behind the biological differences of racism began, as Hazel Rose Markus explains, in the fifteenth century to classify and order the world, but as the conquering Europeans encroached on "new" societies, "the idea of biological differences among people . . . served a wide variety of ideological and social purposes throughout Europe and America."[28] She also points out that early psychologists such as Sir Francis Galton furthered these views and advocated improving the human race through "eugenic breeding practices that he hoped would help elevate the inferior races to approach the level of civilized Europeans."[29] Such perspectives fed the misconception that race constituted fundamental biological differences linked to nationality, language, or skin color.

Social injustices in *Tears* reflect this arbitrary prejudice among human characters, which further draws the reader's attention to her own society. In one example, the Labarí society in *Tears* has established a class system of socially superior and inferior citizens that utterly disregards biology. The elders controlled their people with limited information and rigid class distinctions, and they kept "[their] subjects totally uninformed."[30] By limiting their knowledge, the leaders also limited their power; they further maintained the inferior class's place in society through tattoos that labeled their caste. In the sequel, *Weight of the Heart*, Bruna travels to Labarí and meets a woman with an "S" tattooed on her neck, indicating the servant class, who comments: "This letter is my essence. Thanks to it I know my place in the world. This letter makes me pure and protects me."[31] She believes that her place in society defines her, and as part of a lower class, she is considered inferior to those of higher classes. This arbitrary, socially constructed classism, juxtaposed with android biological racism, foregrounds the irrationality of Labarí—and by extension real-world—racism. Ideas of race and ethnicity are artificial, as Markus explains, because "other people create them, and they are not biologically based 'things' that people 'have.' Instead, they are socially constructed 'doings' or 'historically situated projects.'"[32] Essentially, Montero defamiliarizes the social construction behind race and ethnicity through humanized androids and dehumanized people.

Consequently, like Shklovsky for whom defamiliarization reconnects observer with life and sensation, Montero draws the gaze of the readers back to a ubiquitous real-world racism that has become overlooked, justified, or ignored. Society has essentially swung completely away from old-fashioned, overt racism and considers it unacceptable. Katz and Hass have observed that "public opinion has shifted from widespread acceptance of segregation and discrimination in the 1940s to a broad national consensus in support of racial equality and integration."[33] Similarly, Federico points out that "the success of the civil rights movement has made basic humanitarian concern for blacks a consensual political norm: for the most part, both liberals and conservatives agree that unequal treatment is a violation of basic liberal-democratic values central to American life."[34] People, in general, do not dispute the need for equal treatment and respect; however, this widespread acceptance has relaxed the fight against intolerance and diverted the gaze away from this issue. Many sociologists, psychologists, scientists, and artists argue that the need is as great as ever to address racism because it still has a hold, albeit a more disguised hold, on society. Neville and Awad, for example, point out that "while the United States has made many advances in race relations over the past 150 years, racial inequality persists in all sectors of American life."[35] They refuse to allow racism to become automatic and forgotten; instead they advocate drawing attention to it in order to battle these old tendencies.

AUTOMATIZATION OF REAL-WORLD RACISM

Perhaps the biggest reason racism remains largely unrecognized among the public is that prejudice has become automatic in many ways. Both the individual and people in general are largely unable to recognize personal automatic tendencies such as prejudice in themselves. Shklovsky saw the human tendency to automatize things such as emotions, environments, and cultural viewpoints as a problematic "part of the human condition,"[36] and according to Katz and Hass, our society has automatized racism given that "at least on an unconscious level, some amount of racial bias is still commonplace."[37] Sears and Henry similarly contend that people hold onto "'implicit' measures of prejudice, which presumably tap unconscious, automatic, and uncontrollable forms of prejudice,"[38] and Markus likewise argues that racism "can also be indirect, implicit, and automatic, occurring outside of conscious intention."[39] While society increasingly rejects racial injustice, it still exists and the changes in norms and acceptable speech or behavior have only driven racist sentiments underground.

While the pervasiveness of social commentary against racism may explain why individuals often overlook their own racist tendencies, other scholars—particularly in neuroscience—argue that racism is difficult to recognize because it draws on innate evolutionary instincts to recognize differences among others. Racism itself is not evolutionary, yet neuroscientists Cikara and Van Bavel have looked at racism from cognitive and neurological roots and have explained that humans categorize the social world into in groups and out groups: "one important consequence of the social identification process is that humans reliably divide the world into *us* and everyone else: *them.*"[40] We inherently judge others in relation to ourselves as same or different, and we naturally identify more closely with the similar "us" group—a trait that "has been observed in every culture on earth."[41] People naturally see difference and prefer similarity, which is an evolutionary defense mechanism that has ensured the survival of the human race: "whenever we encounter a novel person or group, we are motivated to answer two questions as quickly as possible: the first is 'friend or foe?'; the second is 'is this agent capable of enacting his or her intentions toward me?'"[42] Classification is inherent and may lead to prejudices and judgments given that group membership "reliably predicts intergroup bias: prejudice and discriminatory behavior that favors the in-group relative to an out-group."[43] However, innate differentiation does not imply inherent racism even though the brain is hardwired for recognizing difference. Judgment is an evolutionary characteristic of fitness, but society molds intergroup biases into a relationship of inferior/superior. Furthermore, recognizing differences is automatic and therefore difficult to notice, which leads to individual unrecognized internal prejudices.

DEFAMILIARIZATION OF RACISM

In *Tears*, defamiliarized prejudice improves tolerance as the characters recognize, face, and overcome their hidden biases. Montero explicitly links prejudice and inequality with deplorable perspectives and treatment of Other while she highlights questions of social injustice. The anti-rep movement designed to stop the production of reps and purge them from society closely resembles genocide, yet it is not because people are technically destroying machines, even though they are human in essence. This technicality defamiliarizes tolerance and prejudice because the lack of essential difference between people and robots emphasizes the social arbitrariness in racism. In this story world, the characters face strange racism centered on literal biological difference in humanized objects, whereas the reader faces real prejudice centered on arbitrary racial differences in dehumanized people. Ultimately, this estranged, and consequently fresh, vision of discrimination can combat prejudice through personal connections. For example, Lizard, the human detective, bridges the gap between human and Other through his personal relationship with Husky. He sees her as an individual because he is emotionally connected to her, but he also explains that because his mother figure, the nanny who raised him, was a rep, "I have nothing against reps."[44] He sees them as people and has overwritten the innate differentiation. Likewise, Bruna eventually sees Lizard as a person and partner rather than a police officer or another prejudiced human. They are companions and friends, and consequently they purge the effects of racism through connections.

This artistic defamiliarization of a real-world issue empowers the reader to overcome racism and see people in place of Other. Shklovsky explained that with defamiliarization, "the artist first separates and extracts a certain set of phenomena from what we call reality," which in this case is racism and prejudice.[45] Montero then defamiliarizes them by taking those "events or objects from real life, [and] arranging them differently and unlike the way they are organized in ordinary life."[46] The reader certainly would not have faced robotic discrimination as a common part of daily life, but she might have overlooked frequently occurring racist tendencies. As she engages this strange human and android prejudice, the reader faces a complex yet compelling new version of racism that brings, as Shklovsky describes, a "sensation of surprise felt toward the world, a perception of the world with a strained sensitivity" that accompanies "the delayed, close examination of the world."[47] This sensation is the renewal that occurs between an observer and her environment, her life, her society, her world, that had faded through automatization. Similarly, scholars fight racism by helping people recognize what they don't see, as Montero does in her novel, through Shklovsky-like defamiliarization and estrangement. Montero highlights the arbitrary nature of biological arguments fueling racism while simultaneously suggesting that recognizing unobserved biases can overcome prejudice. Ultimately, she converts Shklovsky's artistic tool into a social tool that restores awareness and sensation to life.

SHKLOVSKIAN PSYCHOLOGY OF REAL-WORLD RACISM

Similar to Shklovsky's automatization, the ubiquity of racist conversations can lead to either a deadening of their impact or a false security and belief that the individual or society has moved beyond racism. Psychologists, such as Sabina Vaught, point out that people often believe they are free of prejudice because they overlook color and difference; whereas in reality this "refusal to see 'Color'" is a refusal "to see race as language, culture, history, nationality, ethnicity, and so on," which is also refusing to see Other as person.[48] This Colorblindness is a form of discrimination and exacerbates the problem because the refusal to see differences in individuals is also a refusal to see discrimination.[49] If people become comfortable, as with Colorblindness, they overlook lingering tendencies and do not address the problem. Neville and Awad argue that racist perspectives have become hidden because while many Americans

> believe that racism is a thing of the past, . . . racism persists, as illustrated by the disparities in income, health, educational opportunities, and so forth. Moreover, saying that someone does not notice race does not mean that that person is free from racial prejudice. This observation is supported by the growing research linking greater denial of race and racism to increased racial intolerance, endorsement of White privilege, fear of people of color, and lower levels of multicultural counseling and teaching competencies.[50]

If people believe the problem is gone, it pervades unaddressed. To help make it visible, scholars have turned to defamiliarization to raise awareness of racism and effect social change because people must recognize racism in society and themselves first, then they can connect with Others as individuals and move beyond difference and Otherness.

Like Montero, social psychologists pick up the torch against bigotry and defamiliarize racism in real-world society to increase awareness of, and help people face, their prejudice. For example, Neville and Awad advocate new Shklovskian perspectives to force people to see and understand the problem:

> squarely confronting the depth and complexities of the problem of racial prejudice and inequality is one of the first steps to solving this enormous social ill. . . . One way psychologists can help to address this 'gigantic' and 'chaotic' social ill that persists in the United States is to provide people with information and the analytic tools to identify the problem and the language to talk about race. . . . Such an approach encourages people to examine the ways that race and racism are enacted in daily life. Thus, in order to move past race and racism, we must first acknowledge how they operate in society.[51]

They indicate that racism is largely unrecognized, and people must be made aware of its presence and effects by creating new contexts and methods to discuss the recurring issue. Vaught, even more explicitly Shklovskian, argues that the solution resides in estrangement and "the importance of attending to the ruptures in dominant meaning-making, of defamiliarizing practices of racialization in order to discover the ruptures and fissures" (578). This largely unperceived problem can benefit from Shklovsky's tool that helps the public see, recognize, and understand racism. Defamiliarization is not just a tool for art, but for social change as well.

Because defamiliarization restores life to the subject by reconnecting the observer with the automatized elements of her context, making the problem of racism visible could also restore life through deep personal relationships between subject and Other. Like Lizard in *Tears*, Neville and Awad explain that understanding racist roots, tendencies, and effects in society lays the foundation for the solution to prejudice that requires a turn toward humanism, or "a deep concern and commitment to society that is free from racial and other forms of oppression. Thus, to be a humanist is to recognize the humanity of all people and to ensure that basic rights are granted to all."[52] Seeing the Other as Other stems from our innate tendency of seeing him or her as part of an out group, as different, or as a potential threat. However, by seeing Other as a human draws him or her into our own context and enables us to build a close and true connection, as with Husky and Lizard who saw each other as partners and not as members of a differing group. Such connections would undo racism and rewrite boundaries of difference between people of different colors. Shklovsky points out the ills of objectifying another: "a person who is perceived solely as a body has no history—history is created by humanity."[53] Viewing only the physical is incomplete and insufficient; perceiving a person requires getting to know and see the Other. Shklovsky's argument here closely resembles racial colorblindness, or the refusal to see another's differences, which strips the Other of his or her context, ethnicity, language, culture, etc., and ultimately colorblindness exacerbates racism because it makes the Other unreachable to the observer.

Social relations in *Tears* and in a racist society paint color as inferiority whereas recognizing prejudice draws their gaze deeper than the body and into the history and humanity of Other. This deeper view of humanity can erase racism by redefining what is different and what is similar. For example, Cikara and Van Bavel argue that unlike group identification, racism is not inherent and automatic because prejudices change as group lines are redrawn, even when group identification changes at random. They explain that "randomly assigning participants to minimal groups (even when participants know one another prior to the study) produces discrimination in favor of ingroup members. These findings underscore how readily people identify with social groups as well as the context-dependent nature of these identities."[54] They also further comment that among arbitrarily assigned group identities, "most participants take to their identities quickly and maintain them until another identity becomes salient," thus "assigning people to mixed-race teams can even override racial biases on relatively automatic measures of evaluation."[55] Racism does not inherently define groups, and people can override racism because group identity is fluid. Along these lines, and similar to Shklovsky, Lillian Comas-Díaz advocates that becoming closer to others can help connect with them as we rewrite the lines that induce racism. In her book she strives to "increase one's *cultural self-awareness*' . . . [by] becoming conscious of one's reactions to culturally different individuals" which helps "to enhance your [sic] knowledge of self and others to promote sensitivity and responsiveness" to culturally different people.[56] She advocates defamiliarizing personally automatized racism and perspectives in order to reach out to the Other. Robinson identifies such perspectives in Shklovsky's vision of the effects of defamiliarization because this de-automatization has the effect of "blurring the boundaries between self and other, so that experience flows through people and things rather than being rigidly and 'aridly' compartmentalized."[57] Shklovsky, Montero, social scholars, and psychologists argue that breaking down racist boundaries that create the Other forges deeper human connections, which can heal this social ill.

Defamiliarization facilitates connecting with others both in Montero's novel as well as in our society. As we discuss Shklovsky's legacy in the twenty-first century, we must recognize his ideas as more than literary theory but as a groundwork for social justice. Authors and social critics have drawn on Shklovsky's theories, directly or indirectly, as they advocate for social change regarding racist tendencies that often get overlooked. Generally, Shklovsky argues, people do not see their own contexts completely; specific to this study, people do not see their own inherent and commonplace racist tendencies and prejudiced perspectives. To put Shklovsky's legacy into perspective is to recognize how deeply his influence allows us to build a better community. Literary scholars have placed him into conversations of art and philosophy, and social scientists have extended those conversations to effect social change in real-world society. Ultimately, Shklovsky has laid a foundation that can restore the deep sense of life and experience to dominant groups who have failed to see their own prejudiced tendencies, as well as the underrepresented groups that fall victim to social injustices.

NOTES

1. Stone, Bruce, "The Formalist Reformation: Review of Viktor Shklovsky's Bowstring: On the Dissimilarity of the Similar." *Numéro Cinq* 2.7 (2011): n.p.

2. I will be using the English translation by Lilit Zekulin Thwaites: *Tears in Rain*, (AmazonCrossing) 2011, as well as her translation of Montero's second novel *Weight of the Heart*, (AmazonCrossing) 2015. To consult the texts in the original Spanish, see Montero, *Lágrimas en la Lluvia*, (Editorial Seix Barral), 2011; and Montero, *El Peso del Corazón*, (Editorial Seix Barral), 2015.

3. Dwyer, Anne, "Standstill as Extinction: Victor Shklovsky's Poetics and Politics of Movement in the 1920s and 1930s." *Publications of the Modern Language Association* 131.2 (2016): 270.

4. Sherwood, Richard, "Viktor Shklovsky and the Development of Early Formalist Theory on Prose Literature." *Russian Formalism, A Collection of Articles and Texts in Translation.* (Edinburgh: Scottish Academic Press, 1973), 28.

5. Sherwood, 32.

6. Bruns, Gerald, "Toward a Random Theory of Prose. Introduction to *Theory of Prose*." (Champaign: Dalkey Archive Press, 1991), xii.

7. Bruns, ix.
8. Shklovsky, Viktor. "Art as Device." *Viktor Shklovsky: A Reader*. (New York: Bloomsbury Academic, 2017), 79. All quotes attributed to Shklovsky are from published translations of his works.
9. Shklovsky, "Art as Device," 79–80.
10. Montero, *Tears in the Rain*, 63.
11. Montero, *Tears in the Rain*, 63–64.
12. Robinson, Douglas. *Estrangement and the Somatics of Literature: Tolstoy, Shklovsky, Brecht.* (Baltimore: The Johns Hopkins University Press, 2008), 86.
13. Robinson, 87.
14. See Otten et al., "The Uniformity Illusion: Central Stimuli Can Determine Peripheral Perception." *Association for Psychological Science 28* (2017). See also Maxine Sherman, Anil K. Seth, and Ryota Kanai, "Predictions Shape Confidence in Right Inferior /frontal Gyrus." *The Journal of Neuroscience 36* (2016).
15. Shklovsky, "Art as Device," 79–80.
16. Sher, Benjamin, "Shklovsky and the Revolution." Translator's Introduction to *Theory of Prose*, (Champaign: Dalkey Archive Press, 1991): xv.
17. Shklovsky, "Art as Device," 80.
18. Shklovsky, "Art as Device," 80.
19. Shklovsky, "Art as Device," 93.
20. Shklovsky, *Bowstring: On the Dissimilarity of the Similar*, (Champaign: Dalkey Archive Press, 2011), 146.
21. Shklovsky, "Art as Device," 88.
22. Robinson, 115.
23. Robinson, 87.
24. Robinson, 92.
25. Montero, *Tears in the Rain*, 415.
26. Montero, *Tears in the Rain*, 13.
27. Montero, *Tears in the Rain*, 13.
28. Markus, "Pride, Prejudice, and Ambivalence: Toward a Unified Theory of Race and Ethnicity." *American Psychologist* 63.8 (2008): 657.
29. Markus, 659.
30. Montero, *Tears in the Rain*, 217.
31. Montero, *Weight of the Heart*, 162.
32. Markus, 655.
33. Katz, Irwin, and R. Glen Hass. "Racial Ambivalence and American Value Conflict: Correlational and Priming Studies of Dual Cognitive Structures." *Journal of Personality and Social Psychology* 55.6 (1988): 893
34. Federico, Christopher M. "Ideology and the Affective Structure of Whites' Racial Perceptions." *Public Opinion Quarterly* 70.3 (2006): 331.
35. Neville, Helen A., and Germine H. Awad. "Why Racial Color-Blindness Is Myopic." *American Psychologist* (2014): 313.
36. Robinson, 81.
37. Katz and Hass, 893.
38. Sears, David O. and P. J. Henry. "Over Thirty Years Later: A Contemporary Look at Symbolic Racism." *Advances in Experimental Social Psychology* 37 (2005): 144.
39. Markus, 662.
40. Cikara, Mina, and Jay J. Van Bavel. "The Neuroscience of Intergroup Relations: An Integrative Review." *Perspectives on Psychological Science* 9.3 (2014): 248.
41. Cikara and Van Bavel, 245. See also Joao F. Guassi Moreira, Jay J. Van Bavel, and Eva H. Telzer. "The Neural Development of 'Us and Them.'" *Social Cognitive and Affective Neuroscience* (2017): 185.
42. Cikara and Van Bavel, 252.
43. Cikara and Van Bavel, 248.
44. Montero, *Tears in the Rain*, 294.
45. Shklovsky, *Bowstring*, 147.

46. Shklovsky, *Bowstring*, 147.
47. Shklovsky, *Bowstring*, 146.
48. Vaught, Sabina Elena. "'They Might as Well Be Black': The Racialization of Sa'moan High School Students." *International Journal of Qualitative Studies in Education* 25.5 (2011): 577.
49. See Vaught, 577.
50. Neville and Awad, 313.
51. Neville and Awad, 313–14.
52. Neville and Awad, 314.
53. Shklovsky, *Bowstring*, 173.
54. Cikara and Van Bavel, 248, 252.
55. Cikara and Van Bavel, 248–50.
56. Comas-Diaz, Lillian. *Multicultural Care: A Clinician's Guide to Cultural Competence.* (Washington, DC: American Psychological Association, 2012), 15.
57. Robinson, 114.

WORKS CITED

Bruns, Gerald. "Toward a Random theory of Prose." Introduction to *Theory of Prose*. Translated by Benjamin Sher. Normal, IL: Dalkey Archive Press, 1991: ix–xiv.
Cikara, Mina, and Jay J. Van Bavel. "The Neuroscience of Intergroup Relations: An Integrative Review." *Perspectives on Psychological Science* 9, no. 3 (2014): 245–74.
Comas-Diaz, Lillian. *Multicultural Care: A Clinician's Guide to Cultural Competence*. Washington, DC: American Psychological Association, 2012.
Dwyer, Anne. "Standstill as Extinction: Victor Shklovsky's Poetics and Politics of Movement in the 1920s and 1930s." *Publications of the Modern Language Association* 131, no. 2 (2016): 269–88.
Federico, Christopher M. "Ideology and the Affective Structure of Whites' Racial Perceptions." *Public Opinion Quarterly* 70, no. 3 (2006): 327–53.
Katz, Irwin, and R. Glen Hass. "Racial Ambivalence and American Value Conflict: Correlational and Priming Studies of Dual Cognitive Structures." *Journal of Personality and Social Psychology* 55, no. 6 (1988): 893–905.
Markus, Hazel Rose. "Pride, Prejudice, and Ambivalence: Toward a Unified Theory of Race and Ethnicity." *American Psychologist* 63, no. 8 (2008): 651–70.
Montero, Rosa. *El Peso del Corazón*. Barcelona: Editorial Seix Barral, 2015.
———. *Lágrimas en la Lluvia*. Barcelona: Editorial Seix Barral, 2011.
———. *Tears in Rain*. Trans. Lilit Zekulin Thwaites. Las Vegas: AmazonCrossing, 2012.
———. *Weight of the Heart*. Trans. Lilit Zekulin Thwaites. Seattle: AmazonCrossing, 2016.
Moreira, Joao F. Guassi, Jay J. Van Bavel, and Eva H. Telzer. "The Neural Development of 'Us and Them.'" *Social Cognitive and Affective Neuroscience* (2017): 184–96.
Neville, Helen A. and Germine H. Awad. "Why Racial Color-Blindness Is Myopic." *American Psychologist* (2014): 313–14.
Otten, Marte, Yair Pinto, Chris L. E. Paffen, Anil K. Seth, and Ryota Kanai. "The Uniformity Illusion: Central Stimuli Can Determine Peripheral Perception." *Association for Psychological Science* 28 (2017): 56–68.
Robinson, Douglas. *Estrangement and the Somatics of Literature: Tolstoy, Shklovsky, Brecht.* Baltimore: The Johns Hopkins University Press, 2008.
Sears, David O., and P. J. Henry. "Over Thirty Years Later: A Contemporary Look at Symbolic Racism." *Advances in Experimental Social Psychology* 37 (2005): 95–150.
Sher, Benjamin. "Shklovsky and the Revolution." Translator's introduction to *Theory of Prose*, Translated by Benjamin Sher. Normal, IL: Dalkey Archive Press, 1991, xv–xxi.
Sherman, Maxine, Anil K. Seth, and Ryota Kanai. "Predictions Shape Confidence in Right Inferior Frontal Gyrus." *The Journal of Neuroscience* 36 (2016): 10323–336.

Sherwood, Richard. "Viktor Shklovsky and the Development of Early Formalist Theory on Prose Literature." *Russian Formalism, A Collection of Articles and Texts in Translation*, ed. Stephen Bann and John E. Bowlt. Edinburgh: Scottish Academic Press, (1973), 26–40.

Shklovsky, Viktor. "Art as Device." *Viktor Shklovsky: A Reader*. Edited and Translated by Alexandra Berlina: New York: Bloomsbury Academic, (2017), 73–96.

———. *Bowstring: On the Dissimilarity of the Similar*, Translated by Shushan Avagyan: Champaign, Il: Dalkey Archive Press, 2011. https://libproxy.bvu.edu/login?url=http://search.ebscohost.com/login.aspx?direct=true&db=nlebk&AN=802679&site=ehost-live.

Stone, Bruce. "The Formalist Reformation: Review of Viktor Shklovsky's *Bowstring: On the Dissimilarity of the Similar*." *Numéro Cinq* 2.7 (2011): http://numerocinqmagazine.com/2011/07/08/the-formalist-reformation-a-review-of-viktor-shklovskys-bowstring-on-the-dissimilarity-of-the-similar-by-bruce-stone/.

Vaught, Sabina Elena. "'They Might as Well Be Black': The Racialization of Sa'moan High School Students." *International Journal of Qualitative Studies in Education* 25, no. 5 (2011): 557–82.

Part II

Shklovsky's Heritage in Arts

Chapter Twelve

Shklovsky's Dog and Mulvey's Pleasure

The Secret Life of Defamiliarization

Eric Naiman

Since the 1975 publication of "Visual Pleasure and Narrative Cinema" in the sixteenth volume of *Screen*, Laura Mulvey's essay has become perhaps the most frequently cited and anthologized article in contemporary film criticism.[1] Although Mulvey claims in the article that her conclusions are specific to the medium of film and to the conditions of its consumption, she herself soon expanded her work's application, and now, nearly twenty years later, it is a standard item in the repertoire of literary criticism dealing with gender. Mulvey herself appears rather in awe of her article's success. In the introduction to a 1989 collection of articles entitled *Visual and Other Pleasures*—a title insisting that the words "Laura Mulvey" should connote more than this one article—Mulvey looks back at her most famous creation, which, she says, seems "to have taken on a life of its own." "Written in 1973," Mulvey reflects, "polemically and without regard for context or nuances of argument, published in 1975, after many references and quotations in the following years, it has acquired a balloon-like, free-floating quality." "I hope," Mulvey adds, "that publishing it here will not explode it, but bring it back to earth" (vii–viii). Although the essays surrounding "Visual Pleasure and Narrative Cinema" do indeed provide several keys to bringing the article down to the contextual earth of Mulvey's other writings about cinema, here I want to try to take the balloon down a little further—into the underground of its prehistory in theory and, perhaps, into the textual unconscious of its sources.

Mulvey's article has been the object of much discussion, but generally criticism has involved what Janet Bergstrom and Mary Ann Doane have called its "theoretical matrix" (7) rather than close readings of the article's text. In the pages to come, I propose to undertake a "symptomatic" and comparative reading of Mulvey's article in relation to an earlier text that has influenced both Mulvey's writing and film theory in general: Viktor Shklovsky's "Art as Device."[2] In the process I want to consider what the affinities between "Visual Pleasure" and a founding text of Russian Formalism can tell us about both of these texts. How does Mulvey make ostranenie (making strange) stranger or, if two negatives make a positive, how does Mulvey make defamiliarization uncomfortably familiar?

I

"Visual Pleasure and Narrative Cinema" attempts to describe how desire functions in traditional cinema. Explicitly "appropriat[ing]" psychoanalytic theory "as a political weapon" (14), Mulvey examines how the cinema has functioned as a mediating channel for libidinal energy and ego formation.[3] According to Mulvey, the spectator in the cinema derives pleasure in two manners. The first, libidinal, way is through scopophilia—the pleasure of looking at the body of another, a pleasure that in traditional cinema has been directed at the female body. The pleasure is extradiegetic; it tends to work against narrative progression and, since contemplation of the female body arouses fear of castration, potentially threatens the viewer. The second cinematic avenue toward pleasure is achieved through identification with a glamorous, idealized reflection of the self. This identification, which Mulvey treats as a more sophisticated, later variation on Lacan's Mirror Stage, is essential to the reinforcement of the ego. The fear of castration produced by the sight of the other's lack is handled in the cinema in two ways: the male unconscious can "escape" through "preoccupation with the re-enactment of the original trauma (investigating the woman, demystifying her mystery), counterbalanced by the devaluation, punishment or saving of the guilty object (an avenue typified by the concerns of the film noir); or else [through] complete disavowal of castration by the substitution of a fetish object or turning the represented figure itself into a fetish so that it becomes reassuring rather than dangerous (hence overvaluation, the cult of the female star)" (21). While in "Visual Pleasure and Narrative Cinema" Mulvey dodges the question of the female viewer, she returns to it in a sequel in which she discusses the plight of a female viewer who is led to identify with masculine figures on the screen in an ego sustaining move that become second nature, albeit a "Nature [that] does not sit easily and shifts restlessly in its borrowed transvestite clothes" (33).[4]

Critical uses of Mulvey's work may be described as either hard or soft core, depending on whether they explicitly refer to the importance of castration and its Freudian and Lacanian baggage. (The uses of Mulvey made by Slavists, for example, tend to be less orthodox in their use of psychoanalytic theory; Svetlana Boym [165] and Helena Goscilo [211] refer to the gendering of the gaze but not to the psychoanalytic path by which Mulvey reaches her conclusion.) Yet we should not forget that the route by which Mulvey accounts for the gendering of the gaze, and thus by which she herself brings the gendering of the gaze to consciousness, lies through castration—a route that is essential to the article's programmatic import as well as to its analysis.

Having demonstrated that traditional cinematic pleasure works ingeniously to reconcile the patriarchy's Freudian ideological contradictions, Mulvey then proclaims her intention to destroy that pleasure. By exposing the patriarchal contradictions suspended by film, Mulvey in effect attempts to at least make more imminent the fear of castration that the cinema has allayed. Her first sentence announces that her article will analyze the source of cinema's "fascination," and to the extent that that word derives from a Roman, phallus-shaped amulet used to charm or bewitch (American Heritage Dictionary 477), we can say that Mulvey is from the very start out to expose the phallus, to render it vulnerable and undo its charm.[5]

The version of "Visual Pleasure and Narrative Cinema" that appears in Visual and Other Pleasures contains no footnotes.[6] As she progresses through her argument, however, Mulvey is quite open about the texts that have influenced her. She sets up her paradigm of the cinematic view by relying—if eclectically—on Freud and Lacan. She then demonstrates how the paradigm works by briefly discussing Sternberg and Hitchcock. Sternberg serves as an example of fetishistic pleasure, Hitchcock as an example of demystification and salvation through punishment (as well as fetishization), although the Hitchcock films cited are employed by Mulvey for their metavoyeuristic, or metacinematic insight. They do not so much provide examples of voyeuristic cinematic pleasure as serve as parables about that pleasure, and the very sophistication of these films introduces a problem to which we will return.[7] All of these concerns would seem far from the interests of the avatars of modern Russian criticism. Yet when, at the beginning and end of her essay, Mulvey writes less in the genre of scholarly analysis than in the genre of critical manifesto, familiar strains sound. Mulvey calls for "cinematic codes" to be broken down, primarily by foregrounding and thus problematizing "the voyeuristic-scopophilic look" (25). Viewers must continually be reminded that they are watching a film and thus are present as constitutive actors rather than simple observers:

> The first blow against the monolithic accumulation of traditional film conventions ... is to free the look of the camera into its materiality in time and space and the look of the audience into dialectics and passionate detachment. There is no doubt that this destroys the satisfaction, pleasure and privilege of the

"invisible guest," and highlights the way film has depended on voyeuristic active/passive mechanisms. (26)

The resulting cinema must work for "a total negation of . . . ease and plenitude" in its attack on "pleasure" (16). Essentially, this is a call for a politically engaged use of *zatrudnenie* (retardation, or narrative difficulty), of *obnazhenie priema* (baring of the device), and of cinematic delibidinal *ostranenie* (defamiliarization) in which the politically neutral term "automatization" (employed by Shklovsky to refer to that aspect of perception that art must overcome through defamiliarization) has been replaced by the patriarchy-sustaining term "pleasure."

Although Mulvey never directly refers to "defamiliarization" in her famous article, there are other traces, some direct and some indirect, tying Mulvey's article to Formalism, to Viktor Shklovsky and to Shklovsky's foundational formalist article, "Art as Device." In 1989 Mulvey recalled:

> During the sixties the avant-garde returned to the cultural agenda in Britain, not through any direct line or legacy but through a revival of interest in the way that radical art and radical politics had intertwined to create an avant-garde in the twenties. In Europe, to look back to the twenties was to look back across the cold war, the second world war, fascism and Stalinism to "discover," for instance, Russian Formalism and Brecht. ("British Feminist Film Theory's Female Spectators" 69–70)[8]

Mulvey's insistence here on an indirect link to the avant-garde of the first half of the century itself has echoes of Formalist views of literary evolution, in particular Shklovsky's (far from gender-neutral) declaration that in literary evolution "inheritance proceeds not from father to eldest son but from uncle to nephew" (*Za 60 let* 14). No debts are acknowledged to Formalism in "Visual Pleasure," but since Mulvey refers in her article to "recent writing in *Screen* about psychoanalysis and the cinema" (14), it is worth recalling that in the issues of *Screen* that preceded the publication of her article there was a fairly heavy dose of Formalist texts. Volume 15, No. 3, published in autumn 1974, a year before "Visual Pleasure," contained both a collection of articles by Osip Brik (with an introduction and footnotes by Maria Enzensberger that discussed and quoted "Art as Device" [57]) and an interview with Laura Mulvey and her collaborator, Peter Wollen, about their new film, *Penthesilea, Queen of the Amazons*. Wollen was a member of the editorial board of *Screen*, and so might have had access to the Brik articles as early as 1973, when Mulvey says she first wrote "Visual Pleasure." "Art as Device" was first published in English in 1965 (Lemon and Reis 3–24), and the British journal *Twentieth Century Studies* published a special issue devoted to Russian Formalism in December, 1972, just a few months before Mulvey presented "Visual Pleasure" for the first time. (The issue contained three articles by Shklovsky and one about him by Richard Sherwood.) In later articles Mulvey refers to Shklovsky twice by name, most strikingly in the conclusion to a 1983 essay co-written with Wollen on Frida Kahlo and the photographer Tina Modotti, where Shklovsky serves as a bridge between psychoanalysis and feminism:

> It is the discourse of the body, together with its political and psychoanalytic implications, which provides a continuity for us with Mexico between the wars. The history of art, as Viktor Shklovsky observed, proceeds by knight's moves, through the oblique and unexpected rather than the linear and predictable. If the art of Frida Kahlo and Tina Modotti has appeared to be detached from the mainstream, this by no means entails any loss of value. In many ways their work may be more relevant than the central traditions of modernism, at a time when, in the light of feminism, the history of art is being revalued and remade. (105)

In two later works, written without collaboration, Mulvey returns to the image of "the knight's move," which—its source not identified—becomes a quintessential avant-garde strategic move (146, 150). Likewise, in a recent article Mulvey calls the work of artist Cindy Sherman "a re-representation [of femininity], a making strange" (*Fetishism and Curiosity* 67). Most striking, however, is the term "feminist formalism," which Mulvey uses to describe the type of work in which critics and filmmakers must engage if they are to undo the male gaze:

> Politically, a feminist formalism is based on rejection of the past on giving priority to challenging the spectator's place in cinema. From an aesthetic point of view the space and time of realist or illusionist aesthetics have immense limitations they cannot satisfy the complex shifts feminist imagery desires. Splits in the cinematic sign allow ideas to interact with fiction and thought with fantasy. At the same time there is a pleasure in tabula rasa. Structures become visible and the bare bones of the cinematic process force themselves forward. (119)

Mulvey, however, never addresses the question of just what is added or subtracted in the transition from Russian Formalism to feminist formalism. This question would seem important since Mulvey mentions Formalism—a much earlier critical movement—at the same time that she asserts the joy of operating with a clean slate and the necessity of "widen[ing] the gap with the past," "retreat[ing] from forms associated with oppression," and "find[ing] uncontaminated ground on which to build a feminist aesthetics" (118). Moreover, the coining of the term "feminist formalism" is interesting because the place of gender in Russian Formalist theory has remained an almost entirely unexplored topic.[9] I would like to address that issue by turning to that urtext of Russian Formalism, Shklovsky's "Art as Device" ("Iskusstvo kak priem")

(1917), to consider the role gender plays in this manifesto that has had so much impact on critical theory in the twentieth century.

II

For all its rhetorical power, "Art as Device" is a confusing and contradictory article, so confusing, in fact, that the authors of studies of Formalism have kindly more or less refrained from dealing with it as a single utterance. Yet the work seems so contradictory and even haphazard that it begs for close attention to its own strangeness. Beginning with a critique of the school of the Russian philosopher and philologist Aleksandr Potebnya for failing to distinguish between poetic and nonpoetic utterances, Shklovsky makes a case for the presence of defamiliarization as a defining characteristic of the artistic utterance. He then discusses several cases of *ostranenie*, beginning with its use by Tolstoy. In the course of his discussion of Tolstoy, however, Shklovsky cites or mentions several texts that are not artistic at all; what unites these texts is their ethical, not aesthetic, import.[10] Moreover, several of the aesthetic texts are virtually metarhetorical, that is, they foreground defamiliarization by showing how the characters (rather than the readers) experience it. This confusion would seem to be an example of a covertly nostalgic modernist's inability to divorce himself from the primacy of characters within an artistic text,[11] and yet we should note that there is a striking parallel here to Mulvey's use of Hitchcock's texts, which for her are primarily illustrative parables about viewing pleasure rather than examples of how pleasure is made. At any rate, Shklovsky, having criticized Potebnya for analyzing fables rather than real poems, then proceeds himself to discuss the function of defamiliarization in "erotic art," a category that opens with the priest's groping of Solokha in Gogol's "Christmas Eve" and continues through a series of erotic riddles and jokes, including the tale of a peasant who brands a bear, brakes a magpie's leg, and then impales a spider on a stick. The crippled animals sit and watch as the peasant's wife brings him lunch:

The man and his wife finished their dinner in the fresh air, and he began to wrestle with her on the ground.
The bear saw this and said to the magpie and the spider, "Holy priests! The peasant wants to piebald someone again."
The magpie said, "No, he wants to break someone's legs."
The spider said, "No, he wants to shove a stick up someone's rump."[12]

Shklovsky immediately comments: "The identity of the device here with the device of [Tolstoy's story,] 'Kholstomer,' is, I think, obvious to all" *"Odinnakovost' priema dannoi veshchi s priemom 'Kholstomera,' ia dumaiu, vidna kazhdomu"* (literally: "the identity of the device of the given thing [i.e., of the cited text] with the device of 'Kholstomer' is, I think, obvious to everyone")

(20). There are some problems here. According to Shklovsky, the effect of defamiliarization is to make the perceiver of art see an object anew by transferring emphasis from recognition to seeing. And yet in erotic stories and riddles of this sort, the whole pathos is precisely in the final element of recognition, a recognition generically anticipated from the start. The erotic descriptions of body parts such as "Two white miracles appeared from beneath her blouse" seem to belong as much to the realm of cliché as to any category of novel expression. Shklovksy's decision to include his extended description of erotic poetics initially appears puzzling and might be chalked up to a Futurist fellow traveler's penchant for épatage. Yet, as we shall see, the inclusion of the erotic material is consistent with a misogynistic thread that also runs through Shklovsky's earlier discussion of Tolstoy.

Following the extended quotation of the erotic tale, Shklovsky immediately refers to the *"priem dannoi veshchi,"* "the device of the given thing" (i.e., of the cited text), and it is worth noting that priem, the word for "device" in Russian also refers to an act of receiving or taking under one's control.[13] Shklovsky's phrase, *priem dannoi veshchi*, may be read as something of a double entendre, since within the context of the tale the literal *priem dannoi veshchi*, (device/receipt of the given thing) may refer to the burning/tearing/piercing of the female body to which the act of sex is compared. (That *priem*, when used to mean an act of receipt, signifies a relatively passive sort of acquiring possession makes its appearance here especially interesting: the peasant receives his wife's genitals, as it were, on a plate, and he exerts little effort to secure their proximity. The use of this double entendre thus masks the violent context of this particular receipt.) Indeed, Shklovsky ends the next paragraph by telling us that "defamiliarization is frequently employed in descriptions of the sex organs" *"chasto ostranenie primeniaetsia pri izobrazhenii polovykh organov"* (20), and in several of these examples priem functions as both an artistic device and a capture or receipt of the female genitals. Here Shklovsky seems close to Nietzsche, who in *The Gay Science* credits old women with realizing that all truth, virtue and profundity is "merely a veil over the pudendum" (125); wanting to keep this pudendum covered—and in front of us as an object of degradation—at all costs, Nietzsche defines artists as those who value riddles, veils and naming.[14]

In light of Shklovsky's linkage of defamiliarization to sexual description or possession, it is worth recalling that the section on Tolstoy ends with the sentence "Tolstoy's perceptions disturbed his faith when he turned to things he had long avoided touching" *"Tolstovskie vospriiatiia rasshatali veru Tolstogo, dotronuvshis' do veshchei, kotorykh on dolgo ne khotel kasat'sia"* (17), a line that is then echoed at the end of the first quotation (from Gogol's "Christmas Eve") in the next section:

—He, he, he!—and rubbing his hands, the sexton again walked about the room.

—And what have you here, incomparable Solokha? . . .—It is unclear, when the sexton would then have touched with his long fingers.

— *Khe, khe, khe!—i d'iak snova proshelsia po komnate, potiraia ruki.*
— *A eto chto u vas, nesravnennaia Solokha? . . .—Neizvestno, k chemu by teper' pritronulsia d'iak svoimi dlinnymi pal'tsami.* (18)

Although the things that Tolstoy didn't want to touch for a long time and the things toward which the sexton stretches may well be quite different, Shklovsky's language about Tolstoy and his placement of the Gogol quote tie the two images together in a tactile and lexical parallel, one which is reinforced by Tolstoy's well-known decades-long struggle with his own physical and, particularly, sexual urges. Shklovsky's examples of defamiliarization begin, we might recall, with a quotation from Tolstoy's diary in which Tolstoy acts in a manner that is later echoed—or prosaically rhymed—by the sexton who "again walked about the room, rubbing his hands" "*snova proshelsia po komnate, potiraia ruki*":

> I was cleaning [the word here has the same root as rubbing] in the room and, circling about, walked up to the couch and could not remember whether I cleaned it or not. Since such actions are habitual and unconscious, I could not remember and already felt that it was impossible to remember. So that if I had cleaned and forgotten it, that is, acted unconsciously, it would be all the same, as if it had never happened. If a conscious person had seen it, then it would be possible to reestablish it. If nobody saw or saw but unconsciously, if the entire complex life of many people passes unconsciously, it is as if that life had never happened.

> *Ia obtiral v komnate i, obkhodia krugom, podoshel k divanu i ne mog vspomnit,' obtiral li ia ego ili net. Tak kak dvizheniia eti privychny i bessoznatel'ny, ia ne mog i chuvstvoval, chto eto uzhe nevozmozhno vspomnit.' Tak chto, esli ia obtiral i zabyl eto, t.-e. deistvoval bessoznatel'no, to eto vse ravno, kak ne bylo. Esly by kto soznatel'nyi videl, to mozhno bylo by vosstanovit.' Esli zhe nikto ne vidal ili videl, no bessoznatel'no; esli tselaia slozhnaia zhizn' mnogikh proiskhodit bessoznatel'no, to eta zhizn' kak by ne byla.* (12)

The motivation for this parallel resides in the gendered dimension of the activity. Tolstoy finds himself in a moment of everyday life (*byt*), of domestic, normally feminine, activity that becomes for Shklovsky a sort of waking sleep that must be overcome by a scene marked by sexual difference and by objectified femininity—the scene of the groping sexton from Gogol's "Christmas Eve." It is worth recalling here that the categories of everyday life (*byt*) and femininity were repeatedly merged and vigorously attacked by the avant-garde in its Futurist, Constructivist and Proletkul't incarnations. Both woman and byt were identified with a past that could never be purged and whose continued status as "other" was a constant formative feature of the new Soviet being always-in-the-process-of-becoming, a being whom it might be best to call "the new Soviet non-woman" rather than "the new Soviet man." And the avant-garde was not alone in identifying woman with the everyday. *Knizhnaia letopis,'* the official catalogue of books published in the USSR, listed "Everyday Life (*byt*), The Situation of Woman, Folklore" and occasionally "Children's Diseases" under the same heading. In keeping with this tradition, Shklovsky readily identified defamiliarization with masculine resistance to feminizing habit and to feminized everyday life.

In fact, the utopian, anti-quotidian fervor that motivates Shklovsky's quotation of this passage from Tolstoy's diary is such that Tolstoy's chronological marker preceding the entry—"Yesterday was February, 28, 1897" "*Vchera bylo 28 fev. 97*" (1928–1958:53:137)—becomes in Shklovsky's hands "the entry from Tolstoy's diary of February 29, 1897" "*Zapis' iz dnevnika L'va Tolstogo 29 fevralia 1897*"—a date that never existed! Admittedly, Shklovsky was not alone in the mistake; A.M. Khiriakov's edition of the Diary, which Shklovsky had read in the journal *Letopis'* in 1915, also dates the entry "February 29, 1897" "*29 fevralia 1897*" ("Dnevnik" 354). But in the context of "Art as Device" this utopian date is appropriate. The "*priem dannoi veshchi*," the mastery of man over woman, becomes a constitutive factor of true art that shakes Shklovsky's aesthetics out of both habit and the calendar.

The anti-quotidian orientation of the article is evident even in the imprecise nature of the quotation. Where in both his complete works (1928–1958) and in Khiriakov's first publication of the diaries (1915) Tolstoy writes "I was wiping away dust in the room" "*Ia obtiral pyl' v komnate*," in Shklovsky's article we read "I was cleaning [or wiping] in the room" "*Ia obtiral v komnate*" (12). By wiping away Tolstoy's "dust," Shklovsky wipes away an object closely linked to the process of petty accumulation so central to everyday life.

Over the past seventy-five years, this entry from Tolstoy's diary has become—thanks to Shklovsky's use of it—perhaps the best known diary entry in the entire corpus of Russian literature. But in the process the entry has lost any connection to its original purpose: to record a particular moment in its author's life. The entry itself was made during Tolstoy's intensive work on *What Is Art*, a treatise—by the way—that both unexpectedly anticipates Mulvey's in its sustained attack on "art" that seems to provide "pleasure" to only a part (the dominant part) of the populace, and more importantly, specifically targets under the categories of "engagingness" and "strikingness" (*zanimatel'nost'* and *porazitel'nost'*) the sort of aesthetics later to be advocated by Shklovsky. "Engagingness may also reside in the very devices of expression" "*Zanimatel'nost' mozhet zakliuchat'sia takzhe v samykh priemakh vyrazheniia*" (211)—Tolstoy writes. Completely ignoring Tolstoy's aesthetic views and also his horror of erotic art, Shklovsky plugs Tolstoy into an eroticized context and—snipping away the diary's surrounding notes on aesthetics—uses a diary entry contemporary with the composition of *What Is Art* as the foundation for a radically different view of art. Shklovsky's treatment of Tolstoy is thus profoundly parodic, at least in the sense in which Tynyanov uses the term: an echoing that alters a statement, often by recontextualization, so that the original no longer serves its intended use (5–26).[15]

In another respect, though, Shklovsky's article endorses Tolstoy's views and desires. Tolstoy's specific interest in the quoted passage is the importance of consciousness to life and to existence. In essence, he denies the reality of unconscious actions. It is, he says, "as if [unconscious] life had never happened" "*eta zhizn' kak by ne byla*." Yet a peculiar pathos becomes apparent in this statement when we examine what Tolstoy's diaries and letters show was going on in his life at this time. The entry was made at the height of Tolstoy's jealousy over his wife's friendship with the pianist Sergei Taneev, whose playing and views are specifically targeted and denigrated in *What is Art*, although Taneev is not there identified by name but only as the easily recognizable "splendid musician who came to visit us" "*zaekhavshii k nam prekrasnyi muzykant*" (235) and who aroused the entire Tolstoy household with his playing of Beethoven. On February 16, a fortnight before the dusting entry, Tolstoy's wife, Sofia Andreyevna, left him at Nikolskoe to travel to Moscow, and in her absence Tolstoy alternated between depression and jealousy. Earlier in the month, Tolstoy had written an angry letter to his wife accusing her of acting "involuntarily" and "unconsciously" ("*nevol'no*" and "*bessoznatel'no*") in regard to Taneev (1928–1958:84:275). Because he did not want to cease loving her, he said, there was only one possible remedy: "There remains one chance, that you will wake from the somnambulism in which you are walking and return to normal life" "*Ostaetsia odna vozmozhnost',' ta, chto ty prosnesh'sia ot etogo somnambulizma, v kotorom ty khodish',' i vernesh'sia k normal'noi zhizni*" (276–77). In this context, Tolstoy's comments about dusting begin to look somewhat different. If Sofia Andreyevna acted unconsciously, her actions would be (according to the logic of the diary entry) to a fundamental extent less threatening and perhaps even fictitious; "if I had cleaned and forgotten it, that is, acted unconsciously, it would be all the same, as if it had never happened. . . . if the entire complex life of many people passes unconsciously, it is as if that life had never happened."

Thus, the opening piece of evidence supporting Shklovsky's exposition of defamiliarization is essentially part of a spousal squabble that contributes to a denial of the reality of female consciousness and of female desire. Because Shklovsky probably had not read the letter from Tolstoy cited above—it was omitted when Sofia Andreyevna published her correspondence with her husband in 1915—we speak here of a relationship that emerges only from an exploration of sub-textual material repressed in the process of a chain of publication and citation. The effect, though, is still worth considering: on the one hand, Shklovsky—albeit "unintentionally" and "unconsciously"—discards or wipes away the quotidian dust off Tolstoy's life and silences Tolstoy's yearning for the refamiliarization of Sofia Andreyevna and for a return to his "normal," i.e., "habitual" life (of course, to speak of Tolstoy's life as normal is itself problematic); on the other hand, Shklovsky preserves Tolstoy's hostility to female subjectivity. And Shklovsky's oft-cited aphorism immediately following his quotation of the dusting scene—and his requotation of it, as if for emphasis—now also begins to look different, or less familiar, as well:

> Thus life, unnoticed, fades away. Automatization eats up things, clothing, furniture, the wife and the fear of war.
>
> "If the entire complex life of many people passes unconsciously, it is as if that life had never happened." (13)

In other words, the wife, here sandwiched between repetitions of the quote from Tolstoy, may be not only general and indefinite (the wife, our wives) but also a quite specific wife, the subjugation of whose will was an ongoing struggle for the most frequently cited source of Shklovsky's quotations in "Art as Device." In this context, it is worth recalling what Shklovsky represses in his most famous quotations from Tolstoy, those drawn from the scene of Natasha's visit to the opera in War and Peace. Shklovsky reproduces for his reader Natasha's uncomprehending, defamiliarized vision of the opera, but he cuts the scene to eliminate all traces of Natasha's presence. Her name is totally repressed, as are the intervening scenes in which she sees and learns to desire Kuragin. Whereas Tolstoy condemns female desire by showing its subsequent consequences, Shklovsky, working under greater constraints of time and space, wipes the desire away entirely.[16]

The quotation from Shklovsky's article printed in the notes to the translation of Brik's article in volume fifteen of *Screen* begins just after this comment about the loss of a wife: "What is called art exists in order to restore man's sensation of life, to make him perceive things, to make a stone stony." The phallic import here seems not to have been noticed by Mulvey, and the omission of the paragraph with the wife may have precluded her from realizing that in its move from "wife" to "fear of war" to "stone" Shklovsky's article comes about as close as possible to a three word summary of one of Mulvey's most prominently cited Freudian texts—"Medusa's Head."[17] But the dynamic that we have been exploring here suggests another—does art in Shklovsky's view exist to make a wife wifey? And does this wifey-ness consist in a woman's loss of conscious choice and in the appropriation—necessary to patriarchy—of independent female desire? In her reading of

Eisenstein's *Strike*, Judith Mayne remarks that defamiliarization may be profoundly conservative "in the sense that the disruption of a straightforward narrative [may] prevent the political structure of the film from being understood as cliché and stereotype" (68–69). Mayne's point about the avant-garde cinema is that montage can serve as a subterfuge for the perpetuation of traditional values. Our reading of Shklovsky has suggested that this use of a defamiliarizing technique as a patriarchal device was not Eisenstein's innovation but may have been inherent in Shklovsky's and Formalism's early and most famous salvo.

In a memoir included in his 1983 anthology, *On the Theory of Prose*, Shklovsky admits that he made at least one mistake in "Art as Device." Reminiscing about the Formalists' early days, Shklovsky recalls: "It was then that I invented the term 'defamiliarization' [*ostranenie*]. And—today I have reached the point where I can admit that I have made grammatical mistakes—I wrote one n. I should have written *strannyi* [strange, with two n's]. And so off it went with one N, and like a dog with a severed ear, runs about the world" (73).[18] Two pages later he returns to this free-range canine: "One of my articles which was published then, 'Art as Device,' has been republished without any changes up to the present day. Not because it was impeccable and correct, but because, just as we write with a pencil, so time writes with us" (75). In that very same collection, however, "Art as Device" is reprinted with changes. Reprinted for the first time since 1929, this new version, according to the collection's editor, K.N. Polonskaya, offers the reader "an exact copy" "*tochnaia kopiia*" of the 1929 text (8). All that has been changed, she adds, is "the system of citation, to bring it into line with contemporary rules" and to include republications of Shklovsky's sources that are more accessible than the original editions (8). Silently wiped away from the text are many of the symptomatic "mistakes" discussed above. In effect, Polonskaya gives Shklovsky's dog a new, prosthetic ear.[19]

III

Let's close with just one more turn of the screw. Mulvey is extremely cautious in her handling of Freud and Lacan; she is aware that their views are products of the patriarchy and may explode in a feminist critic's hands at any moment. Her implicit embrace of "defamiliarization" does not seem attuned to a similar danger. And yet—perhaps via Shklovsky—a specter of aggression toward woman seems to haunt her programmatic, feminist, formalist solution to the problem of cinema's male gaze. I want to end, therefore, with a brief look at another repressed text in "Visual Pleasure and Narrative Cinema": Hitchcock's *Psycho*.

As reprinted in Mulvey's anthology, "Visual Pleasure" has itself been subtly revised from its original version. One of these revisions concerns the introduction of Hitchcock. The revised version purports to speak of Hitchcock's oeuvre as a whole, supporting its interpretations with references to specific films: *Rear Window, Vertigo, Marnie*. In the original version, Mulvey's remarks are immediately qualified by the statement "in the films which I shall discuss here" ("Visual Pleasure" 15). This initial qualification reveals an awareness that things might function differently in other of Hitchcock's films. The one film that comes to mind as conspicuously absent, given the importance to it of voyeurism—is *Psycho*. As Tania Modleski (73–100) and Marian E. Keane (231–48) have shown, Mulvey's reading of at least two of the films she analyzes (*Rear Window* and *Vertigo*) is rather facile and ignores details that might complicate or undermine her remarks about the gendered gaze. *Psycho* poses an extreme version of this dynamic. Unable to "save" the film for her paradigm through partial repression, Mulvey must repress it altogether.

At the conclusion of *Psycho*, the safe and boring male lead asks a psychiatrist why Norman Bates dressed up in his mother's clothes. "He's a transvestite," a slow-thinking sheriff interjects. "Not exactly," the psychiatrist responds, before explaining how Norman and his mother have coexisted in one body for years until now, when only the mother is left. This explanation is consistent, one supposes, with the killer's name: he is, as Raymond Bellour has pointed out, "Neither woman nor man" (329). And yet there might be another answer consistent with the psychiatrist's "not exactly," an answer that would take seriously the dominance of the mother at the film's ending, in which we hear the mother's voice thinking in Norman's masculine clothed body. The constant copresence of Norman and his mother—together with the latter's dominance—suggest that we treat "not exactly" as a spur to reversing naïve assumptions about what "transvestitism" would mean; reading the film as parable or allegory (as Mulvey would) rather than as psychoanalytic casestudy, we might conclude that throughout most of the movie a woman is disguised and clothed as a man.[20] If this reading is pursued, the famous shower scene, in which Norman uneasily spies on the undressing Marion and then, in women's clothes, kills her, should be understood as follows: Norman's mother, in drag (that is, disguised as Norman), watches Marion undress, and then—having changed back into her own clothes—stabs Marion as she luxuriates in the shower. As perverse as this explanation may seem, it is fully in keeping with Mulvey's female moviegoer, whose "nature," in Mulvey's twice repeated line, "shifts restlessly in its borrowed transvestite clothes."[21] The shower scene has frequently been read as a moment of punishment for the (male) viewer who is identified through his voyeurism with the (murderous) figure that emerges from the other side of the shower-curtain screen.[22] And yet one can see why Mulvey would have had difficulty with

Psycho and why she avoided cinema's perhaps most notorious scopophilic moment as she developed her argument about the male and female gazes; for in P*sycho* the figure who watches an image presumably designed for masculine pleasure and then destroys it appears to be an uncanny reflection of the sort of feminist formalist Mulvey extols. In an article first published in 1960, Jean Douchet quotes Hitchcock's remark that "to appreciate *Psycho*, one needs a great sense of humor" and adds "especially, some Hitchcockian humor which consists, as we know, in reversing wishes, that is to say in realizing them in a way contrary to our expectations" ("Hitch and his Public" 12). Mulvey may have seen and not wanted to see this power in *Psycho*—and looked away to other films.[23]

The syntactic rhyme and pronominal ambiguity in Mulvey's words near the start of her famous article also may point toward the same dilemma: "This article will discuss the interweaving of that erotic pleasure in film, its meaning and, in particular, the central place of the image of woman. It is said that analyzing pleasure, or beauty, destroys it. That is the intention of this article." Is "it," circling almost mirror-like through Mulvey's text and collapsing the specificity of subject and object, "pleasure," "beauty" or "the image of woman"? The analytical knife cutting through the patriarchy's pleasurable defenses against castration finds itself in the uncomfortable position of burying itself in the image of woman. There is a certain logic in Mulvey's anthology which seems inevitably to lead to this moment as the symbolic embodiment of her call for "tearing the veil," "splitting open" "the closed space between screen and spectator," and "splitting the sign." After all, the first essay in her anthology, entitled "The Spectacle is Vulnerable," describes Mulvey's part in a protest at London's Albert Hall that interrupted the 1970 Miss World Pageant: "We had reduced our grandiose plans to the simplest strategy of aiming for the jury and the stage with the comic array of weapons with which we were armed" (4).[24] In P*sycho* this sort of protest looks far more deadly. Yet there is a connection between the writing of "The Kreutzer Sonata" and the killing of Marion Crane: as part of Marion's erasure, her killer, like Tolstoy, must clean up the room, literally wiping away evidence so that life may continue as if nothing had happened.

When using the analytical models of the patriarchy, the feminist formalist may find herself in the paradoxical position of seeking the liberation of her desire through the brutal destruction of a woman's representation. The suppressed question behind Mulvey's avoidance of *Psycho* may be whether killing women—even at a number of representational removes—can be a feminist act. The suppressed question behind scholarly reluctance to look at gender in "Art as Device" may be whether critics under its influence have been working with an aggressively masculine concept of art and have failed to recognize that the essence of the knight's move may be the capture of the queen.[25]

NOTES

This chapter was originally published in *Comparative Literature* 50:4 (1998): 333–352.

1. The special issue of *Camera Obscura* in 1989 devoted to "The Spectatrix" provides ample evidence, if any is needed, for the founding importance of Mulvey's article in feminist film theory. The issue consists of several articles and sixty responses to a questionnaire, all of which repeatedly testify to the impact of Mulvey's article on the work of the authors and respondents.

2. The term "symptomatic reading" has become the hallmark of Jane Gallop's work. Symptomatic reading pays attention to a text's blind spots and repressions. "Where new critical close reading embraces the text in order to more fully and deeply understand its excellences, 'symptomatic reading' squeezes the text tight to force it to reveal its perversities" (Gallop 7). Recently, Mulvey has become interested in symptomatology as a method of critical reading. In her latest collection of essays, the term "symptom" appears in various forms no less than thirty-eight times; at one point it is used six times in a single paragraph (*Fetishism and Curiosity* 25). Mulvey is concerned, however, with only cultural symptoms. The purpose of the present essay is to explore the extent to which our understanding not only of the cinema but also of important writing about it may be enriched by a symptomatological approach.

3. Unless noted otherwise, citations of Mulvey's work will be to *Visual and Other Pleasures*.

4. Mulvey returns to this important image of "transvestite clothes" at the end of the article (*Visual and Other Pleasures* 37). Arguably, the notion of the transvestite female viewer is foreshadowed in "Visual Pleasure," where Mulvey considers the erotic life of the hero of *Rear Window*: "His girlfriend Lisa has been of little sexual interest to him, more or less *a drag, so long as she remained on the spectator side*" (23) (emphasis added).

5. See Gallop's use of this etymology in her analysis of the anthology *The (M)other Tongue* (61).

6. In its original version, the article contained two footnotes. The first, an aside about films with female protagonists, is in *Visual and Other Pleasures* placed in the text of the article as a parenthetical remark. The second, at the article's conclusion, stated that the work was "a reworked version of a paper given in the French Department of the University of Wisconsin, Madison, in the Spring of 1973" ("Visual Pleasure" 18).

7. Tania Modleski (13–14) has noted this implicit use of Hitchcock's films as *metacinematic* support for Mulvey's reading of spectatorship. Compare Marian E. Keane's contention that Mulvey fails to take note of V*ertigo*'s metacinematic dimensions (246).

8. Teresa de Lauretis refers to Mulvey's position as a "Brechtian-Godardian program" (60). This genealogy, though, has its own debt to Russian Formalism. Brecht acknowledged his profound debt to his "teacher," Sergei Tret'iakov, who was a collaborator with Shklovsky on the journal *LEF* and was heavily influenced by the Formalist movement. The crucial aesthetic term "alienation" (*Verfremdung*) was coined by Brecht only after his visit to Moscow in 1934, when he was a guest of Tret'iakov and may be indebted to the Formalist notion of "making strange" (Grimm 211–12; Leach 510; Jameson 58–59; Striedter 441–42). For a sketch of Tret'iakov's life, see Gomolitskaia-Tret'iakova.

9. See Judith Mayne, whose pioneering book (1989) is more concerned with gender's role in the Formalist-informed cinema of Sergei Eisenstein and other early Soviet directors than with a gendered reading of the principal theoretical texts of Russian Formalism. The role of gender is also a prominent focus in Linda Kaufman's analysis of Shklovsky's epistolary, metacritical 1923 novel, *Zoo, or Letters Not about Love*.

10. In this respect, Brecht's reassertion of the ethical, ideological significance of *Verfremdung* would seem to mark a return to the original intent of several of the passages from Tolstoy's writing cited by Shklovsky. See Striedter, 441–42.

11. For a discussion of the extent to which the Formalists turned texts and devices into the equivalents of literary characters, see Rancour-Laferriere, 329–31.

12. Here I have used the very readable translation published by Lemon and Reis (21), emending it only with respect to the spider, which they—following an alternative version of this joke—transform into a "fly." In all other places, however, I have supplied my own, more literal translation. Russian quotations will be taken from the version included in the 1929 collection, *O teorii prozy*.

13. Examples of this usage vary from *priem pishchi* (the ingestion of food) to *priem imeniia* (the taking possession of an estate).

14. For a reading of Nietzsche's veils in the context of female spectatorship, see Mary Ann Doane, 44–75.

15. One may sense a certain degree of mockery even in the placing of Tolstoy, the historical man, at the start of a series of characters that includes many whose access to defamiliarization is narratively proximate to violent, or potentially humiliating, subjugation: a castrated horse, a young woman about to fall prey to a seducer, an imprisoned nobleman, animals violated by a peasant. Only the scholar/critic, it would seem, can have access to insights of defamiliarization through the comforting and inviolable screen of his own acumen.

16. In a book on *War and Peace* written over a decade later, Shklovsky acknowledged that the use of defamiliarization in this scene served the purpose of assisting and was, in part, motivated by Natasha's characterization (*Material i stil'* 28). In this more sober, scholarly book neither sex nor gender play prominent roles, nor does Shklovsky's style bear the mark of an aesthetic manifesto.

17. See the extended epigraph that introduces Mulvey's "Fears, Fantasies and the Male Unconscious or 'You Don't Know What Is Happening, Do You, Mr Jones?'" (6).

18. This dog is probably part of a pun. A few paragraphs later, describing again the process of defamiliarization in Tolstoy, Shklovsky mentions as his first example Pierre Bezukhov [literally Earless, *bez ukha*], the hero of *War and Peace*. It takes an earless creation by Shklovsky to discern the poetic devices of Tolstoy's original.

19. There has been no textological work on "Art as Device." It was first published in the second volume of the Opoiaz (Formalists') *Sborniki po teorii poeticheskogo iazyka* [Anthologies on the Theory of Poetic Language] in 1917, then again with an important supplement (all the material on erotic art) in the third volume in 1919. This erotically supplemented version was reprinted in Shklovsky's critical anthology, *Teoriia prozy/O teorii prozy*, which was published in two editions—in 1925 and 1929. The 1919 text differs from the 1925 and 1929 texts in several minor respects, including punctuation and the use of increasing spacing between letters as a form of emphasis. The most striking difference is the deletion in the later texts of a sexually graphic example in which a soldier orders his wife to strip and mounts her from behind, thus winning a wager with devils, who cannot guess what kind of animal she is. This example, the source of which is cited but not quoted in the 1925 and 1929 texts, directly preceded the tale of the peasant and the three mutilated animals that is said to employ a device "identical" to that of Tolstoy's "Kholstomer."

One wonders what the readers of the third volume of the Formalists' *Anthologies* must have thought in 1919 when reencountering an article they had recently read in the previous tome. Presumably, if they bothered to read it a second time, they would have been struck by the new, "erotic" material, which would at that time have been more notable than it has been for subsequent readers, who encounter the entire text as new when they read it for the first time. My guess is that Shklovsky did not originally intend to include the section on erotic art, because it seems to contradict the piece's opening rebuke of Potebnia for examining similar material. In any event, the article's treatment of women is very much in keeping with the misogynistic dynamics of early Revolutionary culture that were far more developed in the Proletkul't-dominated environment of 1919 than they were two years earlier.

20. Cf. Linda William's suggestion that in *Psycho* "the monster who attacks both looks like and, in some sense, is a woman." Elsewhere in the same article she also makes the point that in horror films women often see in monsters "a potentially subversive recognition of the power and potency of a non-phallic sexuality." She adds: "Precisely because this look is so threatening to male power, it is violently punished" (90). To be relevant to *Psycho*, however, this insight must be projected onto a metacinematic plane: the woman in the film (Marion Crane,

along with her monstrous, frequently trouser-clad double, Mrs. Bates) then becomes all women, and especially the female spectator with access to Mulvey's insights into Hollywood film.

21. The supplementary article, "Afterthoughts on 'Visual Pleasure and Narrative Cinema' inspired by *Duel in the Sun*," in which the two "transvestite" phrases appear, begins with an assertion of Mulvey's subjectivity: "So many times over the years since my 'Visual Pleasure and Narrative Cinema' article was published in *Screen*, I have been asked why I only used the *male* third person singular to stand in for the spectator." Mulvey's emphasis on "male" masks *another* fundamental pronominal change that occurs in this article: in its first paragraph the first person singular appears at least six times. In "Visual Pleasure," on the other hand, Mulvey refrains almost entirely from using the first person singular; it surfaces only in her discussion of Lacan ("the first articulation of the I," etc.) and in the qualification repressed in the anthologized version: "in the films [by Hitchcock] I will discuss here." Elsewhere, the first person appears in the collective plural encouraged by the manifesto genre. The supplement, therefore, restores the first person author and films that she ("I") did not choose to discuss earlier; through the first person it leads the reader into a much closer contact with Mulvey's subjective world.

22. See, *inter alia*, Douchet (*Alfred Hitchcock* 86–95), Durgnat (212), Rothman (292–301), Silverman (206–13), Wood (146–47).

23. In her recent collection of articles, Mulvey *does* mention *Psycho*—in a quite intriguing context. She describes the entry of Marion's sister and the camera into the Bates home as an emblematic moment of female curiosity. She then contrasts this moment with fetishism, which is "born out of a refusal to see." She adds: "These complex series of turnings away, of covering over, not of the eyes but of understanding, of fixating on a substitute object to hold the gaze, leave the female body as an enigma and threat, condemned to return as a symbol of anxiety while simultaneously being transformed into its own screen in representation" (*Fetishism and Curiosity* 64). This moment, I would suggest, is symptomatic of Mulvey's own series of turnings away from, and of finding substitute objects for the shower scene in *Psycho*.

In arguing that Mulvey resisted identification with Mrs. Bates, I am, of course, implicitly projecting Mulvey into *Psycho*. Moreover, by deconstructing her resistance to the film, I am treating her as Mulvey's male viewer treats a female character in a Hollywood film: investigating, mystifying, punishing. My argument, however, follows closely the lesson of much of Mulvey's own work, which insists on the porousness of the screen and the extent to which the spectacle and the spectator are "vulnerable" (3–5, 14–26).

24. The article is elliptical. Because Mulvey never tells her readers just what the "comic" weapons were, the Feminist protest in which she took part has an uncertain status somewhere between "violent action" (3) and comedy. Here too, there is an uncanny echo of Hitchcock: the interruption of a concert at the Albert Hall by Doris Day (of all actresses!) in the second version of *The Man Who Knew Too Much*.

25. I would like to thank Caryl Emerson, Boris Gasparov, Olga Matich, Anne Nesbet, William Nickell, Irina Paperno, Sarah Pratt, Thomas Seifrid, Alexander Zholkovsky and an anonymous reviewer for their helpful suggestions.

WORKS CITED

Bellour, Raymond. "Psychosis, Neurosis, Perversion," translated by Nancy Huston. *A Hitchcock Reader*, edited by Marshall Deutelbaum and Leland Poague, 311–31. Ames: Iowa State University Press, 1986.

Bergstrom, Janet, and Mary Ann Doane. "The Female Spectator: Contexts and Directions." *Camera Obscura* 20–21 (1989): 5–27.

———, eds. *The Spectatrix. Special issue of Camera Obscura* 20–21 (1989).

Boym, Svetlana. "Loving in Bad Taste: Eroticism and Literary Excess in Marina Tsvetaeva's 'The Tale of Sonechka.'" *Sexuality and the Body in Russian Culture*, edited by Jane Costlow, Stephanie Sandler and Judith Vowles, 156–76. Stanford: Stanford University Press, 1993.

de Lauretis, Teresa. *Alice Doesn't: Feminism, Semiotics, Cinema*. Bloomington: Indiana University Press, 1982.

Doane, Mary Ann. *Femmes Fatales: Feminism, Film Theory, Psychoanalysis*. New York: Routledge, 1991.
Douchet, Jean. *Alfred Hitchcock*. n.p.: Editions de l'Herne, 1967.
———. "Hitch and His Public," translated by Verena Conley. *A Hitchcock Reader*, edited by Marshall Deutelbaum and Leland Poague, 7–15. Ames: Iowa State University Press, 1986.
Durgnat, Raymond. *Films and Feelings*. London: Faber and Faber, 1967.
Enzensberger, Maria. "Introduction [to the Selected Writings of Osip Brik]." *Screen* 15.3 (1974): 35–58.
Gallop, Jane. *Around 1981: Academic Feminist Literary Theory*. New York: Routledge, 1992.
Gomolitskaia-Tret'iakova, T.S. "O moëm otse." In *Strana-perekrëstok*, by Sergei Tret'iakov, 554–63. Moscow: Sovetskii pisatel', 1991 (in Russian).
Goscilo, Helena. "Monsters Monomaniacal, Marital, and Medical: Tatiana Tolstaya's Regenerative Use of Gender Stereotypes." *Sexuality and the Body in Russian Culture*, edited by Jane Costlow, Stephanie Sandler and Judith Vowles, 204–20. Stanford: Stanford University Press, 1993.
Grimm, Reinhold. "Verfremdung: Breiträge zu Wesen und Ursprung eines Begriffs." *Revue de Littérature Comparée* 35.2 (1961): 206–36.
Jameson, Frederic. *The Prison-House of Language: A Critical Account of Structuralism and Russian Formalism*. Princeton: Princeton University Press, 1972.
Kauffman, Linda S. *Special Delivery: Epistolary Modes in Modern Fiction*. Chicago: University of Chicago Press, 1992.
Keane, Marian E. "A Closer Look at Scopophilia: Mulvey, Hitchcock and Vertigo." *A Hitchcock Reader*, edited by Marshall Deutelbaum and Leland Poague, 231–48. Ames: Iowa State University Press, 1986.
Leach, Robert. "Brecht's Teacher." *Modern Drama* 32 (1989): 502–511.
Lemon, Lee T. and Marion J. Reis, eds. *Russian Formalist Criticism*. Lincoln: Nebraska University Press, 1965.
Mayne, Judith. *Kino and the Woman Question: Feminism and Soviet Silent Film*. Columbus: Ohio State University Press, 1989.
Modleski, Tania. *The Women Who Knew Too Much: Hitchcock and Feminist Theory*. New York: Routledge, 1988.
Morris, William, ed. *American Heritage Dictionary of the English Language*. American Heritage, 1970.
Mulvey, Laura. "British Feminist Film Theory's Female Spectators: Presence and Absence." *Camera Obscura* 20–21 (1989): 5–27.
———. *Fetishism and Curiosity*. Bloomington: Indiana University Press, 1996.
———. *Visual and Other Pleasures*. Bloomington: Indiana University Press, 1989.
———. "Visual Pleasure and Narrative Cinema." *Screen* 16.3 (1975): 6–18.
Nietzsche, Friedrich. *The Gay Science*, translated by Walter Kaufmann. New York: Vintage, 1974.
Rancour-Laferriere, Daniel. "Why the Russian Formalists Had No Theory of the Literary Personality." *Wiener Slawistischer Almanach* (Sonderband) 31 (1992): 327–37.
Rothman, William. *Hitchcock: The Murderous Gaze*. Cambridge: Harvard University Press, 1982.
Sherwood, Richard. "Viktor Shklovsky and the Development of Early Formalist Theory on Prose Literature." *20th Century Studies*, 7–8 (1972): 26–40.
Shklovsky, Viktor. "Iskusstvo kak priëm." *Sborniki po teorii poeticheskogo iazyka*, Vol. 2, 3–14. Petrograd: Opoiaz, 1917 (in Russian).
———. "Iskusstvo kak priëm," *Sborniki po teorii poeticheskogo iazyka*, vol. 3, 101–114. Petrograd: Opoiaz, 1919 (in Russian).
———. *Material i stil' v romane L'va Tolstogo "Voina i mir."* Moskva: Federatsiia, 1928. Reprint: The Hague: Mouton, 1970 (in Russian).
———. *O teorii prozy*. Moskva: Federatsiia, 1929. Reprint: Ann Arbor: Ardis, 1985 (in Russian).
———. *O teorii prozy*. Moskva: Sovetskii pisatel', 1983 (in Russian).
———. *Teoriia prozy*. Moskva: Krug, 1925 (in Russian).

———. *Za 60 let: raboty o kino.* Moskva: Iskusstvo, 1985 (in Russian).
Silverman, Kaja. *The Subject of Semiotics.* New York: Oxford University Press, 1983.
Striedter, Jurij. "The Russian Formalist Theory of Prose." *PTL* 3 (1977): 429–70.
Tolstoy, L. N. Polnoe sobranie sochinenii, edited by V. Chertkov et al. 90 vols. Moskva: Khudozhestvennaiia literatura, 1928–1958 (in Russian).
———. "Dnevnik L.N. Tolstogo. Izvlecheniia pod redaktsiei A.M. Khir'iakova." In *A. M. Khir'iakov,* ed. *Letopis'* [The Chronicle] Dec. 1915: 332–75 (in Russian).
———. *Pis'ma k zhene.* Moskva: n.p, 1915 (in Russian).
———. *Chto takoe iskusstvo.* Moskva: Sovremennik, 1985 (in Russian).
Tynyanov, Yury. *Dostoevsky i Gogol' (K teorii parodii).* Petrograd: Opoiaz, 1921. Reprint: Letchworth, UK: Prideaux, 1975 (in Russian).
Williams, Linda. "When the Woman Looks." *Re-Vision, Essays in Feminist Film Criticism,* edited by Mary Ann Doane, Patricia Mellencamp and Linda Williams, 83–98. Frederick: University Publications of America.
Wood, Robin. *Hitchcock's Films Revisited.* New York: Columbia University Press, 1989.

Chapter Thirteen

Reading Viktor Shklovsky's "Art as Technique" in the Context of Early Cinema

Annie van den Oever

The Russian writer Maxim Gorky in his essay, "Last Night I was in the Kingdom of Shadows," suggested that the Lumière's cinematograph proved to be a machine that created distortions and disproportions in the representation of people and things, making them look "strange," if not "grotesque."[1] For Gorky, the images created by the new cinema machine had an abundant expressive potential—the potential that soon was unleashed to the fullest by the Futurist performances adding to the already existing "craze" of the early film shows.[2]

This chapter[3] will argue that Viktor Shklovsky's key text "Art as Technique," which revolves around the famous key term *ostran (n)enie* ("making strange"), points at two related phenomena: the way in which the early film show exploited the expressive potential of the new cinema machine to make humans and objects look "strange" if not "grotesque," as Gorky had aptly argued in 1896;[4] and the ways in which this inspired the avant-garde performances celebrated by Shklovsky's Futurist friends (e.g., the poet Vladimir Mayakovsky) from 1909 on. These two phenomena form the context for the inception of "Art as Technique."

To make this point, I will reread "Art as a Technique" within the historical context of the effects of the early film shows and address the question how the new cinema machine functioned to make Maxim Gorky label it as a "grotesque creation."[5] This chapter attempts to create an understanding of Gorky and Shklovsky's relation to the "strangeness" of the early film shows. Therefore, it will present specific fragments of a cultural archaeology of the then new medium and an excavation of its novelty effects. This method is chosen in an attempt to avoid the misunderstandings created by the retrospective perspective. From this perspective, one tends to overlook the novelty experiences triggered by a new medium. As is so aptly explained by Shklovsky in "Art as Technique," novelty/strangeness experiences vanish overtime. Thus, excavations such as in this chapter are needed to remind us of them and to reinvigorate the context from which "Art as Technique" emerged.

IF YOU ONLY KNEW HOW STRANGE IT WAS

Gorky famously described his first "film experience"[6] in 1896 as completely novel and exciting at the same time. As he explained, the new medium provided movement and thus a sudden taste of the animated, of life and of the real. Seeing this completely mute, two-dimensional greyish world made all what's shown seem strange, dead, uncanny, and ambiguous, as if the world were animate and inanimate, proportionate and disproportionate, and real and dreamlike. As Gorky explains in his essay, all those things that in themselves were familiar to the audience were "made strange" by the Lumière's new "cinema machine."[7] Paris, the people, the horses, carriages, the trembling leaves on the tree. . . . If you only knew how strange they were to these early cinema audiences. Echoes of Gorky's words and remarkably similar observations can be found in many turn-of-the-century descriptions of the early movie-going experience, as film scholar Yuri Tsivian has posited.[8] Since twenty-first-century movie-goers are distanced from this moment in time,[9] it seems constructive to cite him once again in an attempt to evoke the taste of an experience of awe and excitement at seeing the first moving images:

> If you only knew how strange it felt. There were no sounds and no colours. Everything—earth, trees, people, water, air—was portrayed in a grey monotone: in a grey sky there were grey rays of sunlight; in grey faces—grey eyes, and the leaves of the tree were grey like ashes. . . . Silently the ash-grey foliage of the trees swayed in the wind and the grey silhouettes of the people glided silently along the grey ground, as if condemned to eternal silence and cruelly punished by being deprived of all life's colours.[10]

In retrospect, it is very difficult, almost impossible, to understand such experiences and exclamations when viewed from our current perspective, as viewing practices have radically changed since 1896. Judging from reception documents, it seems that early movie-goers' experiences were "strange" (Gorky), "uncanny," "astonishing" (Gunning) and often even "stupefying."[11]

SHKLOVSKY AND MAYAKOVSKY

"New phenomena accumulate without being perceived, later they are perceived in a revolutionary way," as Shklovsky wrote in his book on Mayakovsky.[12] "[T]he new arrives unnoticed," he wrote on another occasion.[13] The "new," as early cinema scholar Tom Gunning argues, needs a discourse to be perceived.[14] Hence, very often the "new" cannot be "seen" in its first moment of confrontation. Only much later can we begin to fully understand the extent of its revolutionary impact. Nevertheless, Shklovsky helped provide the discourse to frame the experience of the new by labeling it as essentially estranging.

1909–1912: A SLAP IN THE FACE OF PUBLIC TASTE

Vladimir Mayakovsky and his Futurist friends had a strong impact on Shklovsky, which his memoir, *Mayakovsky and His Circle,* attests to. Moreover, in his *The Hamburg Score*, published in 1928, Shklovsky confirms that film also had a revolutionary impact on him and his Futurist friends. Looking back on the previous decades, Shklovsky writes that the cinema and his work on the cinema "probably modernized me."[15] But in 1928 he had already written, produced and edited films in the 1920s collectives, who made films together.

Much earlier, in the completely different era of the early 1910s, Shklovsky had been a witness to the Futurists' poetry performances. His friends had started "reading" their poetry typically incorporating some of the "crazy" elements of the popular film shows into their avant-garde performances. Yuri Tsivian deemed the Futurists part of the cultural reception of early cinema in Russia, pointing out that they responded in different ways than the Symbolists did. The cultural reception of the Symbolists (who were far more established in the literary world) stayed within the realm of literary tradition, and sometimes well within its margins, as the word 'clichés' used by Tsivian already indicates. In contrast, the Futurists broke with tradition in a rather brisk and bewildering way.[16] Their role in the public debate was radically different: more disruptive, more captivating, more memorable. They moved center stage with great turmoil in the very year Russia's "general craze about the cinema" reached a peak in the year 1913.[17] In the midst of the excitement triggered by the film shows, the Futurists succeeded in captivating the attention of the public once again. They also did so in December 1912 presenting one of their stunningly aggressive manifestos, *A Slap in the Face of Public Taste*. According to Futurism expert Markov, the "aggressive tone of the manifesto and its attacks on everyone from Pushkin to its contemporaries" shocked "everyone" as everyone got a "slap in the face."[18] The Futurists' performances by then were infamous and "crazy." They liked to provoke their audiences and shocking them in a direct address had quickly become one of their specialties. Creating disturbance was an essential part of their poetics and performances. They wanted to trigger a strong audience response and often succeeded, as newspaper articles of the time attest to. According to an influential conservative newspaper, the Futurists stood out as "a bunch of half-wits," in that "crazy" year when cinema was most impressive.[19] So by 1913, the Futurists were closely identified with the cinema, as Tsivian argues, the cinema and the Futurists, together, triggered a sense of "general craze."[20] Both cinema and Futurist poetry were associated with something feverish and vague, with something "incoherent, spasmodic, senseless," with the "[u]ngrammatical, asyntactic"; "these are only some of the features that Futurists and cinema were found to have in common."[21]

Whereas the Symbolists, who "thematized"[22] the uncanny or simply unfamiliar aspects of the viewing experience by attributing meaning to them, the Futurists rather responded to the performative and expressive potential of the new technique itself and mostly with great appreciation for the disruptive perceptual experiences the technique was able to create.

DECEMBER 1913: THE CABARET "THE STRAY DOG"

In December 1913, the young Shklovsky, still a freshman at the University of Saint Petersburg, presented a lecture to his Futurist friends in The Stray Dog, an avant-garde cabaret frequented by the prominent artists of St. Petersburg. It was there "that Shklovsky read a paper entitled 'The place of Futurism in the History of Language.' In his talk he maintained that futurist poetry emancipated words from their traditional significance and *restored them to perceptibility* by calling attention to their sounds."[23] This is to say that Shklovsky provided the theoretical framework for explaining the impact of the new techniques used by the avant-garde poets by drawing from the revolutionary new perspective of perception studies, which was still a very young discipline in academia at that point in time. Interestingly, he came up with a theory the Futurists themselves were not able to provide. It has been argued by Markov that the Futurists in these early years quarreled too much and theorized too little, and that in fact they were not very theoretically proficient,[24] or at least not half as accomplished as the older and much more established Symbolist movement in Russia at that same point in time. They had Andrey Bely and other strong figures to support Symbolism from a theoretical angle. As Richard Sheldon wrote, among the Futurists "[o]nly Khlebnikov had some training in linguistics."[25] Via Shklovsky, they too were suddenly able to at least establish a connection with the Department of Philology at the University of Petersburg, which in fact made Shklovsky an even more interesting "ally." He was properly academically trained, and on top of it, he was brilliant and brash, as they were soon to find out. Until that moment, their poetical reflections were not half as competent as the best-known works by the Symbolists, whose ideas clearly dominated the thinking on poetry and art of the day. In the early 1910s, the Futurists were not yet ready to properly theorize their own radical poetic experiments themselves which was understandable: as part of the broader cultural reception of the technological innovations created by early cinema, these new phenomena easily and almost inevitably escaped conceptualization. Their own reflections on newness were still a bit poor in these early years, but this does not imply that the poetic experiments themselves or their performances were not interesting, effective, or successful. From Shklovsky's own notes on the period (in his memoirs on Mayakovsky, in *A Sentimental Journey*, and other books), it is obvious that it was his great Futurist friend Vladimir Mayakovsky, whose presence, poetry, and poetics had a tremendous and pivotal impact on him, on so many other avant-gardists and on the larger youngster audience of the day (the slightly younger Sergei Eisenstein would be included in the circle of *LEF* about ten years later, when he became Russia's most famous film director).[26]

At the time, Mayakovsky and his Futurist friends had created a revolutionary new performative practice: they were reciting poetry in a way that might remind us of rappers' rhythms. Mayakovsky was showing the audience that a poet need not use meanings, symbols and metaphors in poetry to have an instant impact on his audience; that language itself, its nonsensical sounds and its silly words, could themselves shock & thrill an audience the way an early film show could. Shklovsky provided the conceptual space for framing and explaining the impact in the form of a theory of *ostran(n)enie*—a theory the Futurists themselves were unable to formulate at that point in time, and so Shklovsky filled the niche. Mayakovsky is said to have accepted the new theoretical input gracefully, while also being puzzled and surprised by it.[27]

December 1913, in his Stray Dog talk, Shklovsky introduced the term *samovitoe slovo*.[28] Later, he deepened his thoughts in his 1914 text *The Resurrection of the Word* under the same label of the "self-oriented word." Shklovsky's good friend Boris Eikhenbaum commented on this crucial point in time—crucial to an understanding of Shklovsky's thinking: he now approached the problem of the arts from the perspective of perception studies and he tried to understand the techniques used in the arts to create a specific perceptual experience.

DECEMBER 1916: "ART AS TECHNIQUE"

"Art as Technique" was written in late 1916 and first published in 1917.[29] The text presents Shklovsky's reflections on the twin mechanisms of automatization and de-automatization at the time; today, the two terms are alternatively translated as (de)familiarization or (de)habituation, whereas *ostran(n)enie* is often translated as alienation or estrangement.

> We do not experience the commonplace, we do not see it; rather, we recognize it. We do not see the walls of our room; and it is very difficult for us to see errors in proofreading, especially if the material is written in a language we know well, because we cannot force ourselves to see, to read, and not to "recognize" the familiar word.[30]

What is already familiar to us because we have seen it over and over again, we process habitually, and this process does not really leave much of a trace in our consciousness. However, in the arts, specifically in poetry, where things are made unfamiliar or strange, the smooth and swift process of perception is obstructed, slowed down, deepened and prolonged. This is typical of artistic perception (or what he would label the "art experience," in "Art as Technique"):

> If we have to define specifically "poetic" perception and artistic perception in general, then we suggest this definition: "Artistic" perception is that perception in which we experience form—perhaps not form alone, but certainly form.[31]

Eikhenbaum added an explanatory note to the word "perception" in his 1926 reflections, realizing that most contemporary readers might easily misunderstand Shklovsky's words on perception and form. (In 1926, they were already misread as so-called Formalists, a term coined by Lenin who meant to debunk them, and a label they themselves refused to use without quotation marks.)[32] Eikhenbaum's explanatory words show that they themselves were keenly aware that the new "Formalist" approach to art, from the perspective of perception, was new and even revolutionary, and in fact implied the radical rejection and abduction of the traditional and unfortunate dichotomy of form and content, replacing the "muddled" notion of "form by the notion of "technique" (*priem*).[33] "Perception" here is clearly not to be understood as a simple psychological concept (the perception peculiar to this or that person) but, since art does not exist outside of perception, it should be understood as an element belonging to art itself. Furthermore, Eikhenbaum explains that the notion of "form" here acquires new meaning; it is no longer an envelope, but a complete thing, something concrete, dynamic, self-contained, and without a correlative of any kind.[34] This is to say that the "self-contained word" is a term used in an attempt to get rid of the notion of "form" (it is such a muddy concept, as they kept repeating). Shklovsky tried to pull it out of the mud by replacing "form" by "technique" a few years later, in "Art as Technique." As so often in his life, Shklovsky kept going back to these decisive moments and to his rethinking of the problem of "form." He also had a tendency to rethink and rephrase certain problems over and over again, sometimes in slightly varying formulations. It seems to me that he did not do so to repeatedly stress the same point, but rather to unfold his thinking which he (like Nietzsche) presented in his work, as a process in *statu nascendi*: something happening on the spot, open, never finished, and always open to further rethinking in connection to life itself. He kept returning to one or two fundamental problems, in particular the techniques used in the arts to make the familiar "strange." Throughout his career Shklovsky revisited and reconsidered the (aesthetic) principle and the techniques of *ostran (n)enie* many times, not only in "Art as Technique," but also in a dazzling diversity of works such as *Theory of Prose*, *A Sentimental Journey*, in the memoir written for his Futurist friend, *Mayakovsky and His Circle*; in *Literature and Cinematography*; in his contribution to *Poetika Kino*;[35] in his book on Eisenstein, and so on and so forth. It was not until 1983, however, that Victor Shklovsky reflected on that very moment some seventy years earlier, when he had introduced the term *ostran(n)enie* and had accidentally unleashed a revolution in thinking about the arts. In 1983, he remarked that perhaps he "could now admit to having made a spelling mistake," as he had erroneously spelled *ostranenie* "with one *n*," though the Russian word *stannyi* (strange) is written with a double *nn*.[36] That is how the word entered the history books, with a single *n*, to roam about like "a dog with a ragged ear," as Shklovsky would have it.[37] In "Art as Technique," Shklovsky explored and explained his thoughts on what he was now to call, with an evocative neologism, *ostran (n)enie*.

"ART AS TECHNIQUE" AS AN ESTRANGING AVANT-GARDE MANIFESTO

Though theoretically sound and even brilliant, "Art as Technique" is also quirky and its rhetoric is rather baffling, as if he refused to write a proper academic text and chose to make an avant-garde manifesto for his Futurist friends, in line with the needs of the times. If anything, "Art as a Technique" is a manifesto, in the tradition of the Futurists: scanty, brazen, and provocative by its very generic nature.[38] With brashness,[39] Shklovsky presented his new ideas to the outside world on behalf of a group that was close enough to the Futurists to also be considered as "half-wits," but they did not seem to care. Boldly and with great polemic ardor, Shklovsky—now the leading figure of the Society for the Study of Poetic Language, OPOYAZ—presented his (or their) thoughts in the form of a radical attack on the traditional premises held by the Symbolists and on their idealist poetics. Characteristically, the manifesto is evocative as well as provocative, although not very didactic or impressively coherent. The argument presented is a bit hard to follow, though some parts are solid and of lasting value, in particular the part on "making strange" and its perceptual impact. As he wrote in "Art as Technique":

> If we start to examine the general laws of perception, we see that as perception becomes habitual, it becomes automatic. Thus, for example, all of our habits retreat into the area of the unconsciously automatic.
> [...]
> The process of "algebrization," the over-automatization of [the perception of] an object, permits the greatest economy of perceptive effort. Either objects are assigned only one proper feature—a number, for example—or else they function as though by formula and do not even appear in cognition.
> [...]
> After we see an object several times, we begin to recognize it. The object is in front of us and we know about it, but we do not see it—hence we cannot say anything significant about it.[40]

The most cited part of the text is on how art removes objects from the automatism of perception in several ways:

> The purpose of art is to impart the sensation of things as they are perceived and not as they are known. The technique of art is to make objects "unfamiliar," to make forms difficult, to increase the difficulty and length of perception because the process of perception is an aesthetic end in itself and must be prolonged.[41]

To remove objects from the automatism of perception, the so-called techniques of "deautomatization" are used, the techniques which make objects "strange" (*ostran (n)enie*) or "unfamiliar," as the older translations have it. In this way, art creates the typically prolonged and deepened perceptual experience.

The examples Shklovsky came up with in "Art as Technique" have been studied over the decades with some puzzlement and, at times, even downright irritation,[42] since some of them are "harsh," a fact for which Shklovsky himself apologizes, if only in one particular case.[43] They were taken almost exclusively from the fields of literature (including the folktale) and linguistics, the two fields the members of OPOYAZ had a bit of training in. The choice of samples comes across as incomprehensible if not grotesque in many ways. They were said to be chosen almost randomly, as a way of testing their theory, as Eikhenbaum points out,[44] and in "Art as Technique" they are inserted to merely illustrate their points, as Shklovsky states: "Here I want to illustrate a way used by Leo Tolstoy repeatedly."[45] However, they also seem to be chosen to incite and shock the readers, perhaps to amuse and entertain them as well, bombarding the reader with a set of remarkably incompatible samples, which are taken from Tolstoy and Pushkin as well as Gogol; from a collection of erotic riddles as well as the *Decameron* and *War and Peace*. One instance is taken from folk literature and features that memorable passage in which a peasant tortures a bear, a magpie, and a horsefly, while pretending to do something else to them. Next thing we know is that he is torturing his wife, trying to "shove a stick up [her] rump," or so the horsefly assumes, but readers are of course supposed to know better (the many abbreviated versions of "Art as Technique," available in text books and on the internet, were keen to leave these last samples out).

For many reasons, "Art as Technique" can be considered hard to interpret: because it is ambiguous and provocative; because it is not overtly coherent or didactic; because its examples are baffling; because it turns traditional thinking upside down, and so on and so forth. Possibly, it was even harder to understand and appreciate it in the post-war era of New Criticism and French Structuralism. When one expects a tight-knit text, then one may indeed be easily disappointed as a reader, and may indeed find Shklovsky's enterprise "embarrassingly easy to attack," as Lemon and Reis argued in the 1960s.[46] In fact, cutting "Art as Technique" loose from the turn-of-the century's technological transformations and their cultural impact on the avant-gardes does not help to understand the text. Quite on the contrary: all of Shklovsky's examples expose the potential "ontological instability of all mimetic representation"[47] in the same way new technologies do. As Gunning wrote, new technologies allow for an uncanny "re-animation" of the sense of instability that underlies mimetic tradition.[48] Within this context, it may be argued that Gorky's emphasis on "the uncanny effect of the new attraction's mix of realistic and non-realistic qualities"[49] signaled a crisis in the mimetic functioning of the cinematograph as a new medium. It made most of what was shown appear "alien" or "strange" (note that almost all examples presented by Shklovsky, no less than Gorky's, deal with seeing and the seen and ways of seeing). In effect, the new cinema machine may be said to have caused an epistemological crisis, a crisis for which the cultural explosion of discourses on the shared disruptive viewing experience may well be said to have been symptomatic. Within this historical era and theoretical context, "Art as Technique," stressing the "strange" quality of the seen and its impact on perception, in fact hardly stands out as original. Making strange is basically what the new medium did in the experience of most of its early spectators.

Though the text we have come to know as "Art as Technique" late 1916 and first published in 1917, its preconception too earlier; some of the crucial thoughts were already presented by 1914;[50] and in his lecture in the Stray Dog in December 19 1913 was a significant year in the early cultural reception of th Petersburg and Moscow, as Yuri Tsivian has noted: that yea craze for cinema reached its peak in Russia."[52] It has beco Shklovsky's attempt to rethink the problem of art—in that ve avant-garde cabaret—was deeply embedded in the avant-garc of the perceptual potential of new technologies and technique tive and revolutionary powers and their sudden and strong in ences. As a friend of the Futurists, he approached the problem and "radically unconventional" (Eikhenbaum)[53] perspective and with a "brash irreverence" (Erlich) toward tradition.[54] Th project, with which early so-called Russian Formalism has b connected,[55] is itself a crucial part of what we have come to the tremendous cultural impact of early cinema on writers and revolutionary Russia.[56] The growing academic awareness of cultural impact on the avant-garde movements triggered an u question:[57] If Shklovsky's famous manifesto "Art as Techniqu part of the avant-garde's cultural response to early cinema, t one exactly situate and understand its key premises and *tran(n)enie*, art, technique; its radical opposition to traditi (*form/content*) and practices and methods of interpretation; its cal principles" (to study the new techniques and their imp implications for the studies of the arts, including the replacem by "technique"?

Re-read within this very specific context provided by th responding to the transformations technology brought about, comes clear that "Art as Technique" is not written in suppor method" to enhance interpretation, as some post-war readers think (and as Eikhenbaum already feared might happen).[58] It clear that it is relevant to re-evaluate "Art as Technique" a written in a period of technological transformation, just as th with "new media" and their impact taking center stage. We easily understand, perhaps, than readers of "Art as Technique and 1970s, what Shklovsky was pointing at. My short archa *tran(n)enie* as part of a re-reading of "Art as Technique" defamiliarize it from its long history of misreading. "Misreadi ever, does not express deprecation, but an acknowledgemen reading—including this one—has a specific function in its ov time. We, twenty-first-century passers-by in history, are perhaps better positioned to appreciate these reflections on newness and the de-automatization of perception than the twentieth-century post-war readers were in the heyday of New Criticism, if only because "Art as Technique" created the conceptual space to reflect on the impact of the "new" in culture. If ever there was a field that might profit from the abduction of the traditional ("clumsy") concept of "form" and its replacement by "technique" (apart from the fields of literature and art studies), obviously, it must be the fields of film and media studies: because Shklovsky's theory helps to open up new ways to frame the impact of new technologies in culture. To fields in which the technologies directly interfere with the process of making art, "Art as Technique" provides the conceptual tools to analyze the processes of mutation and appropriation of new techniques in culture, and it brings to light that the genealogies of art and technique are intertwined because they are inherently connected.

I would like to thank Shant Bayramian for his valuable help in preparing this chapter.

NOTES

1. Yuri Tsivian, introduction to *Early Cinema in Russia and Its Cultural Reception,* ed. Richard Taylor (London & Chicago: The University of Chicago Press), 1–14.

2. Ibid., 13.

3. In this reflection, I return to the research work done with a team of (early) film scholars, Yuri Tsivian, Ian Christie, and Frank Kessler among them, for the edited volume on Ostrannenie, published by Amsterdam University Press in 2010. This is a rethinking as well as a reworking of my Introduction and my chapter on "Ostranenie, 'The Montage of Attractions' and Early Cinema's 'Properly Irreducible Alien Quality'" (*Ostrannenie*, pp. 11–20, 33–60).

4. Ibid.

5. Ibid.

6. There were many words for what we call "film" today. See Annie van den Oever, "Introduction: researching Cinema and Media Technologies," in *Technē/Technology: Researching Cinema and Media Technologies—Their Development, Use and Impact,* ed. Annie van den Oever (Amsterdam: Amsterdam University Press), 15.

7. The term "new cinema machine" was coined by Laura Mulvey, see Laura Mulvey, *Death 24x a Second: Stillness and the Moving Image* (London: Reaktion Books, 2006), 68.

8. Tsivian, *Early Cinema in Russia and Its Cultural Reception,* 1–14.

9. Contemporary twenty-first-century audiences are distanced from the viewing experiences provided by the early film shows, but this does not mean that they do not have similar experiences with today's new media.

10. Tsivian, *Early Cinema in Russia and Its Cultural Reception,* 2.

11. Tom Gunning described the *stupefying* effect of early cinema on its early spectator in several places. He also described and analyzed other confrontations with the "new" in similar terms. See Tom Gunning, "Re-Newing Old Technologies: Astonishment, Second Nature, and the Uncanny in Technology from the Previous Turn-of-the-Century" in *Rethinking Media Change: The Aesthetics of Transition,* eds. David Thourburn, and Henry Jenkins (Cambridge, MA: MIT Press, 2003), 40–41. See also Gunning's "The Cinema of Attractions. Early Film, Its Spectator and the Avant-Garde," in *Early Cinema. Space, Frame, Narrative,* ed. Thomas Elsaesser (London: BFI), 1990. See also Tom Gunning, "An Aesthetic of Astonishment: Early

Film and the (In)credulous Spectator," in *Viewing Positions. Ways of Seeing Film*, ed. Linda Williams (New Brunswick, NJ.: Rutgers University Press), 1994.

12. See Shklovsky's *Mayakovsky and His Circle*, trans., and ed. Lily Feiler (London: Pluto Press Limited, 1974), 125.

13. I took this quote from Tom Gunning, who cites Shklovsky's "Electricity and the Theme of Old Newspapers," *Podenshchina* (Leningrad: Pisatelej, 1930), 14–15. See Tom Gunning, "Re-Newing Old Technologies: Astonishment, Second Nature, and the Uncanny in Technology from the Previous Turn-of-the-Century," in *Rethinking Media Change: The Aesthetics of Transition*, eds. David Thourburn, and Henry Jenkins (Cambridge, MA: MIT Press, 2003), 44.

14. Gunning, "Re-Newing Old Technologies: Astonishment, Second Nature, and the Uncanny in Technology from the Previous Turn-of-the-Century," 39–44.

15. The quote is taken from Shklovsky's *The Hamburg Account*, which The Dalkey Archive Press has recently (2017) translated and re-titled to *The Hamburg Score*, but for the reference of the citation of this quote, see Richard Sheldon, introduction to *Literature and Cinematography* trans. Irina Masinovsky. (Champaign & London: Dalkey Archive Press, 2008), xvi–xvii.

16. See, apart from Tsivian, also an expert on the history of the Futurist movement in Russia, Vladimir Markov, "Russian Futurism and Its Theoreticians," in *The Avant-Garde Tradition in Literature*, ed. Richard Kostelanetz (Buffalo: Prometheus Books, 1982), 171.

17. Tsivian, *Early Cinema in Russia and Its Cultural Reception*, 12.

18. See Vladimir Markov, "Russian Futurism and Its Theoreticians," in *The Avant-Garde Tradition in Literature*, 171.

19. Tsivian, 12.

20. Ibid.

21. Ibid.

22. Ibid.

23. See Richard Sheldon's "Introduction" to Viktor Shklovsky's *A Sentimental Journey* (New York: Cornell University Press, 1970), x. [my italics].

24. See Vladimir Markov, "Russian Futurism and Its Theoreticians."

25. See Richard Sheldon's "Introduction," x.

26. The younger Eisenstein became part of the circle surrounding Mayakovsky's LEF in 1923, ten years after Shklovsky's lecture in The Stray Dog, and Shklovsky saw him as a young man, "in wide trousers, very young, gay and with a high-pitched voice," a "versatile" person who brought to this environment of "extreme diversity" his own specialty: "he brought to LEF his ideas on eccentrism." See Shklovsky, *Mayakovsky and His Circle*, 172.

27. See Wellek, "Russian Formalism," 156–159; and Markov, "Russian Futurism and Its Theoreticians," 168.

28. Markov, "Russian Futurism and Its Theoreticians," 171. See also Boris Eikhenbaum, "The Theory of the 'Formal Method,'" 112.

29. Svetlana Boym, "Poetics and Politics of Estrangement: Victor Shklovsky and Hannah Arendt," in *Poetics Today* 26: 4 (Winter 2005).

30. Victor Shklovsky, *Voskresheniye slova* (Petersburg, 1914), 11. See Boris Eikhenbaum's "The Theory of the 'Formal Method'" (112) for a comment and an English translation of this quote.

31. Ibid.

32. As they abducted the notion of "form" and replaced it by "technique," they put "form and "formal" between quotation marks and obviously objected to being called "Formalists" since the word carried the wrong connotations of late nineteenth-century aestheticism and "*L'art pour l'art,*" as preached by some late nineteenth-century autonomists.

33. Eikhenbaum, "'The Theory of the 'Formal Method,'" 115.

34. Ibid., 12.

35. A new and extended edition of *Poetika Kino* [Poetics of Film] was presented in a German translation in 2005. This interesting volume contains many earlier and later writings on the cinema by the Russian Formalists, apart from the texts published in Russia in 1927 under the title *Poètika kino*. A considerable amount is written by Shklovsky. See Wolfgang Beilenhoff, ed., *Poetika Kino. Theorie und Praxis des Films im russischen Formalismus*, trans. Wolfgang Beilenhoff (Frankfurt am Main: Suhrkamp), 2005.

36. Shklovsky is quoted extensively by Yuri Tsivian in "The Gesture of Revolution or Misquoting as Device," in *Ostrannenie*, ed. Annie van den Oever (Amsterdam: Amsterdam University Press), 21–32.
37. Ibid., 23.
38. See Markov on the genre and topic: "Manifestoes in the strict sense of the word were not always concerned with theory. Most of them [by the Futurists of these days] were largely arrogant and vitriolic attacks on proceeding and contemporary literature, more often on fellow-futurists; at other times their aim was to *épater les bourgeois*, rather than declare their aesthetics." Markov, "Russian Futurism and Its Theoreticians," 169.
39. Victor Erlich. "Russian Formalism." *Journal of the History of Ideas* Vol. 34, 4 (October—December 1973), 638.
40. Shklovsky, Viktor. "Art as Technique." In *Russian Formalist Criticism. Four Essays*. [1917] Translated by Lee T. Lemon, and Marion Reis, 3–57. Lincoln & London: University of Nebraska Press, 1965, 3–57.
41. Ibid.
42. See for instance a critique by Eric Naiman, "Shklovsky's Dog and Mulvey's Pleasure: The Secret Life of Defamiliarization." *Comparative Literature* 50, no. 4 (autumn 1998): 333–352.
43. Viktor Shklovsky, "Art as Technique," 13.
44. See Eikhenbaum, "The Theory of the 'Formal Method,'" 115.
45. Viktor Shklovsky, "Art as Technique," 13.
46. Lemon, and Reis, introduction to *Russian Formalist Criticism: Four Essays*, ed. & trans. Lee T. Lemon & Marion J. Reis (Lincoln: University of Nebraska Press, 1965), ix.
47. Tom Gunning, "Re-Newing Old Technologies: Astonishment, Second Nature, and the Uncanny in Technology from the Previous Turn-of-the-Century," in *Rethinking Media Change: The Aesthetics of Transition*, ed. David Thourburn, and Henry Jenkins (Cambridge, MA: MIT Press, 2003), 49.
48. Ibid.
49. Tom Gunning, "An Aesthetic of Astonishment," 117.
50. See Boris Eikhenbaum in "Theory of the 'formal method'" on the crucial passages in and impact of Shklovsky's "The Resurrection of the Word," published in 1914.
51. For a description of Shklovsky's lecture as a freshman in 1913, see Richard Sheldon in his "Introduction" to *A Sentimental Journey* (New York: Cornell University Press, 1970).
52. On the year "the general craze for cinema reached its peak in Russia," see Yuri Tsivian in his *Early Cinema in Russia and Its Cultural Reception*, 12. For a description of Shklovsky's lecture as a freshman in 1913, see Richard Sheldon in his "Introduction" in *A Sentimental Journey* (New York: Cornell University Press, 1970). See also below.
53. Eikhenbaum refers to their violation of traditional notions, "which had appeared to be 'axiomatic,'" in: "The Theory of the 'Formal Method,'" 104.
54. The words "brash irreverence" I took from Victor Erlich's "Russian Formalism." *Journal of the History of Ideas* Vol. 34, 4 (October—December 1973), 638. One must doubt, however, that these words are used by Erlich in any positive way. Most contemporaries and many later scholars took note of the "brashness" of the avant-garde attacks on tradition with great reserve.
55. "Formalism and Futurism seemed bound together by history," as Eikhenbaum wrote in his 1926 retrospective overview of the formative years of Russian Formalism. See Eikhenbaum in "The Theory of the 'Formal Method,'" 104–105: "Our creation of a radically unconventional poetics, therefore, implied more than a simple reassessment of particular problems; it had an impact on the study of art generally. It had its impact because of a series of historical developments, the most important of which were the crisis in philosophical aesthetics and the startling innovations in art (in Russia most abrupt and most clearly defined in [Futurist] poetry). Aesthetics seemed barren and art deliberately denuded—in an entirely primitive condition. Hence, Formalism and Futurism seemed bound together by history."
56. Early cinema studies contributed considerably to our knowledge from this period. Yuri Tsivian is of course of invaluable significance in this field. See in particular his *Early Cinema in Russia and Its Cultural Reception*. Translated by A. Bodger. Edited by R. Taylor. (London &

New York: Routledge, 1994), 217. One must note that in the last two decades, interesting and highly valuable research in this area—also on the connection between early cinema and the avant-garde—mostly comes from Film Studies and so-called Early Cinema Studies in particular, and less from what is institutionally labeled as (continental) "Avant-Garde Studies."

57. This question was not yet posed by avant-garde studies or early cinema studies when we embarked on our research project for *Ostran(n)enie* in a 2006 workshop anticipating the publication of the book in 2010.

58. See, among many others, Victor Erlich, "Russian formalism." In: *Journal of the History of Ideas*, Vol. 34, No. 4, (Oct.–Dec., 1973), 630, 634. Interesting, Erlich complains about "Art as Technique" not being more helpful in this area of interest and he states that he prefers Roman Jakobson's work for this very reason. Erlich (630): "Shklovsky's key terms, e.g., "making it strange," "dis-automatization," received wide currency in the writings of the Russian Formalists. But, on the whole, Shklovsky's argument was more typical of Formalism as a rationale for poetic experimentation than as a systematic methodology of literary scholarship. The Formalists' attempt to solve the fundamental problems of literary theory in close alliance with modern linguistics and semiotics found its most succinct expression in the early, path-breaking studies of Roman Jakobson. For Jakobson, the central problem is not the interaction between the percipient subject and the object perceived, but the relationship between the "sign" and the "referent," not the reader's attitude toward reality but the poet's attitude toward language." Ironically, Jakobson's perspective today is far more passé than Shklovsky's to many.

WORKS CITED

Beilenhoff, Wolfgang (ed.). *Poetika Kino. Theorie und Praxis des Films im russischen Formalismus*. Frankfurt am Main: Suhrkamp, 2005.

Boym, Svetlana. "Poetics and Politics of Estrangement: Victor Shklovsky and Hannah Arendt." *Poetics Today* 26, 4 (winter 2005).

Eikhenbaum, Boris. "The Theory of the 'Formal Method.'" In *Russian Formalist Criticism*, edited by Lee T. Lemon, and Marion J. Reis. Lincoln: University of Nebraska Press, 1965.

Erlich, Victor. "Russian Formalism." *Journal of the History of Ideas* 34, 4 (October–December 1973).

Gunning, Tom. "An Aesthetic of Astonishment: Early Film and the (In)credulous Spectator." In *Viewing Positions. Ways of Seeing Film*, edited by Linda Williams. New Brunswick, New Jersey: Rutgers University Press, 1994.

———. "Re-Newing Old Technologies: Astonishment, Second Nature, and the Uncanny in Technology from the Previous Turn-of-the-Century." In *Rethinking Media Change: The Aesthetics of Transition*, edited by David Thourburn, and Henry Jenkins, 39–60. Cambridge, MA: MIT Press, 2003.

———. "The Cinema of Attractions. Early Film, Its Spectator and the Avant-Garde." In *Early Cinema. Space, Frame, Narrative*, edited by Thomas Elsaesser. London: BFI, 1990.

Lemon, Lee T., and Marion J. Reis. Introduction to *Russian Formalist Criticism: Four Essays*, ix–xvii. Lincoln: University of Nebraska Press, 1965.

Markov, Vladimir. "Russian Futurism and Its Theoreticians." In *The Avant-Garde Tradition in Literature*, edited by Richard Kostelanetz. Buffalo: Prometheus Books, 1982.

Mulvey, Laura. *Death 24x a Second: Stillness and the Moving Image*. London: Reaktion Books, 2006.

Naiman, Eric. "Shklovsky's Dog and Mulvey's Pleasure: The Secret Life of Defamiliarization." *Comparative Literature* 50, no. 4 (Autumn 1998): 333–352.

Sheldon, Richard. "Introduction." In *A Sentimental Journey*. Ithaca, NY: Cornell University Press, 1970.

———. Introduction to *Literature and Cinematography*, xvi–xvii. Translated by Irina Masinovsky. Champaign & London: Dalkey Archive Press, 2008.

Shklovsky, Viktor. "Art as Technique." In *Russian Formalist Criticism. Four Essays*. [1917] Translated by Lee T. Lemon, and Marion Reis, 3–57. Lincoln & London: University of Nebraska Press, 1965.

———. *Mayakovsky and His Circle*. Translated and edited by Lily Feiler. London: Pluto Press Limited, 1974.
———. *Voskresheniye slova* [*The Resurrection of the Word*]. Petersburg, 1914.
Tsivian, Yuri. *Early Cinema in Russia and Its Cultural Reception*. Translated by Alan Bodger. Edited by Richard Taylor. London & New York: Routledge, 1994.
———. "The Gesture of Revolution or Misquoting as Device." In *Ostrannenie:"Strangeness" and the Moving Image: The History, Reception, and Relevance of a Concept*, edited by Annie van den Oever, 21–32. Amsterdam: Amsterdam University Press, 2010.
Van den Oever, A.M.A, ed. *Ostrannenie: On"Strangeness" and the Moving Image: The History, Reception, and Relevance of a Concept*. Amsterdam: Amsterdam University Press, 2010.
———. "Introduction: Ostran(n)enie as an 'Attractive' Concept." In *Ostrannenie: On"Strangeness" and the Moving Image: The History, Reception, and Relevance of a Concept*, edited by Annie van den Oever, 11–20. Amsterdam: Amsterdam University Press, 2010.
———. *Sensitizing the Viewer: The Impact of New Techniques and the Art Experience*. Groningen & Amsterdam: University of Groningen, Amsterdam University Press, & Stedelijk Museum Amsterdam, 2011.
———. *Techn ē/Technology: Researching Cinema and Media Technologies—Their Development, Use, and Impact* . Edited by Annie van den Oever. Amsterdam: Amsterdam University Press, 2014.
———. "The Medium-Sensitive Experience and the Paradigmatic Experience of the Grotesque, 'Unnatural,' or 'Monstrous." *Leonardo* 46, 1 (2013): 88–89. DOI: 10.1162/LEON_a_00495.
———. "Ostranenie, 'The Montage of Attractions' and Early Cinema's 'Properly Irreducible Alien Quality.'" In *Ostrannenie: On "Strangeness" and the Moving Image: The History, Reception, and Relevance of a Concept*, edited by Annie van den Oever, 33–60. Amsterdam: Amsterdam University Press, 2010.
Wellek, René. "Russian Formalism." In *The Avant-Garde Tradition in Literature*. Edited by Richard Kostelanetz. Buffalo: Prometheus Books, 1982.

Part III

Shklovsky's Heritage in Philosophy

Chapter Fourteen

Shklovsky as Philosopher for Tynyanov

Alexander Markov

When Shklovsky, in his manifesto *Art as Device*, changed the cardinal notion of *image* to the notion of *device*, it became seminal for further Russian studies in poetics. We prove that Tynianov's idea of the compactness of the verse series[1] is completely understandable through philosophical presumptions, related to early and late Shklovsky.

COMPACTNESS OF THE VERSE SERIES AS DIALECTICS WITHOUT ARGUMENTS

In his book *The Problem of Verse Language* (1924), Tynyanov gives no definition of the key term. He only describes it dialectically as necessary property of the rhythm but understands this compactness as another name for unity but in the aspect of "dynamization of the word in verse,"[2] "dynamisation of the vocal material."[3] This dynamization is close to Shklovsky's deautomatization of the device but works not as a difference between art and trivial art or non-art, but between verse and prose. He states that a word in verse "bears a particular semantic value"[4] and that a good prosaic writer "will go to great length to be careful that his writing does not have any expressions which resemble verse."[5] Tynyanov writes that unity and compactness of the verse series regroups all distinctions and connections in syntax and semantics:

> coinciding of the verse series with the grammatical unity, they deepen and emphasize the features of the syntactic-semantic connections and articulations.

This dynamization of vocal material draws a sharp boundary between the verse word and prosaic word.[6]

This expressive function of the compact verse leads to oscillating signs of meaning. As Tynyanov states, in a verse "oscillating signs are intensified, but not to the point of obscuring the principal sign."[7] Tynyanov analyzes the following two verses by J. Polonsky, second-row Russian romantic poet:

> The blizzard roars, rushing into the dark
> Precipice of rock with a living wave

Tynyanov remarks:

Here the isolation of the epithet "dark" from the defined "precipice of rock" is not motivated syntactically.[8]

Such semantic double enriching of semantics across the syntax demands not only words but grammar categories. In these examples, we meet verbs for describing not sporadic but continuous actions, such as "roars," and all adjectives are expressive enough to add not only direct but also metaphorical sense. For example, "dark" in Russian often means "obscure, not clear." This additional sense is a result of European grammar as cultural institute, which we will see later.

One of the paradoxes of Tynianov's theory, not discussed in Russian formalist studies, is that he takes different criteria to divide and articulate regular verse with rhyme and irregular verse with free rhythm. He takes as a unit of regular verse its strophic scheme, and of irregular verse only a line, but line and strophe are equally working mechanisms for producing the dynamics of verse. Every verse organization is an unfolding of this compactness, which resembles Shklovsky's famous Unfolding of the Plot (*suzhet* as opposed to *fabula*).[9] In this unfolding, a verse unit is allocated. Tynyanov continues, noting that this unit could be a foot for regular versification or a verse for irregular versification:

We have seen that in systematic verse a part of the series will be such a unit, such as a halt (Abschnitt), or even a foot. In vers libre such a unit is altered. The unit serves each previous series in relationship to the next.[10]

In this fusion of versification and verse organization, Mikhail Gasparov sees a disadvantage for Tynianov's project:

He [Tynyanov] shows how the gaps between the lines and the rhythm inside the lines together emphasize, "dynamize" the words in the line, i.e., give them emphaticity, significance. But when he tries to show that this is not only ambiguity, but also polysemy (or allegiance), it turns out highly unconvincing. He writes the verses of Polonsky into the prose line: "The blizzard roars, rushing into the dark / Precipice of rock with a living wave" . . . and insists that, compared to this, the word "dark" in the verse is amplified with additional emotional meanings, maybe alien and unusual, inspired by e.g. the alliterative word "noise" (how could it be?). All other observations of the game of "fluctuating signs of meaning" in the poetic language are just as vague as this.[11]

Despite this strong abundant criticism, Gasparov, in his own argumentation, comes to less critical conclusions. He examines the "shiftology" (*sdvigologiya*) of the Russian Futurists, in which mishearing turns from misunderstanding into a deliberate method of expressiveness, which makes it possible to discredit the former poets for using this technique often, but unconsciously and not systematically. At the same time, futurists noted shifts for strong positions in verse but refused to observe them throughout the entire line. For example, in Pushkin's verse "To robost'ju, to revnost'u tomim" [tormented with timidity jealous temper] we hear to-to-to (or-or-or) [or to-ti-te in our translation]. If the Futurists would observe these cases, it would mean their need to recognize the appropriate and therefore systematic and conscious use of the shift (*sdvig*).

Gasparov notes another limit of this shiftology: in strong positions we may pay attention only to expressive sound but not to syntactic likeliness of words, and in weak positions syntactic likeliness comes into play. The end of the verse, as the place for rhyme, is a strong position and a point of impressionistic empathic images of pure fantasy, but the central part of the verse demands stability of our syntactical thought, as stable and balanced as walking along a mountain path to the verse edge as to the top of the mountain.

Gasparov's criticism is fully inscribed in Shklovsky's manifesto *Resurrecting the Word* (1914; we cite the translation "The Resurrection of the Word") when he notes that typical figures of late poetry are not generalizations in the full sense but only renovations of mythological or epic imagery:

> It could hardly be said that poetry has made up the damage it has suffered through the loss of the figurativeness of words by replacing this figurativeness with a higher type of creation—for example by the creation of character-types, because in such a case poetry would not have held on so avidly to the figurative word even at such high stages of its evolution as in the era of epic chronicles.[12]

Typical figures pretended to be at the top of the poetic experience, the mountain tops of poetic emphasis and expressiveness, but the disadvantage is that they were all inscribed in the old syntax of figural organization of poetic texts. So, Shklovsky and Tynyanov both demand a more risky and asyntactical way to the top, to the edge, to the rhyme strong position, where our aesthetic experience will be not routine exaltation but the search for new ways of semantical proximity of all that is said and mentioned in previous verses. It is not only compactness, but a risky mountain path, and the Russian words *tesnota* and *tesny* often mean narrow street or path and a lack of empty space at the second place. We will see how the presumed metaphor of compactness includes the mountain path, mosaic, and mountain river as different images of the *sublime* (in the classical sense of Burke and Kant).

ENIGMATIC DIFFERENTIAL OF THE SYNTAX

> Syntax is not for woman's life
> And man is changed in paradigm of his craft.

This quasi-lyrical phrase in the first pages of Shklovsky's *Zoo, or Letters Not about Love* is a kind of Nietzsche-style provocative statement, using gender obsessions for aims of poetics. Woman, for Shklovsky, is a point of strong attention, a strong place of affects in poetry according to Tynyanov, and so she doesn't need any syntactic paradigm. She is the bearer of any complex and oscillating affects and senses, and man, as master of the narrative, must observe dependence of semantics from syntax, without any oscillating or indefinite senses. We may call Shklovsky's philosophy of love a framework for Tynianov's concept of compactness.

Our mention of Nietzsche is not accidental. Nietzsche, and not Tynyanov himself or futurist poet Sergey Bobrov, whom Tynyanov cites, is the real author of the concept, linking semantic and syntactical principles of poetry organization. Tynyanov admired Nietzsche as the inventor of singing phonically conceived prose, a kind of *Sprachgesang*:[13]

> Nietzsche, we suppose, was a mark stone of the outlined topic of Tynianov's book, that poetry is not a rhetorically ornamented artifact in general but a projection of the future norm of melodic speech. All "imminent properties" or "secondary features,"[14] as the phrase was translated, could be attributed both to poetry and ornamented or rhythmical prose, but only verse allows for distribution of strong points and weak points to attract attention to versification as a specific organization. This is the reason that Tynyanov refuses to compare strophic and lines as two principles of poetry-making: for him they were subdivisions, aimed to produce strong points for further differences. Nietzsche writes:

> > This mention of mosaics makes us take into consideration the basic principle of mosaic art: arrangement of heterogeneous pieces, not conceived to be together, in a perfect composition, giving ideal position to each piece. We dare to say about the basic wit of these pieces: their sharpness alludes to humor and semantic games. However, if we take this mosaic assembled, we get performative abundance of semantics. Nietzsche describes this way of strength as "right and left" just as waterfall or mountain river with its relief. For Nietzsche, Horace was a trouba-

dour of aristocracy, and he conceived him not as mosaic master but rather as spiritual top mountain dweller, "noble" and far from the common people.

It's remarkable that the poetic description of a mountain river by Polonsky became for Tynyanov the best sample of compactness. Horace would be useful for Tynyanov as a poet, combining both principles of compactness: verse organization of the local Roman tradition and the elegant strophic borrowed from the Greek tradition. Both principles were conceptualized by the poet as melodic and innovative, as we read in his famous *Monument Ode* (*Odes* 3, 30).

Shklovsky, in his only contribution to art studies, the essay *Space in the Painting and Suprematists*, explains what mosaic is.[15] He explains the absence of a natural (life-similar) perspective in mosaics through strong dependence on a static wall. A painting is, on the contrary, not attached to the wall, but protrudes and overhangs, and this results in an independent perspective and will of the things in the painting as vivid imitations of life. For Shklovsky, as a Marxist thinker, the material basis is key for all superstructures of sense. So Shklovsky insists that a mosaic is not an arrangement of represented things, but an interpretation of the wall as a strong point for the expressiveness of things. Lack of narrative and natural representation in suprematists' paintings (Malevich, Kandinsky) was for him a way back from mimetic oil to mosaic. The only weakness in suprematism for him was that abstract compositions are syntactic in the central part, focusing on abstract construction as specific object, and more expressive only at the edges of the square, and here we can find a parallel to Tynianov's and Gasparov's statement of syntactic priority at the weak points and syntactic and semantic oscillating at the edge, at the point of the rhyme. We find a similar understanding of mosaic art as improvisation at the edge, as a risky way to strong composition, in Sedakova's prose *Opus Incertum*.[16]

Nietzsche's description, like the theory of Tynyanov in its normal use, is generally due to one philological misunderstanding. Our grammatical habits require us to distinguish between the subject and the epithet, and the function of the epithet is clarified further; it adorns, clarifies, or hints at some additional contexts. However, the classical grammar subject, "proper name" (κύριον ὄνομα) was opposed not only to the adjective, but to both "prosegory" (προσηγορία), in the figurative sense, and to an "epithet" (ἐπίθητον), any explanation that could be not only an adjective.

It is this confusion, and not at all underestimation, of syntactic possibilities, flexible syntax, that underlies all the misunderstandings. When Tynyanov mixes "prosegory" and "epithet," considering both of them as additional semantics, and realizing that in poetry words are more often used in a figurative sense than in prose, he believes that explanations, epithets, and any commentary actions of a word will acquire a figurative meaning, and, in strong places, where everything should be clear to us, they will acquire it without fail and in all cases. We will further see how different authors shared this productive fallacy.

Shklovsky was the only Russian theorist who distinguished between *prosegory* and *epithet*, while analyzing Oriental narrative and the juxtaposing of the literary and metaphoric meanings of nudeness. He differentiated the first and the second as historical fact in the narrative and as symbolic act in ritualistic performance. In *The Resurrection of the Word* he simply says,[17] that not only are words and epithets petrified, but statements (*polozheniya*—it means "statement" and "situation" equally) can fossilize also. Shklovsky here mentions the Baghdad edition of Arab tales, where the traveler, whom the robbers stripped naked, climbed the mountain and, in despair, "tore his clothes" (as a sign of despair). In this passage, Shklovsky remarks, the whole picture is stabilized in the unconsciousness, and here we find the top of the mountain as the place of asyntactical organization of speech and *compactness*, that urges metaphor to be a part of statement and the statement to be a situation.

This proximity of Nietzsche's and OPOYAZ's position on going-to-the-edge, realized as ethical extremism in Nietzsche and aesthetical extremism in OPOYAZ, was mentioned by the practicing Russian poet just cited:

> In this instrumentalization of the theory of Tynyanov, two things attract our attention. Firstly, it turns out that Tynyanov does not describe the experience of the poetry of the past, but designs poetry for the future, in which the implied, underlying meanings of words will prove to be more important than immediate dictionary meanings. The syntactic affiliation and semantic ambiguity of a word are not so important in comparison with this gesture of avoiding a ready vocabulary, so that the signs of meanings form the very situation in which a word becomes poetic. Secondly, Sedakova understands this movement as requiring restrictions, while being ontologically and not semantically motivated: these possibilities themselves can exist until they are used, transformed into ordinary material, into chatter, according to Nietzsche, or into an inauthentic condition according to existentialist thought.

In this interpretation, we see influence of the prose theory developed by Shklovsky in his book *The Bowstring*. In the concluding essay "Return the Ball to the Game,"[18] Shklovsky says that the open finale of prose works not only allows characters to act in reality but also with various semantic signs of ongoing actions. All possibilities to act, according to the late Shklovsky, are authentic when they are distanced not only from plot development, but also from these signs, from "playing without the ball." To return to the game means to return from oscillating signs and mountain tops at the edge of the open finale in a novel to the *plain* possibilities of practical syntactical speech.

LEV SHESTOV AND HIS MOUNTAIN EXISTENTIALISM

Nietzsche's philological observations became methodological for one of his most talented and famous Russian admirers, philosopher Lev Shestov, recognized as one of the founders of existentialism, whose aphoristic-paradoxical style is closest to that of Shklovsky. The image of the mosaic and the image of the mountains, as images of Nietzsche, are also key symbols of his reasoning and work.

As an epigraph to his book *Apotheosis of Groundlessness* (translated into English as *All Things Are Possible*), Shestov took inspiration from a warning sign in front of one of the dangerous trails in the Alps: *Not for those who dizzy*. Here he is stylistically close to Nietzsche, the most shocking sayings of which, in form, are the same as warning signs. Like Nietzsche, Shestov contrasts serious speech, based on close interaction with a number of stated words, producing a paradoxical result, to chatter as a non-stop generation of random concepts. Shestov understands chatter as more than simply irresponsible talk about abstract concepts but includes many of the usual and quite desirable social practices, for example, hiding self-interest under a mask of gratitude:

> It is true, in our young days when all was new, light brought us great happiness and joy. Let us, therefore, remember it with gratitude, as a benefactor we no longer need. Do after all let us dispense with gratitude, for it belongs to the calculating, bourgeois virtues. *Do ut des.* Let us forget light, and gratitude, and the qualms of self-important idealism, let us go bravely to meet the coming night.[19]

Shestov further considers Pushkin's line "The Sun, be welcome, Hide thyself, o darkness!" as an example of compactness. Although positive values are produced in this verse, it is important for Shestov that this poem can produce an existential, frightening perception of the world, thanks to such compactness of words, which can even lead to their rearrangement:

> It seems as if, in a short while, man will feel that the same incomprehensible, cherishing power which threw us out into the universe and set us, like plants, to reach to the light, is now gradually transferring us to a new direction, where a new life awaits us with all its stores. *Fata volentem ducunt, nolentem trahunt.* And perhaps the time is near when the impassioned poet, casting a last look to his past, will boldly and gladly cry: Hide thyself, sun! O darkness, be welcome![20]

Shestov here precedes Shklovsky, not Tynyanov, in noting a difference between "prosegory" and "epithet"; for him all future possibilities of a better life come after the existential experience of the edge, of the extreme moving, as epithet, explaining our real-life position. However, prosegory, as characteristics of sun and darkness, are not necessary for the way to the top of life, for the "reach to the light" to a real existence in the truth. Shestov also comments on the strong position of the rhyme as asyntactical affect, leading not to semantical shifts but to real decisions:

> The Secret of Pushkin's "inner harmony"—To Pushkin nothing was hopeless. Nay, he saw hopeful signs in everything. It is agreeable to sin, and it is just as delightful to repent. It is good to doubt, but it is still better to believe. It is jolly "with feet shod in steel" to skate the ice, it is pleasant to wander about with gypsies, to pray in church, to quarrel with a friend, to make peace with an enemy, to swoon on waves of harmony, to weep over a passing fancy, to recall the past, to peep into the future. Pushkin could cry hot tears, and he who can weep can hope. "I want to live, so that I may think and suffer," he says; and it seems as if the word "to suffer," which is so beautiful in the poem, just fell in accidentally, because there was no better rhyme in Russian for "to die." The later verses, which are intended to amplify to think and to suffer, prove this. Pushkin might repeat the words of the ancient hero: "danger is dangerous to others, but not to me." Therein lies the secret of his harmonious moods.[21]

Shestov believes that the word "suffer," standing in a strong position of rhyme, is completely devastated from its own semantics, since the subsequent narration in the poem describes various affects, such as love or sadness, which cannot be reduced to suffering, although they merge with it. As in Tynyanov later with the main fluctuations of meaning, the movement from meaning is in a strong position, whereas in a weak position grammatical accuracy is required to distinguish the content of similar concepts, to compare affects with a set of actions corresponding to the affect and not to the general *compactness*, delight, or dizziness. This now affects epithet, not prosegoria, so it doesn't transform semantics but transforms our experience of danger in real or intelligible mountains, as pure experience.

SHKLOVSKY AS NIETZSCHE: *THE POETICS OF EARLY BYZANTINE LITERATURE* BY AVERINTSEV

Another parallel between Shklovsky and Nietzsche was indirectly mentioned in Averintsev's book *The Poetics of Early Byzantine Literature*. One of the chapters of the book has the title "The Birth of Rhyme from the Spirit of the Greek Dialectic," and already the very title of the chapter parodies Nietzsche's research in ancient culture in *The Origin of Tragedy from the Spirit of Music*.

This remake of the title is not just a clever attempt to attract the reader's attention. Similar to Nietzsche in his meditations on the end of the "tragic era" (high ancient culture), Averintsev speaks about transformation of all aspects of culture after the triumph of the rational analytic principle over irrational ecstatic poetry. The difference is only in temporal localization: if Nietzsche accused Socrates of profanation of the tragic attitude, Averintsev believes that the Gorgian figures rhymed prose and continued the archaic magic speech in the Hellenistic civilization, and only the triumph of Christianity patronized rationalism. Roman the Melodos and especially the anonymous author of the *Akathistos Hymn* subordinated the rhyme to the regular principle of biblical parallelism, used as a tool of rational arrangement of all phenomena. Averintsev advocates his beloved idea on Christian theology as a form of rational anthropology.

A close parallel to this chapter is Shklovsky's essay *A Chinese Novel, First Approaches*. Shklovsky derived main features of plots in this type of Chinese literature from the body of Chinese writing, as arrangement of things and ideas in pictograms, but not an outline of actions and events through grammar, as in European languages. Shklovsky says that we can only say that this literature knows changes, but we can't define the very principles of these changes. The area of contemplation is not an area of rules for actions and their representations, but contemplative content is represented immediately in pictograms without any syntax. We see that, as in Tynyanov, if any pictogram is visible and impressive as an important idea of things and contemplations, then it has no need for syntax. The main argument of Averintsev's book is the same: Byzantine literature is double-sided. Like Western literature, it is highly rational and arranged, but like Oriental literature, it is contemplative and iconic. Byzantine literature needs to be compared not only with other medieval literatures of the West, but with such cases of contemplative asyntaxicism and image conceptualizations as icon veneration and apophatic (negative) theology.

According to Averintsev, late Roman Empire poets such as Nonnos of Panopolis used the technic of contemplative organization of poetic images, where the sense couldn't be reduced to description of actions, but is a subject of fascination and astonishment, just like a masterpiece of visual art. In Byzantine literature as in all traditional literatures, canonic pattern had greater importance that any innovations, but for Averintsev, just as in Chinese literature for Shklovsky, all canonic patterns are visualized as symbols or icons or imaginable concepts. In Byzantium, says Averintsev, all intelligible realities need to be visualized in the human mind to be a subject of amazement and contemplative efforts.

In the title, the word *dialectics*, in the sense of "art of productive discussion, necessary for conceptualization of reality," alludes not only to Hegel, but to Andrey Bely's *Rhythm as Dialectics and Bronze Horseman by Pushkin* (1929). Andrey Bely understood rhythm as part of plot and any change of rhythmic organization in the poem as a sign of change of plot. Plot for him, as for Shklovsky, includes the reader's attitude and intention: for example, the routine rhythm of the pathetic and solemn description of Saint Petersburg in the first part of Pushkin's poem transforms, according to Andrey Bely, this hymn into caricature and turns the very development of the plot from official culture to comic affects and deep psychological studies of the premises of creativity. The reader needs to answer, what coerces him or her to conceptualize this description as serious or ironic, and so he or she reveals the poetic intention as such, understanding poetry not through syntax, but through the general imaginable scheme of poetic intention.

Averintsev cites George Derwent Thomson,[22] opposing folk dialectics important for Christian writers and professional ancient writing, as too cultivated and syntactically overnice to express new Christian ideas as subject for contemplation. Folk dialectics as the art of sharp contrasts, as opposed to softened contrasts in classical literature, was for Averintsev the main source of rhyme as expressive mean, distancing from syntax and introducing its own optics. The only difference between Byzantine and modern rhyme resides in visual characteristics: the old rhyme was more for the eyes, and it was a grammar rhyme. A grammar rhyme means not part of the plot, but a selfish object of contemplation, and not an illusion of the act, but an immediate event of collective psychology. Averintsev describes this rhyme as a kind of ideogram, as self-systematization of language images not for illusion, but for contemplation of unchangeable intelligible reality:

> These words [similar in sound and meaning], so to speak, are betrothed to each other by the collective psychology of the language already in advance, and therefore cannot meet in rhyme suddenly and unexpectedly, like strangers. As a rule, modern poetry prefers rhyming a noun with a verb or an adjective with a verbal adverb to the monotony of a suffixal flective rhyme, especially of a verbal rhyme, condemned at the time of Pushkin. And we are also accustomed to the fact that rhyme is ultimately focused not on the eye, but on the ear, for which reason the consonance of the last stressed syllable is necessary for it, and the identity of the shock end is unnecessary. . . . In the modern European poetics [poetics here means creative and receptive habits, increased in their intentions] of rhyme, the attitude to sensual illusion predominates, much like in European painting from Titian or Frans Hals to the Impressionists, achieving its effect by merging at a certain distance of "inaccurate" strokes.[23]

Averintsev, like his close friend Gasparov and like Shklovsky, Shestov, and Tynyanov, compares the strong position of verse and rhyme with an impressionistic impact, sensual pictorial illusion, and opposing discursive rationality. Thus, he asserts loyalty to the principle of exploring a strong position based on the mixing of "prosegory" and "epithet" when he speaks on ancient poetry, but only *if* speaking on ancient poetry.

NOTES

1. Tynyanov, Jury, *The Problem of Verse Language* (Ann Arbor: Ardis, 1981), 19–20.
2. Tynyanov, 102.
3. Tynyanov, 20.
4. Tynyanov, 92.
5. Tynyanov, 60.
6. Tynyanov, 58.
7. Tynyanov, 95.
8. Tynyanov, 77.
9. Shklovsky, Viktor, *Razvertyvanie siuzheta* [Unfolding the Plot]. Moskva, 1921.
10. Tynyanov, 57.
11. Gasparov, Mikhail, "Syntactic Compactness of the Verse Line." *Poetics. Versification. Linguistics. A Collection of Articles* (Moskva: Azbukovnik Publishers, 2003), 360 (translation is mine).
12. Shklovsky, Viktor, "The Resurrection of the Word." *Russian Formalism: A Collection of Articles and Texts in Translation* (Edinburgh, London: Scottish Academic Press, 1983), 45.
13. Speech-as-song, term of Arnold Schoenberg for his musical oeuvre *Pierrot lunaire* (1910), not actual for Russian Formalism, but here is quite useful.
14. Tynyanov, Yury, *The Problem of Verse Language,* 14.
15. Shklovsky, Viktor, "Space in Art and Suprematists." *Zhizn' iskusstva,* 196–97 (1919): 4.
16. Sedakova, Olga, "Opus Incertum." *Znamia,* 7 (2011): 38–50.
17. Shklovsky, Viktor, "The Resurrection of the Word," 46.
18. Shklovsky, Viktor, "Return the Ball in the Game." *The Bowring: On Unlikeness of Looking Like* (Moscow: Artistic Literature, 1983), 293–6.
19. Shestov, Lev, *All Things Are Possible* (London, 1920), 134.
20. Shestov, 134–35.
21. Shestov, 38.
22. Thomson, George Derwent, *Studies in Ancient Greek and Society. 2. The First Philosophers* (London: Lawrence & Wishart, 1954), 314–20. (Averintsev cites Russian translation of the book.)
23. Averintsev, Sergey Sergeevich, *The Poetics of Early Byzantine Literature* (Moscow: Coda, 1997), 238.

WORKS CITED

Averintsev, Sergey S. *Poetika rannevizantiiskoi literatury* [The Poetics of the Early Byzantine Literature]. Moskva: Koda, 1997 (in Russian).
Gasparov, Mikhail. "Sintaksicheskaia tesnota stikhovogo riada" [Syntactic Compactness of the Verse Line.] In *Poetika. Stikhovedenie. Lingvistika. Sbornik statei* [Poetics. Versification. Linguistics. A collection of articles]. Moskva: Azbukovnik, 2003 (in Russian).
Nietzsche, Friedrich Wilhelm. "Twilight of the Idols: What I Owe to the Ancients." *Philosophical Writings.* New York: Continuum, 1995.
Sedakova, Olga. "Opus Incertum." *Znamia,* 7 (2011): 38–50 (in Russian).
———. *In Praise of Poetry.* London: Open Letter, 2014.
Shestov, Lev. *All Things Are Possible.* London, 1920.
Shklovsky, Viktor. "Vernite miach v igru" [Bring the ball back into the game]. *Tetiva: o neskhodstve skhodnogo* [The Bowstring: on the Dissimilarity of the Similar]. Moskva: Khudozhestvennaia literatura, 1983 (in Russian).
———. "Prostranstvo v iskusstve i suprematisty" [Space in art and the Suprematists]. *Zhizn' iskusstva,* 196–197 (1919): 4.
———. "The Resurrection of the Word." *Russian Formalism: A Collection of Articles and Texts in Translation.* Edinburgh, London: Scottish Academic Press, 1983.
———. *Razvertyvanie siuzheta* [Unfolding the Plot]. Moskva, 1921.

Thomson, George Derwent, *Studies in Ancient Greek and Society. 2. The First Philosophers.* London: Lawrence & Wishart, 1954.
Tynyanov, Yury. "Stikhotvornye formy Nekrasova" [Nekrasov's Verse Forms]. In *Poetika, Istoriia literatury, Kino* [Poetics. History of Literature. Cinema]. Moskva: Nauka, 1977
———. *The Problem of Verse Language.* Ann Arbor: Ardis, 1981.

Chapter Fifteen

Shklovsky as a Technique

Literary Theory and the Biographical Strategies of a Soviet Intellectual

Ilya Kalinin

"Sarnov[1] once said to the aged and decrepit Shklovsky: 'You've done well. You may have had to sell yourself, but at least you had the chance to reach your potential.' Shklovsky responded: 'You sound like a daughter talking to her mother: you've did well—you married papa, while I married a stranger.'"

—Mikhail Gasparov. *Notes and Quotations*[2]

"Life is like Russia. There are no roads, only directions. And everybody tries to find a road for himself."

—Viktor Shklovsky. *A Sentimental Journey*[3]

In the history of Soviet culture, Viktor Shklovsky achieved far more than the status of original theoretician, keen critic and writer who was able to produce literature corresponding to stylistic, or generic, goals he articulated himself. Above all, he constituted a unique and, at the same time, paradigmatic type of Soviet intellectual. This intellectual type was shaped by the extraordinarily severe demands for cultural and political adaptation (and assimilation) dictated by his times. The secret of his survival—which shaped this form of Soviet subject[4]—forces scholars to ponder questions of ethics, over and above questions of lesser significance pertaining to the specific strategies of this survival *per se* (these latter questions do not, however, supersede the first, but rather add a historical dimension to their universal significance).[5]

In this regard, Shklovsky stands out as an ambiguous figure through and through. It seems that the secret of his "creative longevity" lay in his omnipresence: in his being both "here" and "there," that is to say; in his mastery of this effect, which prevents one from locating him in one particular place.

Shklovsky himself wrote about his tricky character at the beginning of the 1920s: "I am a half-Jew and an imitator" (*A Sentimental Journey*).[6] Yet this marked tendency toward imitation can hardly be seen as equivalent to the inauthenticity of the literary or autobiographical character he constructed for himself. Imitating is not the same as faking. Rather, imitation was for him the assertion of a conscious, and therefore free, interaction with history, in which one's personal biography and one's personal "I" turn out to be an effect of this interaction. Given his temperament and political entanglements, it would have been impossible for Shklovsky to steer clear of the whirlwind of history. Yet by the same token he could not enthusiastically embrace it either. The strategy of imitation allowed him to engage history, "to cross-breed with his material" (Shklovsky's *Third Factory*), as he liked to put it, but at the same time to avoid being one with it.

"Life in public was for Victor Shklovsky a way of being, a literary position, and a characteristic literary device all at once."[7] On the one hand, public life allowed him to lay bare the most intimate things, and on the other hand, to render his own biography literary. As a result, his intimate biography became indistinguishable from that very same socially constructed "literariness," the discovery of which was one of Formalism's greatest achievements.

As early as 1928, in his book *The Hamburg Score*, Shklovsky admitted completely openly that, "the Victor Shklovsky about whom I am writing is not quite the same as me, and were we to meet on the street and start talking, we would not quite understand each other."[8] Shklovsky wrote about differing "selves." Moreover, there was no single, stable "self" with which he could fully coincide. Shklovsky's reaction to the sheer turbulence of history was a literary theory that denied the existence of any "eternal aesthetic values," "unchangeable laws of art," "heavenly inspiration," "creative genius," and so on. Alongside these developments, Shklovsky theorized a new conception of the subject, engrossed in history and deformed by it, but also reflecting on that deformation. In other words, Shklovsky breaks with the old concept of a whole and complete subject and the purely external and negative effect of history on that subject.

We are faced with a model of subject-formation in which the very structure of the subject is created and modeled by the movement of history, which the individual inhabits. Shklovsky does not offer this model of subjectivity as a theoretical work. He never offered discursively an open and explicitly anthropological theory. Yet this theoretical construction permeates the literary theory of Formalism. Most importantly for us, it is the result of the superimposition of literary theory and Shklovsky's active biographical participation in the events of the Revolution, First World War, Civil War (and later the construction of the "new Soviet man").[9]

For Shklovsky, literature was more than a field of academic interests. It was a mediating term that allowed him to reconstruct the relationship between his own biography and history. This is precisely why Shklovsky could not limit himself to writing literary theory and literary criticism. Literature had to be a part of his own lived experience. If we note that he read his first scholarly paper, "The Place of Futurism in the History of the Language,"[10] when he was just 20, we must also remark that he published his first non-scholarly autobiographical book, *Revolution and Front,* at 24. In this sense, it was precisely literary writing that rendered Shklovsky's biography an effect of his biographical strategy. Inheriting the Symbolist conception of life-creation, Shklovsky turned it into a conscious device that allowed him to participate in a constantly changing history. Of course, in the case of symbolism, the very life of the poet became a text, in this way gaining the meaning and transcendence it otherwise lacked. In contrast, Shklovsky's literary texts offered the reader a maximally intimate rendering of the authorial persona. Precisely this textually articulated, spectacular presence of the author allowed the "real" Victor Shklovsky to escape unwelcome attention. Furthermore, the poetics of life-creation in everyday life that had been characteristic of the Silver Age came about as a compensation for the semantic inflation of texts and the social ennui of the late empire. Shklovsky's strategy arose as a response to the intensity of social life caused by the Revolution and the dramatic tension between individual biography and history, which constantly defamiliarized typical perceptions of reality. The problem was that this permanent biographical reconstruction and defamiliarization sooner or later led to destructive consequences, turning active participation in the historical process into a compromise with one's past.

Still, Shklovsky managed for a rather long time to turn compromise into a creative stimulus; he had transformed literature into an alibi, in contrast with the usual practice of his contemporaries of taking it as a form of evidence—a *corpus delicti* ("body of the crime"). Having first become a writer, he turned into a literary character, a character who slips away from immediate repressions precisely because he is *literary*. Alexander Arkhangelsky, a writer of the 1920s, penned a witty parody of Shklovsky, playing on Shklovsky's "literary" qualities: "I am very sentimental. I like to travel. This is because I am even more of a genius than I am myself." At another place in the same sketch: "Leo Tolstoy told me: if I hadn't come up with Platon Karataev, I would have written about you, Vitia."[11]

Eikhenbaum noticed this transformation back in the late 1920s: "He is physiological in his writing because literature is in his blood; not in the sense that he is completely literary, but rather in the opposite sense. Literature is as natural to him as breathing or walking. Literature is one of his appetites"

(*Мой временник* [*My dairy*]). Subsequently, Eikhenbaum emphasizes the transformation of the author into himself: "He exists not only as an author but also as a literary character, as a protagonist of some unwritten novel."[12] Here, he references not so much the figure of the author-narrator in Shklovsky's texts but rather the poetics of his everyday conduct, the biographical strategy of his interaction with history. Eikhenbaum's comments bring to mind a comic and symptomatic episode when Shklovsky, hiding from the secret police (the *cheka*), stayed at Roman Jakobson's apartment in Moscow. He asked Jakobson what to do if the *cheka* showed up. "If they come," said Jakobson "just rustle and pretend you are paper."[13] It seems that Shklovsky never forgot this advice to the end of his long life.

I will now focus on just one of Shklovsky's strategies of active and fluid evasion of the epoch—however, it is the most important strategy of all. I will discuss his self-conscious transformation of himself—of his self—into a literary character whose primary identity lies in the constant malleability of identity. Shklovsky's memoirs, which he started writing and publishing at the age of 24 and never abandoned until the end of his life, became his immediate instrument for creating this character. The main devices of this strategy, which was based on erosion of the borderlines between biographical reality and autobiographical fiction, were formed in the first three books of his memoirs—*A Sentimental Journey* (1919–1923), *Zoo* (1923), and *Third Factory* (1926).

It might appear that documentary recording of everything that happens to the autobiographical protagonist is far from the most obvious or safe way to interact with the revolutionary era—especially when this protagonist is engaged in anti-Bolshevik activity, for which he was forced to flee the USSR. However, as a result of this self-exposure, the opposite effect came to pass. Shklovsky escaped so successfully precisely because he was always in sight. His frankness was nonliterary and, though it realized itself in literary form, it made interrogations unnecessary. It seemed as if he had taken Edgar Allan Poe's advice to heart in order to hide the object better, you should put it in the most obvious place.

With their consciousness shaped in the epoch of the historical avant-garde, the Formalists were of a somewhat hyper-historical temperament.[14] Yet further: they were also capable of translating their personal passion for history into a meta-historical reflection: hence, their incredible attention and sensitivity to the rhythms of history, on the one hand, and to the author's biography (as well as to the genre of autobiography) as a way of adapting themselves to these rhythms, on the other. And if earlier Formalism managed to be in tune with the direction of this social development, from the middle of the 1920s it no longer coincided with the contemporary social mainstream.

This brought new theoretical and biographical challenges that related to yet another pivot in the process of understanding one's individual and generational involvement in history's traumatic torrent. This dangerous moment of standing out against the background of the historical era closed the feedback loop between the Formalists' theoretical constructs and the historical context. One key to comprehension of their continued professional wellbeing, as well as their ability to remain productive even after the Formalist method was officially subjected to condemnation, perhaps lies in their emphasis on alteration, demolition, renewal, etc.—qualities that initially characterized Formalist theory. In other words, the Formalists believed that the underlying principles of literariness lay in a kind of motion that constantly negated previous identities, in the ability of literature to cross-breed with other "adjacent realms." Perhaps it was this theoretical definition of their subject of inquiry that also offered them a particular comprehension of their own biographical self-identification.

The hallmark effect of the writings of the Russian Formalists lies in their ability to cross-breed sub-species of theory, history, and biography: their historical accounts were explicit about their theoretical involvements; their theoretical constructions lent themselves to historicization or inclusion into historical and biographical prose, in which they functioned not only as a model but also as a source of defamiliarization. Moreover, this intellectual experience turned out to be existentially necessary and easily convertible into biographical strategies.

The Formalists described literature as "the destruction of habits of perception and interpretation formed by the reiterating rituals of everyday life."[15] In this sense, the mechanisms of literature and history turned out to be isomorphic. The concept of defamiliarization formulated by Shklovsky becomes, then, not only the universal principle of art but also an immanent law of history. The Formalists construed history as a force capable of seizing from literature the prerogative of a drastic modification of traditional patterns of reception. If in the literary field estrangement was usually achieved through revealing and renovating an already "naturalized" literary device, in the field of history and biography the same effect was created through an existential shake-up. When indicating in his manifesto "Art as a Technique" that "automatism eats up things, clothes, furniture, one's wife, and the fear of war,"[16] Shklovsky associated the possibility of refreshing perception's immediacy by means of some form of excess—the dissolution of ordinary life by the discovery of an adultery or the shock of wartime experience.

Defamiliarization, about which Shklovsky spoke so much in 1917,[17] was perceived by the early 1920s as an effect of history itself—and what's more, it became so intense as to rule out the possibility of any historical or biographical continuity. The metaphorical exchange between text and body (not a stable metaphorical equivalence but a dynamic exchange) yielded the hope for a certain narrativization of one's own life. Shklovsky reflects this feeling of defamiliarized personal identity in his *A Sentimental Journey:* "Life flows in scraps belonging to different systems. It is only our costume, not our body, which links the isolated life worlds"; or "All my life is made of pieces linked to each other only by my habits"; or "But my life, too, is united by its madness, I just don't know its name."[18] "Habit," "madness," "name" (or, elsewhere, "dream") make up the literary texture capable of drawing together the centrifugal "pieces" of man's historical experience, resisting the process of decomposition and fragmentation.

In Formalist prose, text and body are described, on the one hand, as systems which permanently exchange centrifugal and centripetal resources with each other. The technique of decomposition lays bars on the fragmentary structure of human experience immersed in history; what's more, history's effect on the body is described as the effect of texts (a textualization of the body, which is what initiates its fragmentation[19]). On the other hand, text can restore lost unity to the body, though no longer as an organic entity but as a certain historical construct. Here is how Shklovsky describes his clandestine experience during the Civil War (an experience of disintegration of self, of loss of unity, of the acquisition of a doppelganger): "It is good to lose oneself. To forget one's surname, to drop out of one's habits. To invent some person and become him. If not for my desk and my work, I would never have become Viktor Shklovsky again. I was writing 'The Plot as a Phenomenon of Style.'"[20] Here, the entry into history is linked to renunciation of one's personal identity, names and habits—i.e., that which is already textually possessed and alienated. However, if the inclusion of man into the space of symbolic substitutions means a permanent and traumatic transgression and redistribution of borders, the urge somehow to prevent the removal of the last frontier of identity, which Shklovsky associates with the creative abilities of the subject, is realized in attempts to gain control over the unpredictable field of textuality itself: the "desk" and work on his book restore an identity lost in the stream of history—if not a biographical identity, then at least the identity of his name (the metonymical link between the name "Viktor Shklovsky" and the works so signed remains the only stable referent of that name; apart from this it is open to all predicates: instructor to an armored battalion, organizer of OPOYAZ, army commissar, member of an underground militant SR organization, etc.). Work on his book is an ordering discursive gesture for Shklovsky, an answer to history's discursiveness gone wild, menacing the very context and background for defamiliarization with disappearance through its alienating pathos.

Lidia Ginzburg writes in her *Notebooks*: "When you listen to him [Shklovsky], you remember his books; when you read him, you think of his conversation. . . . When Shklovsky tells an anecdote, I sense his syntax, the graphic construction of his phrase . . . shifts, moves, and digressions are his typical literary device, to an extent that's no less true than it is of Sterne. They are the products of his intellectual apparatus."[21] Having described defamiliarization as the central principle of literary language, Shklovsky recognizes it as the central mechanism of history *per se*. In fact, his Sternian *A Sentimental Journey* is dedicated to this realization. However, this does not exhaust its significance. Having realized the constructive unity of literature and history, Shklovsky turns this constructive principle—this *device* —into the main principle of his biographical strategy, which consists in synchronizing himself with the defamiliarizing passage of history. This synchronization does not mean an instinctive conformity but implies a conscious conversion of the mechanisms of shift, digression, substitution not only into a mode of thought, but into a form of life.

At the start of 1922, a "memoir" was published by Georgy Semyonov, a former SR and a comrade of Viktor Shklovsky's at a relatively recent moment of anti-Bolshevik underground activity. A wave of arrests began in Moscow and Petrograd. Having escaped arrest thanks to Finland's proximity and the sturdiness of the ice covering the Finnish Gulf, Shklovsky found himself in forced emigration. In early summer, 1922, he was already in Berlin—the city that gave birth to yet another adventurous plot twist for his biography. A year later, with plenty of literary hack work, paid by the day, and numerous connections among the motley but, at the same time, rather tedious world of Russian Berlin, Shklovsky wrote his book *ZOO, or Letters Not About Love, or the Third Eloisa*. This book continues the strategy of contrasting, albeit diffuse, interplay between the autobiographical, literary, and theoretical realms that Shklovsky had discovered already in his *A Sentimental Journey* (1919–1921)—an interplay that exposes the transparency of the lines between these realms. Biography as such is represented here as the source of new literary subject matter—to be put to use in art. Literature becomes a means of shaping a supple identity for oneself, solid enough to retain one's own subjectivity amidst the upheavals of Revolution and Civil War. Literary theory becomes a reflexive effect of lived experience, connected with the intersections of biography and literature and, at the same time, a method that establishes the trajectory of these intersections.

Having fled Soviet Russia thanks to the "documentary truthfulness" of a provocateur's memoir, Shklovsky attempts to return home by writing a book which, on the contrary, rather self-consciously plays with the generic conventions of the epistolary documentary novel; it imitates a correspondence with a real addressee and, at the same time, lays bare the fictitious nature of such imitation. With this in mind, in both cases, the borderline between discursive and socio-biographical practices turns out to be permeable. However, unlike his former brother-in-arms, who had earned forgiveness by means of public denunciations, Shklovsky raises this permeability itself to the level of subject matter, trying to extract a practical effect (permission to return) from the literariness of literature itself. Soon after his return home, Shklovsky commented on the "biographical-political" success of his novel to

Ginzburg, his student at the Institute of Art History: "For once in their lives these people in the All-Russian Central Executive Committee cheered up, and they let me back in as a result."[22]

For Shklovsky, literature and literary theory, as well as his own biography, were products of a struggle with the resistance of the material (when this resistance disappears, literature turns into mere *belles-lettres,* rendering the device automatized; literary theory turns into academic scholastics; and biography into a nonsensical attempt to "heat up ice-cream"[23]—as Shklovsky put it in the last book of his autobiographical trilogy *Third Factory*). In order to live and work, there has to be an impediment: "to write well is difficult, my friends have always said. To live for real is painful. This is something you help me with."[24] The prohibition on writing about love, introduced in the very beginning of the book, is precisely what engenders love, the book itself and the anguished, perverted pleasure that Shklovsky experiences while writing his "letters not about love."

However, our interest is provoked not only by the fact that intimate matters make their way into the literary. In parallel to Shklovsky, Mayakovsky took a similar approach in his poem "About It" ("Pro eto," 1923), revealing his relationship with the sister (Lilia Brick) of Shklovsky's beloved. Shklovsky himself explained this in *Zoo*, drawing his argument from the Formalist theory of the renewal of art: "We have introduced the intimate, that which is given a name and a patronymic, because of ... the need for new material in art."[25] Yet it is not the "new material" of the intimate that informs my interest in the subject but the obstacles that rise on its way, as well as the bypass routes that the intimate takes to avoid these obstacles.

Let us turn now to the interrelation between the emergence of love and the prohibition of its realization, as well as to the relationship between this prohibition and the emergence of literature. Ultimately, the object of my analysis is the interrelation between unrequited love, sublimated into a love of words, and the opportunity to make a political gesture, the success of which depends on the philological competence of a literary theory. In other words, I am interested in the economy of desire, entwined with the traumatic experience of the political subject of revolutionary culture, the traumatic experience of an unlucky lover, and the traumatic experience of a theoretician-innovator trying to take advantage of these other traumatic forms of experience in his work.

Shklovsky turns love into a metaphor for literature, the "prohibition of love" (or "prohibition to write about love") into an analogue of the impediment which makes art *artistic*. His own emigration he portrays as the foundation for all these metaphors. Parting from the motherland means both the impossibility of a reciprocal love and a literary device, a theoretical impediment, the overcoming of which, one hopes, will lead to a positive effect. As a result, his book, saturated with transitions from the intimate into the literary and the other way around, concludes with an evident political gesture, which puts an end to the entire sequence of metaphors and is aimed at reaching for the main absent object—an integral symbolic universe with which one can identify fully and thereby gain a complete identity. For Shklovsky, this symbolic system is revolutionary Russia: "I cannot live in Berlin. I am related to today's Russia by all of my everyday life, by all of my skills and knowledge. It is only for Russia's benefit that I am able to work."[26] Whereas in the introduction the descriptions of the book are defined as metaphors for love, in the concluding letter, titled "Statement to the All-Russian Central Executive Committee," the very expression "I love you" appears as a metaphor for "I want to return to Russia." Emigration turns out to be a realized metaphor for the elusiveness of the object from one or another symbolic system with which one can fully identify. In this sense, however, the return to the motherland had nothing to offer, as is confirmed—two years after *The Third Eloisa*—in *Third Factory*, where Shklovsky also registers the impossibility of approximating this symbolic object of desire ("I lead a dull life, as if shut up in a condom"[27]).

On the real biographical level, however, the masterful transformation of metaphors that Shklovsky had enunciated in order to demonstrate the permeability of the lines between life, literature, and literary theory ultimately worked out. He gained yet another opportunity to expose the permeability of the state border, which he managed to traverse twice in the course of two years: once illegally, through the frozen Gulf of Finland, and the second time on a train from Berlin to Moscow, with the "duplicate of a priceless cargo" (s "dublikatom bescennogo gruza" Mayakovsky) in his pocket. Although even in this instance Shklovsky remained sober in his assessments, perfectly aware of the prospects that his desired return would bring, knowing full well where and to whom he was returning and what awaited him in his motherland. When his request for clemency was satisfied, on September 15, 1923, he wrote to Gorky: "As for me, I am leaving. I'll have to lie, Aleksey Maksimovich. I know I'll have to lie. I expect nothing good."[28]

The last book of Shklovsky's memoir trilogy, *Third Factory*, is an attempt to describe the pressures of the time as a productive factor bringing forth a new type of creative work largely dictated by the historical era. The middle 1920s no longer left room for the adventurous character of the Revolution or for the rejected lover-persona of emigration. Perceiving the new era as a factory deforming subjectivity, Shklovsky attempts to speak of the ethical situation of "unfreedom" in the categories of a productive aesthetic phenomenon. More precisely, he tries once again, as he did in the 1910s and the first half of the 1920s, to model the situation of non-freedom as a result of the conscious construction of a barrier, the overcoming of which ultimately renders the artist free—that is, it renders her "an artist of everyday life" (about which he wrote in "Art as a Technique").

"I want freedom," he writes, "but if I get it, in search of unfreedom, I will turn to women and publishers."[29] The problem here is that toward the middle of the 1920s, unfreedom no longer represented the effect of the artist's interaction with history, in which overcoming the resistance of the material becomes a necessary condition of becoming a free subject. Instead, unfreedom stops being a device and becomes a common place instead—no longer recognizable but, rather, automatized. The whole of *Third Factory* becomes an attempt to compensate for this socially automatized unfreedom—unfreedom as a consciously chosen social task.

Shklovsky describes the post-revolutionary era as a time that has lost the necessary tension between the movement of history and the author's constructible biography. Earlier, he had succeeded in using the traumatic movement of history as a stimulus for biographical plots, which replaced the generic form (Sterne's sentimental travelogue, Rousseau's novel in letters). Now, he recognizes the NEP era as a time deprived of a plot, a time of eclecticism, that accidentally combines the characteristics of pre-revolutionary and revolutionary realities. Shklovsky renders this eclectic space as a space where the creative subjectivity of the protagonist becomes impossible, because the necessary resistance of the material has disappeared. The very material of external reality has become a set of heterogenous elements, devoid of any memory of their own origins and ready to enter into any combination, as dictated by circumstances.

Creating himself as his own literary double, Shklovsky embodies the figure of irony both in his autobiographical prose and in his everyday behavior. This rhetorical figure allowed him to demonstrate the permeability of borders that demarcate different languages and to perform constant moves from one area into another. In fact, his literary self emerged simultaneously as an instrument and an effect of his constant border-crossing. As T. Grits, the author of one of the first books about Shklovsky, acutely observed: "[the theory of literature] evolves on the same plane as does love, and revolution, and the motifs of friendship, and, on the whole, all literary material, always finding a place for itself, always dominating in the end."[30] One can only question the critic's statement about the dominance of the theory of literature. I believe that in Shklovsky's view, the crux of the matter was not the dominance of one or another of these coinciding planes, but the very moment of coincidence—that is, Shklovsky himself. This it is why it is not enough to say that Shklovsky's texts embody the figure of irony, instead, he himself is the figure of irony. "Irony in life, like eloquence in the history of literature, can connect everything"—as Shklovsky wrote in *A Sentimental Journey*.[31] For him, irony represented a universal mechanism of artistic motivation, of the montage of variegated materials, transportation from a historical order into a biographical one, as well as from the intimate plane into the realm of literary theory (as in *ZOO*). That is why he perceives the moment of "solidification" of modernity as the epoch's loss of irony; a new, hierarchical space eliminates the possibility for spontaneous, creative proximity. Modernity becomes anti-ironic and consequently anti-historical; the plot, which for Shklovsky is motivated by the connection between different semantic orders, disappears from literature and life.

Third Factory begins with the words: "I don't feel like being witty. I don't want to build a plot. I will write about things and thoughts. As a collection of quotes."[32] The new reality turns out to be the collection of quotes as well, with the cinema as one of its metaphors. In fact, the "Third Factory" that provided the name for Shklovsky's book was the factory of Goskino, where he worked at the time. Shklovsky describes the office of the director of Goskino: "Two pier-glasses in the corner in the requisitioned gold—baroque. The desk is curved—modern. The chandelier—renaissance. On the floor à la Persian—a rug. On the walls—the portraits of the most eloquent directors."[33] Shklovsky recognizes quotation and eclecticism as more than mere signs of the absence of historical authenticity. Social reality, represented as a cinematographic set, loses its inner meaning, and history loses its direction. The tense connection between the subject and history is destroyed, blocking the very mechanism of mutual defamiliarization, which is essential for the subject-formation of the former and the movement of the latter. Reality takes on the artifice of a cinematographic set, while the cinema itself becomes a metaphor for the mechanical montage of life. Yet here, the axiological marker of montage is changed, in correlation with a shift in the agent of this montage. The Formalists, sharing the fate of the avant-garde, are converted from historical subjects who formulated the theory of montage and took responsibility for its practice, into its objects.

Shklovsky formulates three ways of interacting with historical time: the first is "to leave, to entrench oneself, to earn one's living by non-literature and to write for one's own sake and pleasure at home." This is the path of internal emigration and social escapism. The second approach is "to start describing one's life and diligently look for a new everyday reality and for a correct ideology." This is the path of gradual submission and social mimicry. As for himself, Shklovsky chooses the third path: "To work for newspapers and magazines daily, not to spare oneself but to protect one's work, to change, to interbreed with the material, to change and interbreed with the material again, to rework it over and over, so that literature will be born."[34] In this book Shklovsky regularly returns to the image of processing hemp into a textile. This processing, despite its marked brutality, produces a positive result: after a few stages, hemp becomes cloth, which can be further implemented. The context clarifies the metaphor. Hemp stands for the writer, and its processing, during which it interacts with different chemicals, is the very "cross-breeding with the material" that Shklovsky champions. In addition, in Shklovsky's thinking, it is not the material that is being processed by the author, but precisely the opposite (in Soviet Russia, the material processes you, object processes subject). The author herself functions as the material, whose processing yields both literature and a literary persona, which is, according to Shklovsky, the real subject of history. This subject-forming process occurs at the very moment when the author communicates with history, that is, with extra-literary material. Literature (as a process of creative and free interaction with history) emerges as a sign of the author's deformation, which turns non-literary material (including the author herself) into literary material. In this manner, Shklovsky seeks to return a sense of history's proportionality, as he had experienced it during the Revolution. At that moment, Shklovsky thought that this third, "impossible" path to "freedom as one's self-conscious necessity" would allow him to trick historical time in order to remain himself. But time proved to be stronger.

The historical material with which he cross-bred allowed increasingly less defamiliarizing labor. "The literature of fact," which Shklovsky and other theoreticians of the later LEF supported, left no space for the literary persona. The sheer strength of history presented Shklovsky with an unresolvable dilemma: it was no longer possible to interact with it without aligning himself with it. The remaining options were either to leave or to stay, having so aligned oneself. The third path chosen by Shklovsky in practice meant "cross-breeding with oneself." Veniamin Kaverin, a close friend and relative of Yury Tynyanov, as well as a student of Shklovsky's and a major writer, was among the first to identify Shklovsky's strategy. In the 1928 novel *Scandal-Monger*, in whose protagonist readers recognized Shklovsky, Kaverin gave him the following characterization: "Time helped him. His biography came out better than literature . . . But his literature came to an end. In essence, he wrote only about himself and there was no place left for biography. He blocked his own path."[35]

The drive to preserve his own textually demarcated literary persona at all cost led to his transition from an imitative strategy to a stylizing tactic. In other words, this was a gradual movement from the creative construction of a historically active "I" toward the active reproduction of a recognizable style of writing. Beginning in the 1930s, the presence of Shklovsky's literary persona in his texts takes the form of auto-stylization, a formal reproduction of signature devices that readers associated with Shklovsky's figure. Thus, having at the very beginning of his literary career proposed the "device" as the constitutive principle of literary form, and having extrapolated that principle to history as a whole and to his own biography, Shklovsky himself became a device and became part of his own theoretical construction. Thus, the very drama of this shift toward auto-imitation and auto-stylization lay in the automatization of this device—that is, the very same process which Shklovsky equates with the literary form's loss of its aesthetic function. If we apply Shklovsky's theoretical apparatus to his personal biography, it could be described as a gradual automatization of the defamiliarization device, which he took as the basis for his own life-creation.

While his first autobiographical book, *Revolution and Front* (1921), ended with the words, "Nothing has ended yet," *Third Factory* (1926), according to the spiteful yet insightful emigrant literary critic Georgy Adamovich, registered "the beginning of the end, the beginning of total collapse."[36] Shklovsky's historical uniqueness consists in the fact that he managed to prolong this productive collapse for another 60 years.

NOTES

1. Benedikt Sarnov (1927–2014) was a Moscow literary critic, historian of Soviet literature, and writer.
2. Gasparov, Mikhail L. *Zapisi i vypiski* (Moskva: Novoe literaturnoe obozrenie, 2001), 378.
3. Shklovsky, Viktor. *Sentimental'noe puteshestvie*, In: Shklovsky, Viktor. *"Eshchë nichego ne konchilos'"* (Moskva: Propaganda, 2002), 126.
4. On Soviet subjectivity and mechanism of its production see Hellbeck, Jochen. *Working, Struggling, Becoming: Stalin-Era Autobiographical Texts*, In: *Russian Review*. 2001. No. 6. 340–359; Idem. *Revolution on My Mind: Writing a Diary under Stalin* (Cambridge, MA: Harvard University Press, 2006); Halfin, Igal. *Terror in My Soul: Communist Autobiography on Trial* (Cambridge, MA: Harvard University Press, 2003).
5. I use terms "survival," "adaptation," "assimilation" or "strategies" as ethically neutral descriptive terms referenced to Bourdieuvian perspective, i.e., as particular practices of subjectivization, see Bourdieu, Pierre. *Distinction: A Social Critique of the Judgment of Taste* (Cambridge, MA: Harvard University Press, 1984); Idem. *Other Words: Essays toward a Reflective Sociology* (Stanford: Stanford University Press, 1990); Idem. *Language and Symbolic Power* (Cambridge, MA: Harvard University Press, 1991).
6. Shklovsky, Viktor. *Sentimental'noe puteshestvije*, 195.
7. Panchenko, Olga. *Viktor Shklovsky: tekst—mif—realnost' (K problemam literaturnoi i yazykovoi lichnosti)*. Uniwersytet Szczecinski. Rozprawy i studia. Vol. 267. 1997, 204.
8. Shklovsky, Viktor. *Recenzia na etu knigu*. In: Shklovsky, Viktor. *Sobranie sochinenii*. Vol. 1. (Moskva: Novoe literaturnoe obozrenie, 2018), 522.
9. See Kalinin, Ilya. *Von der Gemachtheit des Textes zum Literarischen Handwerk: Viktor Šklovskij und der Sozialistische Formalismus*. In: Murashev, Jurij, and Liptak, Tomas (Hrsg.) *Schrift und Macht zur Sowjetischen Literatur der 1920er und 30er Jahre* (Vienna: Böhlau Verlag, 2012), 45–69.
10. This paper was published in 1914 under the title "The Resurrection of the Word."
11. Arkhangelsky, Alexander. *Parodii*. (Moskva: Nikitinskie subbotniki, 1929), 97–98.
12. Eikhenbaum, Boris. *Moi vremennik*. (Sankt-Peterburg: Inapress, 2001), 136, 135.
13. Shklovsky, Viktor. *Sentimental'noe puteshestvie*, 158.
14. As Shklovsky wrote in one of his letters to Eikhenbaum: "I am not a literary scholar, I am a person with a fate" ("Iz perepiski Yuria Tynianova i Borisa Eikhenbauma s Viktorom Shklovskim." In: *Voprosy literatury*, 1984, No. 12, 215).
15. Morson, Garry S. *The Boundaries of Genre. Dostoevsky's "Diary of a Writer" and the Tradition of Literary Utopia* (Austin: University of Texas Press, 1981), 52.
16. Shklovsky, Viktor. "Iskusstvo kak priëm." In: Shklovsky, Viktor. *Sobranie sochinenii*. Vol. 1. (Moskva: Novoe literaturnoe obozrenie, 2018), 256.
17. I mean his "Art as a Technique" ("Iskusstvo kak priëm").
18. Shklovsky, Viktor. *Sentimental'noe puteshestvie*, 185, 261, 186.
19. See Kalinin, Ilya. *History as the Art of Articulation (The Historical Experience and Metaliterary Practice of Russian Formalism)*. In: *Social Sciences*, 2006. Vol. 37, No. 1. 43–60.

20. Shklovsky, Viktor. *Sentimental'noe puteshestvie*, 156.
21. Ginzburg, Lidia. *Zapisnye knizhki. Vospominaniia. Esse.* (Sankt-Peterburg: Iskusstvo SPB, 2002), 13.
22. Ibid., 369.
23. Shklovsky, Viktor. "Tret'ia fabrika." In: Shklovsky, Viktor. *"Eshchë nichego ne konchilos'...,"* 372.
24. Shklovsky, Viktor. *Zoo*. In: Shklovsky, Viktor. "Eshjo nichego ne konchilos'...," 323.
25. Ibid., 283.
26. Ibid., 329.
27. Shklovsky, Viktor. *Tret'ia fabrika*, 372.
28. Shklovsky, Viktor. "Pis'ma M. Gor'komu." In: Shklovsky, Viktor. *Sobranie sochinenii*. Vol. 1, 201.
29. Shklovsky, Viktor. *Tret'ia fabrika*, 368.
30. Grits, Teodor. *Tvorchestvo Viktora Shklovskogo (o "Tret'ei fabrike")*. (Baku: Tipografiia OMZAK'a, 1927), 8.
31. Shklovsky, Viktor. *Sentimental'noe puteshestvie*, 226.
32. Shklovsky, Viktor. *Tret'ia fabrika*, 337.
33. Ibid., 394.
34. Ibid., 369.
35. Kaverin, Veniamin. *Skandalist, ili vechera na Vasil'evskom ostrove*. In: Kaverin, Veniamin. *Sobranie sochinenii v 6 t.* Vol. 1. (Moskva: Khudozhestvennaia literatura, 1963), 350.
36. Adamovich, Georgy. *Literaturnye besedy. Kniga vtoraia.* (St.-Petersburg: Aleteia, 1998), 38.

WORKS CITED

Adamovich, Georgy. *Literaturnye besedy. Kniga vtoraia.* St.-Petersburg: Aleteia, 1998 (in Russian).
Arkhangelsky, Alexander. *Parodii.* Moskva: Nikitinskie subbotniki, 1929 (in Russian).
Bourdieu, Pierre. *Distinction: A Social Critique of the Judgment of Taste.* Cambridge, MA: Harvard University Press, 1984.
Bourdieu, Pierre. *Other Words: Essays toward a Reflective Sociology.* Stanford: Stanford University Press, 1990.
Bourdieu, Pierre. *Language and Symbolic Power.* Cambridge, MA: Harvard University Press, 1991.
Eikhenbaum, Boris. *Moi vremennik.* Sankt-Peterburg: Inapress, 2001 (in Russian).
Gasparov, Mikhail L. *Zapisi i vypiski.* Moskva: Novoe literaturnoe obozrenie, 2001 (in Russian).
Ginzburg, Lidia. *Zapisnye knizhki. Vospominaniia. Esse.* Sankt-Peterburg: Iskusstvo SPB, 2002 (in Russian).
Grits, Teodor. *Tvorchestvo Viktora Shklovskogo (o "Tret'ei fabrike")*. Baku: Tipografiia OMZAK'a, 1927 (in Russian).
Hellbeck, Jochen. *Working, Struggling, Becoming: Stalin-Era Autobiographical Texts.* In: *Russian Review.* 2001. Vol. 6. 340–359.
Hellbeck, Jochen. *Revolution on My Mind: Writing a Diary under Stalin.* Cambridge, MA: Harvard University Press, 2006.
Halfin, Igal. *Terror in My Soul: Communist Autobiography on Trial.* Cambridge, MA: Harvard University Press, 2003.
"Iz perepiski Yuria Tynianova i Borisa Eikhenbauma s Viktorom Shklovskim." In: *Voprosy literatury*, 1984, no. 12 (in Russian).
Kalinin, Ilya. *History as the Art of Articulation (The Historical Experience and Metaliterary Practice of Russian Formalism)*. In: Social Sciences. 2006. Vol. 37. No. 1. 43–60.
Kalinin, Ilya. *Von der "Gemachtheit" des Textes zum "Literarischen Handwerk": Viktor Šklovskij und der Sozialistische Formalismus.* In: Murashev, Jurij, and Liptak, Tomas

(Hrsg.) *Schrift und Macht zur Sowjetischen Literatur der 1920er und 30er Jahre* (Vienna: Böhlau Verlag, 2012.

Kaverin, Veniamin. *Skandalist, ili vechera na Vasil'evskom ostrove*. In: Kaverin, Veniamin. *Sobranie sochinenii v 6 t.* Vol. 1. Moskva: Khudozhestvennaia literatura, 1963 (in Russian).

Lipovetsky, Mark. *Charms of Cynical Reason: The Transformations of the Trickster Trope in Soviet and Post-Soviet Culture*. Boston: Academic Studies Press, 2011.

Morson, Garry S. *The Boundaries of Genre. Dostoevsky's "Diary of a Writer" and the Tradition of Literary Utopia*. Austin: University of Texas Press , 1981.

Panchenko, Olga. *Viktor Shklovsky: tekst—mif—realnost' (K problemam literaturnoi I yazykovoi lichnosti)*. Uniwersytet Szczecinski. Rozprawy i studia. Vol. 267. 1997 (in Russian).

Shklovsky, Viktor. *"Eshchë nichego ne konchilos' . . . "* Moskva: Propaganda, 2002 (in Russian).

Shklovsky, Viktor. *Sobranie sochinenii*. Vol. 1. Moskva: Novoe literaturnoe obozrenie, 2018 (in Russian).

Chapter Sixteen

From a New Seeing to a New Acting

Viktor Shklovsky's Ostranenie and Analyses of Games and Play

Holger Pötzsch

I open the present chapter with a quotation on the nature of words and art that, as will be shown later, has a somewhat surprising source. The citation by an esteemed formalist thinker states that

> [w]ords are never a tower, or rather, if they are, they're a watchtower, a tower from which you look out onto the world. In other words, art has always had its vicissitudes, it has always lived in blood. Art has a particular life, a life that doesn't run parallel to real life, but remains in eternal conflict with it. . . . Art is continuous astonishment.[1]

Judging by its content, this quotation could have come from Bakhtin and Medvedev's famous reckoning with formalist thinking, or from Trotsky's charges against what he perceived as a reactionary reductionism of the formal method.[2] However, it does not. On the contrary, rather than constituting a distillation of such and other criticisms, the quotation reflects the position of one of the leading figures of the OPOYAZ movement and creator of some of its most debated and cited texts and concepts. The enunciator of the words above is none other than Viktor Shklovsky during an interview conducted with him by Serena Vitale in 1979[3]—the same Shklovsky who concluded his analysis of *Tristram Shandy* with the statement that "[t]he forms of art are explainable by the laws of art; they are not justified by their realism"[4] and who asserted at a different occasion that "a new form does not emerge to express new content, but to replace old form."[5]

I chose to commence my contribution with reference to these statements by Shklovsky to highlight a certain ambivalence in his thinking that seems to constantly oscillate between an, arguably reductive, art-for-art's-sake position where attention to literariness and estrangement merely reveals a play of form apparently without connections to an extra-literary or extra-artistic reality, and a deeply contextualizing approach that perceives of art's main function as challenging and renewing a reader's or onlooker's view onto, and therefore, being in the world. In this chapter, I will argue that this "doubleness" has been a decisive feature of Shklovsky's thinking from the very beginning.

The chapter will, firstly, trace this ambiguity with reference to the mixed origins and legacies of Shklovsky's key term of *ostranenie*. Secondly, through a comparison with Brecht's V-effect, I highlight important differences between the two thinkers and point to the political implications of these. I argue for a contextual understanding of ostranenie as directed toward the world, yet as different from Brecht's dialectical concept. Finally, I apply ostranenie to analyses of computer games and develop a senso-motoric understanding of the concept—procedural ostranenie—that is specific for this new medium.

SHKLOVSKY'S OSTRANENIE BETWEEN TEXT AND CONTEXT

Ever since its inception in the 1919 essay *Isskustvo kak priëm*, Shklovsky's term *ostranenie* has engendered at times heated debates. In particular, when read together with the earlier *Voskreshenie slova* (1914) and the later texts on *Don Quixote*[6] and *Tristram Shandy*,[7] the question arises whether Shklovsky advocated an understanding of the term that reduces artistic activity to a play of form for the sake of renewing form, or whether he envisioned a context-oriented notion that sees a de-habitualization of readers' and spectators' relations to the world as its main task. There is ample evidence supporting both positions and I will review some of these below. In conclusion, I will argue that *ostranenie* functions both as a text-centric and context-bound concept and that both forms of use are within the frames of Shklovsky's thinking. Which of the two alternatives becomes prominent in any given case depends, among other factors, on specific research interests and which conceptual legacy one sees Shklovsky's work as part of.[8]

Already the title of *Isskustvo kak priëm* has led to some controversy among scholars. In their 1965-translation, Lemon and Reis[9] propose *Art as Technique*. Sher[10] follows up with the suggestion *Art as Device*, while Berlina[11] inserts an estranging comma proposing *Art, as Device* in her most recent translation.[12] Each alternative emphasizes salient elements in Shklovsky's text. While *technique* enables attention to artistic craft and a process of shaping and creating both as a manual and mental activity, *device* directs focus to the formal means through which artistic effects can be achieved. Berlina's[13] additional comma suggests a de-familiarizing strategy by Shklovsky who, according to her, originally published the text with this comma—*Isskustvo, kak priëm*—to enable a different meaning of the title—*Art, how is reception?* I will here opt for Sher's alternative that is also supported by Berlina—*Art as Device*—to emphasize the focus on formal means through which effects of ostranenie can be invited.

Ambiguities such as the ones identified with reference to the title of Shklovsky's text are maintained in translations of the key concept of *ostranenie* itself. Berlina[14] reviews a series of terms that have previously been used—de-familiarization, estrangement, making strange—a list I extend with additional alternatives such as alienation, de-habitualization, distanciation and more.[15] In the end, Berlina[16] choses Sher's suggestion e*n*strangement to retain Shklovsky's initial misspelling of ostranenie with only one "n" in spite of the fact that derivation from the Russian term strannii—strange—would suggest a spelling with two "n"'s—ostrannenie. In addition, e*n*strangement allows for a precise delimitation of Shklovsky's term from related concepts that also suggest a de-familiarizing, de-habitualizing, and renewing effect of artistic form, but that entail competing theoretical and political trajectories—Brecht's V-effect among them.

Besides the term ostranenie itself, also other parts of *Isskustvo kak priëm* pose challenges for translators. In her introduction, Berlina[17] points to several problems connected to key passages of Shklovsky's essay. According to her, difficulties arise due to 1) ambiguities in Russian as to whether a direct or indirect article is implied in a sentence, 2) a tendency by earlier translators to academize Shklovsky's text that, in its original form, deliberately uses straightforward and mundane terminology, as well as 3) an ambivalence in translations of Russian prepositions. In particular the latter aspect leads to a very important ambiguity at a key point of the essay that is relevant for the present inquiry.

Berlina claims that it remains unclear whether Shklovsky's text asserts that "'art exist[s] in order to return the sensation *of* life' or '*to* life'" and explains that the Russian formulation "vernut' oshchushchenie zhizni"[18] allows for both alternatives. The latter translation, she continues, would imply an inherent world-directedness of Shklovsky's term that would put main emphasis on the "after-effects of reading" and, therefore, stands at odds with dominant text-centric strands of early Formalism.[19] In conclusion, Berlina asserts that "in neither text [*Resurrecting the Word* and *Art as Device*] does Shklovsky seem to be fully aware of his concept's ambiguity."[20] At the same time, she, somewhat contradictory, maintains that "the examples he [Shklovsky] cites illustrate all its [ostranenie's] forms" implying attentiveness to a certain breadth of ostranenie's form and scope.[21]

This conceptual ambiguity also comes to the fore in the examples Shklovsky uses in his essays—first and foremost his dependence upon the work of Tolstoy. Striedter[22] and Lachmann,[23] among others, have pointed to a seeming contradiction in Shklovsky's *Iskusstvo kak priëm* that takes recourse to Tolstoy to exemplify a concept aimed at identifying formal devices that slow down reception by drawing renewed attention, not to the world, but to the very devices out of which the work in question is composed. This seems at odds with Tolstoy's technique of re-contextualizing an object with the politically inclined intention of re-inciting readers' awareness for the real world veiled by debilitating habits and can only be explained when assuming an openness of Shklovsky for such contextual understandings of ostranenie. Lachmann[24] then shows that Shklovsky gradually made these apparent tensions in his work more explicit culminating in a re-evaluation of ostranenie in the light of Brecht's work in *Povesti o prose*.[25]

Given his sensitivities for language, I find it very unlikely that Shklovsky was unaware of the semantic ambivalences surfacing both in his formulations and the examples he uses. On the contrary, it appears probable that he deliberately chose to open up a certain leeway for interpretation to maintain relevance of his term for both textual and contextual approaches. In Striedter's words, "two different intentions of e*n*strangement"[26] created tensions in Shklovsky's thinking from the beginning—a fact that can also be traced in debates about possible inspirations, origins, and legacies of his key concept.

The concept of ostranenie has a wider genealogy than originally acknowledged by Shklovsky. In his early essays, he first and foremost set out to delimit the formalist approach from religiously and historically inclined schools of literary criticism (e.g., Chernyshevsky, Pisarev, or Veselovsky) to carve out a disciplinary space for the scientific investigation of literariness. In what Erlich[27] terms a "cavalier treatment of recognized authorities . . . so typical of Russian Formalism,"[28] Shklovsky even disavows the linguistic approach by Potebnya in spite of quite overt common interests and perspectives shared by both thinkers.

Through the years, many possible origins of Shklovsky's ostranenie have been identified. Grimm[29] connects the term to a romantic lineage represented by Shelley and Novalis, a claim that is supported by Fradkin,[30] who cites from an interview conducted by Vladimir Pozner with Shklovsky in 1964 where the latter makes such a connection explicit. Both Helmers[31] and Ungvarí[32] note that estrangement is a cultural concept that has recurred in different forms and varying breadths of application since antiquity and has been used productively for a variety of purposes by among others Socrates, Aristotle, Kierkegaard, Hegel, and Marx.

Such considerations lead Fradkin[33] to assert that, in its widest understanding, estrangement is a "conditio sine qua non" of artistic expressions that will always base intended effects on some form of making strange that "points beyond accustomed circles of association." Estrangement is more than a merely artistic device, but an "indispensable condition" for the acquisition of new knowledge that enables scientific and other progress.[34] Here, estrangement becomes conceivable as a general cultural dynamic and Shklovsky's ostranenie only as a very specific version of it. I account for this by using the translation e*n*strangement to refer to Shklovsky's term and estrangement to account for more general understandings and genealogies of artistic and other practices and forms of making strange. Which tendency in thinking about practices and effects of estrangement Shklovsky's term specifically aligns to can be explored through a comparison with Brecht's concepts of Verfremdung and V-effect.

Willett[35] was among the first to articulate the position that Brecht had been inspired by Shklovsky's *ostranenie*. He argues that a meeting between Brecht and Tretiakov in Moscow in 1935 inspired the former to adopt the terms V-effect and Verfremdung in his work on dialectical theatre. Willet supports his hypothesis by pointing to a series of formal likenesses between V-effect and ostranenie such as a distinction between fabula and plot or the methods of slowing down reception and laying bare the device. This position is apparently supported by Reich[36] who points to the same meeting as an inspiration for Brecht.

On closer inspection, however, it becomes clear that Willett's position is built on rather feeble evidence. Even though Brecht became acquainted with Shklovsky's work in 1935 and might have been inspired to adopt the specific term Verfremdung, he had been working on his own understanding of the estranging potentials of certain devices in stage play since the 1920s (see among others Fradkin[37] and Knopf[38]). Furthermore, while Shklovsky's most salient sources of inspiration seem to have been Tolstoy, Novalis, and Shelley, Brecht took recourse to Hegel and Marx.[39] As such, in spite of certain formal likenesses between ostranenie and V-effect, both terms have very different origins and imply diverging political trajectories.

At a later point in his memoirs, also Reich[40] sows doubts about the importance of Shklovsky's thinking for Brecht. Among other things, he points to significant differences between the concepts of ostranenie and V-effect, thereby relativizing an influence of the former on the latter he had opened for on a general level in the passages cited by Willett. This and similar evidence allow Helmers[41] to conclude that the Shklovsky-Brecht trajectory is possible, but lacks solid evidence. On the other hand, he continues, an opposite influence—from Brecht to a (late) Shklovsky—appears more probable. Helmers then turns to Lachmann's study of Shklovsky's *Povesti o prose*[42] to support his hypothesis.

In her article, Lachmann argues that Shklovsky used *Povesti o prose* to, among other things, re-evaluate his earlier notion of ostranenie and more clearly articulate e*n*strangement as a concept that is also directed at enabling new perspectives on and relations to the world. She writes that, in *Povesti o prose*, "poetics appear as a means of making conscious,"[43] as facilitating a reinvigorating seeing that inhibits an active rising from blinding automatization and debilitating habit and that clearly points beyond the boundaries of aesthetic form. Günther[44] reiterates this position and connects it back to the question of mutual influences between Shklovsky and Brecht. He asserts that articles such as *Obnovlenie poniatiia* or *O novom videnii* (both part of *Povesti o prose*)[45] "absolutely create the impression that he [Shklovsky] had acquired certain self-critical insights from Brecht's V-effects."[46] Günther concludes that both thinkers most likely influenced one another's concepts over time and in trajectories that are difficult to assess with complete certainty.

Pointing to inherent tensions between a *poetics and politics of estrangement*, Boym[47] identifies ostranenie as an important inspiration for practices of resistance in the Soviet Union. Connecting Shklovsky with theorists such as Walter Benjamin, Aby Warburg, Georg Simmel, and above all Hannah Arendt, she asserts that ostranenie constitutes "an existential art of everyday survival and a tactic of dissent in Russia and Eastern Europe [during the Communist era]." According to her, these directly political performances of ostranenie point to the fact that both "estrangement *from* the world and estrangement *for* the world" are key aspects of Shklovsky's thinking.[48] Unfortunately, she does not interrogate possible connections between her overtly political understanding of ostranenie and Brecht's thinking on Verfremdung any further.

It can be argued that, even in its world-directed form, Shklovsky's concept is far from the devices of dialectical theatre devised by Brecht to mobilize and empower spectators. As Tihanov[49] observes, in Shkovsky's thinking, "the end product [of an act of e*n*strangement] is meant as a piece of innovation—arrived at through various artistic devices—that serves, however, to revive and make more palpable the old (and constant) substance of things . . . thus reasserting what is presumed to be the object's timeless substance." According to Günther,[50] this focus on acquiring anew some untarnished original relation to things is strongly at odds with Brecht's didactic and dialectical thinking about the V-effect that was more concerned with shaking up spectators and dissecting complex socio-political realities with the objective to facilitate concrete political interventions and change. While Shklovsky aims at allowing us again to experience the stoniness of the stone in its true nature as something fresh and new, Brecht's work is dedicated at recovering the stone from received ideological frames to facilitate progressive new uses in the politics of class struggle. These differences can be explained with reference to the distinct theoretical lineages of both thinkers—Romanticism in the case of Shklovsky and Hegelian and Marxist dialectics in the case of Brecht.

Finally, there is a historical dimension to all practices and devices of estrangement—Shklovsky's *ostranenie* and Brecht's Verfremdung among them. Once estrangement has taken place, the formal devices behind a renewal of sedimented aesthetic form and naturalized perceptual and cognitive frames quickly wear off and themselves become the source of dominant ways of seeing and thinking. As such, art and reception constantly oscillate between the poles of renewal and customization. Estrangement appears as ultimately contingent upon an ever-shifting background that predisposes what is perceived as normal and what as transgressive at any given moment in history. Much to the vexation of the acolytes of official Soviet ideology, Shklovsky refrained from explicitly excluding socialist society from these inevitable processes of constant automatization and subsequent necessary renewal.[51]

To sum up, in Shklovsky's thinking, estrangement is triggered by innovation that is not only directed at formal conventions, but always also implies a changed relation to the world. This changed relation, however, tends to be backward-looking and bound toward rediscovering and reasserting an allegedly forgotten or hidden original relation to things. In contrast to this specific form of estrangement originating from a Romantic lineage, Brecht's Verfremdung takes recourse to Hegelian and Marxist dialectics to assert a form of estrangement bound to unveiling naturalized and therefore largely invisible power relations and practices of exploitation and oppression with the immediate purpose of facilitating change.

I will now turn toward an application of Shklovsky's concept of *ostranenie* to an analysis of computer games and play to bring forth some medium-specific aspects of games that afford not only a narrative, but also an enacted and performed play of habitualization and renewal.

PROCEDURAL *OSTRANENIE*: FORMS OF ENSTRANGEMENT IN VIDEOGAMES

After having argued for both a textual and a contextual dimension of Shklovsky's *ostranenie*, and after having distinguished the latter from Brecht's dialectical term Verfremdung, I will now move on to show the applicability of the concept of *en*strangement to analyses of digital games. The straightforward use of received theories and methods from established disciplines to a 'new' medium is often riddled with problems. In the slightly polemic formulation of Aarseth,[52] such attempts might "force outdated paradigms onto a new cultural object." In contrast to aesthetic forms such as novels or film, Aarseth argues, games resemble simulations and, therefore, constitute a "radically different alternative to narratives as a cognitive and communicative structure."[53] Consequently, 'old' concepts and methods need to be carefully adapted to enable fruitful inquiries that do justice to the new medium.[54] Below, I will briefly outline the specific affordances of games, before I use Shklovsky's concept of *ostranenie* for an illustrating analysis of the critical anti-war title *This War of Mine*.[55]

Games are actions. In contrast to other media that convey static narratives, games are ergodic[56]—they do not only require interpretation, but in addition enable, and indeed demand, players to act. To play, as such, means to intervene in game worlds of varying complexity and directly engage with emerging events. Possible interactions with diegetic universes, other players, or game characters are pre-structured and predisposed by complex coded rule systems—game mechanics—which, often-tacitly, limit what players can and cannot do. The emergent co-constitutive relation between players, mechanics, and narratives resembles systemic patterns of support and restraint that make possible and motivate some perceptions and actions and disable and de-motivate others. Therefore, Galloway[57] states that, in game studies, "it is no longer sufficient to talk about the visual or textual representation of meaning. Instead the game theorist must talk about actions, and the . . . game-worlds in which they transpire."

In spite of their reliance upon mechanics and code, games also tell stories. Therefore, received instruments from the study of literature, film, and art can productively be applied to the new medium and provide valuable insights into the narrative mechanisms and devices of games. In addition, however, the mechanical frames limiting player freedom to act in fictitious story worlds also require careful scrutiny. After all, according to Bogost,[58] game mechanics and code are the sites where games' specific "procedural rhetoric" conveys and negotiates meaning and ideology. Conscientious attention to the simulation aspects of games requires a careful remodeling of received concepts as well as the design of new methods and theoretical frames.[59]

The stories games tell depend upon active player involvement. Imagine that two different viewers each upload their version of Ridley Scott's war film *Black Hawk Down* (2001) to *YouTube*. Whoever accesses the files later will see exactly the same movie represented as a series of devices formally predisposing spectator experiences. Now imagine a group of players uploading their specific play-throughs of the historical first-person shooter *Call of Duty: Black Ops*.[60] Even though this particular game decisively limits player freedom and ties possible in-game actions to a narrow paradigm of combat-related tactical choices, not two of the uploaded film sequences will ever look completely alike. This example shows what is at stake in the study of games—digital and otherwise—and has led Pötzsch and Šisler[61] to the conclusion that "games' potential effects . . . are contingent upon both the subjective selection of certain variables by designers and developers (aesthetic form) and the active engagement of these textual frames by players (re-appropriative practices of play)."

How, then, can Shklovsky's formalist concept of ostranenie successfully be harnessed for analyses of games and play? I will respond to this question by way of a concrete example—the anti-war title *This War of Mine* (TWoM) released in 2015. By means of a formal analysis, I will develop a notion of Shklovsky's *en*strangement that provides insights into how game mechanics, rule systems, and interfaces enable new perspectives on game worlds and beyond. Inspired by Bogost's[62] procedural rhetoric, I term this game-specific form of *en*strangement *procedural ostranenie*.

TWoM is a simulation game set in an unspecified war zone where players take control of a group of three civilians trying to sustain themselves in a derelict urban environment.[63] The game employs a flat side-view perspective that enables upward-downward and left-right scrolling to access additional areas of the diegetic world, and distinguishes between night and day modes offering different tasks, opportunities, and challenges. During days, game characters can build simple machinery and produce certain tools and goods, or trade, rest, and heal (if they have the necessary resources). During the night, one selected character is sent to scavenge nearby areas for supplies, while the shelter is exposed to occasional raids (figures 16.1 and 16.2).

The game has been lauded for its complex presentation of civilians' hardships in war. In particular, the elaborate feedback system that adds in-game consequences to all player actions and repeatedly enforces difficult ethical

Figure 16.1. Playing Civilians in *This War of Mine*: Day-mode. Courtesy 11 Bit Studios/Wojciech Setlak.

decisions (such as who to feed or heal and who to let die, or by which means to acquire resources vital for the survival of the group) has been reviewed positively. As Toma[64] points out, TWoM enables ethical gameplay and, thereby, successfully counters "mainstream war ideologies which appear in many games"—a move that, according to Kwiatkowski, was an intended outcome of the development process.[65]

As I have shown at a different occasion, forms of estrangement play a key role in the change of perspective on war achieved in TWoM.[66] The move to let players control vulnerable civilians, rather than invincible soldier-heroes, together with a shift of attention to severely negative impacts of warfare at a variety of levels transform a usually expected aggrandizing war-play into an almost unmanageable struggle for survival characterized by a constant lack of resources, mutual distrust, frustration, as well as an inevitable gradual deterioration of moral standards. By these means, TWoM challenges and undermines received power fantasies and celebrations of violence characteristic of the war game genre.[67] The game thoughtfully employs such devices as playable characters, setting, received tropes (damsels-in-distress, player-character heroes), and more to unsettle habitualized perceptions and conventionalized expectations of players.

In this chapter, I will disregard such classical narrative aspects of *en*-strangement in TWoM.[68] Instead, I direct attention to a form of ostranenie that is specific to games, thereby adapting Shklovsky's concept to analyses of a new interactive medium. The game-specific formal device in focus are

Figure 16.2. Playing Civilians in *This War of Mine*: Night-mode. Courtesy 11 Bit Studios/Wojciech Setlak.

controller configurations through which players steer characters and interact with the game world. In TWoM this element is employed for the purpose of enabling not only new perspectives on, but also a *new acting in*, the apparently well-known and familiar frames of pop cultural representations of war and violence.

Controller interfaces bring players into contact with game worlds. Usually, a simplified version of the full game—a tutorial—is used to gradually accustom players to the increasingly complex sequences of accurately timed finger and hand movements required to successfully maneuver an avatar through the various challenges of game worlds. Tutorials are often narratively framed for instance by letting a character wake up after an accident and gradually learn to look around, walk, and pick up or use items again. Tutorials are conventionalized design features that enable entertaining play while incrementally conveying extra-diegetic knowledge and skills necessary for players' in-game success. By these means, the use of controllers is gradually internalized to enable smooth immersion in the various senso-motoric challenges of games.

TWoM breaks with this convention and turns the lack of a tutorial into a powerful enstrangement device that draws attention to the otherwise habitualized and therefore largely unnoticed formal frames that tacitly guide player actions. Once the game has started, players are thrown into a derelict building with no help except a few simple icons indicating potentials for interaction with the game world. From then on, the only option is to try out various affordances to identify the most useful items and the most valuable and vital resources. Similarly, no exposition supports the first scavenging expeditions during night-time, a design-choice that makes occasional hostile encounters almost always deadly for the player. Only after a series of mostly unsuccessful and frustrating play sessions, one becomes accustomed to the basic principles of controller use that gradually recede into the background and lose their estranging function. From then on, play with a more ludic attitude aimed at 'beating the game' becomes possible.

TWoM uses the lack-of-tutorial-device to slow down and complicate the habitualization of game controls. This has the effect that otherwise internalized senso-motoric preconditions for game play are brought to renewed attention of players. However, as one of the lead writers and developers of TWoM, Wojciech Setlak, points out, the move of cutting the tutorial was about more than a mere play with form to enstrange astute gamers. Rather, the immediate purpose of removing sequences of necessary training was political—it was meant as a critical statement about war and about the failings of most popular games to adequately treat this subject.

In an email correspondence with me,[69] Setlak explained that the development team deliberately refrained from adding a user-friendly tutorial to drive home the point that, in actual wars, most civilians will be entirely unprepared for the hardships lying ahead of them. The aim was to create game mechanics that complicate play and force player actions in the diegetic world to reflect precisely this unpreparedness. In leaving out the tutorial, TWoM unsettles conventionalized user experiences and brings forth vulnerability and an inability to act heroically or uphold even the most basic ethical standards as the most salient elements of war situations. By these means, the game issues a sound criticism both of warfare as such and of conventional representations of war in genre films and games that usually treat violent conflict as an arena for heroism and mastery.

In TWoM, a procedural form of ostranenie points beyond a mere play of form and to a complex socio-cultural background. The new seeing and acting invited by the game's enstranged mechanics appears as directed at the world and, as such, entails a political trajectory. This world-directedness, however, is not bound toward recovering an original essence of things apparently lost in blinding custom and habit. As such, a procedural rethinking of Shklovsky's *ostranenie* alone is not enough to grasp the full implications of TWoM's estranging dynamics. In addition, we have to turn to the dialectical dynamics of Brecht's V-effect and its didactic and empowering interconnection of aesthetic form and political practice.

Bringing together Shklovsky and Brecht, it can be argued that the notion of a new acting introduced here essentially refers to two things; firstly, in Shklovsky's tradition, it denominates the effects of a game-specific, mechanics-based form of enstrangement—procedural *ostranenie*—that deploys formal devices to slow down and complicate the acquisition of play skills thereby bringing otherwise internalized frames for interaction with game-worlds to the sudden awareness of players. Secondly, when seen in the light of Brecht's ideas, a new acting point to wider notions of estrangement that complicate form with the purpose of inciting direct political action by unveiling real societal contradictions and interests otherwise obscured by ideology. As such, procedural *ostranenie* in TWoM not only formally challenges received habits of play, but in doing so, also creates a V-effect in the sense of Brecht that re-positions players as active political subjects.

CONCLUSION: FROM A NEW SEEING TO A NEW ACTING

This chapter has argued that both Shklovsky and Brecht see art and life as intrinsically connected. In their views, there is no empty play of form—the realms of artistic creation and world do not run parallel but are in eternal conflict with one another. For both thinkers, art is not static but a lived process and constant struggle. As Shklovsky puts it in the beginning of this chapter, *art is continuous astonishment* and *it has always lived in blood*.

In Shklovsky, this conflict is predominantly backward-looking—a struggle to retain, or regain, an original relation to things now apparently lost. In this process, devices of ostranenie serve to sharpen and reinvigorate perception to make us see anew what habit and custom have tacitly removed from sight. Brecht, in contrast, subsumes art under politics. For him, formal means of estrangement create a V-effect that brings to light naturalized contradictions and power relations. As a didactic and dialectical tool Verfremdung directly promotes education, mobilization, liberation, and progressive change. While Shklovsky advocates a new seeing, for Brecht a new, and inherently political, acting is the most crucial aspect of artistic intervention.

As has been shown in this chapter, this new acting acquires an additional dimension when connected to the aesthetic form of games. Here, a procedural form of ostranenie estranges and, thereby draws attention to, the very devices designed to habitualize and internalize the frames that limit and predispose player interaction with diegetic worlds. I exemplify this notion through an analysis of how the lack of a tutorial in TWoM de-naturalizes received conventions of play and, by these means, opens up not only new perspectives on game form, but also on received ways of representing, and acting in, war. As an increasingly significant cultural form, it seems, also games enable continuous astonishment and are lived in blood.

NOTES

1. Viktor Shklovsky and Serena Vitale, *Shklovsky: Witness to an Era*. (London: Dalkey Archive Press, 2012), 98–99.
2. M. Mikhail Bakhtin and Pavel N. Medvedev, *The Formal Method in Literary Scholarship: A Critical Introduction to Sociological Poetics* (Baltimore: Johns Hopkins University Press, 1978), see, in particular, chapter 4 and Leon Trotsky, *Literature and Revolution*. (New York: Russell & Russell, 1957), see, in particular, chapter 5.
3. Shklovsky and Vitale, *Shklovsky*, 98–99.
4. Viktor Shklovsky, "Stern's Tristram Shandy: Stylistic Commentaries," in *Russian Formalist Criticism: Four Essays*, ed. Lee T. Lemon and Marion J. Reis (Lincoln: University of Nebraska Press, 1965), 57.
5. Viktor Shklovsky, "Der Zusammenhang zwischen den Verfahren der Sujetfügung und den allgemeinen Stilverfahren," in *Russischer Formalismus*, ed. Jurij Striedter (Munich: Wilhelm Fink Verlag, (1965), 51. All translations from German are my own. German version reads: "Eine neue Form entsteht nicht, um einen neuen Inhalt auszudrücken, sondern um eine alte Form abzulösen."
6. Viktor Shklovsky, "The Making of Don Quixote," in *Theory of Prose*, ed. Viktor Shklovsky (Champaign: Dalkey Archive Press, 1990).
7. Shklovsky, "Stern's Tristram Shandy."
8. For a seminal study of Russian Formalism with specific focus on changing notions of estrangement throughout the movement's three constitutive phases, see Aage A. Hansen-Löve, *Der Russische Formalismus: Methodologische Rekonstruktion seiner Entwicklung aus dem Prinzip der Verfremdung* (Vienna: Verlag der österreichischen Akademie der Wissenschaften, 1978).
9. Viktor Shklovsky, "Art as Technique," in *Russian Formalist Criticism: Four Essays*, ed. Lee T. Lemon and Marion J. Reis (Lincoln: University of Nebraska Press, 1965).

10. Benjamin Sher, "Translator's Introduction: Shklovsky and the Revolution," in *Theory of Prose*, ed. Viktor Shklovsky (Champaign: Dalkey Archive Press, 1990).

11. Alexandra Berlina, "Translating 'Art, as Device,'" *Poetics Today* 36, no. 6 (2015) and "Translator's Introduction," in *Viktor Shklovsky: A Reader*, ed. Alexandra Berlina (New York: Bloomsbury, 2017).

12. These differences in translations of the title of Shklovsky's essay are reflected in the German alternatives *Art as Procedure* (Kunst als Verfahren) or *Art as Artistic Device* (Kunst als Stilmittel). See, for instance, Jurij Striedter, "Zur Formalistischen Theorie der Prosa und der literarischen Evolution," in *Russischer Formalismus*, ed. Striedter, xxi–xxii (in particular note 38).

13. Berlina, "Translating 'Art, as Device,'" 151, note 1.

14. Ibid., 152–54.

15. Holger Pötzsch, "Playing Games with Shklovsky, Brecht, and Boal: Ostranenie, V-Effect, and Spect-Actors as Analytical Tools in Game Studies," *Game Studies* 17, no. 2 (2017): 3–4.

16. Berlina, "Translating 'Art, as Device,'" 152–53.

17. Ibid., 155–56.

18. Ibid., 155 (emphasis in original).

19. Ibid.

20. Berlina, "Translator's Introduction," 24.

21. Ibid.

22. Striedter, "Zur Formalistischen Theorie," xxiii.

23. Renate Lachmann, "Die 'Verfremdung' und das 'neue Sehen' bei Viktor Sklovskij," in *Verfremdung in der Literatur*, ed. H. Helmers (Darmstadt: Wissenschaftliche Buchgesellschaft, 1984), 326–27.

24. Ibid., 336–39.

25. Viktor Shklovsky, *Povesti o prose* (Two Volumes) (Moscow: Isdatelstvo Xudoshestvennaja Literatura, 1966).

26. Striedter, "Zur Formalistischen Theorie," xxiii. German original reads: "zwei unterschiedliche Intentionen der Verfremdung."

27. Victor Erlich, *Russian Formalism: History, Doctrine* (The Hague: Mouton & Co., 1969).

28. Ibid., 23.

29. Reinhold Grimm, "Verfremdung: Beiträge zu Wesen und Ursprung eines Begriffs," in *Verfremdung in der Literatur* ed. H. Helmers (Darmstadt: Wissenschaftliche Buchgesellschaft, 1984), 188–89.

30. Ilja Fradkin, *Bertolt Brecht: Weg und Methode* (Leipzig: Verlag Philipp Reclam, 1974), 154.

31. Hermann Helmers, "Einleitung," in *Verfremdung in der Literatur*, ed. H. Helmers (Darmstadt: Wissenschaftliche Buchgesellschaft, 1984).

32. Tamás Ungvari, "The Origins of the Theory of Verfremdung," *Neohelicon* 7, no. 1 (1979).

33. Fradkin, *Bertolt Brecht*, 160–61.

34. Ibid. German originals read: "aus dem gewohnten Kreis der Assoziationen hinausweist" and "unerläßliche Bedingung . . . jeder Erkenntnis."

35. John Willett, *The Theatre of Bertolt Brecht* (London: Methuen & Co. Ltd, 1959), 179–80 and 208–10.

36. Bernhard Reich, *Im Wettlauf mit der Zeit* (Berlin: Henschelverlag, 1970), 371–72.

37. Fradkin, *Bertolt Brecht*, 153–57.

38. Jan Knopf, "Verfremdungen," in *Verfremdung in der Literatur*, ed. H. Helmers (Darmstadt: Wissenschaftliche Buchgesellschaft, 1984), 356–59.

39. Ungvari, "The Origins."

40. Reich, *Wettlauf*, 372.

41. Helmers, "Einleitung," 23.

42. Shklovsky, *Povesti*.

43. Lachmann, "Die Verfremdung," 337. German original reads: "Dichtung erscheint als Bewußtmachung."

44. Hans Günther, "Verfremdung: Brecht und Sklovskij," in *Gedächtnis und Phantasma: Festschrift für Renate Lachmann*, ed. S. K. Frank, et al. (Munich: Verlag Otto Sagner, 2001).

45. Shklovsky, *Povesti*, II: 298–307 & 444–46.

46. Günther, "Verfremdung," 142. German original reads: "Sein [Shklovskijs] Artikel 'Obnovlenie ponjatija' erweckt durchaus den Eindruck, als habe er Brechts V-Effekten bestimmte selbstkritische Einsichten abgewonnen" (142). Reference to *O novom videnii* on page 143.

47. Svetlana Boym, "Poetics and Politics of Estrangement: Victor Shklovsky and Hannah Arendt," *Poetics Today* 26, no. 4 (2005).

48. Ibid., 584 (emphasis in original).

49. Galin Tihanov, "The Politics of Estrangement: The Case of the Early Shklovsky," *Poetics Today* 26, no. 4 (2005), 686.

50. Günther, "Verfremdung, 142.

51. Lachmann, "Die 'Verfremdung,'" 338.

52. Espen Aarseth, "Game Studies, Year One," *Game Studies* 1, no. 1 (2001), n.p.

53. Ibid., n.p.

54. For similar arguments, see Janet H. Murray, *Hamlet on the Holodeck: The Future of Narrative in Cyberspace* (Cambridge: MIT Press, 1997).

55. Released by 11 Bit Studios in 2015.

56. Espen Aarseth, *Cybertext: Perspectives on Ergodic Literature* (Baltimore: Johns Hopkins University Press, 1997).

57. Alexander Galloway, "Social Realism in Gaming," *Game Studies* 4, no. 1 (2004): n.p.

58. Ian Bogost, *Persuasive Games: The Expressive Power of Videogames* (Cambridge: MIT Press, 2007), in particular 28–40.

59. See also Aarseth, "Game Studies."

60. Released by Activision (2010).

61. Holger Pötzsch and Vit Šisler, "Playing Cultural Memory: Framing History in 'Call of Duty: Black Ops' and 'Czechoslovakia 38–89: Assassination,'" *Games & Culture* (online first) (2016), 5.

62. Bogost, *Persuasive Games*.

63. A later version—*This War of Mine: The Little Ones*—includes children that are put in the care of playable characters, a design choice aimed at enhancing the emotional impact of the game.

64. Elisabeta Toma, "Self-Reflection and Morality in Critical Games: Who Is to Be Blamed for War?," *Journal of Comparative Research in Anthropology and Sociology* 6, no. 1 (2015): 216.

65. Kacper Kwiatkowski, "Civilian Casualties: Shifting Perspective in This War of Mine," in *Zone of Control: Perspectives on Wargaming*, ed. Pat Harrigan and Matthew B. Kirschenbaum (Cambridge: MIT Press, 2016).

66. Holger Pötzsch, "Positioning Players as Political Subjects: Forms of Estrangement and the Presentation of War in This War of Mine and Spec Ops: The Line," in *War Games: Memory, Militarism, and the Subject of Play*, ed. Philip Hammond and Holger Pötzsch (New York: Bloomsbury, forthcoming 2019).

67. For a critique of generic representations of war in games, see, for instance, Holger Pötzsch, "Selective Realism: Filtering Experiences of War and Violence in First-and Third-Person Shooters," *Games & Culture* 12, no. 2 (2017).

68. For this perspective, see, for instance, Toma, "Self-Reflection and Morality," Pötzsch, "Positioning Players," and Kwiatkowski, "Civilian Casualties."

69. Email exchange between Wojciech Setlak and me from Sept. 19, 2018.

WORKS CITED

Aarseth, Espen. *Cybertext: Perspectives on Ergodic Literature*. Baltimore: Johns Hopkins University Press, 1997.

———. "Game Studies, Year One." *Game Studies* 1, no. 1 (2001). http://www.gamestudies.org/0101/editorial.html.
Bakhtin, M. Mikhail, and Pavel N. Medvedev. *The Formal Method in Literary Scholarship: A Critical Introduction to Sociological Poetics*. Baltimore: Johns Hopkins University Press, 1978.
Berlina, Alexandra. "Translating 'Art, as Device.'" *Poetics Today* 36, no. 6 (2015): 151–56.
———. "Translator's Introduction." In *Viktor Shklovsky: A Reader*, edited by Alexandra Berlina, 1–50. New York: Bloomsbury, 2017.
Bogost, Ian. *Persuasive Games: The Expressive Power of Videogames*. Cambridge: MIT Press, 2007.
Boym, Svetlana. "Poetics and Politics of Estrangement: Victor Shklovsky and Hannah Arendt." *Poetics Today* 26, no. 4 (2005): 581–611.
Erlich, Victor. *Russian Formalism: History, Doctrine*. The Hague: Mouton & Co., 1969.
Fradkin, Ilja. *Bertolt Brecht: Weg und Methode*. Leipzig: Verlag Philipp Reclam, 1974.
Galloway, Alexander. "Social Realism in Gaming." *Game Studies* 4, no. 1 (2004). http://www.gamestudies.org/0401/galloway/.
Grimm, Reinhold. "Verfremdung: Beiträge zu Wesen und Ursprung eines Begriffs." In *Verfremdung in der Literatur* edited by H. Helmers, 183–215. Darmstadt: Wissenschaftliche Buchgesellschaft, 1984.
Günther, Hans. "Verfremdung: Brecht und Sklovskij." In *Gedächtnis und Phantasma: Festschrift für Renate Lachmann*, edited by S.K. Frank, E. Gerber, S. Schahadat and I. Smirnov, 137–45. Munich: Verlag Otto Sagner, 2001.
Hansen-Löve, Aage A. *Der Russische Formalismus: Methodologische Rekonstruktion seiner Entwicklung aus dem Prinzip der Verfremdung*. Vienna: Verlag der österreichischen Akademie der Wissenschaften, 1978.
Helmers, Hermann. "Einleitung." In *Verfremdung in der Literatur*, edited by H. Helmers, 1–32. Darmstadt: Wissenschaftliche Buchgesellschaft, 1984.
Knopf, Jan. "Verfremdungen." In *Verfremdung in der Literatur*, edited by H. Helmers, 325–92. Darmstadt: Wissenschaftliche Buchgesellschaft, 1984.
Kwiatkowski, Kacper. "Civilian Casualties: Shifting Perspective in This War of Mine." In *Zone of Control: Perspectives on Wargaming*, edited by Pat Harrigan and Matthew B. Kirschenbaum, 691–702. Cambridge: MIT Press, 2016.
Lachmann, Renate. "Die 'Verfremdung' und das 'neue Sehen' bei Viktor Sklovskij." In *Verfremdung in der Literatur*, edited by H. Helmers, 321–51. Darmstadt: Wissenschaftliche Buchgesellschaft, 1984.
Murray, Janet H. *Hamlet on the Holodeck: The Future of Narrative in Cyberspace*. Cambridge: MIT Press, 1997.
Pötzsch, Holger. "Playing Games with Shklovsky, Brecht, and Boal: Ostranenie, V-Effect, and Spect-Actors as Analytical Tools in Game Studies." *Game Studies* 17, no. 2 (2017): 1–19. http://gamestudies.org/1702/articles/potzsch.
———. "Positioning Players as Political Subjects: Forms of Estrangement and the Presentation of War in This War of Mine and Spec Ops: The Line." In *War Games: Memory, Militarism, and the Subject of Play*, edited by Philip Hammond and Holger Pötzsch. New York: Bloomsbury, forthcoming 2019.
———. "Selective Realism: Filtering Experiences of War and Violence in First-and Third-Person Shooters." *Games & Culture* 12, no. 2 (2017): 156–78.
Pötzsch, Holger, and Vit Šisler. "Playing Cultural Memory: Framing History in 'Call of Duty: Black Ops' and 'Czechoslovakia 38–89: Assassination.'" *Games & Culture* (online first) (2016). https://doi.org/10.1177/1555412016638603
Reich, Bernhard. *Im Wettlauf mit der Zeit*. Berlin: Henschelverlag, 1970.
Sher, Benjamin. "Translator's Introduction: Shklovsky and the Revolution." In *Theory of Prose*, edited by Viktor Shklovsky, xv–xxi. Champaign: Dalkey Archive Press, 1990.
Shklovsky, Viktor. "Art as Technique." In *Russian Formalist Criticism: Four Essays*, edited by Lee T. Lemon and Marion J. Reis, 3–24. Lincoln: University of Nebraska Press, 1965.
———. "The Making of Don Quixote." In *Theory of Prose*, edited by Viktor Shklovsky, 72–100. Champaign: Dalkey Archive Press, 1990.

———. *Povesti o prose (Two Volumes)*. Moscow: Isdatel'stvo Xudoshestvennaia Literatura, 1966.

———. "Stern's Tristram Shandy: Stylistic Commentaries." In *Russian Formalist Criticism: Four Essays*, edited by Lee T. Lemon and Marion J. Reis, 27–57. Lincoln: University of Nebraska Press, 1965.

———. "Der Zusammenhang zwischen den Verfahren der Sujetfügung und den allgemeinen Stilverfahren." In *Russischer Formalismus*, edited by Jurij Striedter, 37–121. Munich: Wilhelm Fink Verlag, 1965.

Shklovsky, Viktor, and Serena Vitale. *Shklovsky: Witness to an Era*. London: Dalkey Archive Press, 2012.

Striedter, Jurij. "Zur Formalistischen Theorie der Prosa und der literarischen Evolution." In *Russischer Formalismus: Texte zur allgemeinen Literaturtheorie und zur Theorie der Prosa*, edited by Jurij Striedter, ix–lxxxiii. Munich: Wilhelm Fink Verlag, 1969.

Tihanov, Galin. "The Politics of Estrangement: The Case of the Early Shklovsky." *Poetics Today* 26, no. 4 (2005): 665–96.

Toma, Elisabeta. "Self-Reflection and Morality in Critical Games: Who Is to Be Blamed for War?" *Journal of Comparative Research in Anthropology and Sociology* 6, no. 1 (2015): 209–24.

Trotsky, Leon. *Literature and Revolution*. New York: Russell & Russell, 1957.

Ungvarí, Tamás. "The Origins of the Theory of Verfremdung." *Neohelicon* 7, no. 1 (1979): 171–232.

Willett, John. *The Theatre of Bertolt Brecht*. London: Methuen & Co. Ltd, 1959.

Appendix

List of Russian Transliterated Titles

Adamovich, Georgy. *Literaturnye besedy. Kniga vtoraia.* St.-Petersburg: Aleteia, 1998.
Arkhangelsky, Alexander. *Parodii.* Moskva: Nikitinskie subbotniki, 1929.
Averintsev, Sergey S., *Poetika rannevizantiiskoi literatury* [The Poetics of the Early Byzantine Literature]. Moskva: Koda, 1997 (in Russian).
Belinkov, Arkady, and Natal'ia Belinkova. *Raspria s vekom (v dva golosa).* Moskva: Novoe literaturnoe obozrenie, 2008 (in Russian).
Carroll, Lewis. Kérroll', L'iuis. *Prikliucheniia Alisy v' stranie chudes'* [Alice's Adventures in Wonderland]. Translated by Allegro [P.S. Solovyova]. Illustrations by John Tenniel. St. Petersburg: Tropinka, 1909 (in Russian).
———. Karrol', L['iuis]. *Ania v' stranie chudes'* [Ania in Wonderland]. Translated by V. Sirin [V.V. Nabokov]. Illustrations by Sergey Zalshupin. Berlin: Gamaiun, 1923 (in Russian).
———. Karroll, L'iuis. *Alisa v Zazerkal'i* [Alice in Transmirroria]. Translated by V. Azov [V.A. Ashkenazi]. Poems translated by T.L. Shchepkina-Kupernik. Illustrations by John Tenniel. Moscow-Petrograd: L.D. Frenkel', 1924 (in Russian).
———. Kérroll, L'iuis. *Prikliucheniia Alisy v strane chudes. Alisa v Zazerkal'e* [Alice's Adventures in Wonderland. Through the Looking-Glass, and What Alice Found There]. Translated by N.M. Demurova. Poems translated by S.Ia. Marshak and D.I. Orlovskaia. Introduction by N.M. Demurova. Illustrations by Petar Chuklev. Sofia: Izdatel'stvo literatury na inostrannykh iazykakh, 1967 (in Russian).
———. *Sonia v tsarstve diva* [Sonia in a Kingdom of Wonder]. The first Russian translation of *Alice's Adventures in Wonderland.* [Translated by E.I. Boratynskaia (?).] Illustrations by John Tenniel and Byron W. Sewell. Introduction and notes by Victor Fet. Portlaoise: Evertype, 2017 (in Russian).
Chudakova, Marietta, and Evgeny Toddes. "Prototipy odnogo romana." In *Al'manakh bibliofila. Vypusk X*, 172–190. Moskva: Kniga, 1981 (in Russian).
Efimov, Nikolai. *Formalizm v russkom literaturovedenii.* Smolensk, 1929 (in Russian).
Eikhenbaum, Boris. *Moi vremennik.* Sankt-Peterburg: Inapress, 2001 (in Russian).
———. "Teoriia 'formal'nogo metoda" (1926). *O Literature: Raboty raznykh let.* Moskva: Sovetskii Pisatel,' 1987. 375–408 (in Russian).
Eisenstein, Sergei. "Montazh attraktsionov." In Oushakine, *Formal'nyi metod*, Vol. 1: 337–341 (in Russian).
Galushkin, Alexander, ed., "Viktor Shklovsky i Roman Jakobson. Perepiska (1922–1956)." In *Roman Jakobson: Teksty, dokumenty, issledovaniia,* edited by Henryk Baran, 104–135. Moskva: Rossiiskii gosudarstvennyi gumanitarnyi universitet, 1999 (in Russian).

Galushkin, Alexander. "Eschë raz o prichinakh razryva V. B. Shklovskogo i R. O. Jakobsona." In *Roman Jakobson: Teksty, dokumenty, issledovaniia*, edited by Henryk Baran, 136–143. Moskva: Rossiiskii gosudarstvennyi gumanitarnyi universitet, 1999 (in Russian).
Garzonio, Stefano. "Viktor Shklovsky i Dzhovanni Bokkachcho: Ob istorii odnoi maloizvestnoi stat'i Shklovskogo." In *Epokha "ostraneniia." Russkii formalizm i sovremennoe gumanitarnoe znanie: Kollektivnaia monografiia*, edited by Ian Levchenko and Igor Pilshchikov. Moskva: Novoe literaturnoe obozrenie, 2017 (in Russian).
Gasparov, Mikhail, "Sintaksicheskaia tesnota stikhovogo riada" [Syntactic compactness of the verse line]. In *Poetika. Stikhovedenie. Lingvistika. Sbornik statei* [Poetics. Versification. Linguistics. A Collection of Articles]. Moskva: Azbukovnik, 2003 (in Russian).
Gasparov, Mikhail L. *Zapisi i vypiski*. Moskva: Novoe literaturnoe obozrenie, 2001 (in Russian).
Ginzburg, Lidia. *Zapisnye knizhki. Vospominaniia. Esse*. Sankt-Peterburg: Iskusstvo SPB, 2002.
Gomolitskaia-Tret'iakova, T.S. "O moëm otse." In *Strana-perekrëstok*, by Sergei Tret'iakov, 554–63. Moskva: Sovetskii pisatel,' 1991 (in Russian).
Grits, Teodor. *Tvorchestvo Viktora Shklovskogo (O "Tret'ei fabrike")*. Baku: Tipografiia OMZAKa, 1927 (in Russian).
Hansen-Löve, Aage A. "Perspektivy russkogo formalizma: Logotsentrizm vchera i segodnia." In *Epokha "ostraneniia." Russkii formalizm i sovremennoe gumanitarnoe znanie: Kollektivnaia monografiia*, edited by Ian Levchenko and Igor Pilshchikov. Moskva: Novoe literaturnoe obozrenie, 2017. https://play.google.com/books/reader?id=myMrDwAAQBAJ&pg= GBS.PP53 (in Russian).
Hansen-Löve, Aage. *Russkii formalizm. Metodologicheskaia rekonstruktsia razvitiia na osnove printsipa ostraneniia*. Trans. S. A. Romashko. Moskva: Iazyki russkoi kul'tury, 2001 (in Russian).
Iampolski, Mikhail. "Ischeznovenie kak forma suschestvovaniia." *Kinovedcheskie zapiski* 44 (1999). http://www.kinozapiski.ru/ru/print/sendvalues/656/ (in Russian).
Ioffe, Denis. "Zhiznetvorchestvo russkogo modernizma sub specie semioticae. Istoriograficheskie zametki k voprosu tipologicheskoi rekonstruktsii zhizn'—tekst." *Kritika i semiotika* 8 (2005): 126–179 (in Russian).
"Iz perepiski Yuria Tynianova i Borisa Eikhenbauma s Viktorom Shklovskim." In *Voprosy literatury*, 1984, No. 12 (in Russian).
Jakobson, Roman. "Noveishaia russkaia poezia. Nabrosok pervyi: podstupy k Khlebnikovu" in Oushakine, *Formal'nyi metod*, Vol. 3: 246–304 (in Russian).
Jakobson, Roman. *Raboty po poetike* [Works on Poetics]. Moskva: Progress, 1987 (in Russian).
Kalinin, Ilya. "Viktor Shklovsky kak priëm." In *Sistemy*, edited by Serguei A. Oushakine, Vol. 1: *Formal'ny metod: Antologiia russkogo modernizma*, edited by Serguei A. Oushakine, 63–106. Moskva: Kabinetnyi uchënyi, 2016 (in Russian).
Kaverin, Veniamin. *Epilog*. Moskva: Vagrius, 2006 (in Russian).
———. *Skandalist, ili Vechera na Vasil'evskom ostrove*. In Kaverin, Veniamin. *Sobranie sochinenii v 6 t*. Vol. 1. Moskva: Gosudarstvennoe izdatel'stvo khudozhestvennoi literatury, 1963 (in Russian).
Levchenko, Ian. "Poslevkusie formalizma: Proliferatsiia teorii v tekstakh Viktora Shklovskogo 1930-kh godov." *Novoe literaturnoe obozrenie* 4 (2014): 125–143 (in Russian).
Lvoff, Basil [Lvov, Vasily]. "Literaturny kanon i poniatie strannosti: Russkii formalizm i Kherold Blum." *Zhurnalistika i kul'tura russkoy rechi* 2 (2012): 86–103 (in Russian).
———. "V diskussionnom poriadke." *Voprosy literatury* 2 (2012): 1–21 (in Russian).
Mandelstam, Osip. *Sobranie Sochinenii*. Edited by Pavel Nerler et al. Mandelstam Society edition. 4 vols. Moskva: Art-Biznes-Centr, 1993–1997 (in Russian).
Marshak, Samuil. *Dom, kotoryi postroil Dzhek* [A House That Jack Built]. Illustrated by Vladimir Konashevich. Peterburg-Moskva: Vsemirnaia literatura, Gosizdat, 1923 (in Russian).
Meyerhold, Vsevolod. "Aktër budushchego." In Oushakine, *Formal'nyi metod*, Vol. 3: 566–571 (in Russian).
———. "Balagan." In Oushakine, *Formal'nyi metod*, Vol.3: 522–547 (in Russian).

———. "Doklad o plane postanovki p'esy S.M.Tret'iakova 'Khochy rebënka.'" In Oushakine, *Formal'nyi metod*, Vol.3: 700–701 (in Russian).
———. "Ideologiia i technologiia v teatre" in Oushakine, *Formal'nyi metod*, Vol.3: 580–597 (in Russian).
———. "O paradoksal'nom podkhode v reshenii obraza i stseny." In *Vsevolod Meyerhold, Stat'i. Pis'ma. Rechi. Besedy. Chast' vtoraia, 1917–1939*. Moskva: Iskusstvo, 1968 (in Russian).
Novikov, Vladimir. "Poetika skandala." In *Roman s literaturoi*, 76–85. Moskva: Intrada, 2007 (in Russian).
Oushakine, Serguei, ed. *Formal'nyi metod: Antologiya russkogo modernizma*. 3 Vols. Moskva: Ekaterinburg: Kabinetnyi uchënyi, 2016 (in Russian).
———. "'Ne vzletevshie samolëty mechty': O pokolenii formal'nogo metoda." In *Sistemy*, edited by Serguei A. Oushakine, Vol. 1: *Formal'ny metod: Antologiia russkogo modernizma*, edited by Serguei A. Oushakine, 9–60. Moskva: Kabinetnyi uchënyi, 2016 (in Russian).
———. "Put' formalistov k khudozhestvennoi proze." *Voprosy literatury* 3(2004): 131–150 (in Russian).
Panchenko, Olga. *Viktor Shklovsky: Tekst—mif—realnost' (K problemam literaturnoi i yazykovoi lichnosti)*. Uniwersytet Szczecinski. Rozprawy i studia. Vol. 267. 1997 (in Russian).
Petrovsky, Miron S. "Vladimir Mayakovsky i L'iuis Kérroll" [Vladimir Mayakovsky and Lewis Carroll]. In Kérroll, L. *Dnevnik puteshestviia v Rossiiu v 1867 g., ili Russkii dnevnik*. Stat'i i ésse o L'iuise Kérolle. [Carroll, L. Journal of a tour in Russia in 1867. Articles and Essays about Lewis Carroll], 297–310. Chelyabinsk: Entsiklopediia; St. Petersburg: Kriga, 2013 (in Russian).
Potebnya, Aleksandr. *Iz zapisok po teorii slovesnosti: Poeziia i proza. Tropy i figury. Myshlenie poeticheskoe i mificheskoe. Prilozheniia*. Edited by Maria V. Potebnya. Khar'kov: Parovaia Litografiia i Tipografiia M. Sil'berberg i S-vya, 1905 (in Russian).
Salman, Marina. "Molodoi Shklovsky. (Po arkhivnym materialam)." In *Vienna Slavic Yearbook. 5*, edited by Stefan Michael Newerkla and Fedor B. Poljakov, 148–167. Wiesbaden: Harrassowitz Verlag, 2017 (in Russian).
Sedakova, Olga, "Opus Incertum." *Znamia*, 7 (2011): 38–50 (in Russian).
Shklovskaya-Kordi, Varvara, ed. "K 100-letiiu Viktora Shklovskogo. Izium iz bulki." *Voprosy literatury* 1 (1993): 322–330 (in Russian).
Shklovsky, Viktor. "Bor'ba za formu." In Oushakine, *Formal'nyi metod*, Vol. 1: 222–225 (in Russian).
———. *Chulkov i Levshin*. Leningrad: Izdatel'stvo pisatelei v Leningrade, 1933 (in Russian).
———. *Energiia zabluzhdeniia: Kniga o siuzhete*. Moskva: Sovetskii pisatel,' 1981 (in Russian).
———. "*Eshchë nichego ne konchilos'*..." Moskva: Propaganda, 2002 (in Russian).
———. *Gamburgskii schët: Stat'i, vospominaniia, esse (1914–1933)*. Moskva: Sovetskii Pisatel,' 1990. http://lib.co.ua/memoir/shklovskiyvictor/gamburgskiy-schet.jsp (in Russian).
———. "Iskusstvo kak priëm." *Sborniki po teorii poeticheskogo iazyka*, Vol. 2, 3–14. Petrograd: Opoiaz, 1917 (in Russian), http://www.opojaz.ru/manifests/kakpriem.html#Anchor-%1F%3EMB%3E%3C-17504 (in Russian).
———. "Iskusstvo kak priëm." In *Sborniki po teorii poeticheskogo iazyka*, Vol. 3, 101–114. Petrograd: Opoiaz, 1919 (in Russian).
———. "Iz filologicheskikh ochevidnostei sovremennoi nauki o stikhe." *Germes* 1 (1919): 67–72 (in Russian).
———. *Khod konia*. Moskva and Berlin: Gelikon. 1923 (in Russian).
Shklovsky, Viktor. "Kuda shagaet Dziga Vertov." In Oushakine, *Formal'nyi metod*, Vol. 1: 245–247 (in Russian).
———. *Lev Tolstoy*. Moskva: Molodaya Gvaridiya (Zhizn' zamechatel'nykh lyudei), 1963 (in Russian).
———. *Literatura i kinematograf*. Berlin: Russkoe universal'noe izdatelstvo, 1923 (in Russian).
———. *Marko Polo*. Moskva: Zhurnal'no-gazetnoe ob'edinenie, 1936 (in Russian).

———. *Mater'ial i stil' v romane L'va Tolstogo "Voina i mir."* Moskva: Federatsiia, 1928. Reprint: The Hague: Mouton, 1970 (in Russian).
———. *Matvei Komarov. Zhitel' goroda Moskvy.* Leningrad: Priboi, 1929 (in Russian).
———. *Minin i Pozharskii.* Moskva: Sovetskii pisatel',' 1940 (in Russian).
———. "Monument to a Scientific Error: Context No. 24." Translation of "Pamiatnik nauchnoi oshibke," *Literaturnaia Gazeta*, No. 4, January 27, 1930, by Shushan Avagyan. Champaign: Dalkey Archive Press https://www.dalkeyarchive.com/monument-to-a-scientific-error/.
———. "O Dzige Vertove." In Oushakine, *Formal'nyi metod*, Vol. 1: 248–261 (in Russian).
———. *O teorii prozy.* Moskva: Federatsiia, 1929. Reprint: Ann Arbor: Ardis, 1985 (in Russian).
———. *O teorii prozy.* Moskva: Sovetskii pisatel,' 1983 (in Russian).
———. "Pis'ma vnuku." *Voprosy literatury* 4 (2002): 264–300 (in Russian).
———. *Podënshchina.* Leningrad: Izdatel'svo Leningradskikh Pisatelei, 1930 (in Russian).
———. *Povesti o proze.* 2 vols. Moskva: Khudozhestvennaiia literatura, 1966 (in Russian).
———. "Prostranstvo v iskusstve i suprematisty" [Space in art and the Suprematists.] *Zhizn' iskusstva*, 196–197 (1919): 4.
———. "Potebnya." *Birzhevye vedomosti, utrennii vypusk*, No. 16010 (December 30, 1916), at: http://www.opojaz.ru/shklovsky/potebnya.html. (last accessed 08/10/2018) (in Russian).
———. *Razvërtyvanie siuzheta* [Unfolding the Plot]. Moskva, 1921.
———. "Semantika kino." In Oushakine, *Formal'nyi metod*, Vol. 1: 242–244 (in Russian).
———. "Sentimental'noe puteshestvie." In Shklovsky, V. *Eshchë nichego ne konchilos'.* Moskva: Propaganda, 2002, 15–266 (in Russian).
———. "Sentimental'noe puteshestvie." In *Yu. N. Tynianov. V. B. Shklovsky. Proza*, edited by Vladimir Novikov, 430–641. Moskva: SLOVO/SLOVO, 2001 (in Russian).
———. "Sergei Eisenstein" in Shklovsky, *Zhili-byli*, 466–514 (in Russian).
———. Shklovsky, V.—Yu. Tynianovu in Shklovsky, V. *Gamburgskii schët. Stat'i—Vospominaniia—Esse* (1914–1933), edited by A. Galushkin and A. Chudakov. Moskva: Sovetskii pisatel, 1990: 302–303 (in Russian).
———. *Sobranie sochinenii.* Vol. 1. Moskva: Novoe literaturnoe obozrenie, 2018.
———. *Staroe i novoe.* Moskva: Detskaia literatura, 1966 (in Russian).
———. "Sviaz' priëmov siuzhetoslozheniia s obshchimi priëmami stilia." In Oushakine, *Formal'nyi metod*, Vol. 1: 147–181 (in Russian).
———. *Svintsovyi zhrebii: Dar Viktora Shklovskogo Lazaretu deiatelei iskusstv.* Sankt-Peterburg: Tip. Z. Sokolinskogo, 1914 (in Russian).
———. *Tekhnika pisatel'skogo remesla.* Moskva, Leningrad: Molodaia Gvardiia, 1927 (in Russian).
———. *Tekhnika pisatel'skogo remesla.* Moskva: Molodaia gvardiia, 1930 (in Russian).
———. *Teoriia prozy.* Moskva: Krug, 1925 (in Russian).
———. *Tetiva: O neskhodstve skhodnogo.* Moskva: Sovetskii pisatel,' 1970 (in Russian).
———. *Tret'ia fabrika.* Moskva: Artel' pisatelei "Krug," 1926 (in Russian).
———. "Vernite miach v igru" [Bring the ball back into the game.] *Tetiva: O neskhodstve skhodnogo* [The Bowstring: on the Dissimilarity of the Similar]. Moskva: Khudozhestvennaia literatura, 1983 (in Russian).
———. *Voskreshenie slova.* St. Peterburg: Tipografiia Z. Sokolinskogo, 1914, http://philolog.petrsu.ru/filolog/shklov.htm. (in Russian).
———. *Za 60 let: raboty o kino.* Moskva: Iskusstvo, 1985 (in Russian).
———. *Zametki o proze russkikh klassikov: O proizvedeniiakh Pushkina, Gogolia, Lermontova, Turgeneva, Goncharova, Tolstogo, Chekhova.* Moskva: Sovetskii pisatel,' 1953 (in Russian).
———. *Zhili-byli.* Moskva: Sovetskii pisatel, 1966 (in Russian).
———. *Zhizn' khudozhnika Fedotova.* Moskva: Izdatel'stvo detskoi literatury, 1936 (in Russian).
———. "Zoo, ili Pis'ma ne o liubvi." In Shklovsky, *Zhili-byli*, 165–226 (in Russian).

———. "Zoo, ili Pis'ma ne o liubvi, ili tret'ia Eloiza." In *Yu. N. Tynianov. V. B. Shklovsky. Proza*, edited by Vladimir Novikov, 642–698. Moskva: SLOVO/SLOVO, 2001 (in Russian).

Smirnov, Igor. "Formalizm i nigilizm." *Zvezda* 2 (2014). https://zvezdaspb.ru/index.php?page=8&nput=2243 (in Russian)

Tolstoy, L.N. Polnoe sobranie sochinenii, edited by V. Chertkov, et al. 90 vols. Moskva: Khudozhestvennaiia literatura, 1928–58 (in Russian).

———. "Dnevnik L.N. Tolstogo. Izvlecheniia pod redaktsiei A.M. Khir'iakova." In A. M. Khir'iakov, ed. *Letopis'* [The Chronicle] Dec. 1915: 332–375 (in Russian).

———. *Pis'ma k zhene*. Moskva: N.p, 1915 (in Russian).

———. *Chto takoe iskusstvo*. Moskva: Sovremennik, 1985 (in Russian).

Tretiakov, Sergei. "The Biography of the Object," *October* 118 (Fall 2006): 57–62.

Tulchinsky, Grigory L. 2002. "L' iuis Kérroll: Nonsens kak predposylka istiny" [Lewis Carroll: nonsense as a preliminary condition of truth]. In *Rossiia i Britaniia v epokhu prosveshcheniia. Opyt filosofskoi i kul'turnoi komparativistiki*. Part 1. Filosofskii vek. [Russia and Great Britain in the Age of Enlightenment. Philosophical and Cultural Comparative Studies. Part I. The Age of Philosophy]. Almanakh 19. St. Petersburg: SPb Tsentr istorii idei [Center for the History of Ideas], 2002: 130–150 (in Russian).

Tynianov, Yury. *Dostoevsky i Gogol (k teorii parodii)*. Petrograd: Opoiaz, 1921. Reprint: Letchworth, UK: Prideaux, 1975 (in Russian).

———. "Dostoevsky i Gogol (k teorii parodii)." In Oushakine, *Formal'nyi metod*, Vol. 1: 530–561 (in Russian).

———. *Kiukhlia. Smert' Vazir-Mukhtara*. Moskva: Kniga, 1981 (in Russian).

———. "O literaturnoi evoliutsii" in Yury Tynianov. *Arkhaisty i novatory*. Leningrad: Priboi, 1929, 30–47 (in Russian).

———. "O parodii" in Oushakine, *Formal'nyi metod*, Vol.1: 603–631 (in Russian).

———. "Stikhotvornye formy Nekrasova" [Nekrasov's verse forms]. In *Poetika, Istoriia literatury, Kino* [Poetics. History of literature. Cinema]. Moskva: Nauka, 1977.

Viktor Shklovsky i Roman Jakobson. Zhizn' kak roman. Directed by Vladimir Nepevny. Moskva: Telekompaniia "Gamayun," 2009: https://vimeo.com/154703239 (in Russian).

Yakubinsky, Lev. "O zvukakh stikhotvornogo yazyka." *Sborniki po teorii poeticheskogo iazyka I*. St. Peterburg: 18-aia gosudarstvennaia tipographiia, 1916. 6–30. In Yakubinsky, *Izbrannye raboty*, 163–175 (in Russian).

———. "Skoplenie odinakovykh plavnykh v prakticheskom i poeticheskom iazykakh." *Sborniki po teorii poeticheskogo yazyka II*. St. Peterburg: 18-aia gosudarstvennaia tipographiia, 1917, 15–23. In Yakubinsky, *Izbrannye raboty*, 176–182 (in Russian).

———. *Izbrannye raboty: Iazyk i ego funktsionirovanie*. Edited by A. A. Leont'ev. Moscow: Nauka, 1986 (in Russian).

Zelinsky, Kornelii. "Kak sdelan Viktor Shklovsky." *Zhizn' iskusstva* 14 (1924): 13–14 (in Russian).

Index

Aarseth, Espen, 241
"The Accumulation of Liquids in Practical and Poetic Language". *See* Yakubinsky, Lev Petrovich
Acmeism/Acmeist poets, 12, 17, 113–114. *See also* Formalism; Futurism; poetry
actant, 98
actor, 98, 101, 102, 132, 171
adventure novel, 70, 71, 74, 80
aesthetic(s), 1, 3, 7, 11, 15, 18–19, 69, 100, 110, 115–116, 119, 140, 153, 173–174, 177, 183n8, 194, 212, 220, 227, 230, 240, 241; experience, 95, 209; form, 173, 241, 246, 247; principle, 114, 194. *See also* "Art as Device"; form; perception
affordance, 100, 241, 245
Akhmatova, Anna, 53, 110; "Ode to Stalin", 115
Alexander II, 52
Alice. *See* Characters in Lewis Carroll's *Alice's Adventures in Wonderland*
Alice's Adventures in Wonderland, 3, 51, 54, 56, 60; translation into Bashkir, 55, 56–57; translation into French, 52, 53, 56; translation into German, 52, 55, 56; translation into Gothic, 60; translation into Irish, 56, 59; translation into Middle English, 60; translation into Old English, 60; translation into Russian, 52, 53, 54, 56, 58, 58–59. *See also* Carroll, Lewis; Characters in *Alice's Adventures in Wonderland*
Allegro. *See* Solovyova, Poliksena
All Things Are Possible. See Shestov, Leo
Alonso Quijano. *See* characters in Cervantes's *Don Quixote*
Andreyevna, Sofia, 178
Andropov, Yuri, 41
Ania. *See* Characters in Lewis Carroll's *Alice's Adventures in Wonderland*
Apuleius, *The Golden Ass*, 74, 126
Arac, Jonathan, 143
Aragon, Louis, 53
arbitrio. See non-literary genres
Arendt, Hannah, 240
Aristotle, 12, 66, 238; *Poetics*, 51, 120
Arkhangelsky, Alexander, 221
arms vs. letters debate. *See* non-literary genres
ars moriendi, 5, 131
art, 4, 6, 11, 20, 27, 28, 67, 94, 100, 116, 163, 179, 192, 193, 226, 241, 242; analyzing, 34, 67; and life, 152, 246; art-for-art's-sake, 8, 236; as thinking in images, 11, 51; defamiliarization in, 3, 5, 11, 12, 52, 55, 80, 153, 154–155, 161, 172, 198, 240; erotic, 174, 177, 184n20; Formalist concept of, 103, 194; goal of, 4, 11, 101; history of, 3, 172; laws of, 52, 69, 220, 235; new, 66, 82, 110, 115; of writing, 4, 99; perception

of, 20, 155, 174, 194; purpose of, 80, 140; study of, 116, 211; understanding, 34, 116; verbal (*Sprachgesang*), 116, 117, 120, 235; visual, 215. *See also* "Art as Device"; "Art as Technique"; device; mosaic; Shklovsky, Viktor; "Art as Device", 14, 17, 19, 19–20, 20, 22, 33, 51, 68, 80, 103, 119, 120, 169, 172, 174, 177, 179–180, 182, 184n19, 236, 237; as founding document of Russian Formalism, 2, 11, 51, 172, 173; fame of, 6, 19–20, 32, 140, 207; Yakubinsky in, 14–15, 18; aesthetics; "Art as Technique"; automatization; defamiliarization; device; estrangement; Formalism; image; laying bare; *ostranenie*; perception; plot; plot construction; Shklovsky, Viktor; technique; *Theory of Prose*; thing; threading; Yakubinsky, Lev Petrovich

"Art as Technique" (variant title), 6, 140, 189–198, 202n58, 223, 227. *See also* "Art as Device"; Shklovsky, Viktor

Ashkenazi, Vladimir (Azov), 53

Askers/Turkish soldiers, 29

Association of Proletarian Writers, 111

autobiography, 222

automatization/de-automatization, 15, 19, 32–33, 94–95, 141, 153, 154, 160, 162, 179, 194, 198, 230, 241. *See also* "Art as Device"; defamiliarization; estrangement; making strange; *ostranenie*

avant-garde, 7, 52, 57, 110, 172–173, 176, 179, 189, 191. *See also* Futurism; poetic language; Shklovsky, Viktor

Averintsev, Sergey, 214–216

Awad, Germine H., 158, 160, 161, 162

Azov, V. *See* Ashkenazi, Vladimir

Baker, Peter, 60
Bakhtin, Mikhail, 34, 41, 54, 59, 81, 235; Bakhtin Circle, 27; polyglossia, 54. *See also* Bakhtin Circle
Balagan. See Meyerhold, Vsevolod
Balmont, Konstantin, 52
Barthes, Roland, 73
The Bathhouse. See Mayakovsky, Vladimir

Batyushkov, Konstantin, 139
Bed and Sofa. See Room, Abram
Belinkov, Arkady, 28
Bellour, Raymond, 181
Bely, Andrey, 192; *Rhythm as Dialectics and Bronze Horseman by Pushkin,* 215
Benjamin, Walter, 240
Bergson, Henri, 11, 12, 17
Bergstrom, Janet, 169
Berkeley, George, 22
Berlin, 29, 113, 225, 226
Berlina, Alexandra, 89n1, 236–237
Bhabha, Homi, 96, 142
Black Hawk Down. See Scott, Ridley
Blok, Alexander, 45, 47n19, 52, 139
Bobrov, Sergey, 210
Boccaccio, Giovanni, *Decameron,* 74
Bogost, Ian, 242, 243
Bolshevist government/Bolshevik revolution/the Bolsheviks, 29, 32, 42, 47n12, 52, 222, 225
Borges, Jorge Luis, 83, 85; "Death and the Compass", 3, 79, 82, 85
Boruchoff, David A., 83
Bowstring: On the Dissimilarity of the Similar. See Shklovsky, Viktor
Boym, Svetlana, 170, 240
Brecht, Bertolt, 172, 183n8, 238, 239–241, 246, 247; V-effect, 8, 236, 237, 239–240, 246; *Verfremdung,* 239
Breton, André, 53
Brezhnev, Leonid, 41, 45n2, 115, 119
Brik, Lilya, 45, 47n18, 53
Brik, Osip, 43, 66, 172, 179
Brown, Katherine, 85
Bruna Husky, character in Montero's *Lágrimas en la lluvia,* 153, 155, 156, 157, 159, 162
Bruns, Gerald, 152
Bulgakov, Mikhail, *White Guard,* 56
Burke, Edmund, 209

Call of Duty: Black Ops, 242
Carlton, David Alexander, 60
Carroll, Lewis (Dodgson, Charles Lutwidge), 3, 51–60; *The Hunting of the Snark,* 53; *Jabberwocky,* 60. *See also* characters in Lewis Carroll's *Alice's Adventures in Wonderland*

Index

Alice's Adventures in Wonderland; Through the Looking-Glass and what Alice Found There
Cervantes, Miguel de, 5, 28, 28–29, 70, 73, 74, 125–126, 127, 131, 133–134; *Colloquy of the Dogs*, 127; *Don Quixote de la Mancha*, 5, 34, 42, 125–134; *Don Quixote de la Mancha II*, 125–131, 133–134
Chandler, Raymond, "The Simple Art of Murder", 81
Chaplin, Charlie, 19
character (literary), 69, 71, 102, 157, 174, 221; See also Shklovsky, Viktor
characters in Cervantes's *Don Quixote*: Alonso Quijano (Don Quixote), 70, 72, 126; Diego de Miranda, Knight of the Green Coat, 131; Don Quixote, 5, 28, 34, 125–126, 127–133; Dorotea, as Princess Micimicona, 126; Dulcinea, 34, 129–130, 132; Ricote, 126; Roque Guinart, 126; Sancho Panza, 5, 125, 129–130, 131; Sansón Carrasco (Knight of the Woods, Knight of the Mirrors), 130–133
characters in Lewis Carroll's *Alice's Adventures in Wonderland*: Alice, 51, 52, 53, 56, 57, 59–60; Ania (replacement of Alice in Nabokov's Russian translation), 56; Duchess, 60; Eibhlís (Alice in Irish translation), 59; Hatter, 54; Mock Turtle, 59; Mouse, 56–57; Sonia (replacement of Alice in the first Russian translation), 60; White Hare (replacement of White Rabbit in Middle English translation), 60
Chekhov, Anton, 58, 144; "Chekhov's gun", 71
Chernyshevsky, Nikolay, 238
Childe Harold's Pilgrimage (Byron), 42
children's literature, 31, 57
chivalric romance, 125, 128, 130, 133
Christie, Agatha, 81, 83
Chukovsky, Korney, 54
Cicero, Marcus Tullius, 21
Cikara, Mina, 159, 162
cinema. *See* film
cinematograph. *See* Lumière brothers
Civil War. *See* Russian Civil War

codes, 81, 125, 131, 133, 134, 152, 171, 242
coincidence, 42, 69, 70, 86–87, 228
Collado-Rodríguez, Francisco, 87
Colloquy of the Dogs. See Cervantes, Miguel de
Comas-Diaz, Lillian, 162
Communist Party, 42, 43, 47n13
composition, 34, 65, 67, 68–69, 70, 72, 76, 126, 177, 210, 211
Conan Doyle, Sir Arthur, 80, 83, 144
Congress of Soviet Writers, 113
"Conjectures on World Literature". *See* Moretti, Franco
Constituent Assembly, 113
contradiction as speaking towards, 34
controller/controls. *See* games
convention (literary), 69, 72, 73, 81–82, 83, 85, 88, 89n6, 241, 247
A Conversation with Friends. See Shklovsky, Victor
Cooppan, Vilashini, 141, 142
Covarrubias Diego de, 128, 133
"Cross-Breeding With His Material", 229–230
The Crying of Lot 49, 3, 80, 82, 85, 88, 90n30; coincidence in, 86–87; post-horn symbol, 80, 87–88; Tristero/Trystero, 80, 85–87; W.A.S.T.E., 85. *See also* Pynchon, Thomas
Cubism, 110
cultural archaeology, 189. *See also* novelty effects

Damrosch, David, 142
"Death and the Compass". *See* Borges, Jorge Luis.
de-automatization. *See* automatization
Decameron. See Boccaccio, Giovanni
deceleration/delay/impediment/retardation (in narrative), 70, 72, 74, 75, 76, 80, 172
defamiliarization/defamiliarize/defamiliarized, 2, 3–4, 5, 11–12, 17, 27, 29, 33, 52, 56, 59, 89n1, 119–120, 139–141, 151–152, 153–158, 161–163, 169, 172, 174, 174–175, 176, 178–180, 221, 223–224, 229–230; and racism, 156, 160, 161; and robots, 152,

156–157, 159–160; as out of placeness, 126; in translation, 55, 57, 58; procedural, 236, 243, 246. *See also* "Art as Device"; automatization, estrangement; form; making strange; *ostranenie*
decomposition, technique of, 224
deformation, 220, 229
de-habituation. *See* habitual
dehumanized people, 157, 159
delay. *See* deceleration
Demurova, Nina M., 3, 57, 60
Descartes, René, 22; *Discourse on Method*, 21; *Meditations*, 21
detective fiction/mystery genre/novel, 4, 74, 79, 80–82, 84, 87–88, 143–144; conventions of, 83, 85; cozy, 81–82, 88; hard-boiled, 81–82, 87. *See also* Shklovsky, Viktor
device (*priem*), 7, 12, 17, 29, 30, 68–69, 72–75, 76, 80–81, 83, 99–100, 101, 112, 143, 143–144, 174–175, 177, 179, 207, 221, 228, 236, 238, 239, 240–241, 242, 244, 245, 246, 247; literary, 5, 66, 69, 220, 223, 224, 226, 230. *See also* "Art as Device"; defamiliarization; laying bare; plot; plot construction; Shklovsky, Viktor; technique; *Theory of Prose*; threading
dialectic, 28, 34, 54, 171, 207, 214, 215–216, 241
dialectical theatre, 8, 239, 240, 246, 247
Dickens, Charles, 80, 83
Diego de Miranda, Knight of the Green Coat, character in *Don Quixote. See* characters in Cervantes's *Don Quixote*
discordance (*neviazka*), 99
Discourse on Method. See Descartes, René
discrimination, 157, 158, 159–160, 160, 162. *See also* racism; prejudice
dissimilation (*raspodoblenie*), 99, 100, 101, 102
distant reading. *See* Moretti, Franco
Doane, Mary Ann, 169
Doctor Zhivago. See Pasternak, Boris
Dodgson, Charles Lutwidge. *See* Carroll, Lewis
domestication in translation. *See* translation

Don Quixote. *See* characters in Cervantes's *Don Quixote*
Don Quixote de la Mancha. See Cervantes, Miguel de
Dostoevsky, Fyodor, 44
Douchet, Jean, 181
drama, 69, 72, 230
Duchess. *See* Characters in Lewis Carroll's *Alice's Adventures in Wonderland*
Dulcinea. *See* characters in Cervantes's *Don Quixote*
Ďurišin, Dionýz, 146
Duvakin, Victor, 2, 41–42, 44–45

early film shows, 6, 189, 191, 193, 199n9. *See also* film
Efimov, Nikolai, 95
Efron, Ariadna, 53
Eibhlís (Alice in Irish translation). *See* Characters in Lewis Carroll's *Alice's Adventures in Wonderland*
Eikhenbaum, Boris, 14, 18, 34, 43, 46n9, 52, 97, 114, 118, 146, 193, 194, 196, 198, 221; *The Theory of the Formal Method*, 119. *See also* Formalism
Eisenstein, Sergei, 34, 45, 48n25, 100, 179, 183n9, 192, 194, 200n26. *See also* LEF
emotions, 16, 23n2, 45, 53, 97, 105, 117, 156, 158. *See also* psychologism
Energy of Delusion: A Book about Plot. See Skhlovsky, Viktor
enstrangement, 80, 89n1, 222, 237, 238, 240–241, 243, 244, 245, 246. *See also* defamiliarization; enstrangement; *ostranenie*
enstranging device. *See* games
Enzensberger, Maria, 172
epistemology, 94, 95
epithet, 208, 211–212, 213, 214, 216
Erik Lönnrot, character in Borges's "Death and the Compass", 83–85, 88
Erlich, Viktor, 198, 202n58, 238; error-type story, 84
estrangement/enstrangement (*ostranenie*), 3, 6, 51–52, 55, 72, 80, 89n1, 103, 105, 116, 118–120, 126, 141, 145, 156, 160, 161, 194, 223, 236, 237, 238–239, 240, 243, 247. *See also* "Art as Device"; automatization, defamiliarization,

enstrangement; form; making strange; OPOYAZ; *ostranenie*
Even-Zohar, Itamar, 146
Evertype, 55, 56, 59, 60
evidence, 2, 21, 21–22, 22
evolution, literary, 2, 28, 34, 65, 93, 95, 112, 143, 144, 145, 172, 209

fabula, 3, 67–68, 75, 139, 208, 239. See also sujet; *Theory of Prose*
Fairchild, Terry, 88
fairy tale, 53, 67, 70, 75, 94, 145. See also folklore; folktale; Propp, Vladimir
fame. See non-literary genres
February Revolution, 115
Federico, Christopher M., 154
Fedotov, Pavel, 31, 32
feelings, 96, 97, 103, 104, 105, 110, 117. See also sense
feminism, 172–173. See also film
field (literary), 93, 95, 99, 104, 110, 112, 115, 146, 196, 198, 221, 223, 224
film, 6, 31, 66, 68, 72, 81, 100, 169–172, 179, 181–182, 183n1, 184n20–185n23, 190, 191, 198, 202n57, 241, 242, 245; theory, 48n25, 169, 183n1. See also early film shows; feminism; Futurism
folklore, 52, 54, 59, 66, 69, 176. See also fairy tale; folktale; Propp, Vladimir
folktale, 66, 67, 69, 72, 196. See also fairy tale; folklore; Propp, Vladimir
foreignization in translation. See translation
form, 12, 13, 17, 18, 42, 67–68, 72, 80–82, 95–96, 96, 99–100, 102, 104, 117, 119, 139, 143–145, 151, 152–153, 155, 194, 198, 228, 240–241, 242, 244–246; aesthetic, 240, 241, 242, 246, 247; and content, 16; as step-by-step construction, 74, 84; literary, 99, 222, 230; narrative, 144; new, 95, 235; of enstrangement (*ostranenie*), 241, 243, 244, 246, 247; old, 80, 96, 235; pure, 34, 67. See also aesthetics; estrangement; Formalism; material; plot construction; technique
Formalism/Formalists, Russian, 2, 3, 4, 6–7, 11, 27–28, 33, 42–43, 52, 54, 65, 74, 94–97, 98, 103, 104, 105, 110, 114–120, 126, 139, 143, 146, 151, 169, 172–174, 179–182, 220, 222–224, 229, 235, 243; and Acmeism, 12, 13, 17, 113; and Futurism, 13, 31, 51, 54, 98, 110, 113, 114; Eikhenbaum and, 14, 18, 34, 52, 97, 114, 118, 146, 194; feminist, 6, 173, 180–181; history of, 13–14, 17–18, 104, 180, 194, 198, 222, 237, 238; Jakobson and, 28, 43, 52, 66, 97, 146; Propp and, 66; scholastic, 115; Shklovsky and, 11, 13–14, 14, 27, 28, 30, 43, 152, 155, 226; Tomashevsky and, 66, 146; Tynyanov and, 34, 65–66, 97, 115; Yakubinsky and, 13–16, 17–18. See also "Art as Device"; feeling; form; Formalism; Futurism; literariness; post-Formalism; perception; psychology; thing; fossilization, 81, 95, 96; Fradkin, Ilja, 238–239; freedom, 41, 104, 116, 228; unfreedom
French Structuralism. See Structuralism
Freud, Sigmund, 170–171, 179, 180
Fromm, Devin, 125
function/functionalism, 14, 15, 32, 54, 70, 70–71, 72, 73, 74–75, 76, 98, 139, 152, 174, 211, 245
Futurism/Futurists (Russian), 4, 6, 13, 31, 42, 51–52, 54, 59, 98, 110–111, 113, 114, 118, 174, 176, 189, 191–193, 194, 198, 209, 210, 221; *A Slap in the Face of Public Taste*, 191. See also Formalism; poetic experiments; perceptual experience; poetic language

Galloway, Alexander, 242
games (computer, digital, video), 236, 241, 246, 247; characters (playable characters), 242, 243, 244–245; interface (controller, controls), 243, 245; mechanics, 242–243, 245–246; media specificity, 242; tutorial (as enstranging device), 245, 247; worlds, 242–243, 245, 246, 247
Gardner, Martin, 53
Gasparov, Mikhail, 208, 209, 211, 216
Genette, Gérard, 73
genre, 3, 33, 87–88, 111, 131, 133, 143, 171, 185n21, 201n38, 222. See also

Shklovsky, Viktor; *Theory of Prose*; German, Aleksei, 32
Ginsburg, Lidia, 224, 225
Gippius, Zinaida, 52
globalized reading, 141
Gogol, Nikolai, 144, 174, 175, 176, 196
The Golden Ass. See Apuleius
Gorky, Maxim, 6, 45, 48n23, 58, 113, 115, 139, 189–190, 197, 227; "Last Night I was in the Kingdom of Shadows", 6, 189; World Literature Publishing House, 139, 142
Goscilo, Helena, 170
grammar, 34, 208, 211, 215, 216
Great Purge, 112
Grimm, Reinhold, 238
Gritz, Teodor, 228
grotesque, 6, 32, 101, 111, 189, 196; grotesque creation, 6, 189
group identity, 162
Guild of Poets, 114
Gulag, 32, 121n13
Gumilev, Nikolai, 110, 113, 139
Gunning, Tom, 190, 191, 197, 199n11
Günther, Hans, 240

habitual/habituation/de-habituation, 103, 120, 140–141, 151, 153, 176–177, 178, 194, 196, 223–224, 236–237, 238, 241, 244, 245–247. See also routinization
Hals, Franz, 216
The Hamburg Score. See Shklovsky, Viktor
Hammett, Dashiell, 81
Hansen-Löve, Aage, 34, 95
Hass, R. Glen, 14
Hatter. See Characters in Lewis Carroll's *Alice's Adventures in Wonderland*
Hegel, Georg Wilhelm Friedrich, 215, 238, 239, 240–241
Helmers, Hermann, 238, 239
Henry, P. J., 158
history, 2, 43, 56, 220–221, 221, 222–224, 228–230; of Formalism, 4, 6, 17, 104, 120, 156; literary, 31, 65, 93, 144, 162, 198
Hitchcock, Alfred, 171, 174, 181; *Psycho*, 180, 181–182, 184n20, 185n23
honor code. See non-literary genres.

Horace (Quintus Horatius Flaccus), 11, 210–211
humanity/human race, 18, 156–157, 159, 162. See also humanize
humanize/dehumanize, 157, 159. See also humanity
Hume, David, 21, 22–166
Humpty Dumpty, character in *Through the Looking-Glass and what Alice Found There*), 51, 57. See also Shaltay-Boltay
The Hunting of the Snark. See Carroll, Lewis
Husserl, Edmund, 2, 21–22

Iampolski, Mikhail, 32
I Burn Paris. See Jasienski, Bruno
identity, 33, 93, 155–156, 162, 222, 223–224, 225, 226
ideology, 93, 115, 116, 229, 241, 242, 246
illusion, 44, 155; in literature and art, 73, 216
image/imagery, 11, 12–13, 16, 59, 68, 80, 95, 155, 173, 176, 181–182, 189, 190, 207, 209, 213, 215, 229; poetic, 11–12, 68, 215; thinking in images, 11, 12, 22, 51. See also "Art as Device"
imitation, 27, 211, 220, 225, 230. See also mimicry
impediment. See deceleration
in-group and out-group, 159
inset stories, 5, 126
interface. See games
Iron Curtain, 42
irony, 30, 228
Ivanov-Razumnik, R. F., 98

Jabberwocky. See Carroll, Lewis
Jakobson, Roman, 15, 28, 41, 43, 46n7, 52, 57, 59, 66, 94, 97, 110, 115, 146, 221. See also Formalism; Shklovsky, Viktor
Jameson, Fredric, 145
Jasienski, Bruno, 4, 111, 120n9; *I Burn Paris*, 111; *Mannequin's Ball*, 111. See also Futurism
Jockers, Matthew, 146

Kahlo, Frida, 172–173
Kandinsky, Vasily, 211
Kant, Immanuel, 209

Index

Katz, Irwin, 158
Kaverin, Veniamin, 28, 29, 31–32, 230
Keane, Marian E., 181
Kharms, Daniil, 54, 118
Khiriakov, A.M., 177
Khlebnikov, Velimir, 7, 52, 58–59, 192; *Tiran bez T*, 58
Khrushchev, Nikita, 7, 44, 47n13
Kierkegaard, Søren, 238
King Lear. See Shakespeare, William
Kliger, Ilya, 146
Knight of the Green Coat. See characters in Cervantes's *Don Quixote*
Knight of the Mirrors. See characters in Cervantes's *Don Quixote*
Knight of the Woods. See characters in Cervantes's *Don Quixote*
Knight's Move. See Skhlovsky, Viktor
Knopf, Jan, 239
Kruchenykh, Aleksei, 51
Kushigian, Julia, 83

labyrinth, 3, 79–80, 84, 88
Lacan, Jacques, 170–171, 180
Lachmann, Renate, 238, 239–240
Lágrimas en la lluvia. See Montero, Rosa
La Mancha. See Mancha, La
"Last Night I was in the Kingdom of Shadows". See Gorky, Maxim
Latour, Bruno, 96, 98, 100
laying bare (of devices), 72–73, 76, 80, 102, 152, 220, 225, 239. See also "Art as Device"; device
Lee, Brian, 60
LEF (*Left Front of the Arts*), 115, 192, 230
Lemon, Lee, 139, 172, 197, 236
Leningrad, 111; Siege of, 43, 46n11
Lenin, Vladimir, 45, 113, 194
Levchenko, Jan, 31
linguistic fallibility, 85
literariness, 8, 99, 100, 101, 122n26, 222, 225, 236, 238
literary convention. See convention
literary device. See device
literary double, 228
Literary Evolution. See Tynyanov, Yuri
literary field. See field
literary history, 31, 65, 144

"Literature Beyond 'Plot'". See Shklovsky, Viktor
Literature and Cinematography. See Shklovsky, Viktor
Literature and Revolution. See Trotsky, Leon
Longinus, 12
Lumière brothers (Auguste and Louis), cinematograph, 6, 189, 190

making strange (*ostranenie*), 6, 52, 116, 169, 173, 189, 195, 197, 237, 239. See also automatization, defamiliarization, estrangement; *ostranenie*
Maksimovich, Aleksey, 227
Malevich, Kazimir, 211
Mancha, La, 125, 132
Mandelstam, Nadezhda, 113
Mandelstam, Osip, 17, 113
Mannequin's Ball. See Jasienski, Bruno
marginalization/marginalize, 87, 156
Markov, Vladimir, 191, 192
Markus, Hazel Rose, 157, 158
Marshak, Samuil, 57–58, 60
Marxism, 31, 53, 96, 240–238. See also Marxist critics,
Marxist critics, 28, 30, 116, 211. See also Marxism
Marx, Karl, 43, 238, 239
masculinity, 5, 126, 133
material, 34, 70, 72, 74, 94, 95, 96, 97, 98, 98–99, 100, 101, 103, 104–105, 116, 120, 145, 152, 174, 184n19, 207, 220, 226, 228–230; and form, 3, 67, 102, 178; and texture, 15–16, 17; material world, 100, 104, 155; materialism, 2, 96, 98; materiality, 99, 103, 104, 171; relationship of materials, 34, 67–68. See also form
Matthews, Kristin L., 85
Mayakovsky and his Circle. See Shklovsky, Viktor
Mayakovsky, Vladimir, 4, 7, 45, 52, 53, 111, 112, 113, 120n9, 189, 191, 192–193, 226, 227; *The Bathhouse*, 111. See also Futurism; poetry
Mayne, Judith, 179
McLuhan, Marshall, 37n54
media specificity of games. See games

Meditations. See Descartes, René
Medvedev, Pavel, 235
Merezhkovsky, Dmitri, 52
Merrill, Jessica, 143, 145–146
metaphor, 12–13, 97, 100, 101, 111, 119, 193, 208, 209, 212, 223, 226–227, 229
metonym, 12–13, 101, 224
Meyerhold, Vsevolod, 45, 48n21–48n22, 101–102; *Balagan*, 101
mimicry, 93, 95, 229. *See also* imitation
Mock Turtle. *See* Characters in Lewis Carroll's *Alice's Adventures in Wonderland*
Modleski, Tania, 181
Modotti, Tina, 172–173
Monomakh, Vladimir, 56
montage, 4, 34, 66, 70, 76, 97, 100, 179, 228–229
Montero, Rosa, 5, 152, 153, 155–158, 159–160, 161, 162–163; *Tears in Rain* (*Lágrimas en la lluvia*), 152, 155, 156, 157, 159, 162; *Weight of the Heart* (*El peso del corazón*), 157
"Monument to a Scientific Error". *See* Shklovsky, Viktor
Moretti, Franco, 142–146; "Conjectures on World Literature", 145; distant reading, 142–143; "Network Theory, Plot Analysis", 145; "The Slaughterhouse of Literature", 143; world literature, 142, 144, 146. *See also* literary history; world literature
Morphology of the Folktale. See Propp, Vladimir
mosaic, 66, 209, 210–211, 213
Moscow Association of Proletarian Writers, 111
Moscow Linguistic Circle, 116
Moscow State University, 41
motif, 3, 5, 20, 66, 67, 69, 71, 72, 76, 80–81, 88, 111, 125–126, 134, 228
motivation (of devices), 3, 72–73, 228
Mouse. *See* Characters in Lewis Carroll's *Alice's Adventures in Wonderland*
Mulvey, Laura, 6, 169–171, 172–174, 177, 179, 180–182, 183n2, 185n23; "Visual Pleasure and Narrative Cinema", 6, 169–170, 171, 172, 180–181, 185n21
Murdoch, Iris, 19

music, 11, 115, 117–119; intonation, 118; jazz, 117; rhythm, 118, 193; song, 51, 54, 56, 67, 70, 118; voice, 117
mystery genre/novel. *See* detective fiction

Nabokov, Vladimir, 52; Sirin, V., 56
narrative, 4, 80, 119, 125, 143–144, 145, 244. *See also* narratology; Skhlovsky, Viktor; *Theory of Prose*
narratology, 3, 65, 67, 68. *See also* narrative
NEP. *See* New Economic Policy
"Network Theory, Plot Analysis". *See* Moretti, Franco
Neville, Helen A., 158, 160, 161, 162
new acting, 244, 246, 247
New Economic Policy (NEP),
new man, 110
new seeing, 246, 247
Nietzsche, Friedrich, 7, 175, 194, 211, 212, 213, 214; Shklovsky and, 174–175, 213
NKVD (People's Commissariat for Internal Affairs), 48n20, 120n9
non-literary genres: *arbitrio*, 5, 127–129, 133; arms vs. letters debate, 126, 133; fame, 129; honor code, 133; *razón de estado* (reason of state), 5, 127; swordsmanship, 125, 131. *See also ars moriendi*
Nonnos of Panopolis, 215
Novalis, 238, 239
Novaya Zhizn, 115
novelty effects, 189

Oberiu (*Ob"edinenie real'nogo iskusstva*). *See* Real Art Group
obnazhenie priema (baring of the device). *See* laying bare (of devices)
Ó Cadhla, Pádraig, 59
"Ode to Stalin". *See* Akhmatova, Anna
Odysseus, 33
Oedipa Maas, character in Pynchon's *The Crying of Lot 49*, 85–87
O. Henry, 71
Oleinikov, Nikolay, 54
Once Upon a Time. See Shklovsky, Viktor
"On the Sounds in Poetic Language". *See* Yakubinsky, Lev Petrovich
ontology, 142; object-oriented, 98

OPOYAZ. *See* Society for the Study of Poetic Language
Opus Incertum. See Sedakova, Olga
Orlovskaya, Dina, 60
oscillating signs. *See* Tynyanov, Juri
ostranenie, 6, 8, 11, 52, 55, 79–85, 88, 89n1, 140, 141, 155, 169, 174, 175, 180, 194, 236–241, 243, 244, 246–247; See also automatization, defamiliarization; estrangement; making strange; Shklovsky, Victor
Oushakine, Serguei, 34
out of placeness. *See* defamiliarization

parallelism, 68, 70, 72, 74, 81, 86, 87, 215
parallel story. *See* Shklovsky, Viktor
parody, 3
Pasternak, Boris, 47n16, 52; *Doctor Zhivago*, 44, 47n15. *See also* Futurism
Pater, Walter, 11
Paz, Octavio, 117
perception, 11, 82, 94, 95, 96, 97, 103, 110, 154, 213, 242, 244; aesthetics of, 95, 196. *See also* Shklovsky, Viktor
perceptual experience, 154, 193. *See also* "Art as Device"; Futurism
Perestroika, 29, 41, 46n4
peripeteia. See reversal
personal "I", 220
El peso del corazón. See Montero, Rosa
Petrovsky, Miron, 53
Picasso, Pablo, 43
Pierce Inverarity, character in *The Crying of Lot 49*, 85–87
Pisarev, Dmitry, 238
Platon Karataev, character in Tolstoy's *War and Peace*, 221
Platonov, Sergei F., 7
playable characters. *See* game characters
plot, 7, 79, 81, 86, 88, 145, 208, 215–216, 239; nomadic/roving, 69, 76. *See also* "Art as Device; " device; plot construction; Shklovsky, Viktor; *sujet*; *Theory of Prose*
plot construction (*siuzhetoslozhenie*), 29, 74; stepped, 74, 76. *See also* "Art as Device"; device; plot; Shklovsky, Viktor; *sujet*
Poe, Edgar Allan, 81, 219

poetic experiments, 192. *See also* Futurism
poetic image. *See* image
poetic language, 7, 12, 15–16, 80, 94, 110, 114, 116, 119, 152, 208, 212. *See also* Futurism; prosaic language
poetics, 7, 67, 94, 110, 174, 191, 192, 194, 195, 207, 210, 240; modern, 12, 114, 117, 216; of everyday life, 221. *See also* Aristotle
Poetics. See Aristotle
poetic speech, 14, 79, 174. *See also* Shklovsky, Viktor
poetry, 14, 17, 20, 94, 110, 116–119, 191, 192–193, 194, 201n55, 209, 212, 214, 215–216; ability to focus attention, 15–16, 17; and prose, 12, 15, 53, 119, 145, 207, 208, 210, 211; as a form of thinking, 12–13, 18, 22, 110; image in, 11–12, 22, 68; language of, 15, 51, 52. *See also* defamiliarization; device; Futurism; image; Mayakovsky, Vladimir; poetic language; prose; Shklovsky, Viktor; thinking in images; trans-sense language; Zaum poetry
political gesture, 226
Polo, Marco, 31
Polonskaya, K. N., 180
Polonsky, Yakov, 208, 211
polyglossia. *See* Bakhtin, Mikhail
post-horn symbol. *See The Crying of Lot 49*
post-Formalism/post-Formalist, 2, 27. *See also* Formalism; technique
post-humanism, 96
potboiler literature (*belletristika*), 31
"Potebnya". *See* Shklovsky, Viktor
Potebnya, Aleksander, 2, 11, 12, 68, 95, 155, 174, 238
Pötzsch, Holger, 242
Pozner, Vladimir, 238
Pravda, 111
prejudice, 152, 156, 157, 158–160, 161, 162–163. *See also* discrimination; racism
priem. See device
Princess Micimicona. *See* characters in Cervantes's *Don Quixote*
procedural rhetoric, 242, 243
Proletcult, 113

Propp, Vladimir, 66, 73; *Morphology of the Folktale*, 71. *See also* fairy tale; folktale; folklore; Formalism
prosaic language, 80, 110. *See also* poetic language
prose, 12–13, 15, 119, 145, 207, 208, 210–212, 223, 224, 228. *See also* poetry; Shklovsky, Viktor; *Theory of Prose*
prosegory. *See* rhetorics
Psycho. *See* Hitchcock, Alfred
Psychologism, 13, 93, 94, 96, 105. *See also* emotions; psychology
psychology, 19, 93, 94; collective, 216; of perception, 94, 95, 97–98, 152. *See also* discrimination; psychologism; racism
pun, 29, 55, 56
Pushkin, Alexander, 30, 75, 144, 191, 196, 209, 213, 214, 215
Pynchon, Thomas, 3, 79, 82. *See also The Crying of Lot 49*

racism, 5, 152, 156–162; and colorblindness, 160, 162; automatization of, 160, 162; biological, 157, 159–160; inherent, 159, 162–163. *See also* discrimination
RAPP. *See* Russian Association of Proletarian Writers
razón de estado (reason of state). *See* non-literary genres
Real Art Group (*Oberiu*), 54
realism, 70, 101, 235; Socialist, 4, 111, 113, 115
recognition, 20, 66, 70, 82, 174
Red Scharlach, character in Borges's "Death and the Compass", 83, 88
Red Terror, 112
Reich, Bernhard, 239
Reich, Zinaida, 48n21
Reis, Marion, 139, 172
"The Relationship between Devices of Plot Construction and General Devices of Style". *See* Shklovsky, Viktor
Remizov, Alexei, 52
repetition, 15, 32, 76, 80, 140, 179; epic, 72
"The Resurrection of the Word". *See* Shklovsky, Viktor

retardation. *See* deceleration
reversal (*peripeteia*), 66, 74, 75
revolution, 44, 191; Bolshevik, 4, 42, 44, 52, 220–221, 225, 230
rhetorics (*prosegory*), 211, 213, 216
Rhythm as Dialectics and Bronze Horseman by Pushkin. *See* Bely, Andrey
Ricote. *See* characters in Cervantes's *Don Quixote*
riddles, 76, 80, 174, 174–175, 196
Robinson, Douglas, 153, 155, 162
Room, Abram, *Bed and Sofa*, 32
Roque Guinart. *See* characters in Cervantes's *Don Quixote*
routinization, 96. *See also* habitual
Russia, 2, 21, 29, 31, 48n24, 52, 56, 115, 139, 144, 191, 198, 226, 240; Russian Empire, 41, 52; Soviet Russia, 30, 93, 225, 229. *See also* Russian Civil War; USSR
Russian Association of Proletarian Writers (RAPP), 111
Russian Civil War, 29, 32, 48n24, 53, 56, 221, 224, 225
Russian Formalism. *See* Formalism
Russian Formalism and the Digital Humanities. *See* Stanford Humanities Center
Russian Formalists. *See* Formalism
Russian Futurism. *See* Futurism
Russian Futurists. *See* Futurism
Rychkov, Pëtr, 56

Saint Petersburg, 139, 192, 215
Samovitoe slovo. *See* self-oriented word
Sancho Panza. *See* characters in Cervantes's *Don Quixote*
Sansón Carrasco. *See* characters in Cervantes's *Don Quixote*
Sayers, Dorothy L., 81, 83
Scott, Ridley, *Black Hawk Down*, 242
Screen, 169, 172, 179
sdvigologiya. *See* shiftology
Sears, David O., 158
Sedakova, Olga, 58, 212; *Opus Incertum*, 211
self-awareness, 156, 162
self-oriented word (*Samovitoe slovo*), 193

Semantics of Cinema. See Shklovsky
semiotics, 4, 7, 34, 79, 82, 98, 202n58
Semyonov, Georgy, 225
sense/sensual, 22, 95, 97, 105, 117, 154, 210, 211, 232. *See also* feelings
The Sentimental Journey. See Shklovsky, Viktor
Setlak, Wojciech, 243, 244, 245
Sewell, Byron W., 59–60, 60
Shakespeare, William, *King Lear*, 73
Shaltay-Boltay, Russian translation of Humpty–Dumpty, character in Lewis Carroll's *Through the Looking-Glass and what Alice Found There*, 57–58, 59
Sheldon, Richard, 30, 31
Shelley, Mary, 238
Sher, Benjamin, 89n1, 154, 236–237
Sherlock Holmes, character in Conan Doyle's stories and novels, 71, 85, 87
Sherman, Cindy, 173
Sherwood, Richard, 172
Shestov, Leo, 213; *All Things Are Possible*, 213–214, 216
shiftology (*sdvigologiya*), 209
Shklovsky, Viktor: and detective fiction, 4, 79, 80–84, 86–88, 143–144; and erotic art/literature, 174, 174–175, 177; and genre, 5, 18, 66, 71, 79, 80–84, 117, 120, 125–126, 127; avant-garde, 6, 117, 192, 195, 198, 201n54, 201n56–202n57; biographical strategy, 221, 224; *Bowstring: On the Dissimilarity of the Similar*, 2, 27, 33–34, 75, 119, 212; *A Chinese Novel, First Approaches. Chinese Novel*, 215; *A Conversation with Friends* , 104; *Energy of Delusion: A Book about Plot*, 53, 75; error-type story, 84; *The Hamburg Score*, 68, 191, 220; *Knight's Move*, 28, 115, 173, 182, 222; *Literature and Cinematography*, 67, 94, 194; "Literature Beyond 'Plot'", 144; *Mayakovsky and his Circle*, 115, 191, 194; "Monument to a Scientific Error", 30, 43, 112, 115; *Once Upon a Time*, 27, 104; on character (literary) 72–73, 74, 126, 140, 174, 209, 212, 220; on *Don Quixote* , 5, 28, 34, 70, 72–73, 74, 75, 80, 125–126, 134; on Laurence Sterne, 51, 67, 139, 224, 228; on Leo Tolstoy, 2, 4, 19, 28, 32–33, 72, 73, 74, 75, 103, 104, 144, 174–179, 184n15, 196, 238, 239; on narrative 3, 65–69, 70, 70–71, 72–73, 73–76, 100, 134, 139, 144, 145, 211, 212; on perception, 15, 17, 21, 22, 34, 94, 104, 116, 119, 140–141, 151, 155, 160, 172, 175, 192, 193, 194, 196–197, 198, 221, 223; on Roman Jakobson, 23n12, 34, 44, 73, 202n58; on plot, 3, 29, 33, 65, 67, 68, 69, 71, 72, 75–76, 80, 83, 84, 126, 139–140, 144, 145, 212, 215, 228; on plot construction, 74, 80; poetic speech, 79; poetry, 11–12, 15–16, 18, 20, 22, 34, 51, 53, 66, 68, 115, 116, 117, 119, 145, 192, 194, 210; "Potebnya", 2, 14, 17; "The Relationship between Devices of Plot Construction and General Devices of Style", 29; *"The Resurrection of the Word"*, 14, 17, 18, 51, 80, 81, 95, 193, 209, 237; *Semantics of Cinema.*, 100; *The Sentimental Journey* , 103, 192, 194, 220, 222, 223–224; step-by-step construction, 74, 84; *Techniques of the Writer*, 99; theory of art, 6, 115, 152; wind of revolution, 30; writing style of, 65; *Zoo, or Letters Not about Love*, 2, 27, 30, 72, 97, 100, 210, 222, 225, 226, 228. *See also* "Art as Device"; "Art as Technique"; character; defamiliarization; detective fiction; device; fabula; Formalism; Futurism; narrative; perception; plot; plot construction; prose; Sterne, Laurence; sujet; *Theory of Prose*; Tolstoy, Leo
Shostakovich, Dmitri, 41, 46n11
Shpoliansky, Mikhail, character in Bulgakov's *White Guard* based on Viktor Shklovsky, 56
Silver Age, 45n2, 52, 110, 221
Simmel, Georg, 240
"The Simple Art of Murder". *See* Chandler, Raymond
simulation, 241, 242, 243
singularization, 119
Sinyavsky, Andrey, 44, 47n17
Sirin, V. *See* Nabokov, Vladimir

Sitdykova, Güzäl, 56
A Slap in the Face of Public Taste. See Futurism
"The Slaughterhouse of Literature". *See* Moretti, Franco
social classism, 156
social construction, 157
Socialist Realism, 4, 48n23, 111, 113, 115
social justice, 44, 157, 163
Society for the Study of Poetic Language (OPOYAZ), 14, 65, 113, 115, 116, 118, 120, 195, 212, 224, 235
Socrates, 19, 238
Solovyova, Poliksena (Allegro), 52
Sonia. *See* Characters in Lewis Carroll's *Alice's Adventures in Wonderland*
Soviet Russia. *See* Russia
Soviet subject. *See* subject
Stalin, Joseph, 31, 44, 48n23, 57, 75, 115
Stalinism, 29, 32, 172
Stanford Humanities Center, *Russian Formalism and the Digital Humanities* 146
step-by-step construction. *See* form; Shklovsky, Viktor
Sternberg, Joseph von, 171
Sterne, Laurence, *Tristram Shandy*, 67, 139, 224, 228. *See also* Shklovsky, Viktor
stone, stony, 17, 20, 96–97, 103–105, 140, 154, 166, 179, 210, 240
Stray Dog café, 41, 42, 45n1, 192, 193, 198
Striedter, Jurij, 238
stroph/strophic, 208, 210–211
Structuralism, French, 2, 34, 53, 197
subject, 93, 96, 104, 157, 162, 182, 219, 220, 224, 228, 229. *See also* subjectivity
subjectivity, 29, 178, 220, 225, 227, 228. *See also* subject
Sublime, the, 209
sujet /syuzhet (plot), 3, 29, 67–69, 70, 72, 75, 76, 140. *See also fabula*; plot; plot construction; *Theory of Prose*;
swordsmanship. *See* non-literary genres
Symbolism/Symbolists, 13, 52, 68, 113, 191–193, 194, 221
syuzhet (alternate form of *sujet*). *See* sujet

Taneev, Sergei, 178
Tears in Rain. See Montero, Rosa
technique (*priom*), 29, 67, 72, 74, 85, 101, 140, 141, 154, 192–193, 194, 196, 198, 200n32, 209, 224, 236, 238; defamiliarizing/estranging, 6, 126, 179; narrative, 68, 74. *See also* "Art as Technique"; defamiliarization; device; estrangement; form; Formalism; shiftology; threading
Techniques of the Writer. See Shklovsky
Tenniel, John, 59–60
Tetragrammaton, 83, 84
Theory of Prose, 2, 3, 4, 5, 29, 42, 53, 65–67, 68, 69–70, 72, 73–74, 75, 80, 126, 144, 145, 180, 194; editions of, 27, 34, 65. *See also* "Art as Device"; device; *fabula*; genre; narrative; plot; prose; Shklovsky, Viktor; *sujet*; threading
thing (in Formalism), 4, 15, 17, 18–19, 20, 22, 34, 67, 96, 96–101, 103, 103–105, 114, 139–140, 174–175, 190, 194, 196, 211, 215, 229, 240–241, 246, 247; automatization and, 32, 179, 223; perception/sensation of, 12, 17, 18, 19, 20, 22, 98, 100, 140, 144, 153, 154–155. *See also* "Art as Device"; affordances; automatization; film; perception; stone
This War of Mine (TWoM), 243, 243–246, 247
Thomsen, Mads Rosendahl, 141
threading, 5, 72, 74, 126, 127, 134. *See also* "Art as Device"; device; *Theory of Prose*;
Through the Looking-Glass and what Alice Found There (*TTLG*), 51, 53, 57, 60; transmirrorland (*Zazerkal'e*), 53
Tieck, Ludwig, 11
Tihanov, Galin, 146
Tiran bez T. See Khlebnikov, Velimir
Todorov, Tzvetan, 71, 117
Tolstoy, Leo, 43, 52, 58, 182, 221; "Kholstomer" ("Strider"), 72, 174, 184n19. *See also* Shklovsky, Viktor
Toma, Elisabeta, 243
Tomashevsky, Boris, 43, 46n8, 66, 67, 68, 73, 146. *See also* Formalism;

Shklovsky, Viktor
tonality, 117
translation, 5, 99, 102, 117, 237; domestication in, 55, 56, 59; foreignization in, 55; of Lewis Carroll, 52, 53, 55, 56, 57–58, 59–60
trans-sense language, 117, 118
traumatic experience/traumatic movement, 224, 226, 228
Tretiakov, Sergei, 100, 102, 239
Treviranus, character in Pynchon's *The Crying of Lot 49*, 83, 84
Triolet, Elsa (nee Kagan), 53
Tristero/Trystero. *See The Crying of Lot 49*
Tristram Shandy. *See* Sterne, Laurence
Tropinka, 52
Trotsky, Leon, 113, 116, 235; *Literature and Revolution*, 113
Tsivian, Yuri, 190, 191, 198
Tsvetaeva, Marina, 53
Turkish soldiers. *See* Askers
Turkisms, in Russian language, 58
TWoM. *See This War of Mine*
Tynyanov, Yury, 34, 65–66, 73, 93–94, 96, 97, 99, 100, 104, 115, 146, 177, 207–208, 210–211, 212, 213, 215, 230; compactness of verse, 207, 209, 210, 211, 213, 214; oscillating signs, 208, 210, 211, 212; *Literary Evolution*, 93; *The Problem of Verse Language*, 207. *See also* Formalism; Shklovsky, Viktor

unfreedom, 30, 227–228. *See also* freedom
Ungvari, Tamás, 238
Union of Real Art, 118
Union of Soviet Writers, 43, 47n12, 116
unity (of narrative composition), 16, 33, 66, 69, 76, 224
USSR/Soviet Union, 2, 7, 28, 41, 43–44, 45, 53, 53–54, 176, 222, 240. *See also* Russia

Van Dine, S. S., 81, 83
Vaught, Sabina Elena, 160, 161
V-effect. *See* Brecht, Bertolt
Vengerova, Zinaida,
verbal art (*Sprachgesang*). *See* art
Verfremdung. *See* Brecht, Bertolt
Verschoyle, K., 59

Vertov, Dziga, 98, 100
Veselovsky, Alexander, 69, 238
"Visual Pleasure and Narrative Cinema". *See* Mulvey, Laura
Vitale, Serena, 112, 115, 235
Vitkovsky, Evgeny, 53
Volynsky, Akim, 139
Vvedensky, Alexander, 54

Warburg, Aby, 240
war game (genre), 244, 245
W.A.S.T.E. *See The Crying of Lot 49*
Watson, character in Conan Doyle's stories and novels, 71, 80, 85
Weight of the Heart. *See* Montero, Rosa
White Guard. *See* Bulgakov, Mikhail
White Hare. *See* Characters in Lewis Carroll's *Alice's Adventures in Wonderland*
Willett, John, 239
Williams, Nicholas, 56
William the Conqueror, 56
wind of revolution. *See* Shklovsky, Viktor
Wollen, Peter, 172
word as such, 110
world-directedness, 237, 246
world literature, 5, 33, 139, 141–142, 143–146
World Literature Publishing House. *See* Gorky, Maxim

Yakubinsky, Lev Petrovich, 2, 13–161, 17–18; "On the Sounds in Poetic Language", 14, 15–16; "The Accumulation of Liquids in Practical and Poetic Language", 14, 15, 18. *See also* "Art as Device"; Formalism; Shklovsky, Viktor
Yesenin, Sergei, 45, 48n20, 110

Zabolotsky, Nikolay, 54
Zamyatin, Yesvgeny, 111, 139
Zarathustra, 58
zatrudnenie (retardation). *See* deceleration
Zaum poetry, 117
Zazerkal'e. *See Through the Looking-Glass*
Zhdanov doctrine, 115
Zimmermann, Antonie, 55

Zoo, or Letters Not about Love. See
　Shklovsky, Viktor

About the Contributors

Michael Eskin is award-winning author, translator, publisher, and cofounder of Upper West Side Philosophers, Inc. Eskin has taught at Rutgers, Cambridge, and Columbia Universities. His many publications on cultural, literary and philosophical subjects include: *Nabokov's Version of Pushkin's Eugene Onegin* (1994); *Ethics and Dialogue in the Works of Levinas, Bakhtin, Mandel'shtam, and Celan* (2000); *Poetic Affairs: Celan, Grünbein, Brodsky* (2008); *The Bars of Atlantis: Selected Essays by Durs Grünbein* (as editor; 2010); and *The Wisdom of Parenthood: An Essay* (2013). His translations have appeared in *The New Yorker*, *Sport 40*, and *World Literature Today*, among other venues.

Irina Evdokimova is a lawyer. For many years she has worked as a Criminal Prosecutor for the Attorney General of the Russian Federation, but during all these years she has cherished the idea of writing a book about the period in Russian history that she loves most—The Silver Age of Russian poetry at the start of the twentieth century. Her lively intelligence and extensive knowledge of literary history of this period have made her a valuable contributor to this project.

Michael Everson holds an MA from the University of California, Los Angeles in the history of religion and Indo-European linguistics. He is a linguist, script encoder, typesetter, font designer, and publisher. His central interest is in writing systems useful in formats for computers and digital media. He has a special interest in developing characters for International Standards, including Unicode. He is the publisher and owner of Evertype, and has published many editions of the translations of *Alice's Adventures in Wonderland*.

Victor Fet is Professor of Biology at Marshall University, West Virginia; he teaches Genetics, Evolution, Biogeography, and General Biology, and has over 100 publications on animal systematics and evolution. Dr. Fet has edited and translated from Russian several books on biology. He has published four books of poetry in his native Russian, as well as literary reviews and essays; he is especially interested in the work of Vladimir Nabokov. He has also published translations of poetry by Lewis Carroll and Roald Hoffmann. His poetry has appeared in many expatriate Russian journals and almanacs in Europe and the United States.

Norbert Francis is Professor Emeritus at Northern Arizona University and Visiting Researcher in the Graduate Institute of Linguistics at Chengchi University. His current research project focuses on problems of literary creation in cross-cultural contexts from a cognitive science point of view. In a recent overview of this project in *Bilingual and Multicultural Perspectives on Music, Poetry and Narrative: The Science of Art* (2017) it is proposed that researchers today should recover the work of the Society for the Study of Poetic Language, founded in Russia in 1916, for the study of foundational concepts.

Melissa Garr is an Assistant Professor of Spanish at Florida Southern College in Lakeland, Florida. She specializes in genre fiction, twentieth and twenty-first century Spanish literature, and the work of Mikhail Bakhtin. Dr. Garr's presentations include "Polyphony and Pigeonholes from Innocent Ingénue to Homicidal Sexpot: The *Femme Fatale* in Early Portuguese Detective Fiction" at the International Association of Hispanic Women's Literature and Culture Conference, and "Toward a Philosophy of the Creative Act: Metafictive Dialogism in *El cuarto de atrás*" at KFLC: The Languages, Literatures and Cultures Conference, and her publications include "Power, Privilege, Testimony: Bakhtin's Legacy in Discourses of Privilege in *I, Rigoberta Menchú* and 'Pasión de historia,'" in *Mikhail Bakhtin's Heritage in Literature, Arts and Pscyhology: Art and Answerability* (2018).

David Gorman is Associate Professor of English at Northern Illinois University, where he is a former editor of the journal *Style*. His primary research topic is general poetics, its history, conceptual foundations, and future prospects. In this connection, he has coedited the Norton Critical Edition of the *Poetics of Aristotle* (2018). In addition, he has published essays, translations, bibliographies, and articles in reference works on the contributions made to poetics by Russian Formalists among others. He has an overview of general poetics in progress, as well as a study of the work of Gérard Genette.

Slav N. Gratchev is Associate Professor of Spanish at Marshall University. He is the author or editor of *The Polyphonic World of Cervantes and Dostoevsky* (2017), *Don Quixote: The Re-accentuation of the World's Greatest Literary Hero* (2017), *Bakhtin's Heritage in Literature, Arts, and Psychology* (2018), and *Mikhail Bakhtin: The Duvakin Interviews, 1973* (forthcoming). In addition, he has published numerous articles and essays on Cervantes, Dostoevsky, Bakhtin and other subjects in a variety of academic journals such as *Cervantes, College Literature, The South Atlantic Review, Comparative Literature and Culture, The Russian Review, The Nabokovian*.

Grant Hamilton is Associate Professor of English Literature at the Chinese University of Hong Kong. His teaching and research interests include twentieth-century world literatures and literary theory. His most recent work includes a book on the intersection between speculative realism and literary theory, titled *The World of Failing Machines: Speculative Realism and Literature* (2016) and a co-edited collection of new essays on the Mozambican writer Mia Couto, titled *A Companion to Mia Couto* (2016). In addition, he has published numerous articles and essays in journals such as *Textual Practice, Australian Literary Studies,* and *South Asian Review*. He is currently working on a book provisionally titled *Writing at the End of Capitalism: The Politics of Reconnection in the Contemporary London Novel*.

Ilya Kalinin is Associate Professor at Department of Liberal Arts and Sciences at St. Petersburg State University and at the National Research University "Higher School of Economics." He is Editor-in-Chief of the Moscow-based intellectual journal *Неприкосновенный запас. Дебаты о политике и культуре* (K-Ration: Debates on Politics and Culture). He has published in a wide range of journals including *Ab Imperio, Baltic Worlds, Sign Systems Studies, Social Sciences, Russian Literature, Russian Studies, Russian Studies in Literature, Slavonica, Wiener Slawistischer Almanach, New Literary Observer*, etc. His book *История как искусство членораздельности. Русские формалисты и революция* (History as Art of Articulation. Russian Formalists and Revolution) is forthcoming.

Basil Lvoff is a doctoral candidate in Comparative Literature at The Graduate Center of the City University of New York. He he has taught literature, history, language, and composition at Columbia University, Barnard, Hunter, Baruch, and Bronx Community Colleges. His scholarly work on literary theory and history has appeared in a variety of refereed journals, including *Voprosy literatury, Ulbandus, International Studies in Humour,* and *New Zealand Slavonic Journal*. In 2018, his poems and poetic essays were published in one of Russia's most esteemed literary journals, Novy mir, and in 2017 a collection of his theoretical and philosophical essays was published in

Russia's oldest literary journal, *Zvezda*. His interests in Russian Formalism and literary journalism originated while he was at Moscow State University where he defended his dissertation, and he continues to develop these ideas in his doctoral dissertation.

Howard Mancing is Emeritus Professor of Spanish at Purdue University. He is the author of three books: *The Chivalric World of Don Quijote: Style, Structure, and Narrative Technique* (1982); *The Cervantes Encyclopedia* (2 vols.) (2004); and *Miguel de Cervantes' "Don Quixote": A Reference Guide* (2006). He is also the co-editor of three other books: *Text, Theory, and Performance: Golden Age Comedia Studies* (1994), with Charles Ganelin; *Theory of Mind and Literature* (2011), with Paula Leverage, Richard Schweickert, and Jennifer Marston William; and *Don Quixote: The Re-accentuation of the World's Greatest Literary Hero* (2017), with Slav N. Gratchev. In addition, he has published over seventy articles and essays on Cervantes, Unamuno, Lazarillo de Tormes and the picaresque novel, narrative theory, comparative literature in journals such as *Anales Cervantinos, Cervantes, Celestinesca, Estudios Públicos, Europe, Forum for Modern Language Studies, Hispania, Hispanic Review, MLN, Modern Fiction Studies, PMLA,* and *Semiotica*. Currently he is working on two books: one on cognitive science and literary theory and one on the theory and history of the novel 1475–1700.

Alexander Markov is Professor of Art Theory at Russian State University for the Humanities. He is the author of *Odysseas Elytis: A Biography and Selected* (2013); *1980: Newborn Everyday Life* (2014); *Theoretical Literature Conclusions, 2000–2015* (2016); *Historical Poetics of Spirituality* (2016); *Palms of Zion: 42 Essays on Ekphrasis in Poetry* (2017); and *Postmodern Culture and Postmodern Theory* (2018). He published a number of papers and essays on intellectual history, theory of interpretation, particular questions of art history in journals like *Novy Mir, New Literary Observer, New Philological Bulletin, Questions of Literature.*

Steven Mills is an Associate Professor of Spanish at Buena Vista University. His research focusses on twentieth-century Spanish literature with an emphasis on cognitive approaches to literature, culture, and identity. He has researched eugenics, social thought, and censorship during the Franco dictatorship as well as embodied cognition and contextualized identity as an alternative to Cartesian Dualism when engaging subjectivity and post-humanity in literature. Most recently he has written on Bakhtin as a cognitive theorist who has moved philosophies away from Cartesian dualism and toward embodied cognition consistent with current research in cognitive science. He published a number of articles and reviews in various venues, including

Hispania. He is currently working with projects involving Cartesian and cognitive approaches to identity in Spanish authors such as Rosa Montero and Miguel de Unamuno.

Eric Naiman is Professor of Slavic Languages and Literatures and the Bernie H. Williams Professor of Comparative Literature at the University of California, Berkeley. He is the author of *Sex in Public: The Incarnation of Early Soviet Ideology* (1997) and *Nabokov, Perversely* (2010). He has published articles on Platonov, Bakhtin, Tolstoy, Dostoevsky and Nabokov, as well as on early Soviet culture. His current project is a book tentatively titled *Working Through Nabokov*.

Annie van den Oever is Professor of Film and Head of the Film Archive and Media Archaeology Lab at the University of Groningen. She is also the editor of *NECSUS. European Journal of Media Studies*. She publishes regularly on the history of film theory, film technologies, and film aesthetics. Her most recent book publications and edited volumes include *Life Itself* (2008); *Ostrannenie* (2010); *Sensitizing the Viewer* (2011); *De geboorte van Boontje* (with Ernst Bruinsma and Bart Nuyens, 2012); *Technology* (2014); *Sleutelteksten in Film-en Mediatheorie* [Key Texts in Film and Media Theory] (2015–2016); *Exposing the Film Apparatus. The Film Archive as a Research Lab,* with Giovanna Fossati (2016).

Sergei Alex. Oushakine is Professor at Princeton University. His work focuses primarily on practices of cultural production and consumption. In particular, he is interested in exploring cultural recycling and retrofitting, and he has published extensively on aphasia, nostalgia, pastiches, reconstructions and imitations in contemporary Russian culture. He also studies emotions, analyzing the politics of pity, the patriotism of despair, and different forms of totalitarian (and less totalitarian) laughter.

Holger Pötzsch is Associate Professor in Media and Documentation Studies at The University of Tromsø—The Arctic University of Norway. His main research interests are war films, war games, cultural memory, border technologies, and the politics of digital media. Dr. Pötzsch has published in journals such as *New Media & Society*, *EPD: Society & Space*, *Games & Culture*, *Game Studies*, *Memory Studies*, and *Media, War & Conflict*. He currently coordinates the research projects *WAR/GAME* and *Manufacturing Monsters*.

Rachel Schmidt is Professor in the Department of Classics and Religion at the University of Calgary. Her publications include *Critical Images: The Canonization of Don Quixote through Illustrated Editions of the Eighteenth Century* (1999), awarded a prized from the Canadian Association of Hispanists, and *Forms of Modernity: Don Quixote and Modern Theories of the Novel* (2011). She is working on a long-term project on the presence of non-literary discourses in Cervantes's prose that has been underwritten by the Social Sciences and Humanities Research Council of Canada.

Printed in Great Britain
by Amazon